The Who By Numbers:

The Story Of The Who Through Their Music

Steve Grantley and Alan G. Parker
with Sean Body

Helter
Skelter
publishing

The Who, by Numbers:

The Story Of The Who Through Their Music

This book is dedicated to the memory of
Henry "Harry" Parker (1927 – 2005)

and

Sean Body (1966 – 2008)
founder of Helter Skelter Publishing

and

Norman Grantley (1936 – 2009)

Steve Grantley and Alan G. Parker

with Sean Body

The Who By Numbers:
The Story Of The Who Through Their Music

Steve Grantley and Alan G. Parker
with Sean Body

Helter
Skelter
publishing

First edition published in 2010 by Helter Skelter Publishing
PO Box 50497, London W8 9FA

Copyright 2010 © Steve Grantley and Alan G. Parker

Cover design by Chris Wilson
Typesetting and layout by Graeme Milton
Collages by Graham Perkins
Proof-reading by Graham Perkins

Printed in Great Britain by J F Print Ltd, Sparkford, Somerset

All lyrics quoted in this book are for the purposes of review, study or criticism.

The publishers would like to thank Justin Lewis, Peter Doggett and
Karen O'Brien for their help with this project.

A CIP record for this book is available from the British Library.

Front cover photograph: Harry Goodwin / Rex Features

ISBN 978-1-905139-26-2

Contents

Explanatory Note

This book is not a biography of the Who – for that we recommend you search out Dave Marsh's magisterial *Before I Get Old* – and neither is it an exhaustive discography nor a current-day buyer's guide. We hope this book contains elements of all of these approaches. What we have tried to do is tell the story of the Who through the prism of their key recorded works, charting a unique band's musical progress through five decades, while analysing and evaluating what is quite so special about these records.

There has been no attempt to document unreleased tracks, demo-collections or bootleg recordings, and neither do we look at the band's live performance except where it is inextricably tied up with discussion of the records. Compilations are discussed only where they seem particularly key to the story of the band's career and feature important material not easily available elsewhere, while we have also avoided live albums and rarities collections. Singles are discussed separately very selectively: again, only when they are vital to the unfolding musical journey in their own right, rather than as tracks from well-known albums, no matter how strong they are. All album tracks are covered in due course anyway, and B-sides are discussed in detail only where they are worthy of further investigation.

By critically discussing in detail the Who's major recordings, we are drawing attention to what we consider the key tracks to be, and what is extraordinary about them, while also highlighting which recordings are the best CD editions of these works available. Occasionally, we have added notes on the availability of certain less obvious singles but, generally, it is clear from the narrative where these songs can be found, so we have restrained from going overboard on the various versions and multitudes of outlets for the best-known material. It is worth noting here that available sources do not always agree on the exact release dates of many of the singles – and some albums – especially in the US in the 1960s. We have gone for the most commonly agreed dates, but apologise for any discrepancies.

In terms of the actual versions of the albums, we have tended to look at both the original track listings and the more recent CD remastered editions, and all the additional bonus material. Usually the deluxe remasters are the definitive incarnations of these albums now, but occasionally we have namechecked previous CD versions where some bonus tracks appeared that have subsequently been cropped from the later sets.

Finally, the many solo projects have largely been excluded, except for instances such as when tracks emerged on a Townshend solo album credited to the Who. We occasionally deviate from the album narrative to mention key projects like the film versions of *Tommy* and *Quadrophenia*.

There are plenty of books and websites dedicated to the Who. Every biographical fact and discographical detail is out there if you want it; and yet, sometimes, amid this mass of information, the most important points can get lost. As with Dylan and the Beatles, there are plenty of scholars of the Who around the globe and many who know more of the facts and figures, the discs and dates, than we do. Yet, to use the ultimate cliché, sometimes, amid this forest of information, it can be difficult to see the wood for the trees. Coming from different musical worlds, yet with the enthusiasm of years of Who fan-dom, a critic's hard eye, a professional drummer's technical knowledge, and hundreds of hours of research, hopefully we have been able to shed fresh light on what is most important about this revolutionary group.

Much of the evidence for why and how the Who were so exciting, so groundbreaking, so accomplished, so creative and so important; damn it, so great, is contained in their major studio albums. While fans will always lap up live albums, rarities selections, and archive-trawling CD sets, the major studio recordings are the ones they return to again and again. By looking with fresh critical eyes at these works, we have tried to bring to life the long, strange and often tragic saga of the amazing musical journey of Pete Townshend, Roger Daltrey, John Entwistle and Keith Moon – the story of the Who through their music.

Book One

Prologue: The Arrival Of The Who – 1958-64

Everybody prior to them was polite. The Who just weren't polite.
Shel Talmy

I imagined the band would last two or three records at most. We were like punks: hoping to explode and get on with our 'real' lives.
Pete Townshend

There were few less rock'n'roll parts of London in the early 1960s than the leafy borough of Harrow, on the north-western edge of the city. There was the confidently affluent Harrow-on-the-Hill, inhabited by the famous public school which had educated many British prime ministers and foreign dignitaries. And there was the Harrow where working-class and middle-class families had settled, the Metro-land of commuters that had opened up with the expansion of the Metropolitan railway from the early 1900s. Metro-land was the advertising slogan thought up by the railway authorities to entice workers from cramped homes in central London out into the countryside of Middlesex, Hertfordshire and Buckinghamshire. The idyllic rural setting was inevitably altered irrevocably by the concrete and construction that followed.

But in the summer of '64 as teenagers flocked to a modest brick Victorian pub overlooking the Harrow and Wealdstone station, rock'n'roll history would be made there. With their scooters lined up outside, every Tuesday evening the kids would cram themselves among the local drinkers at the Railway Hotel for the rhythm and blues club night, the Bluesday. This corner of Harrow known as Wealdstone became the place to be for teenagers wanting to hear young bands playing covers and original songs inspired by the American musical import. In a small low-ceilinged bar, they'd watch the musicians squeeze onto a makeshift stage made out of beer crates, to give a very British rendition of songs recorded by mainly American artists.

One June night, a young West London band that had travelled the few miles to Harrow for their residency at the Bluesday club, would give new meaning to the phrase "going through the roof". Just as the lead guitarist pulled an energetically expressive shape during a power chord, the headstock of his expensive Rickenbacker got caught on the paper-thin low ceiling and snapped. Everybody in the audience began to laugh at the flashy guitarist's predicament. An embarrassed Pete Townshend reacted in the only way he knew: he punched an even bigger hole through the ceiling: "I had no other recourse but to make it look like I had meant to do it. So I smashed this guitar and jumped all over the bits and then picked up the

12-string and carried on as though nothing had happened. And the next [time], the place was packed... I've never had any respect really for the guitar. For years and years I didn't care what the guitar was like."

Townshend and his fellow musicians in the Who – bass-player John Entwistle, lead singer Roger Daltrey and drummer Doug Sandon – had been gigging for some years on the local circuit playing mainly R&B covers, first as the Detours then from February 1964, as the Who. But in May, Keith Moon had replaced Sandon, and he was perched on the stage along with the others when Townshend launched what he'd later describe as his "auto-destruction". Soon Keith Moon began destroying his drum kits as well. Townshend said the drummer was "always a great joiner-inner", but Moon simply saw it as great fun.

That simple mishap and Townshend's spontaneous reaction to it would come to shape the trajectory of the band's career. One man who saw that show would come to play an immensely influential role in their lives: Kit Lambert was the posh, Oxford-educated son of the famous composer Constant Lambert. Kit later described that first time he'd seen the Who: "They were playing in this room with just one red bulb glowing and an extraordinary audience they had collected. They were the loudest group I'd ever heard and they gave the whole thing a satanic quality. It just seemed to me that this had to be the face of the late 60s." Lambert claimed to have spotted their potential right from that moment: "I knew they could become world superstars."

That summer, urged on by their then manager Pete Meaden – soon to be replaced by Lambert – the band embraced the R&B-inspired British musical and stylistic off-shoot of Mod, changed their name to the High Numbers, and released a single on Fontana Records. Derek Johnson at the *New Musical Express* was fairly dismissive of the band's debut, declaring, "The High Numbers are highly topical with their novelty lyric about male attire, 'Zoot Suit'." But he thought that the song had an "inconsequential" tune, and that the band had "compelling styling, but weak-ish material".

The band reverted to calling themselves the Who in November and, just seven months after Johnson's discouraging review, the same paper's John Wells would report that the Who represented "a logical musical expression of the bewilderment and anarchy of London's teenagers". There was no easy route from Johnson's disdain to Wells' acclaim.

While the Railway pub incident was believed to be Townshend's first public display of "auto-destruction", he remembers smashing his guitar as far back as 1958: "John Entwistle and I were rehearsing together in the front room of my house. My grandmother came in shouting, 'Turn that bloody racket down!' I said, 'I'll do better than that', and I got my guitar – this was a good guitar that I had paid for myself with money I earned from a paper round – and smashed it to smithereens. I said, 'Now will you fucking get out of my life?' and she stomped out. I looked at John and said, 'What now?' And he said, 'Another paper round, I think'. Once I had done it, it was always there as a possibility. If ever I wanted to deal with any kind of hidden rage, I could always take it out on the guitar. I could always trigger the same little bit of psychotherapy."

The arrival of the Who would be heralded by outrageous, incendiary live performances and brilliant pop singles. Their first few 45s captured all the band's youthful energy and power. Full of teenage frustration and aggression, these records galvanised the idea of the Who in the collective minds of the record-buying public. Within the grooves of these little black discs were spirited songs and dynamic performances, plus musical innovations that would change the landscape of pop music forever.

As the 1960s reached their halfway mark, the Who, a fuel-injected rock'n'roll demolition squad, smashed their way into the headlines with a scorched-earth policy that left a trail of broken instruments, ecstatic fans and outraged media and parents alike. In an age where most bands had an attitude that said, "Love us, love us!", the Who were surly and aggressive. They sneered and snarled, never wanting to be loved. In fact, they wanted to be hated, feared even, but most of all they wanted to be noticed. This wasn't "entertainment"; it was a new rebellion.

The Who were the real deal – wayward lads, sometime delinquents. They were the absolute opposite of the geeky, almost asexual awkwardness of their early influence, the Kinks. And they were the complete antithesis of those lovable mop-tops, the Beatles. Townshend, Daltrey, Entwistle and Moon had been dreaming of escaping their roots, and transcending their dead-end job destiny. Together, with their collective eye on the big prize, they would more than achieve their aim.

Over the next two decades and beyond, the Who continued to survive and thrive in every musical climate. They started in competition with the Beatles and the Rolling Stones, as well as 60s novelty acts such as Freddie and the Dreamers. Later in the decade, they found new adversaries in the shape of supergroups such as Yes, Genesis, Pink Floyd and Led Zeppelin. Then, while many of their own generation grew complacent in tax exile, the Who watched glam replaced by punk, and found themselves trendy again with the re-birth of Mod.

By the early 80s, they were stadium rock stalwarts, touring the US with the Clash in support. Although the underwhelming *It's Hard* album in 1982 seemed to mark the end of the road for the group, they would continue to reunite sporadically, notably at 1985's superstar charity festival *Live Aid* and the *Live 8* show twenty years later. Finally, in 2006, the two surviving members of the original line-up returned to the studio for *Endless Wire*. Forty-one years after their debut album, Pete and Roger had come a long way – and what an amazing journey it had been.

01   Instant Party – 1965

The band's manager Pete Meaden was quickly supplanted by Kit Lambert and his business partner, Chris Stamp (brother of the actor Terence Stamp). When Lambert and Stamp had decided to oust Meaden, they took him out to dinner to persuade him to take a pay-off to bow out of the band's career. "They were prepared to spend £5,000 when they sat down," explained journalist Paolo Hewitt many years later. "Kit started by offering £500 to which Meaden said 'Sure', and they saved £4,500."

As savvy as that move might have been, in the years to come, Lambert's and Stamp's general lack of music business knowledge would work both for and against the band. They may have signed some contracts that would eventually prove detrimental to the group's long-term financial future, but by the same token, they made good things happen too. They had no fear. They would attempt crazy things and what the pair of them didn't know they would make up as they went along. These ideas would often, somehow actually pay off.

Stamp and Lambert originally wanted to make a film tracking a pop group's rise to fame. Chris Stamp explained, "We had seen a number of films about the music business and people in pop music and thought they were terrible trash. We thought we could do better, but we couldn't afford to pay a top pop group ourselves. Our only way was to start from scratch with an unknown group. That was how we came to stumble over the Who."

Keith Moon revealed candidly of the early relationship with the management team, "We didn't like each other at first, really. They were as incongruous a team as we were. You got Chris, on the one hand, who's ya typical East Ender and Kit with his Oxford accent. These people were perfect for us because there's me, bouncing about, full of pills, full of everything I could get my hands on... and there's Pete, very serious, never laughed, always cool, a grasshead. I was working at about ten times the speed Pete was. And Kit and Chris were the epitome of what we were."

For all of their enthusiasm, within a matter of months, Stamp and Lambert seemed to be running out of ideas. They were enormously enthusiastic but were getting nowhere fast. Despite constant gigging the band's bank balance was way into the red. The all-important record deal still eluded them and the young band were at a loss as to what to do next. But they were thrown a lifeline when their managers' secretary, Anya Butler, introduced them to Shel Talmy, an American record producer based in London. He had just produced the Kinks. Pete later observed, "Shel came along at the front of the new wave of recording and of writing and said he was working with the Kinks, whom we admired very much. We didn't like their image but we liked their sound and their music."

It would be Talmy who would render the group's dream of making records into a reality. He first saw the Who in rehearsals in Shepherd's Bush, in West London, and thought they were "raunchier" than most of the "polite" groups he had seen in the UK: "They had everything – the songs, musicianship, a good singer and punch. Easily the most American rock'n'roll band I'd seen since coming to England."

However, Talmy's enthusiasm didn't translate into generosity when it came to contractual terms. He managed to pull enough wool over the collective eyes of Lambert and Stamp to get them to sign one of the worst deals in recording history: the band would receive no advance. Worse, the copyright ownership of the music would revert to Talmy himself. Rock'n'roll contracts were a whole new world to Lambert and Stamp. Both band and management had been stung at the very first turn. The deal Talmy struck would award him the sole right to place the forthcoming album with US label Decca and with Brunswick in Britain. Nobody at the time seemd to notice the four-year contractual option to Talmy's own Orbit Music: a financial time bomb waiting to go off. The band began recording in late 1964 with their new-found saviour/producer at the Pye Studios, near Marble Arch in central London, but with no advance paid by either Talmy or his company, they had to play up to 20 gigs a month to make ends meet.

I Can't Explain
UK Single Release: 15/01/1965 (Brunswick) US Single Release: 13/02/1965 (Decca)
Peak Position: 8 (UK) 93 (US)

The Who's first single finds them at their fledgling pop best. Crammed with inspired melodies, shiny bright crash chords and blistering drum fills, it's a classic that never sounds tired. And what's more, it's all over in just two minutes and three seconds.

John Entwistle divulged the genesis of this pop classic, "When Pete first started writing, his songs were kind of other people's songs badly remembered. We were at Keith's house one night and we were playing 'You Really Got Me' by the Kinks, and Pete went home and tried to remember it but couldn't, he had such a bad memory, and so he came up with 'I Can't Explain'."

Townshend opens with a simple but instantly memorable signature riff played on his metallic-sounding Rickenbacker. "A straightforward copy of the Kinks' 'You Really Got Me' but with a different rhythm," Pete confessed. "I was on my way, but I was just copying." "I Can't Explain" was produced by Talmy who originally planned to use session musicians to cut the backing track. According to Roger Daltrey, Shel didn't think Pete's lead guitar playing was up to it and he even considered replacing Keith Moon.

Townshend takes up the story, "Keith was over in the corner, telling the drummer, 'Get out of the studio or I'll kill ya! On a Who record, only Keith Moon plays the drums'."

Young hotshot session guitarist Jimmy Page was brought in to play the guitar parts but the obstinate Townshend was having none of it. Pete and Jimmy were friends but still Pete demanded of him, "What are you doing here?" Jimmy said he was there to add some weight to the guitar by doubling the rhythm part. They discussed the guitars to be used and Pete said it was "all very congenial" but, nevertheless, Page didn't play the solo.

John Entwistle gave a somewhat different version of events saying Townshend simply "refused to lend (Page) his 12-string Rickenbacker," and so Page didn't get to play on "I Can't Explain". "Jimmy (Page) was there in case Pete couldn't cut it," Talmy confirmed. "But Pete was just fine." Townshend's solo is a nimble-fingered jaunt that's brief but charming as it rings and sparkles, cut with the twang of the Rickenbacker. Keith's 16th-note-couplet snare fills blast out in the brief pauses while Roger gives a controlled, distinctive vocal performance. Daltrey commented years later, "Well, it's that thing – 'I got a feeling inside, I can't explain' – it's rock'n'roll. The more we try to explain it, the more we crawl up our own arses and disappear! I was very proud of that record. It captured the energy and that testosterone that we had in those days. It still does."

Pete describes "I Can't Explain" as a "love song of frustration", a song that inspired his audience to ask for more in the same vein: "They got it and I didn't. When they came to me with that idea, telling me 'you have to write more songs like that,' sort of nailing the nail into my skull for me to get it. What? Songs about the fact that you can't explain what you want to explain . . . 'yes, that's what we mean.' So I was charged with this job." He later remarked that this song represented a process that was akin to an artist receiving a commission to paint a picture.

Lyrically, it deals with the frustrations of a young man who can't explain the romantic feelings he has for a girl. It's wracked with a self-consciousness that all teenagers will recognise. A backing vocal call-and-response (supplied by the Ivy League) is a musical device the Who would utilise frequently. Finally, Daltrey comes clean and says what he means – "I can't explain / I think it's love / Try to say it to you / When I feel blue." But is it love or just teenage lust? Who knows, but the frustration pours from every line and the band's performance is full of youthful arrogance and energy. It's a glorious debut.

The group made several radio and television appearances to promote the single, but their defining spot occurred on 29th January, 1965, when they performed the song on ITV's Friday night music show, *Ready, Steady, Go!* As Pete Townshend later related to Charles Shaar Murray in 1973, "From there on, we never looked back." In the 2007 film *Amazing Journey*, Pete recalled, "Back in those early days I thought, 'I'm not going to write songs forever, y'know, this is boring'. I really thought 'Can't Explain' was quite childish."

Anyway, Anyhow, Anywhere
UK Single Release: 21/05/1965 (Brunswick) US Single Release: 05/06/1965 (Decca)
Peak Position: 10 (UK)

For many years, the only Who song with a composition credit for both Townshend and Daltrey, Peter Townshend upped the ante for this second offering. "We literally wrote it on stage," Roger explained. "Pete had the basic verse structure and I think I wrote the bridge and bits of the chorus. He would do this bit and I would say, 'What about that bit?', and the song came together like that. And we recorded it the next day; that's why there's no demo of it." They never wrote like this again. Years later, when asked if he would have liked to have written more songs with Townshend, Roger replied simply, "Of course I do. Of course I do."

Where "I Can't Explain" was "pop" in its purest sense, the core of "Anyway, Anyhow, Anywhere" contained the beginning of something new. The free-form jam in the song's mid-section was pure rock mayhem. Reportedly inspired by the free-form solos of jazz pioneer Charlie Parker, Pete added Morse code bleeps and gunfire in his solo. The guitar was a 1964 electric 12-string Rickenbacker (also used on "I Can't Explain"), which was also a favourite model for the Beatles, and later used by Paul Weller of the Jam. Then there was the feedback, at that time a rarity on a pop record. "Even before that, we were doing this feedback stuff", Roger said, "We'd be doing blues songs and they'd turn into this freedom, feedbacky, jazzy noise."

"Recording it was a bitch because of the tube equipment we were using," producer Shel Talmy remembered. "But if Pete could play it, I was determined to get it on tape. I had Pete cranking it to the max." In order to ensure that the reverb and signal delays came across in the final mix, Talmy used no fewer than three microphones at the studio session, before mixing to mono and compressing the sound. Baffled employees at the pressing plant for Decca in the United States assumed that the single was from a faulty master. Roger Daltrey: "We said, 'No, this is the fucking noise we want. CUT IT LOUD!'"

"When the big feedback controversy was going on in the mid-60s," Pete later revealed, "[Kinks guitarist] Dave Davies and I used to have hilarious arguments about who was the first to invent feedback. I used to pull Dave's leg by saying 'We both supported the Beatles in Blackpool and you weren't doing it then... I bet you nicked it off me when you saw me doing it.' And Dave would scream that he was doing it long before that." But Townshend was less amused at a similar argument with Jeff Beck. In Townshend's words, Beck would later claim, "'[Pete Townshend] came down to see [Beck's band] the Tridents rehearsing and he saw me using feedback... and copied it'. I never ever saw the Tridents. Obviously, Beck may feel deeply enough that he invented feedback – but for Chrissakes, who gives a shit? It doesn't really matter, it's just a funny noise made by a guitar."

Roger Daltrey backed his band-mate: "Basically, the act that Hendrix is famous for came from Townshend, pre-'I Can't Explain'. 'Anyway, Anyhow, Anywhere' was the first song when we attempted to get that noise onto a record and that was a good deal of time before Hendrix had even come to England."

With "Anyway, Anyhow, Anywhere", Townshend had already taken steps to move the group away from the narrow constraints of a Mod band to the emerging "pop art" movement. Together with producer Talmy, they captured some of the energy and power of their live performances. The song was a resounding success, and was cemented in the psyche of the young British pop fans when, later in 1965, it was adopted as the theme tune for one of Britain's first pop and rock music TV series *Ready, Steady, Go!*, which ran on ITV from 1963 to 1966.

My Generation
UK Single Release: 05/11/1965 (Brunswick) US Single Release: 20/11/1965 (Decca)
Peak Position: 2 (UK) 74 (US)

Speaking candidly Townshend confessed, "If ever there was a period when the

Who might have split, it would have been in the days of 'My Generation'. We had an image of no time for anybody and Mod arrogance, in a period when we were actually a very ordinary group. We hadn't really done anything good, but we knew we were capable so we managed, over a period, to get it together."

"'My Generation' was very much about trying to find a place in society," Pete would reflect years after the record's release. "I was very lost. The band was young then. It was believed that its career would be incredibly brief. The privilege that I had at the time was to be plucked out of bed-sitter land and put in a flat in the middle of Belgravia with two tape machines. It was private, and I could look out at these people who seemed to be from another planet."

"My Generation" 7-inch single

He explained, "Someone came to me and said, 'Make a statement, make a statement'... and I got 'My Generation' together very quickly, like in a night. It's a very blustering kind of blurting thing. A lot of our early records were." Pete said he wrote the lyric "without thinking... scribbling on a piece of paper in the back of a car." Rushed or not, it worked: such pressure paid massive dividends. Townshend had written a song that would define an era. He variously described it "as a talking-blues thing" and "my folk song single", saying it was influenced by the likes of Jimmy Reed, Bob Dylan and Mose Allison (the band would later cover Allison's "Young Man Blues" on the *Live At Leeds* album).

Recorded in London at IBC Studios, "Generation" had started life as a slow blues song with a Bo Diddley beat under-pinning the rhythm. According to Daltrey, Keith wasn't keen on the feel, so he abandoned the original approach and thrashed his way through it. Kit Lambert approved of the drummer's interpretation and the song, as we recognise it now, was born.

One of the ultimate anthems of teenage rebellion and belligerence, "My Generation" finds Townshend cranking out the simple riffs on his Rickenbacker against Daltrey's calculated faltering vocals. The latter's stuttering was manager Kit Lambert's idea, to try and emulate a Mod kid on speed, which would initially result in a ban from an overly anxious BBC which feared upsetting those listeners with genuine stutters. However, Townshend maintained that the stuttering was on his original home demo, claiming he'd stolen the technique from blues master John Lee Hooker. Keith Moon had a further explanation: "Pete had written out the words and given them to Roger in the studio. He'd never seen them before, so when he read them the first time, he stuttered... it happened simply because Roger couldn't read the words."

There were many major musical differences that set this apart from all the other pop records emerging at the time. There's the sneering arrogance, outrageous guitar and drum histrionics plus, of all things – a bass solo. Few other hit singles in pop history have ever boasted a bass guitar solo and certainly not one of such virtuosity. Here's a perfect example of Pete encouraging John to let rip, while he sticks to his powerful rhythmic technique on guitar. It's a monster bass solo that dive bombs its way up and down the neck of John Entwistle's guitar, sounding as if he's trying to emulate Keith's drum fills. Producer/engineer Glyn Johns commented, "If you actually listen to any Who record and isolate the bass, it's pretty astonishing what he's doing, it's nothing to do with what a normal bass player would do."

After a final key change that heralds the last verse and chorus, the band hit the outro section, whereupon Keith kicks into overdrive in his inimitable incendiary style. No one had ever played drums like this on a 60s pop record before. Entwistle commented, "Once Keith turned up, all hell broke loose." Townshend's guitar wails and screams wildly amid the maelstrom of distortion and feedback and, as the band hit the final chord with a satisfying crash, you know that this is no ordinary 1960s beat combo, but a rock'n'roll monster come to eat your children. The single raced to second place in the British charts, but failed to squeeze past the melodic dirge, "The Carnival Is Over" by the Seekers.

The enduring power of "My Generation" was underlined decades later, when American shock rocker Alice Cooper told British DJ Ken Bruce on BBC Radio 2 in 2007 that he thought the song should be the new British national anthem. Cooper described the song as a masterpiece, and its composer as the ultimate rock star. This one song has so many innovations that it alone would later earn the band a place in the Rock And Roll Hall Of Fame.

Townshend later explained another surprising element to the thinking behind these early classic singles: "I found it hard to write for Roger; songs like 'My Generation', 'I Can't Explain', 'Anyway, Anyhow, Anywhere', and lots of songs I wrote that never actually made that period, which I've got on demos, are embarrassingly macho, because I was trying to find things that he would feel comfortable singing."

My Generation
UK Album Release: 03/12/1965 (Brunswick LAT 8616)
Peak Position: 5 (UK)
Out In The Street / I Don't Mind / The Good's Gone / La-La-La Lies / Much Too Much / My Generation / The Kids Are Alright / Please, Please, Please / It's Not True / I'm A Man / A Legal Matter / The Ox

The Who Sings My Generation
US Album Release: 04/1966 (Decca DL 74664)

Out In The Street / I Don't Mind / The Good's Gone / La-La-La Lies / Much Too Much / My Generation / The Kids Are Alright / Please, Please, Please / It's Not True / The Ox / A Legal Matter / Circles

My Generation (Deluxe Edition)

UK Album Release: 09/09/2002 (Polydor 1129262)
US Album Release: 08/2002 (MCA 088 1129262)
Disc 1: Out In The Street / I Don't Mind / The Good's Gone / La-La-La-Lies / Much Too Much / My Generation / The Kids Are Alright / Please, Please, Please / It's Not True / I'm A Man / A Legal Matter / The Ox / Circles (Instant Party) / I Can't Explain / Bald Headed Woman / Daddy Rolling Stone
Disc 2: Leaving Here / Lubie (Come Back Home) / Shout And Shimmy / Heatwave / Motoring / Anytime You Want Me / Anyway, Anyhow, Anywhere (Alternate Take) / Instant Party Mixture / I Don't Mind (Full Length Version) / The Good's Gone (Full Length Version) / My Generation (Instrumental Version) / Anytime You Want Me (A Cappella Version) / A Legal Matter (Original Mono Version) / My Generation (Original Mono Version)

The Who as a group have great potential. They haven't copied anyone. They have had the courage to put together a wild and dynamic stage act that no one would have dreamed of. And they match this colourful form of presentation by wearing equally colourful clothes. Without a doubt they are in a class of their own.
John Emery, *Beat Instrumental*

The Who recorded much of the first album very quickly and were never entirely satisfied with it. Augmenting the group on piano was future Stones collaborator Nicky Hopkins, who would play on all tracks bar the "I Can't Explain" single (Perry Ford featured on piano here). The Ivy League added backing vocals to both that 45 and its flip-side, "Bald Headed Woman" which featured Jimmy Page who added minimal guitar flourishes (late one night in a bar when John Entwistle and Keith Moon were drunkenly contemplating leaving the Who, Entwistle came up with the name Led Zeppelin and Moon had the idea for an album cover featuring the burning Hindenburg airship. They would later encourage Page's band to use both).

Over three days in April 1965, the group plus Hopkins recorded much of what would become the *My Generation* LP. The same team reconvened several months later to complete the record, but it would be the end of the year before it reached the shops, by which time the Who had hit the British Top Ten chart three times. This would help their debut album to reach number five, although it would fail to make any impression when belatedly issued (with its "The Who Sings" prefix) in the USA.

For many years, *My Generation* – when it was available at all – was regarded as a technically shoddy package. Both Shel Talmy and the group believed they were rightful owners of the LP's copyright so plans to improve it were at a stalemate. Had it not been for Who fans Chris Charlesworth and David Swartz, the 2002 deluxe edition might never have seen the light of day. Charlesworth, a former *Melody Maker* journalist who has written extensively about the Who and later became a senior publishing figure with Omnibus Press, knew that someone needed to reason with the record's producer. Swartz visited Talmy in Los Angeles and told him face-to-face that his demands were unreasonable. After some thought, Talmy reduced his asking price to a figure that has been quoted as anything from $50,000 to twice that (one can only wonder at the extent of his original asking price). Finally, Talmy and Townshend could begin to communicate and that proved the catalyst for the album's long-awaited reissue, complete with a plethora of outtakes and rarities.

Out In The Street

The flamenco guitar motif that would also begin "Anyhow, Anywhere, Anyway" features prominently on this opening cut, which had been originally entitled, "You're Gonna Know Me". With a cry of "Out!" from Roger, they're off and running. Townsend's guitar style is already choppy and strident, with the trademark flicking of his pick-up selector switch immediately evident. Echoes of the American guitar pioneer Link Wray can be found here too. Townshend has often cited Wray as a big influence, especially in his distortion and tremolo techniques (for further proof, check out Wray's million-selling "Rumble" from 1958). Roger's vocal delivery offers threatening lyrics, Keith bounces along with John's tight, simple bass lines showing that the band has established itself as an efficient rock'n'roll unit.

I Don't Mind

The first of many covers on the album, "I Don't Mind" had been a hit for James Brown in 1961, as well as providing one of the highlights of his *Live At The Apollo* LP. Brown was one of Daltrey's favourite singers of this period, and he does his best here to emulate his R&B hero. Slick harmony vocals, which will become a Who staple, feature heavily, while Townshend delivers a competent bluesy solo. Nicky Hopkins' piano lurks needlessly in the background.

The Good's Gone

This fairly standard "break-up" song finds Roger sounding deep and gruff. Brittle, chiming guitars arpeggiate as the teenage Moon articulates effortlessly off cranked-up tom-toms and bright cymbals. Already, Keith's style is emerging as a vital part of the band's overall sound scheme.

La-La-La-Lies

As Roger delivers this so-so Townshend-penned ditty, Entwistle is fluidly professional. The energy is maintained with Keith playing intermittent controlled patterns with the snare wound off. There are fleeting glimpses of what's to come later in the group's career, with Pete hitting some tentative crash chords, but it's pretty much a conventional 60s approach. Later in 1966, this would be one of several Who singles to be released by Talmy without the consent of the group, but while only a minor hit in the UK, it would climb into the Top Twenty in Sweden.

Much Too Much

The third consecutive track to have been recorded during the sessions of November 1965, the lyrics describe the rejection of a lover whose feelings are too possessive and claustrophobic. "Your love's too heavy on me," sings Daltrey adopting an affected American accent with Dylanesque overtones. This is typical mid-60s beat boom material, and John's contribution in particular to the sound of the group has yet to really make its presence felt. Once again, Nicky Hopkins' piano part is somewhat unnecessary.

My Generation
Someone has switched the lights on: the superior quality of this song immediately leaps out of the speakers. Now you are listening to the Who – not boys doing what they think people want, but four rock'n'roll geezers, playing how they feel, what they feel, in the way they really want. It's an instant classic, and soars above all of the LP's previous tracks, which have been pleasant enough but little more.

John Entwistle's performance here cannot be over-stated, not only is there the magnificent solo but also his determined 16th notes in the vocal breaks that maintain musical tension and drive the track ever onwards. Getting the right bass sound for the record was arduous and expensive, he recalls, "I was using a Danelectro bass with very thin strings, which were inclined to break, but you couldn't buy replacement strings in Britain then, so I'd have to buy a new guitar. I went through three guitars at £60 a time during the recording of 'My Generation'. In the end, they decided to record it one more time, and I bust a string again and there literally weren't any more Danelectros in the country. I went out and bought a Fender Jazz bass, put the trebliest strings I could find onto it and played the solo on that."

The song's fourth line is one of the most quoted in rock history. Down the years, Townshend has had the "I hope I die before I get old" line thrown back in his face countless times. Talking of his youthfully defiant lyrics many years later he said, "For years I've had to live by them, waiting for the day when someone says, 'I thought you said you hoped you'd die when you got old. Well, now you are old. What now?' Of course, most people are too polite to say that sort of thing to a dying pop star... Perhaps if I had died before I got old, I might have been forgotten. You tend to hope you'll become James Dean or Jimi Hendrix, but a lot of dead people aren't remembered at all... But I've tried to compensate by actually making myself happy."

He said of the most common interpretations of the song, "[It] has always been bandied about as a kind of nihilistic rock'n'roll pre-echo, that leads directly or indirectly to the death of someone like Kurt Cobain... It wasn't nihilistic at all, but exactly the opposite. It was life-affirming: I will be forever young, I hope I die before I get old, I hope I live in this place that I'm in now forever."

The pioneering French electronic artist, Jean Michel Jarre, told BBC Radio in 2008 that this was the first song he ever tried to play with his teenage rock group. He was amazed by what he called the harsh and aggressive sound, concluding that "My Generation" wasn't just an anthem for that particular generation but the anthem for each new generation.

The Kids Are Alright
Recorded at the same time as "My Generation" in IBC Studios, which was fast becoming a home-from-home for the group, they rushed straight from the session to a gig. They were making records so fast in these early days that Roger would have to later listen to the record and write out the lyrics so that he could perform them live, not having had enough time to commit the words to memory.

Townshend's improved writing and the band's inspired playing does not falter. The foursome has found its own voice, with Keith's characteristic fills and Pete's fondness for the suspended chord very much in evidence ("It's just covered in those suspensions", he would reflect on his group's first LP). Pete's unlikely inspiration is said to be the 16th century English composer Henry Purcell.

As well as inspiring the title of the group's 1979 film (see Chapter 11), this was one of Keith Moon's personal favourites and, a decade later, he would cover it for his patchy solo LP, *Two Sides Of The Moon*. It was released as a single in August 1966 without the consent of the group.

Please, Please, Please

With a second cover of a James Brown hit – this time an overwrought remake of his first single from 1956 – "Please, Please, Please" sees the Who returning to playing by the 60s rules. While Moon would deride the covers as "disgusting", Daltrey favoured recording such material and, for the time being, was reluctant to record Townshend's songs – but while fare such as this might satisfy the drinkers and fans at that early gig venue, the Railway Tavern in north-west London, it felt incongruous next to the inspiration of "My Generation" and "The Kids Are Alright". It would only be a matter of time before Townshend's original lyrics would become the bedrock of the group's sound and attitude.

It's Not True

Townshend's song of accusation sees some convincing power chords blighted by even more superfluous honky-tonk piano. Again, this is pleasant, but filler nonetheless.

Keith plays nifty fills around his recently acquired Premier drum kit. The 19-year-old had signed a deal with the company the year this album was released and he took delivery of a resplendent, gleaming red sparkle kit. This was slightly grander than his first drum kit, a secondhand Premier blue mother-of-pearl for which he paid £75. Keith used this kit on his first gig with the group. Entwistle recalled, "He got this little blue drum kit up and then got this huge coil of rope and tied it all together. We couldn't understand why until he went into a drum solo, and everything started to sway backwards and forwards."

I'm A Man

The Who's take on Bo Diddley's braggadocio classic showed that the Stones weren't the only Londoners into authentic blues. A strangled lead vocal with Roger sounding both youthful and surprisingly gruff and commanding, plus some full-on Rickenbacker work and tight playing from the band make this a solid effort, but the musical mayhem during the play-out shows where they really wanted to go.

A Legal Matter

This track marked the first time that Pete Townshend sang lead vocals on a Who song. While he handles his vocal duties with aplomb, the band sound like they've been let off the leash and really let rip to create another early classic.

The painful irony of a song that dealt with divorce – still touchy subject matter in the mid-60s – was that Roger Daltrey was himself separating from his wife at the time. Stylistically not a million miles from the Stones' recent number one hit, "The Last Time", the song would be released as a single in March 1966 without the consent of the group.

The Ox
John Entwistle's nickname – The Ox – gives its name to the closing track on the original LP and the only time a Who song's writing credit would read Townshend/ Moon/Entwistle/Hopkins. This 12-bar blues instrumental is believed by Townshend to represent the first time that the group satisfactorily captured in the studio their free-form live approach.

Keith plays manic 16ths round his toms and Pete's guitar shows Link Wray's influence as it feeds back and buzzes. Keith Moon's biographer, Tony Fletcher, has claimed that the track was based loosely around "Waikiki Run" by the Surfaris. Beneath a penetrating melody lies a powerful bass riff. John claimed, "The track that really epitomised Keith is 'The Ox.'." Pete said this was the only track he enjoyed recording, referring to the rest of the sessions as too disciplined.

Bonus Tracks:

Circles
The final Who song to be produced by Shel Talmy was originally planned to be the follow up to "My Generation". This track, recorded in the second week of 1966, was to be the catalyst in the breakdown in relations between band and producer.

Roger delivers a surly vocal as crash chords ring out from Townshend's guitar and Moon rolls impressively around his tom-toms. All of the Who's trademarks are already here, if in a more restrained form. The other version of this was used as a B-side for the single "Substitute", where there is very little difference apart from Entwistle's morose French horn part.

I Can't Explain
A stereo mix of that startling debut single, this is missing the tambourine part present on the original mix. More than a decade later, the Clash's Mick Jones would steal the song's opening guitar riff for his band's punk classic, "Clash City Rockers".

Bald Headed Woman
Adapted for the B-side of "I Can't Explain" by Talmy from a traditional African-American chain-gang song, "Bald Headed Woman" was rearranged and recorded by numerous other groups during the 60s – among them Sweden's Hep Stars, who included future Abba member and composer Benny Andersson. The Who's version is dominated by a rather mannered, strangulated vocal from Roger, who also contributes a brief harmonica break. John Entwistle later claimed that Roger's solo began with the singer putting the harmonica in his mouth the wrong way round. The tune starts off at a rather pedestrian pace, but then kicks off into an up-tempo rock rave-up of demonic drumming and blues guitar licks.

It may seem odd that a band that was torn between recording their own new material and classic R&B covers would record a song created by their producer. However, in their more innocent early days, the band were prepared to sacrifice almost anything to make a record, including allowing Talmy to gain the publishing royalties.

As well as the Ivy League on backing vocals, this also features the guitar of Jimmy Page, who played the "fuzz" guitar part, apparently because he was the only musician who owned a "fuzz box" in Britain at the time.

Daddy Rolling Stone
A standard rockin' rendition of Otis Blackwell's R&B staple from 1953, although the Who's cover was directly inspired by Derek Martin's 1963 version. First showcased on the flipside of "Anyway, Anyhow, Anywhere", it took until 1987's *Two's Missing* compilation before it was available in the US. Yet again, Nicky Hopkins' superfluous piano-banging detrimentally dominates proceedings.

Leaving Here
Rather underlining a dearth of original material, this additional disc of rarities begins with no fewer than six cover versions. The band is obviously still finding its way on this reworking of a Holland/Dozier/Holland composition, but Roger's bluesy vocal is effective and Keith's drumming is nifty. Young Townshend adds tasty lead guitar breaks and the "Oh yeah" backing vocals are shambolic but fun.

Lubie (Come Back Home)
This song is loosely based on Paul Revere and the Raiders' 1964 US single release "Louie (Go Home)". The Who song – with new title and lyrics – was only issued in the UK as an import. It features fantastic snare work from the teenage Keith, thick and mature lead vocals from Roger, and call-and-response backing vocals echoing the work of the Beatles.

Shout And Shimmy
A staple of the group's early live set – although it was dropped as early as 1966 – and yet another cover of a James Brown composition, this time a song made famous by the Godfather of Soul in 1962. Keith plays some death-defying fills in the build-and-climax section, while Roger's mimicry of Brown is convincing. This was first released in Britain in the autumn of 1965 when it appeared on the other side of the "My Generation" 45.

Heatwave
A professional but unremarkable take on the Holland/Dozier/Holland song first made famous by Martha Reeves and the Vandellas in 1963. While this was considered strong enough to open the Who's live set circa 1965, by 1968, Townshend had dismissed innocuous output like this as "fairly inconsequential music" (a second version of "Heatwave" would feature on the Who's second album, *A Quick One*).

Motoring
This jolly enough reheating of another Vandellas' original (which had been on the

B-side of the "Nowhere to Run" smash hit of 1965) bounces along with a strident feel but there's little spark and few glimpses of Pete's trademark athletic guitar style or the quartet's robust sound.

Anytime You Want Me
The barrage of cover versions concludes with a toothless interpretation of a 1963 album track by Garnett Mimms and the Enchanters. The band hadn't developed their style yet and this track sorely lacks Pete's distinctive guitar, instead it over-relies on Nicky Hopkins' piano. However, the group's American and Australian labels considered it of sufficient quality to appear on the flip-side of "Anyhow, Anywhere, Anyhow".

Anyhow, Anywhere, Anyhow (Alternative)
An alternative reading of the group's second hit single which is soaked with piano embellishments from Nicky Hopkins, but does at least compensate with some abrasive guitars and manic drums.

Instant Party Mixture
Recorded in January 1966 at the same session as the ill-fated "Circles", this was intended to be its B-side, and would in subsequent years escape onto bootleg compilations under the titles "Party And Lies" or "Partyin' Pete". A Townshend-penned doo-wop tune, it metamorphoses into a brief jam of Chuck Berry's "Johnny B. Goode" in its closing section. Undoubtedly throwaway, its sense of fun does anticipate the irreverent content of, for instance, *The Who Sell Out*.

I Don't Mind / The Good's Gone
Full length versions of two tracks curtailed for the original vinyl edition.

My Generation (Instrumental Version)
The backing track of the legendary anti-authority anthem is pushed centre-stage, allowing the listener to fully appreciate the power of the band as musicians. They are tight, energetic and inventive with exceptional collective control.

Anytime You Want Me (A Cappella Version)
The Who often found their combined vocal skills were underestimated. This rare vocals-only take demonstrates Daltrey, Townshend and Entwistle's ease at dealing with three-part counter-harmonies. All three were strikingly skilled harmony vocalists who excelled both live and in the studio.

A Legal Matter (Original Mono Version) / My Generation (Original Mono Version)
To finish off the rarities disc, a chance to hear mono mixes of two very familiar songs, complete with lead guitar overdubs missing from their respective stereo versions.

With hindsight it would seem that the Who simply breezed into a London recording studio, set up and knocked out a few Mod tunes – before posing for the right picture in the right gear and, as if by magic, stardom beckoned. Yet this had been no overnight success. The band were already seasoned professionals on the live circuit before they ever recorded a note.

Local concert poster, 1965

02 Subtitutes And Legal Matters – 1966

The first album marked a move away from the role of the "godfathers" of Mod. In between recording and releasing the *My Generation* album, Townshend declared, "We think the Mod thing is dying. We don't plan to go down with it, which is why we've become individualists." Having cast off their Mod image, the Who would drench their second album in pop art. Its sleeve anticipated the design used by the sometimes-controversial underground magazine *Oz*, which would launch in Britain in 1967. The psychedelic "love-in" of 1967 was still a good six months away, although the cause that would unite the hippies – the war in Vietnam – was already lodged firmly in Pete's mind when the *New Musical Express* (*NME*) interviewed him in March 1966: "Youngsters facing foreign troops about something they don't even understand... They all ought to get out."

With their first album an imperfect ragbag – a handful of genuinely groundbreaking cuts rounded out with covers and filler – the Who quickly realised that competition was ferocious among their peers, especially now that the long-playing record, the LP, was fast replacing the 45 rpm single as rock's most vital currency. The Beatles, barely able to hear their own stage performances due to the deafening hordes of screaming fans, had finally turned their back on touring by 1966, and ploughed all their efforts into studio projects, such as their phenomenal *Revolver* LP. The Beatles' last UK gig was at the *NME* awards at the Empire Pool in Wembley, north-west London. The Who were also on the bill and Townshend and Moon were in full destruction mode: they left the stage strewn with the debris of slaughtered drums and guitars in a desperate attempt to up-stage the headline act. As the old guard began to stand down, the young up-starts were ready and waiting, desperate to fill the breach.

All in all, 1966 would turn out to be, by turns, a frustrating and alarming year for the Who. On the face of it, they were doing well, with a further three Top Ten chart singles in the UK and countless TV appearances. Smashing instruments on stage brought them vital press coverage, but inevitably left them short of cash. They'd adopted many of the trappings of the rock star lifestyle, without the income to match. Recognised at all the trendiest fashion stores in London's Carnaby Street and King's Road, they were on first name terms with every mâitre'd at every top restaurant, and weren't shy of paying for their friends' drinks all night.

Their managers, Kit Lambert and Chris Stamp, encouraged them to act like big stars, believing that if they behaved in this way, that's exactly what they would become. Townshend: "Kit used to brief us before we went into interviews about what to say [and] sometimes to be as objectionable, arrogant and nasty as possible." Townshend would boast to journalists about owning four cars and of spending large sums every week on designer clothes, when, in reality, he would have to borrow cash just to buy a jacket to wear for the papers' and magazines' photo shoots.

Their financial predicament was caused in part by the haphazard nature of the business side of things, which meant that many of the Who's most enduring and popular singles of the 1960s – "I Can't Explain", "Anyway, Anyhow, Anywhere", "Substitute", "I'm A Boy", and later "Pictures of Lily" – were not originally included on their albums. Part of this was due to the timing of the respective releases: there was no coherent structuring of release dates for albums and singles, or any forward planning between artist management and record company executives. Albums or singles were released and they simply hoped for the best. The record companies had still not fully realised the pulling power of the album format; their business was still a singles-led industry in 1966, and it wouldn't be until '68 that albums out-sold singles.

The failure to include singles on the albums created a vacuum; how does a consumer identify with an album if it contains no obviously familiar tracks? Nowadays, not including a single on an album would be considered commercial suicide, but forty years ago this practice was commonplace. Not surprisingly, the Who – like many other bands – found that not including singles on their LPs meant that these albums did not get the attention they deserved, and consequently did not earn the group sufficient funds to support their outrageous antics and expensive tastes.

For the moment, though, the situation called for desperate measures. The hangover from their earlier unfavourable contract with Shel Talmy meant that the band's indulgent lifestyle had to be funded through gigs. Chris Stamp hatched a publishing deal that would earn each group member an advance of £500 – the only drawback being that each of them was obliged to bring a minimum of two songs to the next studio album sessions. The timing couldn't have been worse: just as Pete Townshend was emerging as one of the best new songwriters of his generation, financial imperatives meant that suddenly the other three band members were expected to become songwriters of equal stature overnight. Pete would be allowed only four songs on the original 10-song vinyl version of *A Quick One*.

Daltrey, Entwistle and Moon did well to meet the challenge. John's "Boris The Spider" would become a mainstay of the group's live shows for the rest of his life, while his other composition for this album, "Whiskey Man", was intriguingly surreal. Roger and Keith contributed just one song each to the finished album – "See My Way" and "I Need You" respectively – but got around their contractual obligation through creating rough ideas, which Pete and John would later flesh out into finished songs.

The imposed divisiveness of the songwriting arrangements also reflected the tensions within the band. Arguments erupted constantly as singer and guitar-player wrestled for leadership of the group. Daltrey tried to rule by force, while Townshend intimidated with an acid tongue.

"We were always too unhappy... at loggerheads with one another's ideas," Townshend would later tell *Oui* magazine. "There's a difference between disagreeing with somebody and respecting them, and disagreeing with 'em and thinking they're shit. The first eight years of the Who were like that: very, very,

very unhappy times. And if they were happy, it was explosive happiness."

Daltrey later insisted that his own approach was necessary to keep the band's momentum. "I did used to rule the band with an iron fist," he admitted. "The band needed it. The band wouldn't have got anywhere [otherwise]. And now [Townshend] readily admits that he would have laid in bed all day if I hadn't dragged him out... and forced him to come to a gig. So I don't make any apologies for that behaviour." Music journalist Chris Welch observed: "What people didn't realise when the Who became famous, was that it was Roger's baby. They began as the Detours – his band. By the time they were having hit singles and appearing on TV, Pete was the leader. Thus there was always a power struggle between them."

Such a power struggle between singer and guitarist led to the forming of an unlikely alliance. Keith Moon was a manic teenage tearaway while John Entwistle was often seen as a more distant, calculating character who said very little but observed everything. The Who's rhythm section couldn't have comprised two more different individuals, but faced with the Townshend-versus-Daltrey rivalry, Keith and John closed ranks. "I never really joined in that," explained the latter. "I let Pete and Roger argue about who was the most important person in the band."

Against all the complex odds, the band somehow worked as a musical unit. Chris Stamp had his own theory: "They [had] this incredible, distorted, dysfunctional energy. All of their bad parts and wrong parts worked in this four-man thing... Pete was cerebral. John was very isolated and shut down. Roger was Roger – his anger came through in his voice... Keith, his energy energized them... he was the fucking soul part of it. He was this incredible, emotional human being." But despite such differences and conflicts, all four band members were united by a desire for success. And if they had contempt for each other, this was nothing to the contempt they held for those outside the band. "We trained ourselves to think everyone else was below us," John Entwistle would say.

Albeit partly as a result of the publishing arrangements, at this point in the band's development everyone was contributing songs and ideas, which, though it might result in some inferior material being recorded, can be a healthy way for a group to function artistically. If this trend of all four band members putting forward songs and musical ideas had continued, the tremendous creative pressure Pete was to endure later in the band's career might have been somewhat reduced – though of course the quality may have suffered.

By this time, Pete was using Rickenbacker and Danelectro guitars with Marshall or Selmer amplification. He also used a series of effects including a Colorsound Tone Bender effects pedal, a Marshall Supa Fuzz pedal and a Grampian reverb unit for distortion. John achieved his monstrous bass sound using Fender Precision basses or a Danelectro long horn bass guitar powered through Marshall amps. Keith took delivery of another new Premier red sparkle kit around this time, and the quantity of drums increased. He added a second bass drum that would remain for the rest of his career, and included a third floor tom on his left that was used as a stick and drinks holder. He also dispensed with hi-hats for a time, which was a radical move as drummers rely heavily on them for playing eighth notes – a staple of most pop music. But not Keith, he used a ride cymbal on his left-hand side instead and to hell with tradition. The hi-hats would eventually return but Keith played without them during this period.

Substitute
UK Single Release: 04/03/1966 (Reaction) UK Reissue: 14/03/1966 (Reaction)
US Single Release: 02/04/1966 (Atco)
Peak Position: 5 (UK)

Townshend was greatly inspired by the Rolling Stones' superlative "Satisfaction" and felt compelled to write a riff that would equal Keith Richards' attitude-laden guitar opening. Pete's feeling that the Who were a kind of substitute for the Rolling Stones was the genesis of the song but the roots of "Substitute" lie not only in "Satisfaction" but also in "Tracks Of My Tears" by Smokey Robinson and the Miracles, with its prominent use of the word "substitute" in its lyric.

On the original demo Townshend admitted that he had sung with "an affected Jagger-like accent" and that it was his attempt to write a song to fit what he called a clever and rhythmic-sounding title. John Entwistle shed more light on the subject, "Pete was always being influenced by other artists. 'Substitute' was an attempt to play the introduction from 'I Can't Help Myself' by the Four Tops."

Pete admitted that he had stolen the riff for the verses from a record he was asked to comment on as part of the regular "Blind Date" feature in the *Melody Maker* music paper. "The record wasn't a hit, despite an electrifying riff – I pinched it, we did it and you bought it", he joked. He failed to reveal exactly what song it was but according to Dave Marsh's excellent book, *Before I Get Old*, it was Robb Storme's "Where Is My Girl". Townshend punches out the three-chord riff on a 12-string acoustic guitar, employing subtle voicings including his signature trick of leaving an open D string. Entwistle's bass propels the track as it bounds along enthusiastically.

A tambourine, prominent in the mix, hits the backbeat Tamla Motown-style, complementing Keith's kit, which is further back in the mix than usual, but Moon pumps eighth notes on his bass drum and you can hear him roar as he hits his idiosyncratic, storming fills. Later, suffering from drug-induced paranoia, Moon would insist that he hadn't actually played the drums on this track. The only way the band could convince him that he had in fact done so, was by pointing out his shouting, which was plainly audible in the false end, re-intro section. Townshend commented that, throughout the entire recording, "Keith was out of his head on some cocktail of drugs".

Roger's delivery is tough and streetwise with the aggression of a prototype punk rocker as he delivers the confrontational lyric:

You think we look pretty good together
You think my shoes are made of leather
But I'm a substitute for another guy
I look pretty tall but my heels are high
The simple things you see are more complicated
I look pretty young but I'm just back dated, yeah!

("Substitute"'s proto-punk credentials were endorsed when the Sex Pistols covered it on their *Great Rock'N'Roll Swindle* movie soundtrack album. Townshend's one-note solo on the original would also become a favoured technique of the Pistols' guitarist Steve Jones.)

This was no straightforward hit song. Lyrics of this nature were unknown in pop in 1966: one line from the chorus, "I look all white but my dad was black", was deemed too controversial for audiences in the US – where civil rights battles to gain equality for African Americans were still to be won. Townshend was forced to change them to a more anodyne, "I try walking forward but my feet walk back."

Daltrey says "Substitute" was a very quick song to record, though he found it difficult singing pop tunes like this in those early days, having come from an R&B background with a voice that he would describe as gravelly. Kit Lambert really liked the song and it was his idea to use it as the follow-up to "My Generation".

The history of this classic Who single's release is messy and convoluted and ended in a court case. The band were increasingly frustrated by their five-year deal with Shel Talmy's Orbit Music. They were deeply unhappy with the royalties situation and they'd lost respect for Talmy. Townshend: "We were going in [to the studio] and [Talmy] was just sitting there, and this man called Glyn Johns, the engineer, was doing all the work... [Talmy] used to fall asleep at the desk. Glyn Johns did everything."

Despite the tensions, it seems there were no actual arguments between band and producer during recordings. For his part, Talmy felt they all "worked hard and came up with good things." It was the relationship between producer Talmy and manager Lambert that had broken beyond repair. Shel bemoaned the fact that "Lambert, who was a lot older than all of us, became jealous of my alleged influence with 'his boys' and along with Polydor abetting him, breached my contract. Note that Polydor came on the scene to foment discontent only after the Who were already a huge band... where were they when I was looking for a deal?"

Engineer Glyn Johns agreed with Talmy's production decisions and was frustrated by Kit's constant interjections. Kit would hold this against Glyn Johns for the rest of his tenure with the band but the bad feeling was mutual, neither man liked the other. The band and management knew that recording without Talmy would breach their contract. They needed to release themselves from the constraints of a deal they saw as grossly unfair, and they found an escape route: emboldened by an offer of a £10,000 advance from Atlantic Records, which had been negotiated by Chris Stamp, they broke the contract. Shel Talmy recalls, "I received a letter in the post saying something to the effect that my services were no longer required."

The Who had originally planned to release the song "Circles" as their fourth single. They recorded two versions of it with Talmy; the recordings stuck slavishly to Townshend's original demo. However, after Pete had played Kit his demo of "Substitute" the plans changed and it was agreed that this would be the Who's next single release.

Pete Townshend would for the first time assume producer responsibilities. He revealed, "It was obviously logical that I should produce the Who... 'Substitute' was a bloody amazing session." With Kit Lambert leaning over his shoulder, Pete turned in a shatteringly impressive production debut. This was the Who dream factory in its infancy.

In early March 1966, "Substitute" was released on the Reaction label owned by entrepreneur Robert Stigwood – as opposed to Brunswick which had put out the band's previous releases. This first single featured an alternative version of the track "Circles" on the B-side, oddly with two different titles, "Circles" or in other cases "Instant Party". Within days of its release, Talmy retaliated with a breach of contract lawsuit and a court injunction was issued that immediately halted sales of the single.

As a result, "Substitute" was yet again rush-released, this time "legally" with "Waltz With A Pig" on the B-side credited to the Who Orchestra. Surprisingly, this didn't feature any member of the Who at all but was in fact the Graham Bond Organisation. The GBO was signed to Robert Stigwood's Reaction label and featured Bond, a well-respected jazz musician on saxophone, Ginger Baker on drums and Jack Bruce on bass guitar (soon after, Baker and Bruce joined Eric Clapton to form Cream).

The single's initial progress in the British charts was sluggish, and it was only on its sixth week in the listings that it entered the Top Ten, where it would peak at number five. By this time Brunswick had released "A Legal Matter" as a single in an attempt to claw back some money and sabotage "Substitute" but to no avail. "The Kids Are Alright" was also released by Brunswick to cash in on the Who's success but it only muddied the waters further for the group. Talmy won his injunction. Townshend was furious at Talmy's claims in the court, and was incredulous that the injunction had Talmy claiming not only infringement of copyright but that "on bar 36 I suggested to the lead guitarist that he play a diminuendo, forget the adagio, and play 36 bars modulating to the key of E flat." An outraged Townshend rejected this as "total bullshit." The legal battle stopped the band from recording for only a brief period but the repercussions of the dispute with Talmy would come back to haunt them.

A Legal Matter
UK Single Release: 07/03/1966 (Brunswick)
Peak Position: 32 (UK)
Released without the band's permission after they changed record companies from Brunswick to Reaction. Sales were slow in Britain.

The Kids Are Alright
UK Single Release: 12/08/1966 (Brunswick) US Release: 07/1966
Peak Position: 41 (UK)
Released without the band's permission after they changed record companies from Brunswick to Reaction. As above, this failed to chart in the States and sold poorly in the UK.

I'm A Boy
UK Single Release: 26/08/1966 (Brunswick) US Single Release: 10/12/1966
Peak Position: 2 (UK)
This song peaked at number two on the official UK chart in 1966, but many people

saw it as a natural number one: *Melody Maker* had it at the top of its chart and all the radio stations had "I'm A Boy" at number one on their playlists. On the official national chart, "All Or Nothing" by the Small Faces held it off the top spot.

Townshend was in the producer's chair for this as he was for "Substitute" but the situation was soon to change due to internal band politics. Kit was keen to produce the band and Pete was prepared to give up the role in an effort to reduce his workload and remove himself from the firing line of being the producer as well as writer.

There were two versions recorded at IBC Studios in the August of '66, the longer of the two featured horn parts played by Entwistle. He referred to this version as "a forerunner to *Tommy*". This track was to be part of a larger Townshend concept piece called "Quads": set in a future where parents could order their children, the mother and father request four daughters but get three girls and a boy. The disappointed parents refuse to accept the reality of the child's gender, and raise their new son as a girl. The character cries, "I'm a boy but my Ma won't admit it" and declares "my name is Bill and I'm a head-case!"

The lead vocal bounces back and forth between Daltrey and Townshend, the protagonist and narrator respectively. The Beach Boys-style harmonies and exuberant musical performance belie the twisted subject matter of this bizarre and darkly humorous tale of gender confusion and enforced cross-dressing. It was hardly the stuff of a 60s hit but nonetheless it was a huge success.

La-La-La-Lies
UK Single Release: 11/11/1966 (Brunswick)
Released without the band's permission after they changed record companies from Brunswick to Reaction. Failed to chart in US or UK.

Ready Steady Who EP
UK EP Release: 11/11/1966 (Reaction)
This featured the tracks "Circles", "Disguises", "Batman", "Bucket T" and "Barbara Ann". Failed to chart in 1966 but reached 57 in the UK when re-released in November 1983.

Happy Jack
UK Single Release: 09/12/1966 (Track) US Single Release: 18/03/1967 (Decca)
Peak Position: 4 (UK) 24 (US)
Recorded at CBS Studios early in November '66, this was the Who's first hit in the US, reaching 24 – and a smash in Britain hitting the number four spot. Pete remarked that during this period he had been "writing novelty songs for my own amusement". The single he said was "a very different sound for us, it became obvious that the musical direction of the group was going to change. I'd gone back to being influenced by the Stones again."

For Daltrey, it was the drummer's contribution that was compelling: "Listen to Moon... in those days he was so distinctive. It was such instant chemistry. Really, we couldn't have had any other drummer. He was incredible." After the success in Sweden of the *Ready, Steady Who* EP, which featured Keith's lead vocal on "Bucket T", Moon was full of vocal confidence and determined to sing on "Happy Jack".

They tried to include him on backing vocals but it just didn't work so eventually he was banished to the control room, much to his dismay. Ever the prankster, Keith decided to make mischief and distract the other three while they tried to complete their vocal parts. Realising that they'd never get the track done unless Moon was reined in, Kit Lambert eventually ordered him to lie still on the studio floor and behave himself. Moon complied but in the final bars of the song he could contain himself no longer and slowly peered over the recording console at the musicians around the microphone. A bemused Townshend utters, "I saw ya!" The comment was left on the master and is audible – it became so much an integral part of the song, that Pete would repeat the line when they performed the song live.

On the same day that this entered the US chart – 20th May, 1967 – "Pictures Of Lily" reached number four in the UK. The band were playing a festival in Belgium that night, fired by the realisation that their hard work was beginning to bear fruit.

A Quick One
UK Album Release: 09/12/1966 (Reaction 593002)
Peak Position: 4 (UK)
Run Run Run / Boris The Spider / I Need You / Whiskey Man / Heatwave / Cobwebs And Strange / Don't Look Away / See My Way / So Sad About Us / A Quick One, While He's Away / Happy Jack

Happy Jack
US Album Release: 05/1967 (Decca DL 74892)
Peak Position: 67 (US)
Run Run Run / Boris the Spider / I Need You / Whiskey Man / Cobwebs And Strange / Don't Look Away / See My Way / So Sad About Us / A Quick One, While He's Away / Happy Jack

A Quick One (Remastered Edition)
UK Album Release: 06/1995 (Polydor 527758-2) Reissued: 14/04/2003
US Album Release: 06/1995 (MCA MCAD-11267) Reissued: 09/2002
Run Run Run / Boris The Spider / I Need You / Whiskey Man / Heatwave / Cobwebs And Strange / Don't Look Away / See My Way / So Sad About Us / A Quick One, While He's Away / Batman / Bucket T / Barbara Ann / Disguises / Doctor, Doctor / I've Been Away / In The City / Happy Jack (Acoustic Version) / Man With The Money / My Generation – Land Of Hope And Glory

Gone is the breezy, slightly aggressive but youthful sound of four young Mods. This is a natural development for the Who, a group with the most interesting LP ideas since the Beatles.
Penny Valentine, *Disc & Music Echo*

An incredible album that captures the Who's humour, cynicism, nervous drive, violence and delicacy.
Chris Welch, *New Musical Express*

Run Run Run
This album-opener is musically close to "My Generation" but lyrically it is pure pop with an infectious chorus and a wonderfully energetic shuffling rhythm. It would have been a sure-fire hit had it been released as a single. Penned by Townshend, and recorded – like much of *A Quick One* – at IBC Studios in early October 1966.

It's rumoured that, once again, Jimmy Page was called in to play the bluesy solo in the middle section. However, considering Kit Lambert was the producer on this record, it's highly unlikely that he would have considered replacing Townshend. The song had been covered earlier that year by a band called the Cat, recording it on the Reaction label.

Boris The Spider

Recorded at Pye Studios, the ominous but charming "Boris" was for a long time acknowledged as the first solo song John Entwistle wrote for the Who, although it has since transpired that he wrote "Whiskey Man" earlier.

"I really made up 'Boris The Spider' on the spot," John explained. "I had to run home from rehearsals and demo it before I forgot it." He had been drinking with Bill Wyman of the Stones the previous night. "We got to the stage where we were making up silly names for animals. I thought of this name for a spider, Boris, after Boris Karloff."

The final verse tells of the spider's "sticky end" and, during later live performances, the band would duly kill Boris in effigy. Although by then, the whimsical "Boris" was rather at odds with the group's more boisterous or emotionally charged material, somehow it remained a live favourite, perhaps because it brought a little light relief.

"Young kids love 'Boris The Spider'," said its composer, "and a lot of the other songs I'd written. So we were gonna release a children's album, a project Kit Lambert thought of, with all these snakes and spiders and creepy things... It certainly does have a nursery rhyme charm to it."

I Need You

A rare Keith Moon composition – which started life under the longer title "I Need You (Like I Need A Hole In The Head)" – tells of the various drinking dens across London that he was already frequenting. It's a Beatles-meets-Beach-Boys tune, which is hardly surprising considering what a huge surf music fan he was. Daltrey commented years later "The funny thing about Keith, though, he was a total Beach Boys nut. Even in the 70s, if the Beach Boys had asked Keith to join them and leave the Who, he'd have left us. He was an absolute fanatic... that's all he ever wanted to do, was be in the Beach Boys. He never wanted to be in the fucking Who, we played rubbish!"

With some rather silly lyrics, it is partially redeemed by Keith's own madcap vocal. Moon also claimed that its middle section was designed to evoke "a musical illustration of a transport café". Harpsichord touches also abound from Nicky Hopkins.

John Entwistle: "Keith had gone through an experience with the Beatles where they were talking their own language. He had gone through all this paranoia thinking that the Who could speak the language as well. Everything you said, [he'd respond] 'What does that mean? What does that mean?' He was on these little yellow paranoia pills at the time."

Keith didn't write much for the group but one can't help wondering that if he had put more effort into writing, no matter how off-the-wall, he may well have produced something of worth somewhere down the line. Perhaps all Moon needed was a little more encouragement to give him the confidence.

In these early days of trying to capture the band's performances on tape, it was often difficult because of Keith's lethal technique. Having never encountered such a wild player before, engineers at the time just couldn't handle his style. This problem is evident here with Keith's ride cymbal distorting, ridiculously loud in the mix as he crashes away.

Whiskey Man

It's John Entwistle's turn to write about alcohol intake, in a rather bizarre tale of a man being consigned to a padded cell because of his relationship with an invisible friend who lives at the bottom of a whiskey bottle. Its inspiration came from a violent Western film which had opened in London in the spring of 1966 called *Ride Beyond Vengeance*, in which Elwood Coates (played by Claude Akins), the foreman of a local cattle ranch, has an imaginary friend with the nickname "Whiskey Man". Entwistle's speech difficulty in singing words containing the letter "r" resulted in his vocal being double-tracked.

Heatwave

The band injects a spirited and youthful energy into its second recording of the Martha Reeves classic (the earlier version would remain unreleased until the *My Generation* deluxe edition), but perhaps inevitably, their version doesn't measure up to the exuberant original.

"Almost every group played 'Heatwave'," said Roger. "We just stuck with it longer than most." This very brief track – which struggles to reach the two-minute mark – became, at the very end of August 1966, the first to be completed for this LP.

Cobwebs And Strange

Zany musical antics dominate an instrumental officially conceived by Keith Moon, although thirty years on, John would tell Ken Sharp of *Goldmine* magazine that "'Cobwebs And Strange' was me. I made the brass part up and it just went on from there." In fact, there's a weird and wonderful mix of instruments present: Pete contributes penny whistle and bass drum, Roger the trombone, John trumpet, and Keith orchestral cymbals and tuba. The latter also added some frenetic drum parts that sound like an express train at full speed. For early takes of the track, which began life under the title "Showbiz Sonata", the four musicians marched back and forth past a mono microphone, but the experiment was unsuccessful. This was used in the film *The Kids Are Alright* during a section illustrating the drummer's offbeat, offstage lifestyle. It's crazy and shambolic, but tons of fun with Moonie at his uninhibited best.

Don't Look Away

A cheerful, if uninspired, countrified ditty, adapted from their crowd-pleasing live set, recorded at IBC that shows how short of songs they were. An underwhelming guitar solo doesn't help.

See My Way
A rare solo Daltrey composition, "See My Way" is, in the words of its composer, "basically the demo I did over at Pete's", although after the basic track had been laid down at Townshend's flat in Wardour Street in the heart of Soho in central London, Moon added a drum part. Daltrey had requested that Moon try to emulate the sound of Jerry Allison in Buddy Holly's Crickets, but he only managed that sound when he used cardboard boxes as substitute drums. Entwistle told the story, "Roger wanted the drums to sound like cardboard boxes, but Keith's drums always sounded like biscuit tins being hit. We couldn't make them sound like cardboard boxes. So Keith went out the back of the studio for a while, and when he came back, he started playing and Roger said, 'That sounds perfect! How are you doing that?' It was two cardboard boxes Keith had found outside."

So Sad About Us
The well-crafted pop of Townshend's "So Sad About Us" was originally written earlier in 1966 for Liverpool group the Merseys (formerly the Merseybeats), but their reading failed to follow its predecessor "Sorrow" into the hit parade. The Who's version is a highlight of *A Quick One*, starting with a riff reminiscent of the Searchers' 1964 chart-topper, "Needles And Pins". It showcases a heartbreaking lyrical sentiment: "Apologies mean nothing when the damage is done / But you can't switch off my loving / Like you can't switch off the sun."

Daltrey was impressed with "So Sad About Us" calling it a great song, and saying, "It's very melodic but there's angst behind."

In late 1978, the Mod heroes, Rickenbacker users and Who fans, the Jam would cover this song as a tribute to the by-then deceased Keith Moon. First contained on the B-side of the Jam's "Down In The Tube Station At Midnight" single, it can now be found on the deluxe CD edition of their third LP, *All Mod Cons*, issued in 2006, where a demo version of the song is also captured for posterity.

A Quick One, While He's Away
By November 1966, with the sessions for the album otherwise complete, the Who realised they were still some ten minutes short of an LP's standard playing time, so Kit Lambert suggested that Pete write an extended piece in the classic operatic tradition to fill the gap. Initially reluctant, Townshend reconsidered and opted for a series of short pop songs which would be linked thematically to form one complete piece.

Six songs were rapidly created – "Her Man's Been Gone", "Crying Town", "We Have A Remedy", "Ivor The Engine Driver", "Soon Be Home" and "You Are Forgiven" – but the recording budget was exhausted; indeed, "You Are Forgiven" features Roger and John singing the word "cello" over and over, because the group couldn't afford to bring in a string section!

This extended piece was innovative and revolutionary at the time and the inclusion of "A Quick One, While He's Away" did not just spice up a somewhat uneven LP, but would also spark Townshend's imagination to contemplate even more grandiose and ambitious extended musical projects in the years that followed. The six-song cycle would be performed in its entirety by the Who in late 1968 for the Rolling Stones' *Rock'N'Roll Circus* film and, although their electrifying performance was initially consigned to the cutting-room floor, it would ultimately surface in the band's own movie *The Kids Are Alright*.

Bonus Tracks:

Batman

Just months after the American TV adaptation of Gotham City's superhero had debuted in Britain on ITV, the foursome hurtled through its signature tune in barely more than 90 seconds for inclusion on their EP of late '66, *Ready, Steady Who!* (the EP's other three tracks follow in sequence on this CD reissue).

For a time in the second half of 1966, "Batman" came to replace "Heatwave" as the group's traditional live opener. The original TV theme had been composed by Neal Hefti, one-time Count Basie arranger and composer of the jazz hit, "Cute". The Jam would also include their own version of the theme song on their 1977 debut LP, *In The City*.

The same year, the legendary US surf music duo Jan and Dean had recorded their own song, "Batman", inspired by the TV series; it included a brief homage to the Hefti guitar part.

Bucket T

"Bucket T", the B-side to Jan and Dean's own "Batman", had also inspired the Who and they covered it, with their resident fan of surf music – Keith Moon – as the obvious choice for singing lead vocal. And when it became an unlikely number one hit in Sweden – one of the few times the Who reached number one anywhere – Moon briefly gained teen pin-up status. Pete quipped, "We only played surf music to humour him." This track was included on the *Ready, Steady, Who!* EP.

Barbara Ann

Although the Beach Boys had recently scored a major hit in the UK with "Barbara Ann", the song dates back to 1961 when the Regents had taken it into the US Top 20. This was recorded largely to appease Keith Moon and his passion for all things surf. He loved the Beach Boys and shares much of the lead vocal here with Roger. In 1977, footage of the band playing this song during rehearsals for the movie *The Kids Are Alright* would portray the Who in unguarded, carefree mode, genuinely enjoying themselves.

Disguises

The only Who original on the *Ready Steady Who!* EP, this apes the tuneful pop of the Beatles nicely enough. It was recorded at the end of July 1966, marking co-manager Kit Lambert's debut as the group's producer.

Doctor, Doctor

The B-side to the later single "Pictures Of Lily", Entwistle's "Doctor, Doctor" is the only track on this reissue which does not date from 1966 (it was recorded in April 1967). With a simple beat-boom approach, falsetto harmony vocals and clanging Rickenbacker guitars crowd this tale of a hypochondriac's pleas.

I've Been Away
Written by Entwistle, this quirky little tune in waltz time barely sounds like the Who at all. It was originally issued in the UK in late '66 when it appeared on the B-side of the "Happy Jack" single.

In The City
Another former single B-side – this time for "I'm A Boy" – written by Entwistle and Moon. The lyric praises "the pretty girls of the city" while Keith and John emulate a surf arrangement that the latter would later dismiss as "a real Jan and Dean rip-off". Keith Moon features on lead vocals, further indulging his desire to be in the Beach Boys. John and Keith recorded the backing track between them, only later did the others participate in its recording, with Pete adding guitar, and all four contributing harmony vocals (the Jam would later co-opt this title for both their debut single and album).

Happy Jack (Acoustic Version)
Pete attempts to play cello on this, an alternative, calmer acoustic version of what would shortly become the group's sixth Top Ten single. Recorded at IBC Studios, Keith adds percussion as well as kicking up something of a racket behind the kit.

Man With The Money
A staple of the group's live set, this is an unremarkable remake of what had been the flip-side to "Love Is Strange", the final Top 20 hit by the Everly Brothers in late 1965.

My Generation – Land Of Hope And Glory
To finish off, something of an oddity: for a mimed *Ready, Steady, Go!* appearance in October 1966, the group recorded a basic version – with no stuttering from Roger – of their call-to-arms Mod anthem, which in the coda segues into Edward Elgar's paean to the British Empire. At the end of the take, Kit Lambert is heard to say, "That's perfect!" (however, for their actual appearance on the show, they used a take which segued into a different expression of patriotism: Thomas Arne's 1740 arrangement of the James Thomson poem "Rule Britannia").

While an undoubted improvement on the covers-heavy and somewhat anonymous *My Generation* album, *A Quick One* feels rather unfinished, a mishmash of ideas that illustrates how the Who had still to find their way. There are flashes of greatness though, most notably "Run Run Run", "So Sad About Us" and the closing six-song cycle, "A Quick One, While He's Away". However, even though they hadn't hit their stride just yet in the studio, the band were still delivering blistering live performances and these propelled them through this comparatively barren recording period.

03   Cynical Psychedelia – 1967

Nineteen sixty-seven was a year when it seemed that only the beautiful people made pop music. The Beatles released their classic groundbreaking album *Sgt Pepper's Lonely Hearts Club Band*, which was regarded as an early example of a concept album, and which, after its June release, barely left the number one spot for the rest of the year. It was light years ahead of the instant pop of previous boy-meets-girl Fab Four hits like "She Loves You" and "Can't Buy Me Love" and would influence and inspire a whole generation of musicians.

Another group in residence at Abbey Road Studios that year was the new EMI signing the Pink Floyd, then at the beginning of a very long career with a space-age debut album called *The Piper At The Gates Of Dawn*. The Floyd had emerged from a London underground music scene that was trying to capture the excitement of the American West Coast. In California, where LSD-inspired acid rock and psychedelia were the order of the day, bands like Jefferson Airplane and the Grateful Dead inspired their fans to tune in, drop out and turn on. Meanwhile, *The Velvet Underground And Nico* may have barely registered at the cash tills but seemed to inspire nearly everyone who heard it to form a group of their own.

Against this "tripped out" backdrop of "Happenings" and "Psychedelic Freak-Outs", the Who released *Sell Out*. The record had fashionable psychedelic leanings but ultimately it dealt far more with the burgeoning new trend of consumerism than the "free love" philosophy expounded by the hippies and flower children. "You could write a song that went, 'Weee love you, weee love you', and it would get to number four in the charts," bemoaned Pete Townshend. "I knew I was too much of a cynic to ever be able to do that (the Rolling Stones released a single in the US and UK in August '67 entitled "We Love You")."

"Psychedelia was a bit too spongy for me," Roger Daltrey later complained. "I found it pretentious and I couldn't wait to get back to a good bit of Otis Redding. We did get into it in some ways but the difference was that, though we were all into the anti-war movement, every time we went on stage we were showing them what war was really like!"

Although the group dallied with the psychedelic, hippy fashions of the day, the paisley, sequins and ruffles were soon replaced. Townshend came to sport a boiler suit and bovver boots, with the others displaying attire far more suited to their streetwise, working-class roots. These were arrogant, tough, talented boys with ambition, from the London streets and keen to prove themselves, not tripped-out hippies espousing peace and love. The four members of the Who were no strangers to drugs of various kinds, but Townshend wasn't that impressed with the prevalent "acid" scene in 1967. In December, he told *Melody Maker*'s Chris Welch, "A lot of people in pop have taken acid, and all of them have softened up and lost their basic ambition."

If psychedelic acid rock didn't excite the Who, an American session guitarist with rock roots, certainly would. Jimi Hendrix was a rock'n'roll guitar virtuoso that nobody had ever seen the like of before. Townshend, along with his wife and fellow guitar hero Eric Clapton, had attended some of Hendrix's early London dates in the autumn of 1966. Townshend recalls, "[Hendrix] was astonishingly sexual, and you could just sense this whole thing in the room where every woman would just [applauds] at a snap of a finger. He wasn't particularly in control of his ego at the time, [although] I found him a very charming, very easy, a very sweet guy. I just kept hearing stories, [like] the night that he went up to Marianne Faithfull when she was there with Mick [Jagger], and said in her ear, 'What are you doing with this asshole?' He just couldn't resist trying. There were no boundaries, and that really scared me. You know, I don't like that kind of megalomaniacal perspective... I think it's important to respect other people's relationships."

But Townshend also felt insecure about Hendrix in terms of talent: "I just sort of felt that I hadn't the emotional equipment, really, the physical equipment, the natural psychic genius of somebody like Jimi, and realised that what I had was a bunch of gimmicks which he had come and taken away from me... I did actually feel stripped, to some extent, and I took refuge in my writing. The weirdest thing of the lot is that, although people really, really value those early years, the Who was not a particularly important band at that time. We were at the end of an era; under normal circumstances the band should have disappeared. But because he just swept everything aside, like in early punk, I had to learn to write from a new angle, and what that actually did was provide me with records that sold in America, somehow. I don't know why that is."

The Jimi Hendrix Experience were the first group to be signed to Kit Lambert's new record label, Track Records – on which label they would enjoy three Top Ten British hits in 1967 alone, as well as two mind-blowing LPs in *Are You Experienced?* and *Axis: Bold As Love*. The second group on Track would be the Who.

Pete Townshend had written a collection of songs that he felt were to a large extent "weak and occasionally cheesy". But he found the dynamic unifying idea that would give the next Who album an edge, in Chris Stamp's office early in 1967. Townshend decided to, "turn the entire album into a pirate segment and actually sell advertising space to manufacturers and fashion houses". This unique idea enthralled his fellow band mates and management alike. They all quickly added a myriad of inspired supercharged ideas to the core theme and the album that became *The Who Sell Out* finally found its direction.

Despite his own dismissive description of some of his songs, with *The Who Sell Out*, Pete Townshend targeted the British pop lover with a set of songs unlike any other. There are no sentimental ditties about love, flowers-in-your-hair and the hippie dream. Instead, we have sexual jealousy, suspicious minds, tattooed flesh, masturbation, the population boom, baked beans and body odour. There's a love song or two in there somewhere but they're mostly submerged in frustration, cynicism and disappointment.

Side one was a sequence of songs interspersed with specially-made spoof advertisements and very brief jingles. The intention was to evoke the sound of Radio London, a pirate commercial radio station which had been broadcasting off the coast of Essex, but had – like all other pirate stations – been forced to close down in August 1967 when the Marine Broadcasting (Offences) Law came into effect (many of its DJs, including Tony Blackburn, John Peel and the anarchic Kenny Everett, were to find a new home that autumn when the BBC launched its first pop music radio station, Radio One).

John Entwistle: "I had an idea for a couple of tribute jingles to the pirate stations that had just been deposed. We owed a lot to the pirate stations because the BBC wasn't very good to us at all. And then we decided to put other little bits of commercials in." In keeping with this theme, the album sleeve – designed by David King and future *Spitting Image* creator Roger Law – photographed each group member in a mocked-up advertisement. Roger Daltrey got to know the meaning of the phrase "suffering for your art" while his contribution was being shot. Sat waist-deep in a bath of cold Heinz baked beans, he protested that he was freezing. Keith brought in a heater and placed it behind the bath, but because the bath was made of tin, the heater merely cooked the beans behind him, leaving the rest still freezing, "Talk about ham and beans!" he said later. By the time the photo shoot ended, a shivering Daltrey was showing signs of coming down with a nasty bout of flu.

Entwistle had had a narrow escape: "I was supposed to be in the beans," he later claimed. "I rang up and said I was going to be a bit late and they said 'You're going to have to hurry up because the baked beans are drying up.' And I said 'What baked beans?' And they said, 'The baked beans you're going to be sitting in.' So I figured if I left it a little bit longer someone else would arrive and have to sit in the beans. So I got there real late and I got the girl and Roger got the beans."

Recordings took place from late May through until early November 1967, but the scheduled release date in November was postponed when Track was obliged to obtain written permission from the various companies whose products had inspired the jingles. When finally issued just before Christmas, early copies contained a psychedelic poster designed by Adrian George of Osiris Visions.

Pictures Of Lily
UK Single Release: 22/04/1967 (Track) US Single Release: 24/06/1967 (Decca)
Peak Position: 4 (UK) 51 (US)

To promote the band's first release for Track Records, Moon took delivery of his specially-made Premier "Pictures Of Lily" drum kit, which featured Day-Glo pictures of naked women, and was emblazoned with the legend "Keith Moon, Patent British Exploding Drummer". The fact it was a unique kit didn't stop the irreverent drummer from purposely smashing it up at the end of performances on a frighteningly regular basis. Check out the section in *The Kids Are Alright* movie where you will see Moon's demonic destruction of these drums. He tops off this "smashing" performance by recklessly throwing the kit into the audience.

Around this period Pete was using various guitars that included a Gibson ES345 plus a Fender Stratocaster and Jazzmaster. His amplification now came compliments of Sound City amps with Marshall cabs: a classic combination.

"Pictures" was an obvious choice for a single but for the lyric, which dealt publicly with the daring (for the time) subject matter of teenage masturbation. Roger Daltrey would tell *Uncut* magazine many years later: "I saw the words and I knew what it was about. So I deliberately thought I'd sing it the opposite way, with complete innocence. Instead of it being something suggestive, it tweaks it the other way and it gives it a little more intrigue." He added: "It's another rip-off from the Kinks".

The lyric specifically details a conversation between an adolescent boy and his father in which the former tells of his "frustrations". Dad advises that "pictures of Lily" may be the solution and sticks the pictures on to the boy's wall. However, uninhibited joy is halted when the father informs the lad that the Lily in the photographs is in fact dead. There's a whimsical, dreamy quality to the whole proceedings that overrides the subject matter and eschews smutty innuendo. John Entwistle bluntly exclaimed, "It's all about wanking – Townshend going through his sexual traumas – I sometimes think you could say that record represents our smutty period or, to be more refined, our blue period."

The record returned the Who to the top five in the charts in their homeland, and became a moderately-sized American hit but, as Daltrey later reflected, it "never sat well on stage for some reason." Townshend regarded it as a novelty: "It was written purely to test out a demo recorder system I'd put together."

The Last Time
UK Single Release: 30/07/1967 (Track)
Peak Position: 44 (UK)

This track and "Under My Thumb" were recorded as a protest after Mick Jagger and Keith Richards were convicted on drugs charges, following their arrest in February that year. Jagger was sentenced to 90 days, and Richards was sentenced to a full year behind bars. Roger explained, "We did it as a gesture. All the proceeds were gonna go to legal things to mount a campaign to get them out. We thought it was a disgraceful sentence."

The band released an official statement: "The Who consider Mick Jagger and Keith Richards have been treated as scapegoats for the drug problem and as a protest against the savage sentences imposed on them at Chichester yesterday, the Who are issuing... the first of a series of Jagger/Richard songs to keep their work before the public until they are again free to record themselves." The single was recorded rapidly at De Lane Lea Studios in London in late June 1967; Entwistle was on his honeymoon so Townshend replaced him on bass. Daltrey concluded, "It was fun to play someone else's song."

Mick and Keith were freed on the same day that the single was released; Richards' conviction was quashed on appeal and Jagger's was reduced to a conditional discharge. The song reached the lower end of the UK chart and was the only Jagger and Richards compositions recorded and released by the Who. It was not issued in the US.

I Can See For Miles
UK Single Release: 13/10/1967 (Track) US Single Release: 18/09/1967 (Decca)
Peak Position: 10 (UK) 9 (US)

This song had been around since before "Pictures Of Lily" but Pete had kept it in reserve. Townshend was so pleased with the demo of what he considered to be his best song to date that he wanted to wait until Kit Lambert was supremely confident as a producer. In 2007 Pete told *Record Collector* magazine, "I think it's the best thing I've done. Apart from anything else, the demo I made at home was extraordinary. Kit responded by making the best record we made together with him as our producer."

The recording had a gestation period of four months during which time the backing tracks were laid down (May 1967 at London's CBS Studios), vocals added (in August that year at Talent Masters in New York) with the final mix being completed in early September at Goldstar in Los Angeles. This was by far the lengthiest recording of anything to be included on *The Who Sell Out*. "I think it's one of the best-produced singles we ever did," Roger enthused. "We spent literally a whole day putting down layer and layer of harmonies on the 'miles and miles' section."

Townshend called it a "fiery Wagnerian piece" on jealousy. This expression of distrust, suspicion and deceit begins tensely with droning guitars and snare fills, before Roger claims omniscience towards his straying lover. The song's narrator is the ultimate stalker figure, a precursor to Sting's "Every Breath You Take" fifteen years later.

Pete Townshend regarded "I Can See For Miles" as nothing short of "a masterpiece" concluding that it was "the ultimate Who record." Daltrey agreed, "It's probably our best single." When issued as a single two months ahead of *Sell Out*, it continued the band's run of Top Ten hits in Britain, but only just, peaking at number ten. For Townshend, who aspired to being number one, it had failed. "I spat on the British record buyer," he would later lament. "We were confused about why we'd stopped selling singles when we'd felt that the quality of the singles was going up. Broadcasting reacted to [it] very favourably. We'd just lost the pirate stations, but it was on the radio all the time, *Top Of The Pops* played it every fucking week. But it still made only a very low showing in the charts. I felt it was a very powerful single from the band, but people had obviously got bored with hearing the Who do that sort of single." Bitterly disappointed and deeply frustrated, he revealed, "That was the real heartbreaker for me."

The recording of *The Who Sell Out* would take more than six months to complete, during which time the band was touring on both sides of the Atlantic. The Who hit the US Top 30 for the first time with "Happy Jack" which reached number 24 in June, and in the same month they played a career-defining set at the Monterey Pop Festival in California. Other artists there included the Jimi Hendrix Experience (Jimi all but stole the Who's act by burning and smashing his guitar) and the Mamas & The Papas. On stage, the Who were introduced by Eric Burdon of the Animals saying, "I promise you, this group will destroy you in more ways than one."

Burdon's words were not simply hyperbole: while in the US the band performed on the *Smothers Brothers Comedy Hour* TV show. At the finale of "My Generation" Keith's bass drum – packed with his favourite "Cherry Bomb" explosive – ignited and chaos ensued. Townshend's hearing was permanently damaged by the blast but it did catapult the Who firmly into the minds of America's youth.

The Who Sell Out
UK Album Release: 15/12/1967 (Track 612002)
US Album Release: 06/01/1968 (Decca 74950)
Peak Position: 13 (UK) 48 (US)
(Radio London) / Armenia City In The Sky / (Radio London) / Heinz Baked Beans / (More Music) / Mary-Anne With The Shaky Hand / (Premier Drums – Radio London (Instrumental)) / Odorono / (Radio London) / Tattoo / (Radio London (Church Of Your Choice)) / Our Love Was / (Radio London (Pussycat) – Speakeasy – Rotosound Strings) / I Can See For Miles / (Charles Atlas) / I Can't Reach You / Medac / Relax / Silas Stingy / Sunrise / Rael / (Track Records)

The Who Sell Out (Remastered Edition)
UK Album Release: 06/1995 (Polydor 5277592)
US Album Release: 06/1995 (MCA 11268)
(Radio London) / Armenia City In The Sky / (Radio London) / Heinz Baked Beans / (More Music) / Mary-Anne With The Shaky Hand / (Premier Drums) / (Radio London (Instrumental)) / Odorono / (Radio London) / Tattoo / (Radio London (Church Of Your Choice)) / Our Love Was / (Radio London (Pussycat)) – (Speakeasy) – (Rotosound Strings) / I Can See For Miles / (Charles Atlas) / I Can't Reach You / Medac / Relax / (Rotosound Strings (Demo)) / Silas Stingy / Sunrise / Rael / Rael 2 / (Top Gear) / Glittering Girl / (Coke 2) / Melancholia / (Bag O'Nails) / Someone's Coming / (John Mason's Cars (Rehearsal)) / Jaguar / (John Mason's Cars (Reprise)) / Early Morning Cold Taxi / (Coke 1) / Hall Of The Mountain King / (Radio 1 (Boris Mix)) / Girl's Eyes / (Odorono (Final Chorus)) / Mary-Anne With The Shaky Hand (Alternate Version) / Glow Girl / (Track Records)

This new LP puts the Who well into the upper pop bracket. The interesting development of ideas linking up with commercial advertising and use of mass media is completely original for a pop group.
Record Mirror

(Radio London)
With its mantra of pop art and love of pirate radio writ large, the album begins with a Radio London jingle that features an electronically altered voice exclaiming the days of the week. This gradually falls away as backwards guitars buzz from one speaker to the other, a testament to the early days of stereo recording.

Armenia City In The Sky
John "Speedy" Keene, Townshend's friend and driver, wrote the eerie "Armenia City In The Sky". It features him on lead vocals coupled with Roger's high-pitched, studio-treated trippy vocal. The "tracked" voices float over a psychedelic backing track with the drums hard-panned over to one side, while weird, backwards brass lines fade in and out menacingly (this backwards effect was an easy studio trick in which the engineer would turn the tape over to record. Once the master tape was placed the correct way, any instrument recorded previously would appear backwards). Entwistle quipped of the song's title: "Everyone thought it was 'I'm an ear sitting in the sky'."

In 1969, Keene would go on to enjoy sparkling if short-lived success in his own right with Thunderclap Newman. Pete Townshend would produce their number one hit "Something In The Air", and would be credited on bass guitar under the pseudonym "Bijou Drains".

(Radio London)

The legend "Wonderful Radio London... whoopee!" appears in the same "electronic" voice and the band launches into their first spoof commercial for, of all things, baked beans.

Heinz Baked Beans

With a count-in from Keith and a trumpet fanfare from John, "Heinz Baked Beans" is one of the silliest moments in the Who's entire canon. This finds the band in a wacky, humorous mood. The backing track clangs along with a military snare drum and stick clicks from Moon, with brass and banjo embellishments contributed by John and Pete respectively. Various comical voices enquire, "What's for tea?", only to be finally told – inevitably – that it's "Heinz baked beans". John Entwistle would be responsible for much of the Who's more humorous output so it's not surprising to learn that he penned this absurd but amusing throwaway vignette.

(More Music)

As a corny segue, an original Radio London jingle finds a barbershop quartet exclaiming "More Music! More Music! More Music!"

Mary-Anne With The Shaky Hand

The song was recorded several times in both Electric Studios and Talent Masters but this version was finally nailed at De Lane Lea Studios, London, late in October '67. Let's just say that Mary-Anne's wrist action is not solely reserved for stirring her coffee: "Mary Anne with the shaky hands / What they've done to a man, those shaky hands". Written by Pete, the arrangement features an acoustic folksy approach, with flamenco flourishes and exotic percussion to boot. The ensemble vocals are somewhere between the Mamas & The Papas meets Simon & Garfunkel. They're obviously aiming at a more *Pet Sounds* vibe but to no avail.

(Premier Drums "Advert" – Radio London (Instrumental))

Keith batters out a syncopated tom-tom pattern that fades in as he and John Entwistle cry out in rhythm, "Premier Drums... Premier Drums... Premier Drums." Keith always used British-made Premier Drums and he was their biggest and most famous patron. Moon's relationship with Premier would last his entire career. An original Big Band Radio London jingle follows, ringing out briefly as a preface to the next cut.

Odorono

You can't get much further from the en vogue subjects of the time – love and peace – than a paean to an under-arm deodorant. Set against Townshend's comical lyrics, "Odorono" is a melancholy story of a female singer whose deodorant lets her down at a crucial point backstage when she meets a man – Mr Davidson – who really was "quite handsome". Pete's laidback vocal is offset by some stark rhythm guitar and a hard-panning backing track.

(Radio London)

A scintillating string orchestral jingle with a beautifully cheesy female vocal that reminds us, "It's smooth sailing with the highly successful sound of Radio London".

Tattoo

Townshend says of the inspiration for this, "When I was eleven or twelve, street guys always had a mass of tattoos down one arm," he explained. "You really felt, 'Jesus, that's gonna happen to me sometime'. It was such a relief when I finally got to be sixteen or seventeen, and you didn't have to do that anymore. There were marches for Ban the Bomb and against impending nuclear war, bigger issues than going down to the fun fair and standing there with your arm covered with tattoos listening to Elvis Presley records..."

A lament of male teenage angst unfolds as two brothers discuss, "What makes a man a man". After much deliberation, they decide to get tattooed, but their parents have mixed feelings about their decision:

> My dad beat me cos' mine said "Mother"
> But my mother naturally liked it and beat my brother
> Cos' his tattoo was of a lady in the nude
> And my mum thought that was extremely rude

The story ends with the revelation that not only is the narrator tattooed; so is his wife. Pete explained another inspiration for the track: "'Tattoo' was written as an album track. I wrote it when we were on the road with Herman's Hermits in 1967. Jimi Hendrix was already in our lives... I was feeling eclipsed by him as a guitar player... so I decided to write a different kind of song, which is why I started to write story-songs, cameos, essays of human experience, and 'Tattoo' was one of those songs, concerning not only what it's like to be young, but trying to look at the generation divide and what made men. 'Tattoo' again is me examining what divided me and Roger, and his idea of what made a man a man and my idea. I thought it was going to be one of those songs where Roger would turn around and say to me, 'No, you sing this. I don't need to question whether I'm a man or not.' But he did sing it, and he sang it really well. And I realised then, 'Hey, he doesn't know. He doesn't know if he's a man or not. He's got the same insecurities I have."

This wonderful, quirky, if subdued Townshend song is full of pathos. Often overlooked, "Tattoo" remains one of Pete's personal favourites. Like the work of the Small Faces' Steve Marriott and the Kinks' Ray Davies, it stands as an excellent example of Townshend finding in the humdrum something of universal resonance and appeal. Daltrey's vocal delivery intrigues and seduces, extending his range; always more than able to belt it out, "Tattoo" finds him in a passive, pensive mood. As a vocalist, Roger was improving beyond even his own expectations and here's the proof.

The song would become a popular addition to the live set. A great version of this would later appear on *Live At Leeds* where, even in a rock'n'roll concert setting, the band would deliver the song with depth and sensitivity.

(Radio London (Church Of Your Choice))

A sombre, reverent church choir instructs us, "Radio London reminds you, go to the church of your choice!" This was an original jingle that the radio station ran regularly.

Our Love Was

A handful of tracks on *Sell Out* were recorded in the late northern summer of 1967 at various studios in the US. "Our Love Was" is one such track, being captured in mid-August at Columbia Studios in Los Angeles. Known as "Our Love Was Is" for the LP's Stateside release, it's one of the few love songs on the record, with finely-crafted lyrics and uplifting musical motifs to match.

A melancholy descending bass and guitar motif opens this Townshend song of a barren love affair that transforms itself into renewed passion. Pete's vocal delivery is understated as he traces an affair that went from "imitation" and "famine" to "shining, like a summer morning". Finally, Keith blitzes his kit before Pete tears into a guitar solo reminiscent of Jimmy Page.

(Radio London (Pussycat) – Speakeasy – Rotosound Strings)

An original radio jingle delivered in hip, glib tones advertising the London club "Big L" informs us in faux American accents that we are at turns "Pussycats... where it's at... the ins, out," finally stating "BIG L". Following immediately, Entwistle and Moon supply an original Who spoof jingle: "Speakeasy, drink easy, pull easy", referring to the Speakeasy drinking den in London where the band would regularly go in the early days to party with young women who were interested in getting more than just an autograph from the assorted pop star clientele. The final spoof ad in this trilogy interlude finds the band comically announcing, "Hold ya group together with Rotosound strings", a reference to their guitar strings of choice.

I Can See For Miles

For Pete Townshend, the final track on side one of *Sell Out* was always his ace in the hole. It fits perfectly into the album's running order and gives a hardcore injection of latent rock'n'roll violence. With all its menacing drones, ethereal crescendos, sublime rotating backing vocals and its overall atmosphere of intimidation, it towers above the more lightweight pieces.

However, once released as a single it slowly crawled up the UK chart absolutely confounding its composer. Pete believed it was deserving of the number one spot but the British baby-boomer buying public simply didn't respond. Townshend's musical pride had taken a severe battering. It wasn't all bad news, though. In America, it became the first – and only – Who single to reach the Top Ten on the *Billboard* charts, where it would peak at number nine. Perhaps just as surprising was its relatively brief stay in the group's live act. By early 1968, it was already on its way out of the set-list.

(Charles Atlas)

A brief ditty spoken by Pete and John over an almost country-and-western backing track tells us that "The Charles Atlas course with 'Dynamic Tension' will turn you into a beast of a man." It was a hymn to Charles Atlas, the famous American body-builder whose advertisements in the back pages of the less classy magazines of the 60s depicted an "8-stone weakling" getting sand kicked in his face by bullies on the beach. The balance was redressed after the weakling had completed Atlas's "Dynamic Tension" course, and with his new manly physique, he could then stand up to the thugs.

I Can't Reach You

This sweet, simple 60s tune sounds like many other pop songs of the era. Compared to the Who's new musical direction demonstrated on "I Can See For Miles", this is a lightweight slice of pop; whimsical rather than radical and lacking the magic of the band's earlier pop classics.

Medac

An Entwistle-penned tune that is firmly in the quirky, black-humoured area of the band's repertoire and keeps the commercial *sell* theme going. Henry is an adolescent battling with acne and spots. Once he starts using Medac, his "current bun" face becomes smooth "like a baby's bottom". John features on lead vocals here but "Medac" is not one of his best tunes (it was titled "Spotted Henry" on US release).

Relax

Beginning with a swaggering, cool Hammond organ part, this has a strutting, cocky vibe. Roger's lead vocal is supported by smooth backing vocals until the mid-section where Pete takes over the lead. Some musical madness follows as John builds tension by vamping on the stomping riff while Pete solos over the mayhem, his feedback wailing somewhere in the distance. This is a competent 60s pop tune that has a laid-back charm but the usual Who guitar and drum histrionics soon become the order of the day.

(Rotosound Strings (Demo))

The spoof commercials were recorded in London at Kingsway Studios. According to John, he and Keith "thought them up in the pub next door." Here, they perform the ad a cappella.

Silas Stingy

Silas is a Scrooge-like miser – his name borrowed from George Eliot's character, Silas Marner – who "carried all his money in a little black box / which was heavy as a rock with a big padlock". Bearing more than a passing musical resemblance to "Boris The Spider", this is another Entwistle composition, sung by him, and showcasing his off-the-wall humour far more successfully than "Medac". He explained, "My family... we've got rather a sick sense of humour. The whole family that is: my father, my grandfather before him." John had recently moved on to a Fender Precision bass but one of his favourites was a guitar that he had constructed from the remains of five smashed basses, which he promptly named Frankenstein. He changed the finish from the traditional sunburst to a less than tasteful baby pink. "I have about thirty-five Precisions," he explained, "but I always go back to Frankenstein."

Sunrise

This is arguably one of the greatest understated moments of Pete Townshend's entire career. Here he is in reflective mood, with this heartbreakingly beautiful ballad of unrequited love featuring him singing solo with nothing more than his own expertly delicate finger-picked acoustic guitar for company.

Lyrically he reveals himself as sincere without ever sounding mawkish on this tragic tale of finding it impossible to move beyond a failed relationship, and find love again. The subject of his longing takes his breath away and haunts his dreams, but come sunrise, "Once more you'll disappear, my morning put to shame."

Pete's acoustic guitar solo rips at the heart as he continues:

Sometimes I fear this will go on my life through
Each day I spend in an echo vision of you
And then again I'll turn down love remembering your smile
My every day is spent thinking of you all the while

Townshend neatly moves into the middle-eight, bemoaning the chances he's lost because he was so rooted in the past, in some of his most mature and finely crafted lyrics. This was the final track to be recorded for the album; with its memorable tune and the haunting delivery, it's stunningly beautiful.

Rael

Legendary session man Al Kooper, who played keyboards on this track, discloses in the liner notes that after working on this recording, engineer Chris Huston returned to the studio the next day, only to find that the cleaning lady had inadvertently put the master tape in the bin. It was covered in cigarette ash and soft-drink splashes – the first 15 seconds of the song was ruined and would have to be re-recorded. When Townshend arrived, Chris took him to one side and explained the situation, saying, "Pete, I'm sorry but sometimes these things happen."

According to Kooper, Pete fumed for a while and then picked up the engineer's chair and hurled it through the control room glass partition causing thousands of dollars worth of damage. He turned to Huston and said, "Don't worry Chris... sometimes these things just happen."

There has been much speculation as to what "Rael" is actually about. Journalist John Swenson wrote, "It's about 'overspill'," meaning some kind of population boom, however Townshend claimed, "No one will ever know what it means; it has been squeezed up too tightly to make sense." This has the pretensions of a possible mini-opera but ultimately you could call it a suite. It has a regal feel to it with the obligatory harmony vocal layers plus, what had become for this album, the de rigueur hard panning of drums. The track takes a left turn and becomes the blueprint for what would eventually be the track "Sparks" on *Tommy*.

Overall, "Rael" is intriguing at best but lacks a clear direction for the listener.

This is a Townshend experiment and, as he mines his imagination, you can hear fragments of *Tommy* buried deep in the melodies and musical movements.

Bonus Tracks:

Rael 2
The solemn melody that Pete sings here will eventually mutate into "I'm Free" also on *Tommy*.

(Top Gear)
Keith plays manic "Wipeout"-style toms as the others shout "Top Gear" advertising the BBC radio show of the same name. *Top Gear* was an "in session" show where the popular groups of the day would go into the BBC studios and record tracks exclusively for the programme. This is where the spoof ads stop featuring the lush orchestral arrangements and super-smooth 60s female voices and it's the band, only, who perform the rest of the advertisements on the record.

Glittering Girl
This skips along in a jolly fashion and hints at a riff that will eventually appear on *Tommy* as "I'm Free".

(Coke 2)
The band launch headlong into a spectacularly muscular riff and "acid" guitar solo, which as it gathers force is interspersed with chants of "Coke, after Coke, after Coca Cola." This excellent backing track is wasted here.

Melancholia
Recorded at Advision Studios in London, this tough, raucous rock track finds Pete delivering more acid guitar licks. Moody and foreboding, the band satisfactorily work through their repertoire of rock moves on this sprawling cut.

(Bag O'Nails)
John and Keith have fun in the studio messing with the spoof ad idea promoting the well-known London drinking den, the Bag O' Nails.

Someone's Coming
The B-side to "I Can See For Miles" was the first time Daltrey had provided the lead vocal to an Entwistle-penned song. Recorded in New York and Nashville it relies heavily on Entwistle's brass contributions.

(John Mason's Cars (Rehearsal))
The rhythm section attempts to advertise a local car dealer in the West London suburb of Ealing – John Mason: "John Mason, we got the best cars 'ere!"

Jaguar
This was the first song that Townshend wrote for this album. In the final choruses

the band vamp on the riff as they all chant "Ja, Gu, Ar". Townshend commented, "As things progressed, we realised the whole album could be built around this aspect of commercial advertising."

(John Mason's Cars (Reprise))
Keith suggests they "should do it a bit faster". More laughs as John and Keith attempt the "John Mason" ad... again.

Early Morning Cold Taxi
Written by Roger Daltrey and friend Dave "Cyrano" Langston (a former Who roadie), this was recorded at IBC Studios in London. It's a vibrant, optimistic tune that bounces along light-heartedly as the lyric tells of coming home with friends in the early morning after a wild night out – something this band knew all about.

(Coke 1)
A further ad for Coke appears as the band intones, "Things go better with Coke."

Hall Of The Mountain King
Starting with the riff from the 60s American TV comedy *The Munsters*, this instrumental goes on to borrow the title and theme from Edvard Grieg's "In The Hall Of The Mountain King" section of his *Peer Gynt* suite. One of the most unlikely credits in rock is shared with composition by Grieg (who died in 1907) and arrangement by the Who.

(Radio 1 (Boris Mix))
John announces "Radio 1" in his Boris voice to the tune of same. These later ads failed to make the original album and that's no surprise – they're half-finished and often ill-conceived.

Girl's Eyes
This is one of the few Keith Moon-penned songs the band would ever record. John and Pete both made contributions but the credit goes to the drummer. Keith takes the lead vocal with Roger in close support on this happy little pop tune that features acoustic work from Townshend and some drum theatrics from Moon at the fade.

(Odorono (Final Chorus))
A reprise of the "Odorono" chorus that was chopped off the end of the original recording makes a brief appearance.

Mary-Anne With The Shaky Hand (Alternate Version)
Played faster than the original album version and featuring superfluous Al Kooper Hammond organ, this take appeared on the US release of "I Can See For Miles". It doesn't have the languid, sweaty vibe of the album cut and it's no surprise they relegated this version to B-side status.

Glow Girl

This was the first glimmer of the idea that would eventually become *Tommy*. "'Glow Girl'," Townshend explained, "led me to the idea of 'It's a boy Mrs Walker'... I rarely leave any good idea unused. 'Rael' themes crop up in *Tommy* and so do the last lines of this."

(Track Records)

After the last bonus track, the extended CD version of the album finishes with a constant repeat of the legend "Track Records, Track Records, Track Records" by John and Keith to the fade-out.

In March 2009, a 2-CD deluxe edition was released, compiled for the first time from the original stereo and mono masters. The 28-page booklet that accompanied it contained previously unpublished photos and 60s advertising images. The CD sleeve featured outtakes from the photographic sessions for the cover of the original album.

Nik Cohn wrote in *Queen* magazine at the time that the album could be paralleled with Andy Warhol's Campbell soup cans. Richard Barnes declared that the Who had produced "a truly Pop Art album" but the album attained minimal success. *Sell Out* peaked at number 13 in the UK chart and reached a disappointingly low 48 in the US. "I love *Sell Out*, I think it's great," Roger Daltrey told music critic Ken Sharp in 1994. "I love the jingles. The whole thing as an album is a wonderful piece of work. The cover, everything about it. It's got humour, great songs, irony."

A cathartic process for band and management, this aurally arresting album with its ambitious ideals had moved the band away from the traditional pop idiom into a whole new area of creativity. The band had developed new skills; harmonies were tighter, arrangements slicker and Pete had finally got to grips with playing the piano which added much to the sophistication of the record. The band's idea of itself was broadening and deepening; the musicians were more cohesive as a unit and, even though the personality clashes remained, they had diminished somewhat. Most importantly, they could no longer escape the awareness that the Who was bigger than the sum of its parts.

But "I Can See For Miles" failed to be the huge money-spinning commercial hit that Townshend believed it would be and although *Sell Out* had helped the band to grow, he still felt they were in danger of getting lost. He felt the Who needed something phenomenal to save them and he felt it was he, and he alone, who could do it.

04 Opera Rocks – 1968-69

In spite of their success, by 1968 the Who found themselves drastically in debt, amassing bills approaching a million pounds. They were living so far beyond their means that, despite six Top 5 UK singles, their appetite for destruction – of drums, guitars, hotel-rooms – simply could not be sustained by their income. The band wasn't earning enough money from their British hits and were seriously lagging behind other big British groups when it came to any chart action in America.

Although "I Can See For Miles" had edged into the *Billboard* top ten – incredibly, their only 45 ever to do so – their best placing on the US albums chart up to now had been a measly 48, for *Sell Out*. It was felt that a major factor in their albums' relative failure in America was the omission of the single releases. Stateside label Decca really didn't know what to do with the Who. Decca's last resort was to re-package a collection of previously issued material and release it in 1968 under the title *Magic Bus: The Who On Tour*. The group had jokingly dubbed it "The Who's Greatest Flops" because most of the singles included on it had failed in the USA. Pete was furious with the release, but under contract he had no choice but to go along with it. His anger was made even greater by the choice of cover photo – a clumsily chosen image of the group standing next to a "magic" tour bus. Nonetheless, after a few weeks of media attention and some steady radio play, the album made it to number 39, giving them their first Top 40 album in the US.

The much-vaunted never-ending "summer of love" had really only lasted a year, and, by the end of 1968, the flower power era was all but over. Meanwhile, the Who's Track Records label-mate Jimi Hendrix was keeping up the pressure. This US guitar hero wasn't just smashing guitars; he was fucking and then burning them! Townshend admitted that the force of the Hendrix super-nova had prompted in him something of an identity crisis. He said he felt "very confused for a bit. I kind of groped around, I had a lot of spiritual problems, I asked my [girlfriend] to marry me before it was too late, and started work on *Tommy* a bit later."

Nineteen sixty-eight was also the first year that rock fans in England bought more albums than singles. This change in buying habits signalled a new future, one which Townshend knew his band had to embrace. Earning money from gigs was also proving to be difficult: over-exposure through incessant gigging in the UK now meant that universities, who would once have happily paid the Who more than £100 per show, were now booking them for as little as £50 per night. The band needed to break America; they needed a huge hit.

Townshend had a plan: "I went away and I thought I have to save this band, I have to do it, Kit can't do it, Keith can't do it, Roger can't do it. I have to do it!" Both the Beatles and the Beach Boys had recently released albums with a central unifying concept. Pete decided to take this idea further still, to link every song on an album with a central character and narrative. His dream was to produce something previously unheard of: a full-length rock opera. In 2002, Pete would tell *Uncut* magazine, "If I'm accused of being pretentious because I write a rock opera, I find myself wondering what I am pretending to be. I invented rock opera, then wrote one. No pretence there. Mad? Of course I'm mad (though what would become *Tommy* is widely acknowledged as the first rock opera, many fans of the Pretty Things believe their album *SF Sorrow*, which predated the Townshend opus by a year, actually deserves this accolade, though it barely registered in the popular consciousness)."

Back in 1966, the nine-minute "A Quick One, While He's Away" had been seen almost as a mini rock opera, but in terms of ambition and scale, that would be dwarfed by *Tommy* (and later *Quadrophenia*). It was a brave first attempt at a time when most groups were still obsessed with the three-minute pop song, and it was a useful warm-up. At first glance, the rock opera *Tommy* may have appeared to be the fastest way to get dropped by a record company. A storyline based on the life and times of a "deaf, dumb and blind kid", who excels at pinball and is acclaimed as a messiah? Surely this was commercial suicide?

Townshend's concept for a rock opera had started life as a rough idea in its creator's mind during 1967. There had been many working titles – "Amazing Journey", "The Brain Opera", "Omnibus" and "Deaf, Dumb And Blind Boy" – before Kit Lambert settled on *Tommy*. Townshend wanted the piece to be intellectually entertaining, have the feel of a fairy tale but to ultimately contain a spiritual message. This was a tall order for a band more used to churning out singles. Townshend took a long time to settle on a plot and the songs came in dribs and drabs. A key inspiration was Indian guru, Meher Baba. Townshend had been aware of Baba since late 1967 and had been introduced to his teachings by Mike McInnerney, the artist who would later create the cover artwork for *Tommy*. "It was in the knowledge that [Mike] was a Baba lover," Townshend explained, "and able to grasp the needs of the evolving album, that I asked him to do the artwork."

Meher Baba would become a huge influence on Townshend's life and work. In a 1970 *Rolling Stone* piece, Townshend gave his own take on the background to the guru's rise: "He was born in a town in India called Poona in February, 1864. While in college, he built up an affection for an old woman named Hazrat Babajan, who was in reality a Perfect Master. One day she kissed him on the forehead, and from that moment he was changed. He neither ate nor slept for months, and spent the next seven years in study with the five Perfect Masters of the time [a Perfect Master, according to Baba, is a God-realised person – someone whose consciousness has merged with that of God – who can use his or her divine attributes of infinite power, knowledge and bliss for the spiritual uplifting of others]. One of these Masters, Upasni Maharaj, threw a stone at Baba, hitting him at the spot where Babajan had kissed him, between his eyes. It was at this moment that Baba became aware of his role and destiny as a Perfect Master himself."

Baba lived a life of extreme simplicity. He spent long periods in seclusion, often fasting, but he also travelled extensively with a close-knit group of followers, and spent a lot of time working with the sick and the poor. From 1925 to the end of his life, Baba remained silent, communicating with an alphabet board or by gesture. Baba said, "You have had enough of my words, now is the time to live by them." In 1954, Baba declared that he was the Avatar of the Age – the incarnation of God on earth, in bodily form. Fourteen years later, he announced that he had completed his work in this world to his complete satisfaction. He died on 31st January 1969, with a wish to "live eternally in the hearts of those that love me."

The later stages of *Tommy*'s messianic experiences would draw particularly heavily on Baba's life and teachings (Townshend wasn't the only rock star to come under the guru's spell; Ronnie Lane of the Small Faces was another devotee). Pete was also fascinated by the writings of the American writer of Polish descent, George Adamski, who wrote the bestseller *Flying Saucers Have Landed* in 1953. Herman Hesse's novel, *Siddhartha*, also inspired him, with its study of spiritual matters amid the harsh reality of everyday life.

Recording sessions for the new album began at IBC Studios in September 1968, with the intention to release it in time for that year's lucrative Christmas market, but work was slow. The band had a busy gigging schedule to keep some much-needed money trickling in, and that meant more time away from the studio. Kit Lambert started to tire of Townshend's constant rewriting, and eventually turned up at the studio with a film script entitled "Tommy 1914-1984". At that moment, the project finally found its direction. By the time the completed double LP was ready for release in May 1969, it was five months late. The band's huge debts and the massive investment of time and money in this album meant that it had to be a hit – and a big one at that.

With imaginative production by Kit Lambert (with Damon Lyon Shaw as engineer), *Tommy*'s distinctive sound was, according to Townshend, "easy to come by. I thought I was going to have to make concessions, but not once did I have to. I mean, ideas were made much more powerful than they were originally." However much later, in 1989, he would admit with hindsight: "*Tommy* would have been so much better if I had had modern equipment. I can't tell you how hard that was for me. I'm not a great memory man, I'm not very good at music, I'm not very good at ordering my thoughts. I'm very flitty, and I found it so difficult to write. I mean, just to write the two or three bits where there was an element of through-composition, like 'Go To The Mirror', having 'See Me, Feel Me' in it, and the 'Overture'. It was just a nightmare, because I had to write stuff on paper and I had no training. That's my one great regret."

Tommy did feature many of the more sophisticated studio techniques of the day, some of which were more successful than others. The vocal sound is slick with Kit utilising multi-tracking facilities plus backwards guitar effects. But the hard panning of the drums to one side, which he uses constantly here, immediately reduces the stereo picture making the sound somehow smaller, and detracting from the overall power of the record. This studio trick was quickly discarded, and is only ever used now in modern production as a nostalgic nod to rock'n'roll days gone by.

Considering the relatively limited technology available at the time, the end result was a tremendous achievement on the part of Townshend and Lambert. The major difficulty was keeping the musical continuity between all the different sessions that took place over the months of recording. They made a good, innovative team, with Pete's youthful energy offset by Lambert's sophisticated thinking, effortlessly utilising the contrasting dynamics of the studio and the limited options offered by a four-piece rock group in order to create a grandiose feel.

The album relies heavily on acoustic guitars, with little in the way of axe heroics from Townshend (he used an array of guitars that included a Gibson SG special, Gibson ES355, Fender Jazzmaster and a Fender electric 12-string). The musical performances are controlled but effective, with the focus firmly on the vocals, and the character-based narrative to which everything else is subordinated. Townshend commented: "Kit deliberately mixed it like that, with the voices up front. The music was structured to allow the concept to breathe."

Keith Moon, however, saw it quite differently: "A lot of the songs were soft. We never played like that."

Call Me Lightning
US Single Release: 16/03/1968 (Decca)
Peak Position: 40 (US)
According to Townshend, "What's really interesting for me about 'Call Me Lightning' is realising how hard from the very beginning it was, writing for Roger's voice."

Recorded at Goldstar Studios in California in late February, this was a US release only with "Dogs" being its British counterpart. Townshend was floundering artistically but the band had to have "product" in the shops so they released what they had. Manager Chris Stamp recalled, "We had to have records. At that time the Who were falling apart. We weren't going anywhere."

Pete explained his artistic dilemma: "'Call Me Lightning' was among the batch of songs that I submitted for the Who's first single. It tries to be a slightly surfy, Jan and Dean kind of song, to satisfy Keith Moon's and John Entwistle's then interest in surf music, which I thought was going to be a real problem. Being a trumped-up Mod band was bad enough for us to handle, but trying to be a trumped-up Mod band playing R&B but with surf overtones was almost impossible.

"Anyway, I was trying to write this song which was all things to all men, and I came up with this kind of Shadow Morton backing track and then wrote the lyric for Roger. All of the lyrics are about things that I thought would help Roger portray himself in the way he thought he should be portrayed. So this kind of braggadocio, grandiosity, aggression, flash, empty kind of figure is obviously what I took Roger to be at the time."

Townshend saw himself as writing for "the characteristics which Roger carried which I thought were lacking in me. I don't have what Roger has. I don't have his conviction that if he gets into a fight, he can win... I didn't have his looks. I didn't have his magnetism. I just had talent."

Dogs
UK Single Release: 14/06/1968 (Track)
Peak Position: 25 (UK)
Possibly the most bizarre composition of the band's entire catalogue and a baffling choice of single, "Dogs" was a complete failure. Townshend himself referred to it

as corny. He admitted that the band were, in his words, "going down the drain" at the time, and this painfully barren artistic period for Townshend resulted in having to release this music hall knock-about track, where the hero of the piece falls in love with a kennel maid at the local greyhound-racing track and admits that, until he met the girl, "there was nothing bigger in my life than beer." This was later remixed and included on the expansive *Thirty Years Of Maximum R&B* box set.

Magic Bus
UK Single Release: 11/10/1968 (Track) US Single Release: 27/07/1969 (Decca)
Peak Position: 26 (UK) 25 (US)

John Entwistle hated this track, bemoaning that it was "eight minutes, playing A". He did indeed have to play the basic Bo Diddley ostinato for what seemed like an eternity but his low-end rumblings underpinned the track perfectly. Recorded at IBC Studios in the summer of '68, Keith played a basic clave pattern while Townshend and Daltrey exchanged call-and-response lines back, with Daltrey repeating "I want it, I want it, I want it" and Townshend replying, "Ya can't have it!"

This was always a real crowd-pleaser and the band included an enthusiastic version of it on their *Live At Leeds* album. At one gig in Liverpool late in 1968, the band invited all the acts on the bill to join them in a huge ensemble 20-minute version of "Bus". The acts included the Small Faces, whose drummer Kenney Jones played alongside Moon. Within a decade, Keith would be dead and Kenney would have joined the Who.

1969:

Pinball Wizard
UK Single Release: 07/03/1969 (Track) US Single Release: 22/03/1969 (Decca)
Peak Position: 4 (UK) 19 (US)

Townshend originally dismissed "Pinball Wizard" as "awful, the most clumsy piece of writing I've ever done." He felt it was going to be "a complete dud" and tentatively presented the demo to everyone in the studio where the consensus was undoubtedly that they had a hit on their hands. A bemused Townshend asked himself, "Have I written a hit?" He'd been furious that the band had been denied a smash hit with "I Can See For Miles" but "Pinball Wizard" would restore his confidence that the Who could still create the perfect single.

Recorded at Morgan Studios in London, in February 1969, "Wizard" was vitally important because nothing else on the record sounded like a chart hit. And, although the band had obviously moved on with larger concepts and ideas, they still needed singles chart success. "Pinball Wizard" reached number four in the UK and remained on the British charts for 13 weeks. Constant airplay and various TV performances secured its success. In the US it managed a respectable 19 and thrust the band back onto the radio playlists there.

"Pinball Wizard" starts with a melancholy, slightly threatening series of chords all with a B-note in the root, a technique influenced by the English Baroque composer Henry Purcell (and also employed on "I'm A Boy"). For Townshend it was "just an exploration of how many chords I could make with a running B". The now-famous celebratory rhythmic guitar fanfare which Townshend referred to as "a bit of vigorous kind of flamenco guitar", rings out as he utilises his favoured suspended chords to the maximum; the effect is incendiary. Once the song truly kicks off, the melody is the focal point to which all else is sacrificed. The irresistible "sure plays a mean pinball" hook with counterpart backing vocals, draws you in and lodges firmly in your brain, never to be forgotten.

Musically beguiling, "Wizard" is confident and assured with the young band's commanding playing demonstrating how much they had improved as musicians. Sonically, it's clean and crisp with a deft, no-nonsense arrangement, "Kit's production on 'Pinball Wizard' is absolutely tremendous," Daltrey insisted. "The whole montage of sounds he got in emulating the pinball machine is extraordinary. I don't think he got enough recognition for his work on that. Not necessarily the sound he got – because most of the time making *Tommy* we were out of our boxes, God knows what we were doing – but the actual arrangements and the ideas, the harmonies and the structures."

Townshend was doing various interviews at the time of the single's release and talking endlessly and excitedly about his forthcoming "rock opera". Music media interest was mounting and "Wizard" benefited from this attention but, as a stand-alone song, it was destined to become a generation-spanning classic: one of the greatest rock'n'roll records of all time (as an example of the song's genre-defying appeal, in 1973 the saccharine pop group the New Seekers released a single that segued "Pinball Wizard" into "See Me, Feel Me". It reached number 16 on the UK chart, and 29 in the US).

I'm Free
US Single Release: 05/07/1969 (Decca)
Peak Position: 37 (US)
This was released in the US only.

Tommy
UK Album Release: 23/05/1969 (Track 613013/4)
US Album Release: 17/05/1969 (Decca DXSW 7205)
Peak Position: 2 (UK) 4 (US)
Overture / It's A Boy / 1921 / Amazing Journey / Sparks / Eyesight To The Blind (The Hawker) / Christmas / Cousin Kevin / The Acid Queen / Underture / Do You Think It's Alright? / Fiddle About /Pinball Wizard / There's A Doctor / Go To The Mirror! / Tommy Can You Hear Me? / Smash The Mirror / Sensation / Miracle Cure / Sally Simpson / I'm Free / Welcome / Tommy's Holiday Camp / We're Not Gonna Take It

Tommy (Deluxe Edition)
UK Album Release: 19/01/2004 (Polydor 9861011)
US Album Release: 28/10/2003 (Geffen B0001386-36)
Disc 1: Overture / It's A Boy / 1921 / Amazing Journey / Sparks / Eyesight To The Blind (The Hawker) / Christmas / Cousin Kevin / The Acid Queen / Underture / Do You Think It's Alright? / Fiddle About / Pinball Wizard / There's A Doctor / Go To The Mirror! / Tommy Can You Hear Me? / Smash The Mirror / Sensation / Miracle Cure / Sally Simpson / I'm Free / Welcome / Tommy's Holiday Camp / We're Not Gonna Take It / See Me, Feel Me – Listening To You
Disc 2: I Was / Christmas (Outtake 3) / Cousin Kevin, Model Child / Young Man Blues (Version 1) / Tommy Can You Hear Me? (Alternate Version) / Trying To Get Through / Sally Simpson (Outtakes) /

Miss Simpson / Welcome (Take 2) / Tommy's Holiday Camp (Band's Version) / We're Not Gonna Take It (Alternative Version) / Dogs (Part 2) / Stereo Only Demos: It's A Boy / Amazing Journey / Christmas / Do You Think It's Alright? / Pinball Wizard

The Who should ignore the seductive attention of critics who want to tell them they're artists.
Charlie Gillett, *Record Mirror*

Overture

This energetic attention-grabbing overture kicks off with some trademark Who percussion and guitar before staccato band and orchestral riffs seize the listener. The band then run through the cycle's key musical motifs – among them "See Me Feel Me", "Listening To You", "Go To The Mirror" and even the introductory riff to "Pinball Wizard" – during this grandiose, dramatic introduction.

"This clues you into a lot of the themes and gives continuity to the individual tracks," Townshend explained. "You think you've heard them before because they've been stated in the overture. It gives more of a flow and strengthens the whole thing." John Entwistle's horn flourishes are heavily featured, with angelic vocals in the intermittent breakdowns. Keith's drums sound crisp, tight and clean as do the in-your-face acoustic guitars on which Pete demonstrates his excellent, action-packed country blues picking technique. Here, he was using a Gibson J-200 and Harmony Sovereign guitar.

It's A Boy

Based on the original album alone, some of the details of Tommy's story were sketchy and implied rather than specifically stated. Though Townshend has filled in some of these gaps subsequently, one should be wary of considering the *Tommy* album to have one sole and clear narrative meaning.

In the first song on the album, the unseen Captain Walker is missing in action during World War I. Shortly after hearing this news, Mrs Walker gives birth to their son Tommy in this very brief reworking of 1967's "Glow Girl" – unreleased at the time, but later to appear on *Odds & Sods* and the remastered version of *Sell Out* – though the gender of the child is changed to fit with the exclamation, "It's a boy, Mrs Walker". Indeed, other than the final refrain "A son, a son", this exclamation forms the song's entire lyric – less, in this case, is more. Musically delightful but more a snippet than a proper song, wistful horns and plaintive acoustic guitar arpeggios accompany the few words.

1921

The title here reinforces the timeframe for the events that are unfolding. Also known under the title "You Didn't Hear It" in the USA, "1921" begins with the quiet optimism that "'21 is gonna be a good year", but as the chorus approaches, there's an air of foreboding.

When his father, Captain Walker, returns from the war to find his wife has a new lover, he flies into a rage and murders the man. The child Tommy witnesses the events through a mirror (in a major change, the later movie version would reverse this violent encounter and depict Tommy's father as being killed by his mother and her new lover). As Tommy is told emphatically that he saw and heard nothing of the event that has just taken place, and is forbidden from ever mentioning it again, he suffers such deep psychological trauma that he is ultimately rendered "deaf, dumb and blind" (though this new affliction is not mentioned until the opening of the subsequent track, "Amazing Journey"). There is a painful irony in the repeated refrain of the opening line, "Got a feeling that '21 is going to be a good year", darkly shorn of the original optimism.

"What about the boy?" is the final line. The answer to this question is the story of Tommy. Although not of the rock classic calibre of "Pinball Wizard" and some other *Tommy* highlights, this is a strong tune and lyric set against some very simple but effective backing that includes a beautifully understated rolling piano riff. While it pushes the story considerably forward, it can also stand alone as a memorable Who track.

Amazing Journey

At the age of 10, Tommy's new life – the amazing journey of the title – begins with him "deaf, dumb and blind... in a quiet vibration land". The subtle, shaking rhythm matches the words exactly. Appropriately for a Messiah in the making, with rock star parallels, Tommy's "musical dreams ain't quite so bad". His journey, like that of many spiritual pilgrims, is a chance to "learn all [he] should know..." In a vision he is confronted by a mysterious stranger dressed in a long glittering silver robe that trails down to the ground – a manifestation of his subconscious or his alter ego perhaps, this spiritual figure would be Tommy's guide on his journey (though Meher Baba was far more ascetic, his influence is evident in the presence of Tommy's new mentor).

As the tempo picks up, Keith throws in some inspired, wild fills that shouldn't work but do and Roger gives a restrained vocal performance resisting the temptation to belt it all out. A change of pace and the band set off on a half time feel with a backwards guitar solo. By now, the band is in full pop mode with harmonies reminiscent of Keith's favourites the Beach Boys. Subtle and gently melodic, it shows how far the band had travelled from the maximum R&B with which they made their name.

Sparks

This understated instrumental has its origins in riffs found on "A Quick One" and "Rael". Keith plays dramatic rolls and fills on tympani and all the while the tension builds in preparation for the next instalment of the story...

Eyesight To The Blind (The Hawker)

This started life as a blues song by Sonny Boy Williamson II before the Who added the subtitle in parenthesis. Townshend tweaked the lyrics and transformed the tune into a more up-tempo rock song, the signature tune of a cult leader at a church where Tommy's parents take him in search of healing.

Christmas

Bizarre and disturbing backing vocals set an uneasy atmosphere as Tommy's parents bemoan that on Christmas Day "Tommy doesn't know what day it is". If Tommy isn't aware of Jesus, how can he be saved from this "eternal grave"? Later, Pete interjects the increasingly desperate demands, "Tommy can you hear me?" This track adds another dimension to Tommy's journey. It features a lightning drum break from Keith and tight, choppy acoustic guitars from Townshend.

Cousin Kevin

Tommy is left in the care of his cousin, self-proclaimed school bully Kevin, who tortures him out of boredom and spite – "We're on our own cousin, let's see what games we can play!" This is more of a standard musical theatre exposition piece than a straightforward rock song; it is packed with information to push ahead with the narrative of Tommy's experiences, all laced in very dark humour. It was written by John Entwistle, who apparently took inspiration from memories of a cruel schoolmate.

Of this and John's other contribution, "Fiddle About", Townshend commented, "They're ruthlessly brilliant songs because they are just as cruel as people can be." He revealed that Kevin's spiteful line, "There's a lot you can do with a freak!" would have been one he would have avoided in his own writing. Townshend praised John saying he, "came up with two really incredible songs about abuse and bullying, which I couldn't write myself because of my own childhood tenderness on the subject." The subject matter here was well suited to John's musical persona – dark, macabre – and perhaps only he could have captured Kevin's gleeful contempt at how his blind cousin found it so hard to play hide and seek – "To find me, it would take you a week..." or thrown a humorous veil over a bully's malicious delight in wondering what it would be like to give his victim a shove from the top of the stairs.

"We hope that people's pre-conceptions will get screwed around by this," Townshend added. "This sick humour thing which John's got is so important to the album."

Acid Queen

Tommy's parents take him to a woman of questionable morals to see if her lascivious attentions can make a man of him and shock him out of his walking coma state. Could she be his salvation? Pete commented, "The song's not just about acid. It's the whole drug thing, the drink thing, the sex thing, wrapped into one big ball. It's about how you haven't lived if you haven't fucked forty birds, taken sixty trips, drunk fourteen pints of beer – or whatever. Society – people – force you. She [the Acid Queen] represents this force." The carnal corruption fails to awaken the boy and his plight continues. Pete takes on the lead vocal as the Acid Queen.

Underture

Representing Tommy's experiences on acid, this long and complex instrumental track adds weight to the already epic feel of the album. Here, parallels with "Rael" are evident as the piece chops and changes, evoking a feeling of disorientation while building narrative tension and intensifying the drama.

Do You Think It's Alright?

This brief interlude finds Tommy's parents asking themselves with more than a tinge of doubt: "Is it alright / to leave the boy / with Uncle Ernie?" Of course, it isn't. It's a very bouncy and jolly little musical theatre-style song-excerpt; although very melodic, it consists of little more than a tuneful rendition of the above lyric. Shorn of all Who trademarks, this would sound very out of place on any other of their albums.

Fiddle About

The answer to the question posed by the previous track is answered almost immediately in a Paul McCartney-esque knockabout melody, when Tommy is indeed left with his self-proclaimed "wicked" Uncle Ernie. The old reprobate takes advantage of the fact that Tommy won't be able to see or hear anything that he does and abuses him in the euphemistic "fiddle about" and "down with the bed clothes, up with your night shirt".

Written by John Entwistle at the very closing stages of the album's composition, Townshend apparently knew what he wanted to say but felt he couldn't summon the requisite callousness – "I didn't think I could be cruel enough" – and delegated the task to Entwistle who he knew could dispassionately come up with very dark lyrics:

"I wanted to show that the boy was being dealt with very cruelly and it was because he was being dismissed as a freak. The kid is having terrible things done to him, because that's life as it is... 'Fiddle About' represents a whole feeling of family callousness and lack of respect for the kid because he's not like they are."

"Cousin Kevin" and "Fiddle About" are defining moments in Tommy's mistreatment (the subject matter took on a new level of dark poignancy in the light of Townshend's 2003 revelations that he had accessed a website showing images of child abuse in order to investigate possible abuse he had suffered in his own childhood as part of the research for his autobiography. Following a police investigation, he was cleared of any offence. "As I made clear at the outset," Townshend stressed at the time, "I accessed the site because of my concerns at the shocking material readily available on the internet to children as well as adults, and as part of my research towards the campaign I had been putting together since 1995 to counter damage done by all kinds of pornography on the internet, but especially any involving child abuse...").

Perhaps his own childhood experiences were crucial both in choosing the specific nature of Tommy's maltreatment and in delegating the task of writing about this to his fellow band member.

Pinball Wizard

Told from the point of view of a hardened pinball champion, "Wizard" documents Tommy's amazing intuitive mastery of the game: "that deaf, dumb and blind kid sure plays a mean pinball", notes the observer as he questions how the senses-deprived kid can be so good. Ushered to the machine by his "disciples", Tommy isn't distracted by the buzzes, the bells or the flashing lights and simply focuses on his intuitive instincts, far surpassing any player who could see and hear. Faced with the extraordinary skills of this newcomer, the narrator hands his pinball-champion "crown" to Tommy.

The critic and author of seminal rock'n'roll primer *Awopbopaloobop Alopbambaoom*, Nik Cohn, was a key influence in the choice of subject matter. Cohn had heard a rough mix of part of *Tommy* and apparently wasn't impressed. Knowing Cohn was a fan of pinball, Townshend came up with the idea of Tommy being an exceptional player. Cohn liked the idea and Townshend wrote "Pinball Wizard" to prove a point:

"I was caving in by writing it because it put the fairly small idea of a blind man playing pinball – or any such game – into too clear a frame," the composer confessed. "But in the end it worked. I really did write it to try and get my friend Nik Cohn to accept rock opera."

Guru Meher Baba's great emphasis on the value of games would also influence Pete in having his hero play pinball. "The whole point of 'Pinball Wizard'," Townshend elaborated, "was to let the boy have some sort of colourful event and excitement. Suddenly things are happening... 'Pinball Wizard' is about life's games, playing the machine – the boy and his machine, the disciples with theirs, the scores, results, colours, vibration and action...

"This is Tommy's big triumph. He's got results. A big score! He doesn't know all this; he stumbled on a machine, started to pull levers and so on, got things going, and suddenly started getting incredible affection – like pats on the back. This hasn't happened to him before, and the kids are his first disciples."

Many of *Tommy*'s tracks are vehicles to move the opera's plot onwards rather than songs in their own right. But while "Wizard" tells of a pivotal stage in Tommy's development – dramatically, indeed even operatically – its success as a single proved it had a life of its own away from the narrative. It's one of the few tracks on the record where the group actually sound like a rock band.

There's A Doctor
This is another very short, Music Hall-style, plot-pushing snippet. Pete sings this piano-based number describing Tommy's parents' intention to take him to a local specialist "a doctor I've found can cure the boy / a man I've found can remove his sorrow." But can he? We'll find out "tomorrow"...

Go To The Mirror
The doctor explains that there is nothing physically wrong with Tommy, but that he has "an inner block", that no machine or doctor can fix. Tommy responds by crying out inwardly the plaintive refrain, "See Me, Feel Me, Touch Me... Heal Me." The doctor also anticipates the shock that Tommy's senses returning will bring to the young man before explaining that only Tommy can cure himself and urges him to "smash the mirror, boy" and free himself.

Opening with a pounding electric guitar riff, this goes off on a number of melodic tangents as it grows into a hook-laden, classic rock number driven along by some blistering playing and fine singing. There is sensuality in Roger's double-tracked vocals, contrasting with the innocence of Townshend's "See me, Feel me, Touch me" refrain. Keith adds some fantastic triplets to the mix (he had now switched to a Premier champagne silver kit that had the same spec as the "Pictures Of Lily'"'kit). The band head off into a slight return to the insistent "Listening to you" refrain as the track reaches its climax (this outro was lifted by a younger generation of rebel-rockers the Clash on the play-out section of "White Man In Hammersmith Palais").

Tommy Can You Hear Me?

The title is a plea from Tommy's anguished mother, whose conscience is pricked by her son's plight. Her guilt increases because she knows she played a part in the violent events that caused her son's trauma-induced affliction.

With a simple bass and acoustic guitar arrangement, this breezy country-rock ensemble vocal piece has the band singing tight harmonies in a style similar to that which would be showcased by Crosby, Stills and Nash in their eponymous debut album released the same month. Melodically upbeat, this is yet more evidence of Townshend's innate pop sensibility. John continued to use his "Frankenstein" bass, and his tight staccato style of picking is well demonstrated here. The track concludes poignantly with Roger alone singing, "Tommy... Tommy... Tommy."

Smash The Mirror

Tommy's mother voices her frustration at how he doesn't answer her calls with "even a nod or a wink"; he doesn't hear or see her and yet he appears to be transfixed – Narcissus-like – by his own reflection. "How can the mirror affect you?" she cries out in frustration, threatening to retaliate against his silence by following the doctor's suggestion and smashing the mirror.

This compelling blues-flavoured piece begins with some funky playing – Keith kicks it off with a distinctive roll and is immediately joined by some acid-fried rock guitar riffing. Roger pushes his voice almost to breaking point, appropriately, on the word "Mirror". Like the country-rock of "Tommy Can You Hear Me", this acid-rock showcases the band's versatility. It ends with a resounding smash, the sound of a mirror shattering!

Sensation

The cathartic breaking of the mirror becomes an epiphany for Tommy, liberating him from the trauma of the violent act seen reflected in the mirror when he was a child. With the return of his senses comes an awareness of his own messianic status. Previously devoid of sensation, Tommy has become the embodiment of sensation itself – his approaching presence is felt by others like new vibrations. He exclaims the upbeat affirmative refrain: "I'm a sensation!" With the clear influence of Meher Baba's spiritual journey, Tommy achieves the status of a guru, attracts disciples who worship him, claims to offer "the answer" and declares himself to be "the Light".

"'Sensation' is the song Tommy sings after he's regained his senses," Townshend explains. "He realises who he is and becomes totally aware. The sound of the song is like the Beach Boys; the moment is that of divinity. Tommy is worshipping himself, knowing what he is and speaking the truth... I used all the sensation stuff because, after all this time where Tommy's just been getting vibrations, now he's turned the tables. Now you're going to feel me! I'm in everything; I'm the explosion; I'm a sensation."

Leaving behind the dark frazzled funk of "Smash The Mirror", the music here reflects the elation of the lyrics, as it breezes enthusiastically along driven by John Entwistle's multi-layered brass section. Townshend sings the lyric that celebrates Tommy's liberation.

Miracle Cure

"Extra! Extra! Read all about it! The pinball wizard and the miracle cure..." – the tabloid press hails Tommy's recovery, voiced by a chorus in the style of a 1940s Broadway musical, in a very brief musical snippet – this one lyric repeated twice with a final, emphatic "extra!" added for good measure. A useful point is made about Tommy's burgeoning fame, but this is hardly a song at all and one might wonder why this simple harmonious refrain justifies separate track status.

"It would have been tedious but simple to have run the whole album into one big long kibosh," Townshend explained, "but I wanted to retain track-by-track action. I was really pleased that it had a musical form from beginning to end; separate tracks with separate action and separate musical strength and, at the same time, track-by-track unity, links across time and shunt-backs, all going smoothly."

Sally Simpson

Sally is a Tommy fan who wants to see him preach. Although her father forbids her from going and she "knew from the start that she and Tommy were worlds apart", she is emboldened by her mother's encouragement and goes along anyway. Sitting in the front row, Sally bites her nails and weeps as various gospel groups warm up the crowd in anticipation of Tommy's appearance. When the spot-lit Messiah hits the stage to preach – a rock show in all but name – the crowd go crazy and when Sally moves forward to try to show Tommy how much she loves him, she's thrown back by the security guards and her face is gashed. An ambulance speeds her to hospital, where her wound receives 16 stitches. That Sally ends up marrying an American rock musician shows the parallels Townshend is drawing between Tommy the Messiah, and successful rock stars; the power, the adoration of fans and the fury and potential violence of the massed crowd – the latter in particular would haunt the Who's career much further down the line... Musically, it's another country-rock-style ramble with some great bar-room piano and a breezy rhythm. Like some of the other *Tommy* songs, it works best as part of the opera and would sound very unusual on any other Who album. Pete referred to the more sedate sections as deliberate blandness.

I'm Free

Tommy starts to come to terms with the power of his new role as a Messiah, revelling in the freedom of the title refrain and offering to enlighten his growing band of followers, showing them how to "reach the highest high" by having the guts to "leave the temple".

It begins with a staggering rock guitar riff that shows some Kinks influence and, like all the great Motown singles, opens with the chorus riff of the title: "I'm Free". In its driving beat this is reminiscent of the earliest Who singles but with a much warmer sound, and the verses are far more sophisticated, lyrically and musically.

"'I'm Free' came from [the Rolling Stones'] 'Street Fighting Man'," Townshend would later confess. "This has a weird time/shape and when I finally discovered how it went, I thought 'well blimey, it can't be that simple'." Townshend adds some country-blues picking and the song finally twists back into a slight instrumental refrain of the album's other highlight, "Pinball Wizard", with some Beatles-esque vocal harmonies at the outro. It's a truly liberating anthem, and was later co-opted for a Saab car commercial: *The Who Sell Out* come full circle...

John Entwistle told Chris Jisi in 1989, "On 'I'm Free', me and Pete had to play the drums and Keith played the breaks because he couldn't get the intro. He was hearing it differently from how we were, and he couldn't shake it off. So we put down the snare, the hi-hat and the tambourine part and he came in and added all the breaks. When we did it live, the only way to bring him in was for Pete and I to go like this (makes an exaggerated step), which must have looked completely nuts."

Townshend would describe "I'm Free" and "Pinball Wizard" as "songs of the quiet explosion of divinity. They just rolled off the pen."

Welcome

With the catchy rock chorus of "I'm Free" still ringing in the listener's ears, "Welcome" is another plot-progression track, musically untypical of the Who, that might struggle to stand alone away from the rock-opera setting. Arpeggiated guitars ring out in the distance as Tommy sweetly and melodically welcomes all to his house; indeed, parts of this might not sound out of place in a rather mild West End musical until Roger rips into the vocal and the band finally step things up with some driving piano, menacing backing vocals and blues harmonica.

While Tommy extends his welcome to all, young and old, his following is growing at an exponential rate: "There is more at the door /... We need more room / Build an extension / A colourful extension / Spare no expense now..."

"The institution of the church comes up in 'Welcome'," Townshend explains. "The followers want to know how to follow him and he tells them very simply what to do. He's telling them what they want to hear – it's going to be all smooth and fun and we're never going to speak, we're going to drink all night and have the time of our life... Rama Krishna, Buddha, Zarathustra, Jesus and Meher Baba are all divine figures on earth. They all said the same thing; yet still we trundle on. This is basically what Tommy is saying. But his followers ask how to follow him, and disregard his teaching. They want rules and regulations; going to church on Sundays – but he just says, 'Live life!'"

Tommy's Holiday Camp

As hordes of disciples continue to descend upon Tommy and demand guidance, he comes up with a novel way to accommodate them: "[Tommy] knows they're way off track," Townshend explained, "and is trying by his very presence to make them aware of what they should be doing – coming into the house and then getting out again. Instead of that, they want more action, so he gets the bright idea of extending the house into a huge holiday camp where he can accommodate thousands who want to come and be brainwashed..."

Scarily, though, the would-be converts are greeted by the camp's somewhat inappropriate host, wicked old Uncle Ernie who declares enthusiastically, "Good morning campers!" Keith came up with the concept of portraying what was once a great British working-class institution, the holiday camp, as the setting for Tommy's home for his disciples. Townshend wrote the song – though he credited it to Moon anyway – and sings it in a comical voice reminiscent of comedian Spike Milligan or other Goons, backed by jolly banjos and a cheesy, pier-end, comic Farfisa organ, so cheesy it actually sounds quite creepy – like many parts of *Tommy*, it's a good reminder of what legendary critic Charles Shaar Murray called the Who's "masterly combo-platter of high concept and low comedy". The track concludes with a particularly sinister final "Welcome". It's an accomplished theatrical song a long way from the trademark rock records of the Who, though it is a little anachronistic: set in the 1920s but more reminiscent of the 1950s era setting that would be used in the celluloid version.

We're Not Gonna Take It

Tommy recounts his recent epiphany and tells his would-be disciples how to follow him by replicating his experience: "Play pinball [with] earplugs [and] eyeshades [and a] cork [in the mouth]." He makes it clear that alcohol and drugs are not the answer, but his followers are beginning to question these new pronouncements. "All the time they demand more and more," Townshend said of Tommy's disciples, "and so he starts to get hard: 'Well if you really want to know what to do, you've got to stop drinking for a start. You've got to stop smoking pot.' And he starts to lay down hard moral facts – like Jesus did – but nobody wants to know."

Tommy's way bears the considerable influence of Meher Baba's teachings: "Ask for nothing and you have everything" and "Drugs are harmful mentally, spiritually and physically".

Before long, Tommy's devotees rebel, first whispering, then chanting "We're not gonna take it" as they reject the rules and regulations they once demanded of him. Instead of accepting his teachings, they choose to defy them. In line with the spirit of the age, the message seems to be anti-organised religion, but pro-spiritual enlightenment. It's when Tommy's thoughts are formalised and followed that things go awry, as Townshend explained: "The disciples become disillusioned with Tommy; that is often the way with heroes. They feel that the whole idea has become commercialised and begin to question their hero worship."

Throughout a number of Tommy's experiences, there are parallels between his role as messiah and that of a major rock star. Particularly on this track, a correlation can be drawn between Tommy's rise and fall and the arc of a rock'n'roll career where artists become heroes but are often dropped by their fans as quickly as they were taken up. Perhaps Townshend feared this could happen to his band; although the Who were heroes, rejection could be just around the corner.

"We're Not Gonna Take It" may not have one of Townshend's most memorable melodies, but it's a powerful piece and the band's driving musical accompaniment is building towards a climax. Finally, it slows and seamlessly segues into...

See Me, Feel Me – Listening To You

Abandoned by his followers, Tommy arrives at a new level of spiritual enlightenment as he offers his final Meher Baba-inspired message of hope, "Listening to you, I get the music...".

Roger Daltrey sings with profound authority in his moving, awe-inspiring finale. The intensity builds to a climax of joyous celebration, blurring the lines between the experience of rock'n'roll and the sacred experience of religion in the closing moments of another of the album's highlights (never was this more powerfully illustrated than at Woodstock where the song was performed at sunrise to an overwhelming response).

In summing up the band's performance on *Tommy*, Townshend would reflect: "The singing is better than ever on this album – there are some incredible performances of diction from Roger, aggressively sung but perfectly phrased. And it was an incredible surprise to find that we could all do it live. Such a relief... Keith's playing has never been better, John's playing has never been better, Roger's singing has never been better. They were so incredibly true to form, and as a member of the Who, I was true to form... It really does show how flexible rock'n'roll is, and what a lot of bullshit is talked about what it can and can't do. Although the sound itself has limitations, it has flexibility and malleability... four musicians totally involved with one another's limitations, lives and emotions...

"I mean, what other three musicians would have put up with all my bullshit in order to get this album out? It's my apple, right? It's my whole trip, coming from [Meher] Baba, and they just sat there, let it all come out, and then leapt upon it and gave it an extra boot. It's an incredible group to write for, because you know it's going to work out right. And although I've written other songs, which I won't mention, I've only ever had hits with the Who. And hit records are very near and dear to me."

During the recordings, Pete had turned to Keith and said, "We have a huge hit on our hands." Roger was equally confident: "I don't think there's any way it could have failed." It didn't. *Tommy* was such a success commercially and artistically that it saved the band from their waning 60s novelty pop stardom and propelled them into the rock stratosphere. It also brought the Who the sort of wealth they had previously only fantasised about. Perhaps Townshend's most enduring creation, it inspired huge critical acclaim from highbrow circles and the rock press alike, and secured the Who's status as the thinking man's rock band.

"It was our first attempt," Townshend commented in 1975, "at something that wasn't the same old pilled-up adolescent brand of music." He later added: "We were actually shocked that it did what it was supposed to do, which was to shatter the preconception that people had of the band. Remember, we'd only really existed in the UK at that point as a singles band."

The Who would play most of the double LP in their live set throughout the rest of 1969 and 1970, including the legendary performance at Woodstock. Its finale was at London's Camden Roundhouse on 20 December, 1970. The performance at that last show was dedicated to the support act of the evening, a little-known singer-songwriter named Elton John (who was to have an even closer connection with the *Tommy* story a few years later).

In spite of its success, the band soon discovered that you can't please everyone: over at the *NME*, Richard Green had mixed feelings about the new LP. Under the headline "Who's Sick Opera" he wrote, "I really was looking forward to this 'pop opera', which has occupied Pete Townshend's mind for so long. Really I was. But what a disappointment, even though I did tip it for the *NME* LP charts. Admittedly, the idea is original – even though other groups seem to be jumping on the bandwagon now – but it doesn't come off. Running at over an hour, it goes on and on, and isn't totally representative of the Who. Maybe it's time for a change in style but, if this is it, I long for a return to the old days. 'Pretentious' is too strong; maybe 'over-ambitious' is the right term, but 'sick' certainly applies. One line goes: 'Sickness will surely take the mind'. It does".

Though *Tommy* was billed as a rock opera, in many ways it is really more of a musical – with many melodies and arrangements that are a long way from classic rock'n'roll. Though it features a number of classic rock songs, it is most definitely not a rock album. For the band, however, its historical importance cannot be over-emphasised – it changed their world. Their profile soared and they were suddenly seen as purveyors of "serious" music. Townshend was a media darling and the Who were rich. Their terrible financial situation had finally been resolved. No-one – least of all the musicians themselves – could have predicted that the Who would have reached respectability like this.

The record was released as two separate discs, parts one and two, to make it a cheaper option for those who couldn't afford the double album price. It was performed as a ballet in Canada and consequently the production toured the USA. *Tommy* stayed on the *Billboard* chart for more than two years and sold in excess of 2,000,000 copies. Despite its enormous success and the fact that it saved the band and guaranteed their future, *Tommy* would become something of an albatross around the group's neck. In the long term it did so much for the Who that escaping the character had become impossible.

05 Tougher, Harder, Heavier – 1970

Pete Townshend admitted that the reason for the seminal live album, *Live At Leeds*, was that, "It was all we had. My writing had gone completely apeshit – I won't say it had completely stopped, but I was definitely coming out with some really weird stuff like 'Dogs', 'Magic Bus', bits and pieces..." Maybe it was just as well the band had nothing else, because this is one of the finest live rock records ever made. Or, as *Mojo* put it, "Perhaps the most revered in-concert album ever".

It was released as the burning embers of the 60s cultural counter-revolution began to cool. There was something in the air. A new "heavier" style of music was emerging that was tougher and edgier than anything that had gone before and, with *Live At Leeds*, the Who delivered a slab of unremitting hard rock that was both seductive and thrilling. Meanwhile, the beginnings of what would become known as "heavy metal" were brewing as Black Sabbath, Deep Purple and Led Zeppelin shifted millions of LPs. In May, just before *Live At Leeds* was released, another symbol of the end of an era emerged when the Beatles' final album, *Let It Be*, was issued.

The Who's plan was to draw an LP's worth of material from two deliberately unglamorous gigs in the north of England. The tapes of a Hull show weren't up to scratch, so the Valentine's Day 1970 show at Leeds University refectory was used instead. The original plain brown cardboard sleeve primitively hand-stamped "The Who - Live At Leeds" in simple blue capital lettering, aped the cheap counterfeit image that was prevalent among bootleg sleeves of the time; its contents consisted of letters, photos, contracts, tickets, advertising and handwritten lyrics.

Within the humble packaging were six blistering tracks played with almost telepathic interaction and unprecedented intensity. Yet, given the amount of material recorded at Leeds, some fans were puzzled at the brevity of the work; in an era of in-concert double albums, this was curtailed to just four originals and two covers.

Mojo's Phil Sutcliffe later summed up the original LP incarnation with a succinct description of "metallic 'Young Man Blues', stroppy sharp 'Substitute', pumped-up 50s jiving 'Summertime Blues', beat-boom scruffy 'Shakin' All Over', sprawly, mad 15-minute 'My Generation' and roots-redolent Bo Diddley leaper 'Magic Bus'". Sutcliffe saw it as "a history of the Who woven into a history of rock'n'roll in just six tracks". But it was a very selective history; most obviously absent was any trace of the album that had made stars of the Who, even though they played it in its entirety at Leeds. *Tommy*'s immense international success had overshadowed the band's other achievements. Though they were rich and famous beyond their dreams, like Tommy himself, the Who were now at the mercy of the masses: their shows playing to tens, and sometimes hundreds, of thousands of fans.

As Townshend put it to Sutcliffe, the transformative power of *Tommy* and

Woodstock, had meant that Roger was now a superstar that every groupie wanted to have sex with, while Townshend himself had a hot line to the cultural movers and shakers like the *Rolling Stone* editor Jann Wenner. All four band members had it all – but they were uneasy about their new status. Townshend in particular felt alienated from his audience and developed a terrible feeling that "stadium rock was gonna kill us". He also missed art college, his old mates and the Mod scene.

The full extent of the Leeds performance was only truly reflected three decades later with the 2001 deluxe edition. Suddenly the original half-dozen songs on the vinyl version, ballooned to no fewer than 33 songs on the new double CD set. This deluxe edition reorders the evening's set slightly. The group's encores – covers of "Summertime Blues" and "Shakin' All Over", plus epic performances of "My Generation" and "Magic Bus" – close the first disc so that their live rendition of *Tommy* can be housed on the second disc. Live outings for the latter tended to sequence the rock opera in a slightly different order – as well as dropping a couple of songs ("Cousin Kevin" and "Welcome") which were rarely played in concert.

The expanded two-disc deluxe incarnation of this legendary live record is all the better for the fine added material, but the original LP made a statement that the Who were not just the makers of a concept album about that "deaf, dumb and blind kid". They were a rock band that were still in touch with their R&B roots. Worried at what they and their audience had become, the live record release was a back-to-basics no-nonsense affair, as reinforced by the no-frills packaging. As Townshend's old art school pal and acclaimed Who biographer Richard Barnes put it, "It was 'The 'Oo goes back and kicks arse!'" Indeed it was...

Live At Leeds is an accurate document of the blistering live show. The entire album is mixed with John's bass and Pete's guitar panned hard into left and right speakers with Keith's metallic-sounding kit bright and clear. Roger's voice, meanwhile, is centre stage. The record's adrenalin-fuelled passion and boundless energy are truly remarkable.

Throughout this mix of classic tracks and marathon jam sessions, Keith runs riot around his expansive Premier drum kit. Roger's vocals are a heartfelt roar while Townsend's guitar playing is lethal – vicious in its attack. The Entwistle bass resonates with tons of bottom, filling in the gaps left by Pete's unmistakable, often open, broken power-chord approach. All four band members gel together thrillingly, and while there are the inevitable imperfections of a live performance, these add to the album's robust charm. This is what the Who are really all about.

"*Live At Leeds* is my favourite Who album," Entwistle would later say, "and it's the only one I still play."

The Seeker
UK Single Release: 21/03/1970 (Track) US Single Release: 21/03/1970 (Decca)
Peak Position: 19 (UK) 44 (US)

"I've always found it a bit ploddy... I don't like it that much", Roger stated candidly of Townshend's bouncy tune about his search for spirituality in the modern world. Pete would later praise Roger whom he said would still sing a song with complete commitment even if he didn't particularly like it. John felt much the same way as the singer, saying, "I never liked that song. I hated playing it on stage." He felt that the band never got "the feel" right and believed that it should have remained a demo.

The track was recorded several times; Pete explained "We did it once at my home studio, then at IBC where we normally worked, then with Kit Lambert producing. Then Kit had a tooth pulled, breaking his jaw, and we did it ourselves."

Townshend had mixed feelings about the song, while on the one hand acknowledging, "The results are impressive" he also admitted to liking it the least of all the songs that they were recording at that time. None the less, they played it live briefly in 1970 – and it would reappear in their set, almost four decades later when they played it on stage in 2007.

The carefree country feel of this is a precursor to songs such as "Going Mobile" and "Squeeze Box" to be found later on *Who's Next* and *The Who By Numbers* respectively. The light-hearted musical approach belies the angst of the lyric that finds Townshend explaining how he's asked "Bobby Dylan" and "the Beatles", searched low and high desperately trying to find an answer to life's questions, but all to no avail. He said, "'The Seeker' is a bit like back-to-the-womb Who, not particularly good, but it's a nice side." Joking years later, "I wrote it in a swamp in Florida. At the time, I really was seeking. Really. It was no fun."

In other incarnations of the song, Townshend included a solo version on a limited edition record released as a birthday tribute in memory of Meher Baba. Scottish vocalist Fish, formerly of Marillion, rendered a decent cover regularly in concert during his 1993 *Songs From The Mirror* tour. Eighties progressive techno-flash band Rush uncharacteristically covered this on their 2004 R30 tour and included it on their *Feedback* EP released the same year. The Smithereens also included this on their *Attack Of The Smithereens* rarities record.

Summertime Blues (Live)
UK Single Release: 10/07/1970 (Track) US Single Release: 11/07/1970 (Decca)
Peak Position: 38 (UK) 27 (US)
This was culled from the *Live At Leeds* album and served as a stop-gap while the band continued to tour and promote *Tommy* in the US.

See Me, Feel Me
UK Single Release: 09/10/1970 (Track) US Single Release: 26/09/1970 (Decca)
Peak Position: 12 (US)
Taken from the climax of *Tommy* this also bought the band some time as they continued to tour including playing the legendary Isle Of Wight festival. This was absent from the UK chart but made a fairly respectable number 12 in the US.

Live At Leeds
UK Album Release: 22/05/1970 (Track 2406001)
US Album Release: 16/05/1970 (Decca DL 79175)
Peak Position: 3 (UK) 4 (US)
Young Man Blues / Substitute / Summertime Blues / Shakin' All Over / My Generation / Magic Bus

Live At Leeds (Deluxe Edition)
UK Album Release: 11/2001 (Polydor 112 6182)

US Album Release: 17/09/2001 (MCA 088 112 6182)
Disc 1: Heaven And Hell / I Can't Explain / Fortune Teller / Tattoo / Young Man Blues / Substitute / Happy Jack / I'm A Boy / A Quick One, While He's Away / Summertime Blues / Shakin' All Over / My Generation / Magic Bus
Disc 2: Overture / It's A Boy / 1921 / Amazing Journey / Sparks / Eyesight To The Blind (The Hawker) / Christmas / The Acid Queen / Pinball Wizard / Do You Think It's Alright? / Fiddle About / Tommy Can You Hear Me? / There's A Doctor / Go To The Mirror / Smash The Mirror / Miracle Cure / Sally Simpson / I'm Free / Tommy's Holiday Camp / We're Not Gonna Take It

Quite simply one of the great rock albums. A perfect follow-up to Tommy *with a typical live performance by the Who. All the power, excitement and sheer command of the group are amply demonstrated with total cohesion between Daltrey, Townshend, Entwistle and Moon. The most integrated rock band in the world.*
Rodney Collins, *Record Mirror*

Original Album:

Young Man Blues

This marked the first time that the Who's cover of the Mose Allison standard had been released officially. Here, the band has mutated into the ultimate power trio and deliver an exhilarating, jet-propelled version of the Allison song. It's a storming performance with Pete playing some exquisite blues guitar in the quieter moments while Keith contributes stunning fills around his cranked-up tom-toms.

Here, Entwistle, Moon and Townshend reveal the massive influence that Cream had had upon them. The two bands had often played the same shows and Cream had shown them how far rock music could be taken in terms of improvisation. But perhaps on one point they differed: where Cream had often seemed to be musically competitive, the Who line-up was more complementary.

Substitute

Here the band play an extremely short version of their 1966 hit. In concert they would immediately segue into concise versions of both "Happy Jack" and finally "I'm A Boy" as a nod to previous chart hits. As a stand-alone track away from the mini-trilogy idea of the original live performance, "Substitute" sounds all too brief and ultimately, throwaway. The medley appears in full on the deluxe edition.

Summertime Blues

The late, great Eddie Cochran's rock'n'roll classic is given a full-on Who treatment, as the band takes ownership of this simple 1950s pop song, and positively rip it to shreds. Issued as a single six weeks after the LP's release, it scraped into the British Top 40 as one of the group's more modest hits. It was always a favourite of Entwistle's.

Shakin' All Over

Another cover, this time of Johnny Kidd and the Pirates' number one hit from 1960. Kidd was one of the very few pre-Beatles British pop stars to achieve success abroad, and his group had a considerable influence on the Who (Kidd was an early youthful loss to fledgling rock'n'roll, when he died in a road accident in Lancashire in 1966). There's a real swagger to the Who's version here as they assault and contort the song, again stamping their identity on a cover version.

My Generation

A testosterone-fuelled 14-minute take that sticks faithfully to the original version before it sets off on numerous musical tangents interspersed with false endings: a short-lived jam gives way to a section of "See Me, Feel Me" from *Tommy* featuring a soulful vocal from Roger. Next comes a slow blues manoeuvre which gathers pace as Townshend vamps and solos. Eventually, the band drops out abruptly, leaving only Pete and his guitar, which rings out, gently delayed, building tension.

The other three pile back in for yet another jam session, cranking out this rock riff only to drop out once again, leaving Townshend alone to noodle some more. Suddenly Pete hits an inspired monster of a riff and the others are back in with Townshend's guitar leading the way. They head off into an exhilarating version of "Sparks", again from *Tommy*, there's one last breakdown and kick-off, and the band finally bring the whole 14.45 minutes of rock mayhem to a breathtaking end.

"The only time I ever really enjoyed myself on stage," Entwistle reflected, "was when I was allowed to do something freeform. I didn't like playing set arrangements, I couldn't get off on the other stuff."

Magic Bus

Townshend said of this many years later, "I played this to Mick Jagger after I wrote it in 1964. He loved it, I think, said it sounded like Bo Diddley-meets-Eddie Cochran. But I was embarrassed by the silly words." Based around the Bo Diddley beat motif, this grand finale is a real crowd-pleaser. The band tear off into a hot rock'n'roll jam halfway through which features a brief harmonica solo from Roger, an instrument the group should have utilised more often. The band come to a shuddering halt, finishing what is arguably the most exciting live album of all time. As the *NME* review of May 16th, 1970 put it, "A beautiful album that is going to be an absolute monster, without doubt".

Deluxe Edition: Disc 1:

Heaven And Hell

This Entwistle composition, a muscular rock workout, was a regular opener for the band during this period. This is its first official appearance on record, although shortly afterwards, when "Summertime Blues" was unleashed as a stand-alone single, this was its flip side. John, also the song's lead vocalist, said, "I basically wanted to write a song with a big subject, an important subject rather than spiders or drunks. The original version of 'Heaven And Hell' had a different chorus. It was, basically, I'd rather stay in the middle with my friends because I don't like the sound of either of them. I still don't. Maybe there is an in-between place."

Keith and John jam relentlessly as Pete solos over the top with a definite Cream influence in evidence. John explained, "We were a three-piece band with a singer, so we had to cover a lot of ground. I eventually became a lead bass player."

I Can't Explain
Tight and punchy, an instantly recognisable riff rings out, and the band set off at a controlled pace giving a typically crisp and concise approximation of their debut hit from 1965.

Fortune Teller
Roger's intro on this explains that the tune was "done by a guy called Benny Spellman" and made famous by the Rolling Stones, Wayne Fontana… "and the Merseybeats!" interrupts a voice from behind the drum kit. They kick around this 60s favourite (written by Naomi Neville) and then segue directly into one of their finest tunes.

Tattoo
First recorded three years earlier for the *Sell Out* LP, this is a fine rendition of the male rites of passage tale.

Young Man Blues
As above.

Substitute – Happy Jack – I'm A Boy
Here's the full medley of three of their early hits, featuring a clutch of highly structured pop songs. They kick off into a tight concise arrangement, shifting gear between each of these seminal tracks with ease. Townshend refers to "I'm A Boy", commenting that it was "our first number one for about half an hour."

A Quick One, While He's Away
Preceded by an introduction and explanation from its composer, this live version of their 1966 mini-opera is an unforgettable eight-and-a-half minutes crammed with complex three-part vocal harmonies, twists and turns of tempo changes and radically different musical styles. Pete and Roger share lead vocals as the band blast through the dynamic, convoluted arrangement. Worthy of special note is John Entwistle's excellent falsetto vocal.

Summertime Blues
As above.

Shakin' All Over
As above.

My Generation
As above.

Magic Bus
As above.

Deluxe Edition: Disc 2:

Tommy (Live)

Disc one was re-shuffled to enable disc two to take in the whole "live" version of what was heralded that night as "Thomas, the pot-opera!" To which Keith calls for some order and quiet, "It's a bleedin' opera, isn't it?"

At the start of this second disc it appears the group have returned to the stage after an interval. Townshend also mentions that having performed their short opera ("A Quick One, While He's Away"), they'd now like to do the real thing. The genuine running order for this gig on the night was tracks 1 through to 9 (of disc one), followed by the opera, with tracks 10 through 13 (again, disc one) played as an encore.

The 1970 live version of *Tommy* shows the obvious progression from its original and rather clinical studio incarnation of the previous year. The four band members sound like they're having the time of their lives. One of the highlights is the madcap rendition of "Tommy's Holiday Camp" which, though it flashes by in just one minute, is likely to put a smile on the listener's face. As with most of their live outings of the "opera", four items are missing from the set list – "Cousin Kevin", the lengthy "Underture" instrumental, "Sensation" and "Welcome" – while the running order of parts of the middle section has been re-jigged. Otherwise, however, it's the perfect way to flesh out the second disc.

Live albums can be a perilous business, usually representing either awkward contractual obligations or a thin disguise for a dearth of new material. In one sense, *Live At Leeds* certainly falls into the latter category, but otherwise, the awe-inspiring performance on display here renders it a vivid snapshot of a quartet at the peak of its powers. In all its various incarnations, it remains one of the very few live LPs to deserve the accolade of "essential".

06 Brave New World, Brave New Sound – 1971

A lot had happened since the May 1969 release of the Who's last studio album, *Tommy*. The previously financially strapped and struggling West London Mod band were now rich and famous international rock gods who had triumphed at the era-defining Woodstock and Isle of Wight festivals. They acquired large homes in keeping with their new rock aristocracy status and threw themselves into rock'n'roll hedonism. Keith was at his hotel room-wrecking best, living the lifestyle that would earn him his Moon the Loon moniker. Only health fanatic Roger would steer away from the booze and drugs enjoyed by his band-mates.

Townshend seemed almost schizophrenic [not yet Quadrophrenic] in his ability to combine the contradictions of his love of the pub with his devotion to his anti-drug, ascetic guru Meher Baba. He wrote in *Rolling Stone* in 1970 of having Baba devotees come to his hotel room, greeting him with the words "Jai Baba" – victory to Baba – and shocked to behold the hangers-on, the detritus of smashed TV sets, broken guitars, and whiskey bottles strewn everywhere. His fellow Baba followers couldn't equate the two conflicting lifestyles and, increasingly, neither could Townshend.

His affinity for Baba at least partly drove him in a new direction: this time the subject matter would be the power of music itself, particularly as an antidote to teenage dissolution. Given Townshend's sense of post-*Tommy* alienation and the success of the Who's back-to-their-roots *Live At Leeds*, it's puzzling that he decided the group's next studio project should be yet another intense and complex rock opera, *Lifehouse* – a double album, theatrical production and an epic film. At the August 1970 Isle of Wight festival, where the Who premiered a song off this project, Townshend claimed that the band were half way through the new album.

"I believe rock can do anything," Townshend declared in 1970. "It's the ultimate vehicle for everything. It's the ultimate vehicle for saying anything, for building anything, for killing and creating." More worryingly, considering his own contradictions, the guitarist added: "It's the ultimate vehicle for self-destruction."

"He would test all sides of that equation to their limit over the next few years," critic Peter Doggett wrote in his fine study of the counter-culture *There's A Riot Going On*. "Ploughing his creativity and his band's reputation into ever more portentous projects that might solve the mystery of what rock meant. Townshend's mind was under siege from a mass of competing impulses – the band's daredevil hedonism, his own intake of drink and drugs, his spiritual debt to his guru Meher Baba, his generation's political yearnings, and his music. All of these factors came together to form the... life-changing self-examination that was *Lifehouse*."

Years later, Townshend explained, that *Lifehouse*'s story was about how "rock, pop, whatever you want to call it, offers a moment of perfect reflection that allows us to see ourselves." Influenced by Sufi musician Inayat Khan, one of the keys to this was the search for a "perfect note" that would encapsulate all that was good in humanity. Another key would be to break down the gap between performer and fans. Like John Lennon, he was questioning why he, as a superstar, should be on a pedestal with the worshipping fans at a distance. He planned to develop the *Lifehouse* material in concert, revising and expanding it to take in the input of the audience. In the ultimate spiritual communion, performer and audience would, as author Peter Doggett concisely put it, "become one transcendent note that could change the world…"

"The essence of its storyline," Townshend explained in *Penthouse*, "was a kind of futuristic scene, a fantasy set at a time when rock'n'roll didn't exist. The world was completely collapsing and the only experience that anybody ever had was through test tubes. They lived TV programmes, in a way, everything was programmed. Under those circumstances, a very, very, very old guru figure emerges suddenly and says, 'I remember rock music, it was absolutely amazing; it really did something to people.' And he talked about a kind of nirvana [that] people reached through listening to this type of music. The old man decides that he's going to try to set it up so that the effect can be experienced externally. Everybody would be snapped out of their programmed environment through this rock'n'roll-induced liberated selflessness. Then I began to feel, 'Well, why just simulate it? Why not try and make it happen? If it doesn't, well okay, we'll spoof it.'

"And so I became obsessed with really making it happen, and *Lifehouse* would be the film of the event. I was talking wildly about a six-month rock concert, hiring a theatre for it, and having a set audience with a closed house of maybe 2,000 people. I was going to write a theme for each individual, based on a chart that told everything from their astrological details to alpha waves, to the way they danced, to the clothes they liked, the way they looked, everything. All these themes would be fed into a computer at the same moment, and it was all going to lead to one note. All these people's themes put together would equal one note, a kind of celestial cacophony. I did a lot of experiments, and it was practical; it wasn't just a dream. I was working at it."

Townshend had just one problem: getting anyone else – the band, the critics, the audience, anyone – to understand what he was trying to communicate and how he could possibly achieve it. *Lifehouse* had such a complicated storyline that the composer found it almost impossible to explain to any of his collaborators, but to himself, his vision was clear:

"A self-sufficient, drop-out family group farming in a remote part of Scotland decide to return south to investigate rumours of a subversive concert event that promises to shake and wake up apathetic, fearful British society. Ray is married to Sally, they hope to link up with their daughter Mary who has run away from home to attend the concert… They travel through a dystopian wasteland in a motorised caravan listening to old rock records. The family's freedom had been tolerated by the authorities as they were producing essential food while life in the cities was much more repressive.

"Urban dwellers were forced to live in special space suits. These suits are interconnected in a universal grid, a little like the modern Internet, but combined with gas-company pipelines and cable-television-company wiring. The grid is operated by an imperious media conglomerate headed by a dictatorial figure called Jumbo who appears to be more powerful than the government that first appointed him... The grid delivers all the people's essential needs such as food and medicine as well as providing a lavish programme of entertainment which allows the recipients to 'live out' virtual lifetimes in a short period of time, though sometimes this has adverse consequences – causing emotional and spiritual problems.

"A vital side-issue is that the producers responsible for the programming have ended up concentrating almost entirely on the story-driven narrative form, ignoring all the arts unrestrained by 'plot' as too complex and unpredictable, especially *music* [author's italics]. Effectively, these arts appear to be banned. In fact, they are merely proscribed, ignored, forgotten, no longer of use. A young composer called Bobby hacks into the grid and offers a festival-like music concert – called The Lifehouse – which he hopes will impel the audience to throw off their suits (which are in fact no longer necessary for physical survival) and attend in person. 'Come to the Lifehouse, your song is here'...

"The concert begins, and indeed many of those watching at home are inspired to leave their suits. But eventually the army break in. As they do so, Bobby's musical experiment reaches its zenith and everyone in the building, dancing in a huge dervish circle, suddenly disappears. It emerges that many of the audience at home, participating in their suits, have also disappeared."

It's perhaps no surprise that neither musicians nor managers understood where Townshend was going with this new idea. It was hard to see it ever reaching completion. "Everybody was behind it," Pete counters, "they just didn't understand it. The fatal flaw, though, was getting obsessed with trying to make a fantasy a reality, rather than letting the film speak for itself."

In Townshend's own mind at least, *Lifehouse* was going to be bigger than anything the Who had attempted to date. But a few low-key public outings of the material at London's Young Vic Theatre – a small venue chosen to emphasise the interactive experience – early in '71 baffled audiences and confused the composer. When the idealistic Townshend took the stage one night, he was greeted by a shout from someone in the audience: "Capitalist pigs! Bastards! Get off the stage!" In every show, the audience failed to live up to Townshend's ambitious hopes for interaction and gradually he lost sight of *Lifehouse*'s initial inspiration.

An abortive trip to the States in the hope that Kit Lambert might save the day, resulted in disaster when Townshend discovered that Kit was denigrating *Lifehouse* behind his back, in favour of Lambert's own ambitions to make a film of *Tommy*. Distressed and disillusioned, Townshend crumbled to the point of breakdown. He and the band continued to work on the *Lifehouse* songs and showcase them live but he soon abandoned his plans to make anything more than a concept-free rock album out of the material. The failure to realise his vision for *Lifehouse*, would haunt him for years.

Townshend conceded that it was an incredibly ambitious project that got entirely out of hand and may simply have been too far ahead of its time. "*Lifehouse* failed because I couldn't get it to work dramatically," he would tell Stephen Gallagher in 1996. "The problem that I had with it was that I jumped ahead in time so far that I was describing things like the internet and virtual reality and the karmic and psychological consequences of exposing naïve minds to more experience and information than they were capable of taking in, 20 years before anybody had thought it was ever possible."

Lifehouse has subsequently been revisited on more than one occasion by its creator and is now available as a solo live concert on DVD. It also took on a new life in the form of a BBC Radio 3 play which was first broadcast in December 1999. Roger observed in the movie *Amazing Journey* "The trouble is with *Lifehouse*, no-one I've ever met, apart from Pete, understood it."

Crucially, the failure of the cherished *Lifehouse* project would affect Townshend's view of his audience; to his dismay, they weren't interested in an interactive transcendent spiritual experience; instead, they wanted to have a few drinks and sit back while their favourite band played some rock'n'roll. "So," as Who biographer Dave Marsh put it, "the Who toured in continuing comfort, and their audience (like all rock audiences at this time) became increasingly irrelevant, except as a means of footing the bills. The bonds between band and fan were severed now." It was a sad state of affairs for a band that had prided itself on remaining in touch with its fans, as exemplified by *Live At Leeds*.

Who's Next was a chance to salvage something from the wreckage of the *Lifehouse* project, but it would be unwise to try to comprehend the story of *Lifehouse* by simply listening to *Who's Next*. The two projects have little beyond a few common songs to tie them together. When listened to out of context, these tunes won't help unravel the enigma that is *Lifehouse*. Instead, *Who's Next* was a rock'n'roll record comprising apparently unrelated songs that the Who's fans – whose response to his grandiose spiritual quest had so disappointed Townshend – could easily get. Instead of the purely artistic imperatives of Townshend's ambitious interactive multimedia experience, this would be a commercial hit record. Pete would give the fans exactly what they wanted. The basic title, punning on a common question, would tell fans that, instead of a great concept, this was simply the new record by their favourite band.

The ill-fated March '71 trip to New York had seen the band recording *Lifehouse* material at the Record Plant with Kit Lambert at the controls. The results were unfocused and unsatisfactory, according to Townshend, because of Lambert's growing drug habit. Kit was also preoccupied with the thoughts of a *Tommy* movie at the time. The band, too, had their distractions, not least partying with the New York glitterati.

On their return to London, more studio time was booked at Olympic Studios in Barnes, and some tracks would also be recorded at Mick Jagger's mansion, Stargroves, this time with producer Glyn Johns, who had worked with the Beatles on some *Get Back* sessions. It was here that the new album really took shape. Concentrating on Townshend's best new songs, and with Johns at the helm, the band recorded some of their finest work.

Townshend began experimenting with new equipment, utilising the synthesizer in an innovative way, adopting the Sequence Arpeggiator function on the ARP synthesizer as the basic rhythm track and melodic backdrop for entire songs. Years ahead of later currents in rock, pop and dance music, this was the first marriage of electronics and a four-piece rock'n'roll band and, more importantly, it worked. Roger, though, was less enthusiastic for Pete's adoption of this avant-garde technology.

"I used to hate that fucking thing," he would confess to writer Ken Sharp in 1994, "Oh God, it used to drive us nuts! All it could do is go 'weeeeing...' [imitates high-pitched sound]. I mean, I could do the same thing with a paper and comb."

In terms of its musical "progress" and the ambition of the songwriting – taking complex pieces such as "Won't Get Fooled Again" at eight minutes-plus, way beyond the traditional scale of a rock song – this album was a huge leap forward for rock music and its influence is still very much in evidence in today's contemporary music scene. It was hard to believe that the Who were once pop chart competitors with the likes of Herman's Hermits and the Tremeloes. Now, the band were aiming for rock'n'roll super-power status.

Though the hugely complex *Lifehouse* concept had been ditched, Townshend still had an ambitious scale in mind for the new record. "We were gonna do a double album because we thought this is eight months of our lives, right?" he explained. "Then we figured it would be far better, much more solid, to just pick the best stuff out and make it a good, hard, rock album 'cause we were very, very afraid of doin' what the Beatles did, just layin' ourselves wide open like they did with their double albums and making it so that it was too much, too many unlinked ideas which to the public would look like untogetherness, despite the fact that it's always there in the background...

"We decided on a single album because, really, it was the straightest thing to do, basically every single angle, every tangent that we went off on, we eventually arrived back, if you like, to where the group used to be. The more times this happened the more times it reinforced Roger's stand that the group was perfectly alright as it was, and that basically I shouldn't tamper with it... So really what my position is at the moment is... obviously very, very happy that the group got over the hump and that I had the guts to back down, if you like. It's a lot harder to back down sometimes than it is to back up."

After the disposable bootleg-type packaging of the live album, *Who's Next* has a memorable cover image – indeed in 2003, VH1 voted it the second-greatest album sleeve of all time. Ethan Russell's cover photograph shows the band apparently just having urinated on two sides of a large rectangular concrete block protruding vertically from a slag heap at Easington Colliery, in north Yorkshire – a location the band spotted when driving back from a gig on 8 May 1971. According to Russell, it was Pete's idea to pee on it but some of the members were unable to oblige as well so rainwater was tipped from a film canister to achieve the effect. The photo is often seen to be a reference to the monolith discovered on the moon in Stanley Kubrick's movie *2001: A Space Odyssey*, which John and Keith are said to have been discussing when they glimpsed the block. In spite of the white clouds and blue skies, the landscape does indeed have an unearthly quality. Townshend later joked that the cover was the band's revenge on Kubrick for refusing to direct *Tommy* (alternate cover images that were rejected included one featuring photos of obese nude women and another featuring Keith Moon dressed in black lingerie and wig, holding a whip).

One of the defining characteristics of *Who's Next* is the massive improvement in sound quality. Compared to all of the band's previous recordings, the album sounds superb. This is in no small part as a result of working with engineer and associate producer Glyn Johns. Pete referred to the sessions with Johns as highly disciplined and sober. It was Johns' talent and vision that helped forge the Who's new sound and thanks to his efforts, for the first time ever, the power of the Who as a live band was captured in the studio.

Roger Daltrey was less than enthusiastic about the entire finished album, though his loathing for the synth sound may have coloured his judgement. More surprisingly, Townshend dismissed it bitterly as "the first ordinary Who album" – still smarting from the failure of his more ambitious *Lifehouse* project. Compared to his original vision, any mere rock record would seem ordinary. *Who's Next* is truly remarkable – a landmark achievement. Indeed, it is often cited as the Who's best album. Pete Townshend's ideas on this album revitalised rock'n'roll, and the critics loved it. *Melody Maker*'s Ray Coleman was particularly enthusiastic about the band's new sound: "Roger Daltrey no longer shouts so coarsely. The result is that we can now hear his words. A superb Who album, then. Turn the bass down and the treble up to maximum to get that cutting, abrasive sound, and you can imagine the guitar smashing at the end."

In the US, the press was even more enthusiastic. The highly respected *Village Voice* critic, Robert Christgau, saw it is as a "triumph of hard rock [that] is no more a pure hard rock album than *Tommy*." Christgau put it at the top of the Who's work to date, "It's got more juice than *Live At Leeds*," he wrote, and gave it a rare A rating. When *Who's Next* won the *Village Voice* annual critics' poll for best album – by a huge majority – Christgau concluded that it "was clearly the only popular masterpiece of the year."

The album was a commercial triumph, reaching number one in the UK and number four in the US. It would go on to earn the group an unprecedented 28 gold and four platinum discs. Fortunately, the Who didn't seem to take their new status too seriously. They destroyed the gold and platinum disc just after midnight on December 10th, 1971, during a party in their honour at the Continental Hyatt House in Hollywood.

"Christ Almighty!" Townshend said to *NME*'s Nick Logan earlier in the year, "we thought, here we are being told we are musical geniuses, when all we are is a bunch of scumbags."

Posterity has been kind to the album, which has aged extremely well and it is now considered to be an essential part of the classic rock canon, particularly in the US. It has been cited as one of the best albums of all time in polls collated by the TV channel VH1 (number 13) and *Rolling Stone* magazine (28). Included in the book *1001 Albums You Must Hear Before You Die*, it was also chosen by *Time* magazine in 2006 as one of the 100 best albums of all time. Tracks including the original album's opener and closer, "Baba O'Riley" and "Won't Get Fooled Again", have been rock radio playlist favourites for decades.

Won't Get Fooled Again
UK Single Release: 25/06/1971 (Track) US Single Release: 17/07/1971 (Decca)
Peak Position: 9 (UK) 15 (US)

"Won't Get Fooled Again" was released a couple of months before the album as a brief taster of the magnificence to come. The band succumbed to alleged technical constraints and commercial pressure agreeing to edit the track down from its original 8 minutes and 21 seconds to the more radio-friendly length of 3.35. "I hated it when they chopped it down," Roger bemoaned. "I used to say 'Fuck it! Put it out as eight minutes,' but there'd always be some excuse about not fitting it on or some technical thing at the pressing plant. After that, we started to lose interest in singles because they'd cut them to bits. We thought, 'What's the point? Our music's evolved past the three-minute barrier and if they can't accommodate that we're just gonna have to live on albums.'"

The savage editing undoubtedly diluted the song artistically, but worked in terms of chart success, leading to the single cracking the Top Ten in Britain and the Top 20 in the US. The full-length version is now a staple on UK and US radio stations.

Who's Next
UK Album Release: 27/08/1971 (Track 2408 102)
US Album Release: 14/08/1971 (Decca DL 79182)
Peak Position: 1 (UK) 4 (US)
Baba O'Riley / Bargain / Love Ain't For Keeping / My Wife / The Song Is Over / Getting In Tune / Going Mobile / Behind Blue Eyes / Won't Get Fooled Again

Who's Next (Deluxe Edition)
UK Album Release: 12/2003 (Polydor 113 0562)
US Album Release: 25/03/2003 (MCA 088 113 056-2)
Disc 1: Baba O'Riley / Bargain / Love Ain't For Keeping / My Wife / The Song Is Over / Getting In

Tune / Going Mobile / Behind Blue Eyes / Won't Get Fooled Again / **Record Plant Sessions:** Baby Don't You Do It / Getting In Tune (Previously Unreleased) / Pure & Easy / Love Ain't For Keeping / Behind Blue Eyes / Won't Get Fooled Again (Previously Unreleased)
Disc 2 (Live At The Young Vic): Love Ain't For Keeping / Pure And Easy / Young Man Blues / Time Is Passing / Behind Blue Eyes / I Don't Even Know Myself / Too Much Of Anything / Getting In Tune / Bargain / Water / My Generation / (I'm A) Road Runner / Naked Eye / Won't Get Fooled Again

Who's Next *is a superb album. A lot of people who have never got into the Who's music in the past because they thought of them as a rough bunch of rockers who smash up their guitars and have a mad drummer who kicks his kit offstage should forget that and give* Who's Next *a chance... and don't get fooled again.*
Billy Walker, *Sounds*

Baba O'Riley

A key survivor from the *Lifehouse* project and half of what journalist and critic Charles Shaar Murray called *"Who's Next*'s devastating one-two punch of zeitgeist-defining epics" – along with "Won't Get Fooled Again". This is one of the great rock side-one/track-ones of all time.

Townshend, though, was keen to dismiss its anthemic status, "On stuff like 'Baba O'Riley' the lyrics mean fuck-all... but it's probably one of the best vocal performances I've ever heard Roger do, and yet he's singing about nuthin'... It's a bit of the script of the movie [*Lifehouse*] which never happened." In the *Lifehouse* project this was to have been voiced by Ray, the Scottish farmer, at the beginning of the album as he prepares his wife Sally and two children for the journey to London.

The title is never mentioned in the song lyrics though it appears to derive from two of Townshend's key inspirations: Meher Baba and musical influence Terry Riley, the groundbreaking minimalist American composer who had also studied Indian classical music. The song is often mistakenly called after its repeated refrain of "Teenage Wasteland". This, the song's most famous line had an interesting genesis: "The line 'teenage wasteland' came from a photograph of one of our roadies trying to clear up litter after the Isle of Wight festival," Townshend would explain to writer Phil Sutcliffe years later. "This place is three feet deep in shit these teenagers have left behind. I just thought, 'What a fucking load of wankers!'"

A similar but different song, titled "Teenage Wasteland", was scheduled for the *Lifehouse* project. Also, if the words themselves really do have no meaning, the song certainly had a clear inspiration and purpose in Townshend's mind. He told *Penthouse* magazine in 1974, "['Baba O'Riley'] was a theme that I put together in reaction to Meher Baba himself. That was his theme. That was the sound I thought represented the power and, at the same time, the ease of his personality."

A source on *thewho.net* puts it more succinctly: "Pete wrote it as an example of what might result if the biography of his avatar, Meher Baba, was fed into a computer and turned into music. The music would, therefore, be Meher Baba in the manner of Terry Riley or "Baba O'Riley'." What sounds like an ARP synthesizer arpeggiates the now-famous opening melody adorned by additional electronic melodic trills (though Townshend was using the huge modular ARP 2500 synth at the time, some sources suggest it was not actually used on the album recording of this famous riff. It has been posited by Rich Rowley on *thewho.net* that, though it sounds like the ARP, these riffs were played on a Lowrey Berkshire Deluxe TBO-1 organ which was then filtered through the ARP. Pete is using a setting called "Marimba Repeat" and a "Wow-Wow" setting that works like a guitarist's wah-wah pedal and that is being used as a tone control; in his original demo, the effect is used in the regular way).

Though the sound is contemporary, the droning tune evokes Eastern origins. "I like synthesizers because they bring into my hands things that aren't in my hands – the sound of the orchestra, French horns, strings," Townshend commented. "There are gadgets on synthesizers which enable one to become a virtuoso of the keyboard. You can play something slowly, and you press a switch and it plays it back at double speed."

Glyn Johns was full of admiration for Pete's eager embrace of the new technology: "Townshend is the only musician I've met before or since who really knows how to work one, he really knows it. He's really got it down."

The synth part – like that of the same album's "Won't Get Fooled Again" – bears the likely influence of Terry Riley pieces from the 1960s, including the experimental *In C* (1964) and *A Rainbow In Curved Air* (1969), and also of another great American musical innovator, John Cage. "Baba O'Riley was originally thirty minutes long," Townshend would say. "And the way you hear it now is all the high points just shoved together... I was trying to do what is really a very John Cage type thing... it was my 'make rock more reflective' crusade. We bypass all the bullshit and go straight down to the 'soul' as it were, and get the music from there. In 'Baba O'Riley' that's about as near as I ever got to it."

Against the rolling waves of synthesizer-generated rhythms, Moon demonstrates his control and technical ability as he plays along freely with the machines, at no time sounding metronomic. John plays simple but effective root notes and Roger gives a no-nonsense vocal performance as he voices Townshend's [apparently "meaningless"] words of defiance. "I don't need to fight / To prove I'm right / I don't need to be forgiven." As they hit the second section, Pete makes his grand entrance on guitar with some killer power-chords and then takes over lead vocals for the lines: "Don't cry! / Don't raise your eye! / It's only teenage wasteland!" As the band gather pace, Pete adds more adrenalin-filled licks to the musical invective. Roger's chant of "Teenage wasteland" comes as the F-C-Bb power chords ring out and he rips into the line "They're all wasted" as the band belligerently hit a series of precise, monumental, accent crashes.

On the outro, a violin solo from Dave Arbus (of East of Eden) fades in and then moves to centre stage, conjuring visions of gypsies and vagabonds. The violin was Keith Moon's idea and he gets a production credit for it. "What did he do?" mused critic David Fricke, "chase the poor fiddler around the studio?" The band return and together they all rip it up. Dave's solo swells, as the band builds the intensity to an almighty crescendo and a sudden stop. In concert Roger would replace the violin with his own harmonica solo.

Years later the song would be used as the theme tune for American TV show *CSI Crime Scene Investigation, NYC*.

Bargain

Bearing the Baba influence, the titular "Bargain" is a man's trading of all his earthly possessions in exchange for spiritual enlightenment. "This song is simply about losing one's ego as a devotee of Meher Baba," Townshend commented. "I constantly try to lose myself, and find him. I'm not very successful, I'm afraid, but this song expresses how much of a bargain it would be to lose everything in order to be one with God."

Lyrically, the structure is a familiar litany of all the things the singer would give up, or the pains he would willingly suffer, in order to get "you", but instead of a lover, the "you" is God. "I'd gladly lose me to find you / I'd gladly give up all I have. To find you... / I call that a Bargain / The best I ever had."

The band recorded at least nine versions between April and June of '71 until deciding that this one could not be bettered. A gentle acoustic guitar introduces this classic rock ballad while an Eastern-influenced drone intones quietly in the background. Pete praised producer Johns for the sound: "Glyn Johns was a real genius at recording acoustic guitars. He got a fantastic sound for everybody he worked with. It's still his best thing." This lush, understated intro, however, is the calm before the storm. Keith steams around his kit and the band kicks into gear with Pete setting the pace with his rhythm guitar. Roger gives a throat-ripping performance as he makes his way determinedly through the poignant Townshend lyric.

There's an effective Moog keyboard solo; Pete plays some splendid blues licks and Keith demonstrates some incredible double kick drum playing. Townshend punches out a glorious riff surrounded by an octave jumping-synthesizer fanfare before the song closes as it began, on the calm, acoustic vibe of the intro. "Bargain" is a faultless masterpiece of songwriting and performance.

One of the guitars used on this track was a vintage 1959 Gretsch given to Townshend by Joe Walsh, the American guitarist from the James Gang and later, the Eagles. Pete has said that, while his acoustic sound was influenced by Glyn Johns, his electric sound had more to do with Joe Walsh, "Joe was the guy that gave me the most help... Joe was always the one who would actually give me complete set-ups to try..." (Townshend used a range of guitars on this album including a 1955 Les Paul Junior, 1969/70 Gibson SG Special, plus various acoustics, including one of his favourite guitars, the Blonde Guild 12-string).

Love Ain't For Keeping

Recorded in March at the Record Plant studio soon after it had opened, this was another *Lifehouse* relic originally to be sung by Farmer Ray. With hippy overtones and an optimistic carpe diem message, the lyric has a chilled-out vibe of contentment: "Rain's comin' down but I know the clouds'll pass... / Lay down my darlin', Love ain't for keeping." The subtext? If love's not for keeping, then it is for sharing...

Skilfully picked, multi-tracked acoustic guitars dominate here on this intimate blues-tinged country love song that bears the influence of the Band's first two albums and the Grateful Dead's *Workingman's Dead*. Keith and John are restrained but effective: for the Record Plant session, Moon uncharacteristically used Ludwig drums instead of his Premier kit; Entwistle stuck with his favourite "Frankenstein" bass. Some fine cascading backing vocals support Pete's outstanding bluesy acoustic guitar solo.

My Wife

Recorded at Olympic in the June of '71, this song was added to the tracklisting after *Lifehouse* had been abandoned. John commented, "It was decided that I'd have a track on the album. I only had one song ('My Wife'), which I wanted to keep for my album." He wasn't completely happy with the band's version feeling that it didn't "swing" in quite the way he wanted. He later re-recorded the song for his solo album *Rigor Mortis Sets In*.

Entwistle's inspiration for the song was loosely autobiographical; he'd come up with the idea while walking his dog in the woods after an argument with his wife, Alison. The song's narrator has been out partying too much and his wife isn't happy; she suspects he's been with another woman and she's in pursuit, hell-bent on retaliation. The idea is simple enough but it's the humorous hyperbolic imagery that Entwistle conjures to describe this predicament that marks this out as some of his finest lyrics:

> *Gonna buy a tank and an aeroplane*
> *When she catches up with me there'll be no time to explain...*
> *Give me police protection, gonna find someone to look after number one*
> *Give me a bodyguard, a black belt judo expert with a machine gun!*

When asked about his wife's reaction to the song, Entwistle said, "She always thought it was very funny. She always had the ambition to come on and hit me over the head with a rolling pin halfway through it when I was doing it on stage."

Entwistle's mid-paced rocker rumbles along with a casually gathering momentum. He plays several instruments: bass, brass and piano, and sings the lead vocal.

The Song Is Over

"When you listen to 'The Song Is Over'," said Townshend, "you are only literally hearing the end of the film [*Lifehouse*]." The backing track and overdubs for this song were recorded at Olympic in May. The clarity of the recordings is fully demonstrated here with the complex, dynamic arrangement. Townshend raved to music journalist Penny Valentine that the band were astounded at the quality of the sounds that Johns was getting in the studio: "For the first time, the Who were recorded by someone who was more interested in the sound than in the image of the group... when Kit was producing us, that [image] was all he cared about."

A simple piano part, supplied by stalwart Who sideman Nicky Hopkins supported by a VCS3 synthesizer, gently introduces this rock ballad of lost love and missed opportunities initially sung by Townshend, who mourns the loss of love – as represented by the "song" in the title – and the fact that it has gone, that it's over. Pete's tasteful lead guitar breaks fit the reflective mood until Keith and John join in with uncharacteristic heavy fours. Daltrey takes over the soaring lead vocal on the joyous chorus. The song, which was never performed live, features as its finale the moving chorus from the *Lifehouse* centrepiece, "Pure And Easy".

Getting In Tune
Originally titled "I'm In Tune", this featured in the February '71 Young Vic shows in London and was recorded a month later during the abortive New York sessions. The melancholy opening mood features Nicky Hopkins on piano. Roger sings Townshend's lyrics which initially claim to be designed, like the notes of the song, just to fit the chords: "I can't pretend there's any meaning to the things I'm saying ... but I'm in tune..."

The narrator is tired of superficialities, of making small talk at boring parties, and wants to strip away the non-essentials by "Getting in tune to the straight and narrow" – whether with a lover or a spiritual figure. Again, the lyrics mirror Townshend's own search for greater understanding of himself as both a spiritual person but also a man tempted by the excesses of the rock'n'roll world. This perceived contradiction would frustrate, confuse and haunt him for many years to come. Townshend found it difficult to reconcile his private, sensitive, spiritual self with his public, larger-than life, drunken, drug-taking, rock star persona for whom the "straight and narrow" would often prove an elusive path.

While arguably one of the lesser songs on the album, this is still an accomplished mid-tempo [late] Beatles-esque number and the spiritually questing lyrics are matched by some strong playing. Hopkins' piano is augmented by some deft and increasingly frenetic guitar work, while Keith Moon plays some laid-back snare beats on the 2 and 4 of his Premier kit, showing his mastery of a slower tempo. He anchors the track, as it gathers into an all-guns-blazing improvisational jam before the fade.

Going Mobile
Originally conceived as part of the *Lifehouse* project, to be sung by Farmer Ray as he and his family drove south, it's also a hymn to the open road. Pete had bought a mobile home in the summer of 1970 and would sometimes drive it to the band's British gigs:

Keep me moving... I'm going mobile...
Watch the police and the taxman miss me

Recorded at Stargroves on the Rolling Stones' mobile studio in April 1971, this bounces along with a country-rock flavour that prefigures the sound of the later *Who By Numbers* album. The sunny melody of "Going Mobile" is shot through with an optimistic mood, and sung by an exuberant Townshend, unadorned by backing vocals other than his own occasional yelp of joy.

The instruments are stripped down to a minimal bass, drums and acoustic guitar line-up, with additional musical texture supplied by a VCS3 synthesizer. Townshend also generated an interesting synth sound for his solo, playing his guitar through an "ARP synthesizer called an Envelope Follower," as he explained, "where you plug the guitar in and you get a sort of fuzzy wah-wah sound." Overall, it's one of the album's slighter tracks and was never played live.

Behind Blue Eyes

This is one of Townshend's best-known songs and features one of his most beautiful melodies and most memorable lyrics. Written for *Lifehouse* (and premiered at the Young Vic that February), Pete explained, "'Behind Blue Eyes' really is off the wall because that was a song sung by the villain of the piece [Jumbo], the fact that he felt in the original story that he was forced into a position of being the villain whereas he felt he was a good guy."

This, however, is also a dark slice of autobiography: a first-person cry for help from the lonely pinnacle of rock stardom and brimming with self-loathing, self-castigation and self-pity. In this, it echoes themes explored on John Lennon's 1970 angst-ridden work of primal scream therapy, *Plastic Ono Band*. The song's origins spring in part from an occasion when Townshend struggled with that "straight and narrow" path he had praised as his salvation in "Getting In Tune." Tempted by a groupie after a Who show, and perhaps mindful of his failure to always live up to Meher Baba's spiritual teachings, Pete returned to his hotel room alone, full of self-recrimination and penned a prayer that began "When my fist clenches, crack it open... " This prayer was incorporated into the climactic rocking section.

Recorded during the Record Plant sessions in New York, this haunting song is book-ended by finger-picked acoustic guitar and a solo Roger delivering the key lines: "No-one knows what it's like to be the bad man / to be the sad man behind blue eyes"; no-one other than the song's protagonist. As the song gathers pace, Daltrey rails against being hated, fated and telling only lies, through restrained, gritted teeth, then vents his vitriol as he blames the listener before asking for help. It's a sublime showcase for Roger's impassioned vocals.

The accompaniment features block-backing vocals, John's fluid, tasteful bass fills and the much-copied section where Moon rampages round his drums, Pete slams into power chords and they all hit the dynamic accents together as one.

This bleak piece was released as a single in the US where it remains a staple of rock radio playlists. It featured in the band's live set for years afterwards.

Won't Get Fooled Again

Despite having shoved counter-culture revolutionary Abbie Hoffman off the stage at Woodstock, in what Townshend later described as "the most political thing I ever did", he had become wracked with contradictory feelings about his role as a rock star. At times, he felt convinced of his omnipotence but also questioning whether he was misusing or wasting this power. He revealed, "The first verse sounds like a revolution song and the second like somebody getting tired of it. It's an anti-anti song; a song against the revolution because the revolution is only a revolution and a revolution is not going to change anything in the long run and a lot of people are going to get hurt."

"Bursting on to the radio like a natural successor to 'Street Fighting Man'," as Peter Doggett put it, "'Won't Get Fooled Again' virtually begged for clenched fists to be thrown into the air." The headline-grabbing soundbite lyrics – "Meet the new boss, same as the old boss" – saw it interpreted as a revolutionary call to arms: don't be fooled by the empty promises of a staid capitalist society; don't be fooled by the establishment, by the Man. More convincingly, however, the song reflects Townshend's disillusion with both his own political and spiritual idealism that had inspired the grandiose vision of *Lifehouse* and the counter-culture in general. It's a wake-up call to himself: don't be fooled by such naivety again.

Pete revealed, "I wrote [it] at a time when I was getting barraged by people at the Eel Pie Island commune. They lived opposite me. There was like a love affair going on between me and them. They dug me because I was like a figurehead... and I dug them because I could see what was going on over there. At one point there was an amazing scene where the commune was really working, but then the acid started flowing and I got on the end of some psychotic conversations. And I just thought, 'Oh, fuck it!'."

Radical counterculture mainstay, Mick Farren, argued with Townshend about what he saw as the song's politically conservative message, during a party at Keith Moon's house. He followed up his criticism with an open letter to Townshend, co-signed by a number of associates: "Whereas the music is still strong, kicking out, aggressive music," Farren wrote, "the lyric is seemingly defensive and negative, even potentially damaging to the consciousness of kids who strongly identify with the Who as an extension of their lifestyles. In fact it's calculated to bring down anybody seeking radical changes, in what we know you agree is a depressingly corrupt society. Why?"

Farren had a point: what sounded like a stirring rebellious clarion call to the kids to fight the system was actually a more complex critique of the pitfalls of revolution. As Townshend put it in his response to Farren, he was not actually with the radical movement; author Peter Doggett points out, Pete explained that it was not for him to provide false hope. Instead, the Who leader felt his band's role was to represent the negativity felt by "the kids [about] the fight for power which is being waged in their name, but not on their terms, not using their ethics..."

Pete Townshend would continue to be bemused to see this song adopted as a defiant "rock anthem" when he had in fact written it as a world-weary warning – and that, like the other songs on *Lifehouse*, it was originally conceived as a theatrical piece, rather than an autobiographical lament, and was designed to be voiced by a particular character. In *Lifehouse*, this was sung by rock concert organiser Bobby as he denounced the evil dictator Jumbo's attempt to pass himself off as a spiritual seeker.

The song achieved another life as an anthem for the young and disaffected precisely because it was such an uplifting and energetic, ferocious piece of music; the rebellion is in the rock'n'roll rather than the words; the medium is the message:

"I felt my guitar sound, and the band's edge," Townshend commented, "came from and reflected its essentially working-class audience of non-intellectuals, who knew they might have to fight and die like their fathers. They would not be fooled by university graduates telling them what to think..."

Musically, this seminal piece develops this sound and edge into an action-packed eight-minute rock meisterwerk of epic proportions (a musical sibling of "Baba O'Riley") that became a live mainstay for the rest of the band's career and one of the most popular tracks they ever recorded. It's a truly defining moment in the Who's history.

With his search-and-destroy guitar work – "Captain Powerchords", as he deemed himself – Townshend is relentless with the vintage Gretsch guitar and an Edwards volume pedal (the gifts from Joe Walsh that were also used on "Bargain"). John Entwistle's basslines flow effortlessly, holding everything down, and Keith's adventurous fills are played with manic excitement. If John Bonham and Ginger Baker wrote the rock'n'roll book of drumming, Keith Moon tore it up in this fierce onslaught. Townshend solos on gritty chords over a half-time feel, but the keyboards are the musical centrepiece here, and Townshend utilises all of their creative possibilities. It was Daltrey's gut-wrenching performance however, that became the motif of the song, as the singer roars, "Meet the new boss, Same as the old boss."

"That big scream I did on 'Won't Get Fooled Again' was totally instinctive," Roger explained, "but it became kind of the focal point of the song. It pisses me off because I didn't get any royalties for it!" While dynamic recordings often come out of internal pressures and stressed conditions, Roger attributes this track's power to the relaxed recording set-up. "We did it at Stargroves," he explains. "Jagger had this big old house in the country and they used to have a mobile studio. It was good because we were kind of hanging out." Further overdubs were recorded at Olympic with the final mix being completed by Glyn Johns at Island Studios in London late in May.

"Won't Get Fooled Again", alone, merits the Who's legendary status and it remains one of the band's most well-known songs and is a firm part of the classic rock canon. VH1 voted it number 17 in their list of the 100 Greatest Rock Songs; it was in fifth place on a *Rolling Stone* poll of the 500 Greatest Songs of all time, while *Q* magazine had it at number seven in its list of the 100 Greatest Guitar Tracks. Years later it would feature in an advert for Nissan and an episode of *The Simpsons*, as well as being used as the theme tune for American TV show *CSI, Miami*.

"Won't Get Fooled Again," Pete concluded, "that really is the feather in my cap." Along with "Behind Blue Eyes", it was one of two Who songs Roger wished he had written.

The New York Record Plant Sessions:
In order to include these recordings, the 2003 deluxe edition of *Who's Next* now boasts an extra 20 tracks. A second disc is added to cover the group's February '71 performance at the Young Vic. These recordings document the origins of the ill-fated *Lifehouse* project, but they are not just of historical interest. For all of the fine musicianship – the band's performance is often electrifying – these versions aren't as strong as the original release. "We did it once before," Entwistle commented, "but we weren't satisfied with it."

Baby Don't You Do It
This Marvin Gaye song written by the veteran Motown tunesmiths, Holland, Dozier and Holland, is transformed by the Who: Roger's throaty blues vocal is accompanied by some great Moon moments. Guest musician, Mountain's Leslie West, joins Townshend on lead guitar.

Getting In Tune
A similar, alternative, take of the cut that was eventually used on the album. The musicians' banter reflects the relaxed performance.

Pure And Easy
Originally known as "The Note", this was the defining song of the abandoned *Lifehouse* project – focusing on the "chords of life" and the search for the perfect musical note that would bring audience and performer together in perfect spiritual harmony: "The simple secret of the note in us all". The lyric identifies music as an eternal force with the power to create, unite and destroy. "There once was a note," the singer begins, "pure and easy / The note is eternal / I hear it, it sees me / Forever we blend it / Forever we die." The narrator hears "music in a word, and words when you played your guitar...".

Musically, "Pure And Easy" lives up to its name with a catchy, sweet rolling melody, a shiny upbeat country-rock sound and some fine guitar licks showing the influence of James Gang guitarist and future Eagle, Joe Walsh. It would have been a worthy addition to the original album.

"I think stuff like 'Pure And Easy' and a lot of the stuff around *Who's Next* are very sort of James Gang structures," Townshend has said. He and Joe Walsh were good friends and used to hang out, but they never worked together, though Joe would add guitar to Keith's solo album.

"Pure And Easy" was previously released on the *Odds & Sods* collection and here is in a slightly different mix from the 1995 reissue CD.

Love Ain't For Keeping
This particular version is a full two minutes longer than that used on the final record, thanks to an overlong outro jam that, though entertaining in places, was indulgent and wisely cut for the definitive album take. The band sound relaxed but it's still a muscular performance.

Behind Blue Eyes
This is the original take of the Who classic, devoid of the magic, power or confidence of the version used on the final album. The band were wise to give it another go once they were more familiar with the material.

Won't Get Fooled Again
Another alternative take which is markedly different to the better-known version. Townshend explains in the liner notes of the deluxe edition, "This version used a non-taped backing track (the organ was processed in real time through a synthesizer,

not taped). That is why it is a different shape and length." As with many of the other songs here, the final version used on *Who's Next* clearly benefited from the band having rehearsed and recorded the song before.

The synthesizer part and overall arrangement seems to lack focus and this early version sounds tentative. The musicians are, as a consequence, all over the place in the breakdowns and are obviously unsure of exactly what happens next. The song hasn't quite settled into their collective subconscious yet and they are still having to think about the arrangement.

The Young Vic – Live:
An additional disc included in the 2003 edition of *Who's Next* covers the group's 26th April '71 performance at the Young Vic. After the New York trip, Townshend's grip over his new project was faltering, but the Who still returned to this London theatre for another low-key show of *Lifehouse* material, playing to invited fans and members of London youth clubs. The performance was recorded using the Rolling Stones' mobile studio by Glyn Johns' younger brother Andy, though the tape was not meant for later release (after this, there would be one more *Lifehouse* concert at the Young Vic on May 2nd after which Pete and the Who finally abandoned the project to concentrate on turning its highlights into *Who's Next*).

Love Ain't For Keeping
In a relaxed and confident mood, the band work their way with ease, through this tightly controlled take on the Townshend tune.

Pure And Easy
A strong performance of the poignant *Lifehouse* keystone – Entwistle's bright, top-end bass sound is very much in evidence as Moon plays some clean, crisp fills throughout.

Young Man Blues
Though the band had been playing this live favourite as far back as 1964, here it doesn't have the crunch and power of the *Live At Leeds* recording.

Time Is Passing
An untypically country-sounding tune, this is a solid performance of an unusual Townshend composition that first appeared on his *Who Came First* solo record.

Behind Blue Eyes
In the final seconds of the previous track, Townshend stated that "Behind Blue Eyes," would soon be released as the first single from the *Lifehouse* material. However, this would not happen until October, and then only in the US and parts of continental Europe.

The band tear through a fine rendition of this live favourite. As they finish the song, Townshend demands that a man in the audience stop dancing: this enthusiastic fan is distracting him and Townshend insists that he's still trying to "remember all the chords". This was a free concert but it does seem a bizarre request for a band member to ask of his appreciative audience and didn't bode well for Townshend's *Lifehouse* aim for band and audience to come together through one eternal note.

I Don't Even Know Myself
Roger plays a great, all-too-brief, harmonica solo in the opening section of this slightly cheesy 1970 tune, and there's the usual power-chord bluster. This song would get a release in the summer of '71 on the B-side of the "Won't Get Fooled Again" single.

Too Much Of Anything
This country-flavoured rock ballad pushes Roger's voice to its absolute limit.

Getting In Tune
The extended mid-section features a Jimmy Page-like guitar solo from Townshend and includes a "blues jam" breakdown not found on the studio cut. Roger delivers a belligerent, throat-stripping vocal which never once eases up.

Bargain
This particular version feels awkward and clunky; Moon sounds uncertain of the arrangement and unsure of exactly where the groove sits. It clicks into place eventually and the band do get it together but very late in the take.

Water
The band first started playing this around 1970 but it wasn't until 1973 that this song appeared on the B-side of the "5.15" single. Here they give a solid performance of this rocker, but it's the youthful Roger who claims the laurels as he sings like an ageing blues man.

My Generation
An adequate enough rendition of their classic 60s hit.

(I'm A) Roadrunner
This Bo Diddley classic is given the Who treatment, though a superior version can be found on *The Kids Are Alright* soundtrack.

Naked Eye
Added to the band's repertoire around 1970 and recorded in '71, this didn't find a release until 1974 when John included it on the *Odds & Sods* compilation. It's a fine bluesy rocker with some frantic scything guitar work; Daltrey's on strong raspy form.

Won't Get Fooled Again
This embryonic version hasn't got the magic, atmosphere or spark of the version eventually used on the final album. Here, they are still feeling their way, not familiar

enough with the arrangement to do the song justice.

Who's Next may not have been what they'd originally planned and, when it was first released, Townshend described it as the first ordinary Who album, while Roger Daltrey succinctly declared, "We'd lost one bollock!" But both came to reassess a collective performance that is arguably the best they'd ever delivered. The album spent more than 40 weeks in the charts – it was the Who's only UK Number One album, and reached number four in the US.

Many fans believe it secured the band's enduring status as one of the greatest rock groups on the planet. In 1987, *Rolling Stone* gathered rock media critics together and they placed *Who's Next* in their top twenty rock albums of all time. *The Great Rock Discography* described it as the band's "most constant and cohesive work" and since its release it has sold in excess of 3,500,000 copies. A musical salvage operation turned out to be the group's biggest success, proving to Pete Townshend that there was more to his writing, and to the Who, than fancy concepts and complicated storylines.

There is a unity deep in the grooves of this recording that comes from years of shared musical experience. "What's great about *Who's Next*", said Roger Daltrey, "is that it was the only album where we played all those songs over and over again. They were our songs. They weren't just Pete's songs. That's the difference with *Who's Next*. We had that freedom to do that. We were never allowed that freedom after that."

Behind Blue Eyes
US Single Release: 06/10/1971 (Decca)
Peak Position: 34 (US)
Pete claimed this beautifully twisted rock ballad was "too much out of character" for the UK singles market. It did, however, find a release in the US where it scraped into the Top 40. This has been played in concert regularly since its release and still remains a firm live favourite.

Let's See Action
UK Single Release: 15/10/1971 (Track)
Peak Position: 16 (UK)
The song was from Townshend's first collection of *Lifehouse* demos; he described it as a call to arms. "I was pretty fucking hard," he said. "We all were." It hints at the radical anthem that Mick Farren and his cohorts were hoping Townshend would come up with: "Let's see action, let's see people / Let's see freedom, let's see who cares". Although this was written as part of a *Lifehouse* character's story, it did mirror Townshend's own endeavours, not to change the world but to change himself, seeking solace in the mysticism and spirituality of his guru, the self-styled avatar Meher Baba: "I have learned it, known who burned me / Avatar has warmed my feet / Take me with you, let me see you / Nothing is everything, everything is, nothing is."

The message was self-focused rather than outward-looking, accepting that embarking on a spiritual journey requires a surrendering to the impossibility of always knowing where it would take you: "I don't know where I'm going / I don't know what I need / But I'll get to where I'm gonna end up / And that's all right by me".

Roger explained, "Pete was going through a terrible bitterness about the fact that Kit Lambert and Chris Stamp hadn't got behind making *Lifehouse* as a film. But the reason they didn't get behind it was because they couldn't get to grips with the narrative, and I still feel to this day – even though Pete's done his *Lifehouse Chronicles* box and done it as a radio play – well, I'm sorry but, though there's some incredible music in there and some sparks of theoretical and theological ideas, I think the narrative thread of the story is about as exciting as a fucking whelk race! But I always liked 'Let's See Action'. It's got that texture of explosive rock'n'roll bits mixed in with a laid-back, almost country feel. I still love the sentiment behind it, too."

Meaty Beaty Big And Bouncy

UK Album Release: 11/1971 (Track 2406 006)
US Album Release: 10/1971 (Decca DL 79184)
Peak Position: 9 (UK) 11 (US)
I Can't Explain / The Kids Are Alright / Happy Jack / I Can See For Miles / Pictures Of Lily / My Generation / The Seeker / Anyway, Anyhow, Anywhere / Pinball Wizard / A Legal Matter / Boris The Spider / Magic Bus / Substitute / I'm A Boy

Cementing the Who canon, this is the first of many greatest hits compilations. It concentrated on the singles – some not available on any other Who album, including new versions of "I'm A Boy" and "Magic Bus" – and as a result, it sold particularly well at the time. In direct contrast to the grandiose *Lifehouse* material, it's a reminder of the Who's Mod roots right down to the inside cover photo of the north-west London pub, the Railway Hotel in Wealdstone, where they had played so regularly in the early days.

07 Tantrums, Tapes And Tranquilisers – 1972-73

After the intense mixing sessions at Olympic Studios for *Who's Next*, the place became Pete's musical home. In May 1972, after returning from an extended holiday, the band recorded both "Join Together" and "Relay" there; Townshend also laid down a demo of "Long Live Rock".

"I remember when Pete came up with 'Join Together'," Roger told *Uncut* magazine decades later, "he literally wrote it the night before we recorded it. I quite like it as a single, it's got a good energy to it. But at that time I was still very doubtful about bringing in the synthesizer. I just felt that, with a lot of songs, we'd end up spending so much time creating these piddly one-note noises that it would've been better just doing it on a guitar. I mean, I'm a guitar man. I love the guitar; to me it's the perfect rock instrument. I don't think Pete did much with those sequencing things that he couldn't have done on his guitar anyway."

Featuring a glorious sing-along chorus, some idiosyncratic broken beats from Keith and, of all things, a lamellophone (mouth harp), "Join Together" showcased the Who's brighter, lighter side. That year it proved an apt anthem to be adopted by the World Affairs Council of America – an inclusive non-profit, non-partisan organization dedicated to fostering grassroots understanding and engagement in international affairs and global issues, across all communities in the US.

Join Together
UK Single Release: 17/06/1972 (Track) US Single Release: 08/07/1972 (Decca)
Peak Position: 9 (UK) 17 (US)

Lou Reizner's Tommy
With the London Symphony Orchestra and English Chamber Choir
US Album Release: 27/11/1972 (Ode Records)
UK Album Release: 08/12/1972 (Rhino Records)
Peak Position: 5 (US) 8 (UK)

Kit Lambert was still determined that *Tommy* would be made into a film and he'd been working tirelessly on a script. Townshend however had lost interest in it as a concept and wanted to move on. Lambert was furious and the tensions between them lead to an insurmountable rift. Pete admitted, "It was *Tommy* that destroyed the relationship." Lambert's script was eventually rejected by Universal Studios and, for the time being, that halted any plans for a film.

But *Tommy* would not be easily consigned to the dustbin of musical history: the respected American record producer Lou Reizner wanted to record *Tommy* with a full symphony orchestra and choir, with an all-star cast performing the piece.

Reizner had produced two albums for Rod Stewart and, originally, he wanted him to take the lead role as Tommy, but Rod refused saying there were too many words to learn. Pete suggested that Roger Daltrey be given the chance to play the lead if he wanted to, and Roger eagerly agreed: "It's part of me. I was only too glad to do it. I could never get tired of it."

Townshend approved of Lou's concept and felt that this production could be the perfect distraction for the fans who repeatedly demanded that the band perform *Tommy* in concert. A theatre production would help the Who to leave *Tommy* and the other characters behind...

The album took eight months to record with the London Symphony Orchestra and the English Chamber Choir conducted by David Measham. Daltrey and Townshend were an almost constant presence during the recordings. Wil [sic] Malone painstakingly completed the orchestral arrangements with extra parts added by session guitar player "Big Jim" Sullivan. The stellar cast included Ringo Starr as Uncle Ernie, Stevie Winwood (Traffic) as Tommy's father, Maggie Bell (Stone The Crows) as Tommy's mother, the famous Irish actor Richard Harris was cast as the Doctor, Fairport Convention's Sandy Denny played the nurse, and John Entwistle played evil Cousin Kevin. The album was a huge hit reaching number five in the US charts, and eighth place in Britain (with the single "I'm Free" climbing to number 13 on the UK pop chart).

The Rainbow theatre in North London became the venue for the stage production in December 1972. Pete Townshend was the narrator, with Peter Sellers taking over the role of the Doctor. Keith Moon assumed the role of Uncle Ernie and Rod Stewart was cast as a local lad who sang "Pinball Wizard". Roger had been singing the Tommy part with the band since '69 but this was the first time that Townshend had seen him from the audience's perspective and he was amazed: "I'd always thought Roger was a bit naff. That was the moment I realized that, through Tommy, Roger had made his connection to the audience and became a theatrical performer. I had much greater respect for him after that."

(*Tommy* was staged with a different cast in Australia where it was televised by Channel 7 and won a TV award for most outstanding creative production. A further production was staged in Britain again with a different cast that included pop star David Essex and Steve Marriott of the Small Faces.)

The Relay
US Single Release: 25/11/1972 (Track) UK Single Release: 23/12/1972 (Track)
Peak Position: 39 (US) 21 (UK)

Titled as "Relay" in the UK it would be released as "The Relay" in the States. This average slice of typical Townshend fare features some Clapton-influenced guitar breaks and some spiky synth work. The band performed this early in 1973 on British TV, on the mainstream *Russell Harty Plus* and the cult rock series, *The Old Grey Whistle Test*. This single made a poor showing on both the US and UK charts. Daltrey said, "I love 'Relay'" but Pete told *Melody Maker*, "I've got to get a new act together for the Who... we've got to get something fresh."

1973:

5.15
UK Single Release: 05/10/1973 (Track)
Peak Position: 20

Love, Reign O'er Me
US Single Release: 27/10/1973 (Track)
Peak Position: 76

These singles were released in advance of the epic double album. Roger claimed, "Really, it (5.15) was the only single on *Quadrophenia* we could have released." "5.15" with its powerful chorus and memorable punch line, "out of my brain on the 5.15", would remain a staple of the band's live set for years to come. However in America a radio-friendly shorter remixed version of "Love, Reign O'er Me" appeared instead, reaching a paltry 76 on the charts.

Quadrophenia
UK Album Release: 02/11/1973 (Track 2657 013)
US Album Release: 27/10/1973 (MCA2 10004)
Peak Position: 2 (UK) 2 (US)

Quadrophenia (Remastered Edition)
UK Album Release: 07/1996 (Polydor 531 971-2)
US Album Release: 07/1996 (MCAD2 11463)
Disc 1: I Am the Sea / The Real Me / Quadrophenia / Cut My Hair / The Punk And The Godfather / I'm One / The Dirty Jobs / Helpless Dancer / Is It In My Head? / I've Had Enough
Disc 2: 5.15 / Sea And Sand / Drowned / Bell Boy / Doctor Jimmy / The Rock / Love, Reign O'er Me

Get a copy and, if you're listening on your own, use your headphones and turn the volume knob sharply to the right. If you don't feel better at the end of side four then you must be a very difficult person to please. Finally, to sum up, I would just like to say, 'Wow!'
Rob Mackie, *Sounds*

After Townshend put out a Baba-dedicated solo album, *Who Came First* in October 1972 – featuring three *Lifehouse* highlights "Pure And Easy", "Let's See Action" (which was the October '71 single) and "Time Is Passing" – he settled down to work on the next Who album at his studio in his new riverside home at Goring-on-Thames. He pooled all his resources using stockpiled ideas from endless jamming and past musical experiments. Many of the synthesizer sounds included on the final album are from these original demo sessions, a few piano parts also survived plus many of his sound effects.

"He was always writing notes till four in the morning," his friend Richard Barnes told *Mojo*'s Phil Sutcliffe, "getting all these ideas together, something he'd just written, something he'd put in a drawer two years ago, bits he'd recorded, a nice riff, a song he didn't release where he could take the middle section and put it in this new one here. He gets them all together and comes out with this new concept..."

Townshend told *Circus* magazine that this process became "a sort of musical

Clockwork Orange." The new project would be a musical and social explanation of the British Mod cult, the backdrop to why and how "My Generation" had come to be written, and the effect it had had on the band and fans alike. Townshend told *Uncut* magazine in 2007, "What made Mod essential to my story was the idea of the uniform, the desire to sublimate oneself into a group in order to grow." Specifically, it would evoke the 60s Mod movement as seen through the eyes of a confused teenage pill-popping London Mod called Jimmy. "It's about growing up," said Pete. "At the end of the album, our hero is in danger of maturing." But as Jimmy's journey begins, he's unable to relate to either his fashion-conscious, fastidious Mod peers or his drunken parents; he fights the rockers at Brighton Beach but does so with far less enthusiasm than his mates. He gets his heart broken and grows disillusioned with Mod culture itself, feeling alienated and confused: "Schizophrenic?" Jimmy rails, "I'm bleeding Quadrophenic..."

The album title, *Quadrophenia*, would thus describe the multiple personalities of the central figure, as well as alluding to the four different characters that made up the Who and to the plans to record it in quadraphonic sound (i.e. using four channels to output sound, two at the front on left and right and two at the back on either side, simulating 360-degree sound).

The character of Jimmy was loosely based on the short life of a North Londoner Barry Prior, who abandoned plans for a career as an accountant to reinvent himself in Brighton, and who was found dead at the foot of cliffs in 1964. But Jimmy was also a composite of some of the many characters Pete knew from those early days in Goldhawk Road in West London, and to whom he dedicated the album. Among them was "Irish Jack" Lyons, a former West London Mod and Goldhawk Club regular who would later co-author a book on the Who's live shows.

Quadrophenia would also serve as a form of public psychological cleansing for Townshend, who was coming to terms with both his and his band's history. In its early gestation, Townshend revealed years later, he conceived the record as being an autobiography of the band themselves, allegedly to be called "Rock Is Dead – Long Live Rock", but by the time it was finished, the band's presence was only symbolic.

"I think our album clarifies who the real hero is in this thing," the composer commented. "It's the kid on the front cover. He's the hero... It's his fucking album. Rock'n'roll is his music." If *Tommy* had been an ambitious first try at a full rock opera, then *Quadrophenia* found Pete pushing the boundaries even further: "I still have the same ambitions for rock and roll and for the group. The Who is gonna keep climbing 'cause you can't stop just because somebody's decided that that's a pinnacle". The songs he devised for *Quadrophenia* would leave behind the experimentation with electronic equipment he had used so effectively on *Who's Next*.

The band took up residence in what was once St Andrew's parish church hall in Battersea, South London. They'd bought the building for next to nothing and were converting it into their own studio space to be called Ramport Studios. Their ambitious plan was to turn it into the first bespoke quadraphonic recording studio, purpose-built for the album whose name would be inspired by the sound system. But the studio was still incomplete, which meant that sessions had to be split between Ramport and Ronnie Lane's mobile studio which they'd parked outside the building.

As both producer and composer, Townshend had an elaborate idea for the music which he was struggling to record in a new format: "*Quadrophenia*, as far as I was concerned, was going to be the first creative use of quadraphonic sound in rock," he explained. "I had divided the character of our hero into four narrative voices, each one of which had attributes of a member of the Who. Each one had a musical theme, and each one occupied an oral space in the sound picture. At the moment when the character finds himself, when the story ends, the four themes would come together and emerge in the middle with a great big glorious shower of sound."

However, the new technology was not 100% reliable. Quadraphonic sound was in its infancy in the early 70s and the bottom line was, it simply didn't work with vinyl records. Quad sound wouldn't come into its own until more sophisticated digital systems arrived in later years.

While the band grappled with technical issues, tensions again surfaced with their management. When Roger delivered his solo album, *Daltrey*, early in 1973, Lambert and Stamp tried to bar its release, claiming it was substandard – but perhaps more concerned that if it was a hit, Roger might quit the band for a solo career. Daltrey was livid and insisted that the album must be released; his persistence was vindicated when it came out in April and spawned a Top 5 hit single with "Giving It All Away" (the album was in the Top 50 on the US chart). The success didn't curb Roger's anger, and matters escalated when he insisted that Lambert and Stamp open their accounts for the band to inspect. Roger insisted that if Pete didn't join him in suing the two managers he'd leave the Who.

Townshend hesitated – he was keen to have Kit's creative input on the new project, and Lambert was scheduled to produce the next album. But, after the manager wrote a large cheque to fund the work at Ramport before flying off to his new home in Venice, Townshend gave way – the cheque had bounced despite the vast sums the band should have accumulated. So began the legal action which would result in one of Lambert's employees, Bill Curbishley, eventually becoming the Who's manager in 1976.

Tensions spilled over into the studio, with arguments over production values: Roger accused Pete and the engineer Ron Nevison of burying his vocal in the mix and would later reflect, "It was the biggest recording mistake we ever made. The echo diminishes the character as far as I'm concerned. It always pissed me off. From day one I just fucking hated the sound of it. He did that to my voice and I've never forgiven Ron for it."

On the original mix of the album the vocal is quiet, buried in reverb. Roger felt that this was a deliberate act on Townshend's part. However, it was eventually discovered that this was due to a technical problem, specifically, according to Townshend, "a phase fault". It was all a little too late, though. Relations between Roger and Pete slipped another notch. Twenty years on, Daltrey still had mixed feelings. "I love the album," he would concede, "but I still think *Quadrophenia* should be remixed... I think a lot of the vocals are very low." Entwistle was also disappointed with the final mix, feeling that his bass wasn't prominent enough. He remixed the album in 1979 for the film's soundtrack, but Daltrey didn't approve of that either.

Townshend had total control in the studio but it was hard going for him trying to balance the competing demands on the producer – getting the best out of the musicians, making music the fans will want to hear and the record company will promote and sell, while never losing sight of your own goals for the songs. It was made even harder by the fractious relations with his singer and managers. The band had recorded 15 hours of music; Townshend was surrounded by stacks of 16-track tape piled as high as the ceiling. Trying to whittle it down too was a gargantuan task. He flew to Los Angeles in September for the all-important mastering sessions with Arnie Acosta at the Mastering Lab. Townshend was taking no chances, he knew that the record could be ruined during this process and he was there every step of the way. He was not disappointed. Years later, he said, "I've really had more control over this album than any other Who album. I've directed it, if you like, and certainly, the people in the band have contributed fantastic amounts in roles that they normally wouldn't play... This is the first album when the Who have used each other's capabilities as musicians to the full."

There are critics who believe that many of the songs sound the same but, melodically, they are diverse and the arrangements are more grandiose than anything previously recorded by the band. What does bring a feeling of similarity to the album, however, is the fact that many of the songs are played at roughly the same tempo, with recurring musical and lyrical motifs. However, unlike *Tommy*, where many of the songs rely on each other to make sense of themselves and the narrative, the songs on *Quadrophenia* stand up on their own with no explanation or context needed from the story or other songs.

In a break with tradition, John Entwistle did not contribute any original songs to this album but Pete Townshend was full of praise for the bass player's new role: "He's done a fantastic piece of arranging work, sitting in the studio writing out and then dubbing on 50 horn parts." Entwistle himself quipped that *Quadrophenia* was "the best thing Wagner ever wrote!" And, as a bass player, the new project came at a time when he was ready to stretch himself: "I was playing in a completely different way on *Quadrophenia* because I'd got stuck in one of my bass ruts and changed my equipment and I was finding a new me... [It was] the first time I really let myself go on the bass..." For this record, John dropped his beloved workhorse "Frankenstein" bass and began using Gibson Thunderbirds; his amps were now provided by Sunn. Keith Moon's performance on this album has also been the subject of much debate, but his more dedicated fans point to kamikaze drum fills on a vastly-expanding kit, contrasting with light cymbal flourishes and inspired counter-rhythms.

Townshend used a wide range of guitars on these sessions including a 1957 Fender Stratocaster with a sunburst finish, which was a gift from Eric Clapton – a present for helping with Clapton's comeback gig at the Rainbow Theatre in Finsbury Park, London, in 1973 (in 2000, Townshend allowed the British charity Oxfam to auction the guitar; he promptly bought it back in a joint syndicate with David Bowie and Mick Jagger, and the three gifted it to the then British Prime Minister, Tony Blair. For his part, Blair promptly returned the guitar to auction where it raised £75,650 for Oxfam when it was bought by a private collector).

Quadrophenia hit the shops in a lavish package: a gatefold sleeve housed the two discs and a substantial booklet which contained a written version of the story, the song lyrics and a collection of evocative photos to illustrate Jimmy's tale. The front cover featured "Jimmy" (as played by "Chad" aka Terry Kennett), astride his scooter, his parka bearing a Who arrow logo painted on the back (Roger's idea). The band only appeared one by one in miniature, their faces reflected in the scooter's mirrors.

The double album was a critical and commercial success, earning rave reviews and hitting the number two spot on both sides of the Atlantic, becoming the band's third best-selling album to date. Only David Bowie's *Pin Ups* kept it from being a UK number one. Some sources have suggested that US sales of this vinyl-intensive two-record set may have been affected by a shortage of copies in the shops caused by the vinyl scarcity brought on by the OPEC oil embargo.

Quadrophenia would fail to capture the imagination of mass rock audiences in the way that *Tommy* or *Who's Next* did. The tours would see the band failing to convince their fans of the worth of the new material, in the absence of an irresistibly catchy single like "Pinball Wizard" or an anthem like "Won't Get Fooled Again". Instead of a call to arms, or a call to party, the message appeared to be that the kids' troubles were not the fault of the system, nor of The Man – their lack of fulfilment was their own problem, caused simply by adolescent inner turmoil. The solution was neither fight nor flight; neither turn on nor drop out. Instead Townshend appeared to be telling his fans – young Mods and rock fans alike – that it was time to grow up.

"Love, Reign O'er Me" (Pete's theme) is the touchstone song here. Arguably the album's highlight and now generally appreciated as one of the Who's greatest songs, it's a mature work that has Jimmy realising it's time to go home in search of love and "cool cool rain". Uplifting but decidedly bittersweet, this slow-building epic ebb and flow marks Jimmy's growing maturity, but singing along to the slow descending drawn-out refrain of the title was far less attractive to audiences than punching the air in time to the uplifting rhythmic yells of "It's A Teenage Wasteland" or "Won't Get Fooled Again". Fans, looking to rock'n'roll for escapism, vicarious rebellion, and an uncomplicated great night out, were unreceptive and unimpressed.

Townshend's disappointment would be long lasting, but *Quadrophenia* has aged well and retains a place in the classic rock pantheon. In 2000, *Q* would feature it at number 56 in its list of the 100 Greatest British Albums Ever, while it would also feature in Best Album Of All Time polls on VH1 and in *Rolling Stone* magazine.

I Am The Sea (The Four Themes)

All that can be heard at the start is the sound of the sea crashing on the shores, then rainfall (the engineer Ron Nevison and Townshend recorded some of the real-life sounds by taking Ronnie Lane's mobile studio down to the beaches of Cornwall; Pete captured natural sound effects at his home on the banks of the Thames in Twickenham). Out in the eerie distance Roger asks "Is it me for a moment?" before themes from "Bell Boy" and the closing "Love, Reign O'er Me" drift in and out. A threatening Roger demands, "Can you see the real me? Can ya! Can ya!?" – and the band comes crashing in, making a startling beginning to Townshend's most ambitious work to date.

The Real Me

Pete described this song as "a boast, a threat," and that's exactly how Roger belts it out. There's venom and passion in his performance as the singer stretches his vocal chords near to breaking point. And never has a rhythm section been so inventive: Keith and John work together seamlessly on this inspired and inventive rock onslaught, in an illustration of what Townshend once described as the key to good rock'n'roll – abandonment.

Keith and John's extemporising leaves Townshend to pin everything down with power chords and rock-solid rhythm guitar work. John: "We constructed our music to fit round each other. It was something very peculiar that none of us played the same way as other people, but somehow, our styles fitted together. On 'The Real Me', I was joking when I did that bass part – that was the first take. I was sitting on top of my speaker cabinet playing a silly bass part and that's the one they liked." In 1989, Pete described John as "much more loquacious as a bass player than most," explaining that the band's habit of letting John run riot on the fret board while Pete laid down the groove "really was the secret of our sound, because the rhythm sound that I produced and his sound moulded together and created a rash of random harmonics which is very attractive."

Not once sounding cluttered, "The Real Me" bristles with fervent energy. It finds Jimmy beginning his troubled search for identity, seeking help from a doctor and a holy man, and discovering that his angst is hereditary when his mother sympathises, "I know how it feels son 'cause it runs in the family". Given no concrete answers, however, Jimmy's only salvation is the Mod code to which he clings.

Quadrophenia

Tightly played acoustic guitars open a long instrumental that introduces the four main musical themes which purport to represent Pete, Roger, John and Keith. Townshend said of Jimmy that there were "four distinct sides to his personality" and in Jimmy's words, not "schizophrenia... Quadrophenia!"

Roger is cast as the aggressor, John the quiet one, while Keith is firmly set in his maniac role with Pete as the insecure character with all the questions. All four members were a complex mix of all of those traits, but Townshend diluted them down to the base elements. He expanded further: "One side of him is violent and determined, aggressive and unshakable. Another side is quiet and romantic, tender and doubting. Another side is insane and devil-may-care, unreasoning and bravado. The last side of him is insecure and spiritually desperate, searching and questioning."

Despite its length and the labyrinthine arrangement, this instrumental piece holds the attention. However, Pete often harboured serious doubts about his melodic and harmonic gifts on instrumentals: "Lyrics come very easy to me but music is always very tough, and so stuff like 'Quadrophenia' and 'The Rock' were fucking incredibly difficult for me to get together without feeling that I was on a Keith Emerson trip." Even so, a grand feel is lent to the track by the complex mixture of pianos, synthesizers, timpani, guitars and sound effects. Despite this, the end result is neither pompous nor cacophonous.

Cut My Hair

"Most of the guitar solos I just did at three o'clock in the morning, raving drunk," Pete confessed of guitar motifs like the one that opens this track, and makes various appearances throughout.

Ironically, for a Mod diatribe, this song title bears a nod to David Crosby's hippy anthem "Almost Cut My Hair" – but there is no "almost" about it. Jimmy's soliloquy here shows him torn between pressures to fit in with the youthful rebellion of the Mod scene and wanting to do the right thing by his parents. Essentially he is split between adolescence – fashion, pills and street fights – and more adult-like responsibility – tidying his room, conforming to normal society. Marking his mood swings, the music switches from slow and reflective piano, tentative cymbals and poignant guitar backing as Jimmy, sung by a wistful Pete, ponders his life's contradictions, to drum-driven, stuttering rock rhythms and Roger's more aggressive vocals for Jimmy's angry outbursts. Townshend called this a "domestic interlude... The boy recalls a row with his folks that culminated in his leaving home."

It's one of the album's strongest lyrics and shows Jimmy knowing he should fight his parents but hesitating as his "old man, he's really alright". Even dressed in his sharpest Mod finery and ready for a beach fight, Jimmy experiences "an uncertain feeling". The teenager wants to fit in with the Mods but finds himself taking tremendous pains to impress "a crowd of kids that hardly notice I'm around – I have to work myself to death just to fit in!" It's a powerful and moving evocation of a feeling recognised by many an awkward teenager, desperate to feel part of the cool crowd.

The Mod descriptions are packed with references to past Who songs ("zoot suit", "out on the street again", "I just can't explain"). For Who fans who were expecting anthems of teenage rebellion voiced in simple soundbites, this generally downbeat song may disappoint. But, it's a sophisticated musical number with some subtle hooks and changes. It also contains some of Pete's finest lyrics so far. The character of Jimmy really comes dramatically to life here.

As the song finishes, a radio news bulletin talks of the clashes at the coast between Mods and leather-clad rockers. The BBC radio presenter John Curle recorded this announcement for the band at Ramport Studios. Finally, the sound of a kettle coming to boil marks the song's end and leads into the next track. As well as fitting with the song's final line about Jimmy's breakfast making him sick it also effectively symbolises an increase in the pressure both between Mods and rockers and in terms of what Jimmy is facing. Duly, the next track begins with a crash.

The Punk And The Godfather

"Mixed up in *Quadrophenia* was a study of the divine desperation that is at the root of every punk's scream for blood and vengeance," Pete later explained. This song encapsulates the tension between the kids in the audience and the out-of-touch performing stars that would lead to punk rock itself.

Staccato accented guitars punctuated by ominous drum rolls set a dramatic opening scene for Townshend's inner dialogue, where he sees himself as both Mod kid Jimmy (the Punk) and rock star (the Godfather). It's one of the Who's – and rock's – great intro riffs and returns as the song's defining musical refrain. The Punk wants the rock star to know "you only became what we made you." He's tired of being a "slave" to "phoney leaders." The Godfather is the "guy in the sky, flying high," whose condescending pronouncements from on high further rile the youngster – though he does also proclaim himself, in a nod to "My Generation", "the punk with a stutter." Townshend explained that the punk had gone to see his favourite band but was shunned by them backstage and he leaves, disillusioned.

Like the previous track, this switches between the full-on rock'n'roll of the "Punk" and the slower, quieter ruminations of the "Godfather". This would mark the end of side one, disc one, on the original vinyl.

I'm One

Side two of the original double album begins in a downbeat mood on this lilting country-tinged ballad; finger-picked acoustic guitars accompany Pete's plaintive autumnal cry that he is "a loser". He's a classic frustrated adolescent, painfully aware of his own shortcomings – "ill-fitting clothes… fingers so clumsy, voice too loud," and yet defiant, as he is not only a Mod, "I'm One", but he's a somebody, a face in Mod terminology, "I'm The One". Townshend would often perform this solo during the first *Quadrophenia* tour and it proved to be a firm favourite of his for many solo appearances throughout his career.

The Dirty Jobs

Musically, this is untypical of the Who. The sophisticated arrangement features highly effective chopping violins played by Townshend, piano by Chris Stainton of Joe Cocker's Grease Band (Stainton played piano on these sessions as their usual keyboard player, Nicky Hopkins, was in the States), some horn-type synthesizer riffs and Keith's typically relentless, idiosyncratic playing. John plays some masterful bass runs as Daltrey delivers an empathetic vocal. The final coda briefly features a full brass band which Pete once said was to evoke, in the absence of appropriate sound effects, the "stink" of the dump.

Having been kicked out of his parents' home, Jimmy takes a "dirty" job working on the rubbish trucks for the local council (though this job is mentioned by name only in the sleeve notes, not in this song's lyric). The song voices his frustrations as well as those of a number of characters who are torn between the demands of working-class employment – "Usually I get along ok" – and frustration at such dead-end "dirty jobs" as looking after the pigs or driving a local bus. It also voices Jimmy's anger at those in authority who would put him down and push him around.

Being a Mod or listening to rock'n'roll is no longer rebellious enough for Jimmy. Refusing "to sit and weep again" he drifts into politics – Roger would comment that this was going from one stink to another – and starts lecturing his older workmates who are not impressed with his revolutionary rhetoric. The sleeve notes describe him as being amazed that men, brave enough to fight in the war, won't strike for better pay. Jimmy may be young and mixed up, but he knows "what's right".

"The Dirty Jobs" was played only once on the *Quadrophenia* tour before being exiled from the band's live set until the 90s.

Helpless Dancer (Roger's Theme)

Pete decided that each member of the band should go into the studio and improvise; the end result would be that person's theme for the album. The band, however, promptly vetoed the proposal. The singer's own theme here is heralded by dramatic rolling piano and John's haunting brass parts. There are no drums; the track relies on hammered, almost operatic, staccato piano chords and stabs of acoustic rhythm guitar to propel it forward.

Daltrey spits out Townshend's heartfelt, hate-filled lyric as an increasingly alienated Jimmy rages against the machine and the modern world that drives him mad – "running from his boss", bombs being dropped, "computers and receipts", being "beaten up by blacks" – who, he acknowledges, have their own reasons for being angry. Structurally, the form is highly effective as a series of conditional clauses that is followed by a long pause and then finally resolved by the adamant conclusion that, when faced with all of this, "You stop dancing". Roger delivers the line suddenly, after an instrumental break has built to a crescendo and then left him alone in the spotlight...

Is It In My Head?

This was recorded at Stargroves, rather than Ramport, using the Rolling Stones' mobile with Glyn Johns at the controls. An introspective Jimmy demands of himself, "Is it in my head or my heart?", in an increasingly desperate search for the answers to his creeping malaise. He appears to be getting paranoid, hearing voices at the end of a dead phone line, feeling like he's being followed. There's a trademark Townshend pun when Jimmy says "Every word I say turns out a sentence." There's a surprising amount of self-awareness for a young Mod and he is astute enough to appreciate that perhaps he doesn't have a problem after all. This was only played once on the *Quadrophenia* tour and then dropped.

I've Had Enough

The closing track on side two is an irascible rocker that crackles with tension. Entwistle's bass pins down Townshend's dramatic chord progressions while Moon flails around his Premier drum kit. Roger sneers through the ranting lyrics in typical bruiser fashion and there's also a brief premonition of the "Love, Reign O'er Me" theme.

Lyrically, the song is dramatic, switching between the voice of an anonymous authority figure who gives advice to Jimmy, and the boy's own story of despair. There is a lot going on at this stage of the plot, not all of it clear from the lyrics alone. The album sleeve notes explain that Jimmy had been reduced to sleeping rough and surviving on pills. When he sees a girl he really likes (and had once slept with), who is now with his best mate Dave, it's the last straw. Worse is to come: Jimmy crashes and demolishes his beloved scooter, and in the pouring rain, he walks to the railway station where he is tempted to simply throw himself under a train. But, instead, he buys a ticket to Brighton and heads off to his "land of dreams".

The song's two key verses are litanies of everything Jimmy has had enough of, in short he's had enough of life itself. As the authority figure insists, "Get a job and try to keep it", Jimmy begins to understand his feelings of despair and alienation: he's had enough of "dancehalls", "pills", "street fights", "fashion", and "acting tough". He's basically had enough of being a Mod.

This powerful song climaxes with a spine-chilling wail from Roger: "I've had enough of trying to LOVE", followed by the sound of an Inter-City train roaring by. According to the engineer Ron Nevison, Roger sang so loudly in places he actually blew up two microphones.

5.15

Pete's driver at the time, bribed a British Rail train driver with a five pound note to sound his train's whistle as it pulled out of Waterloo station in London – breaking all station rules – to provide the opening of this track.

The plot sees Jimmy travelling to Brighton on the 5.15 train from London, sandwiched between two respectable City gents, out of his mind on purple hearts, overwhelmed with thoughts, observations, impressions of what's inside the carriage, in the tabloid newspaper he is reading, and passing by outside the window. He muses over the great times he's had on the coast with the massed tribe of Mods. There's also a knowing nod to "My Generation".

Sea And Sand

"This is 1965 and the Mod scene is already falling apart," Townshend explained. "And what does he do but go to Brighton just to remember. The crazy days when 300,000 Mod kids from London descended on that little beach town were only three weeks ago, but he's already living in the past."

The sound of seagulls confirms that Jimmy is now at the seaside in Brighton, "but nothing ever goes as planned". As he says in the sleeve notes, "Brighton cheered me up. But then it let me down." Jimmy is soon full of regrets as he thinks back to the night that his drunken parents threw him out of the house. He's again torn between the supreme confidence of having the superior Mod status known as a "Face" but also a deep awareness of his own shortcomings. The girl he loves "is a perfect dresser" and he knows he has to match her with the perfect-cut, slim, checked jacket. Yet for all his efforts, "dressed up better than anyone within a mile", he feels the other Mods "look so much better".

"I should have split home at fifteen", he bemoans as he reflects on his life's disappointments. But, our young hero remains defiant: "I'm wet and I'm cold / But at least I ain't old". Finally, a musical coda reprises the early High Numbers single "I'm The Face" – "I'm the face that you wanted..."

Drowned

In 2007, Pete told *France Metro* how quickly he had written this song: "Because I record at home I have often knocked songs together quickly simply so I can enjoy some recording... 'Drowned' happened that way, and yet it is one of the most powerful songs I've written... "

Film director Ken Russell was present sporadically during the recording of *Quadrophenia*, discussing the final script for *Tommy*. In the studio when the band were recording "Drowned", he remembered how, "there was a cloudburst, and they wanted a stereo rain effect. We were in this caravan outside and, bit-by-bit, the playing stopped except for the piano, and I went in and the floor and the roof had caved in as they were singing and the rain had really deluged them. They were soaking wet, and there were firemen with a hose pumping it out except for [Chris Stainton] in the cubicle playing the piano, and he was gamely playing on, and when they opened the door, it poured like a waterfall."

This song places Jimmy on Brighton beach, disappointed that he hasn't caught a glimpse of his hero, the Ace Face. He looks out at the ocean, seeing it as a symbol of cleansing redemption: "Let the tide in / And set me free". The band included this in their live set for a while until Townshend got so frustrated playing along with tapes that he trashed them on stage.

Bell Boy (Keith's Theme)

This much-aired live favourite closes side three. Moon's theme fittingly begins with a storming tom-tom fill, and offers the drummer a sizeable guest vocal spot. This is one of the album's more theatrical and dramatic encounters, as the different voices are more clearly delineated than on some of the other tracks. Jimmy's still wandering the seafront, when he recognises somebody: "I see a face coming through the haze / I remember him from those crazy days". It's Ace Face, a Mod hero who led the charge against the rockers on Brighton beach, but Jimmy realises that this Mod rebel is now proudly dressed in a hotel porter's ugly uniform with a job as a "bell boy", carrying guests' suitcases. The fastidious code adopted by the Mods is tarnished forever for Jimmy.

The Face offers a vociferous defence – "People often change" – but can't hide his regret at being reduced to servant-status, "licking boots for my perks". Let down by everyone else in his life, Jimmy reflects in Townshend's sleeve notes, that he "never thought he'd feel let down by being a Mod". Roger sings Jimmy's part in the verses while Keith takes over on the choruses in the Ace Face role, hamming it up in a working-class Cockney burr. Moon delivers the raspy refrains with remarkable sensitivity, adding a particular poignancy when he drops the cartoon voice for the song's closing line, the Face's rueful, "always running at someone's heel".

Though another mid-paced rocker, this is an often-overlooked minor Who classic, featuring some fine work from Keith, delicately muted horns, and a simple rhythm guitar riff. It's packed with a myriad of hooks, from the catchy bellowed "Bell Boy" refrain to the soaring Roger vocal on Jimmy's key lines, "A beach is a place where a man can feel / He's the only soul in the world that's real".

Doctor Jimmy (Including John's Theme "Is It Me?")

"'Doctor Jimmy' was meant to be a song which somehow gets across the explosive, abandoned wildness side of his character," Townshend commented. "Like a bull run amok in a china shop."

After a few brief sound affects evoking a storm on the seafront, side four explodes with this splenetic rocker. The longest track on the double album, "Doctor Jimmy" includes the bass player's theme. Dramatic, shock-tactic, razor-sharp power chords and a tense groove usher in one of the album's most powerful anthems. Trippy synthesizers work well within the overall arrangement and complement the rolling piano very effectively. Roger also delivers some wonderful falsetto lines towards the end. With its raging guitar riffs, crunching horns and catchy "Dr Jimmy and Mr Jim" chorus, this stand-alone rock epic would satisfy any Who fan disappointed with the album's many more mid-tempo songs.

Jimmy may be down but at the song's opening, he is defiant, as Roger's bloodcurdling vocals swagger with braggadocio:

> *Laugh and say I'm green*
> *I've seen things you'll never see*
> *I'll take on anyone*
> *Ain't scared of a bloody nose*

Lyrically, this is Townshend at his most aggressive – "What is it? I'll take it. Who is she? I'll rape it" and "her fella's gonna kill me / Oh, fucking will he?" – and makes explicit Jimmy's schizophrenia or Quadrophenia, in a direct reference to Robert Louis Stephenson's metaphorical tale, *Dr Jekyll And Mr Hyde*.

The "Doctor Jimmy" side of the dual character is self-aware and thoughtful, even when on pills, but, after a few gins, an angrier character emerges: "Mr Jim" is violent and destructive – he wants to fuck all the women and fight all the men; try all the drugs and take any bets on. He wants violent revenge on all those who've hurt him and he plans to get it... Or is it just drunken bravado?

Though this incorporates John's theme, Pete saw the Mr Jim side of the character as being more relevant to his drummer: "[Jimmy's] damaging himself so badly that he can get to the point where he's so desperate that he'll take a closer look at himself.

The part where he says, 'What is it? I'll take it. Who is she? I'll rape it'. That's really the way I see Keith Moon in his most bravado sort of states of mind."

With a sense of menace throughout – including the threat of sexual violence – this was shocking stuff for 1973, and retains a certain power even now.

The Rock

A despondent Jimmy pops some pills and steals a boat, swigging gin as he heads towards a jagged rocky outcrop off the Brighton coast. The soundtrack to this adventure is a six-and-a-half minute instrumental which incorporates all four main themes in a series of complex and atmospheric ebbs and flows, which shows Townshend in particular at his most musically dextrous, notably on a brief but heartbreaking blues solo over the chords of "Love, Reign O'er Me". The overall feel is grandiose but not pompous, in a passionate performance packed with pathos and vigour. The track ends with the empty, lonely sound of rainfall as Jimmy finds himself marooned on the rock which gives the track its title.

Love, Reign O'er Me (Pete's Theme)

As Pete's theme, it is no surprise that this is the album's key song and central recurrent refrain. Piano chords ring out as the rain pours down like it can only do in an out-of-season British seaside town. Keith plays orchestral rolls on tuned timpani, ending on a huge gong crash. The band give a "rough-house" rendition of this rousing rock epic, complete with anguished, impassioned career-highlight vocals from Roger (who had just recovered from a dose of German Measles), searing guitars, soaring keyboards, and an anthemic chorus.

An uplifting, elated mood is tainted by sadness and regret, as our hero, still alone out on the rock in the rain, comes to terms with himself and his many different personality traits; he's growing up – or, as Townshend put it, "in danger of maturing." Jimmy is discovering new things, but also leaving something precious behind him: his youth. He could choose to either surrender to the suicidal prospect of drowning or he could leave the beach in search of a home and in search of love. Pete is at his most poetic in this paean to the healing power of water, "cool, cool rain" inspired by a tenet of Meher Baba's that rain was a blessing from God.

The track ends with an orgy of guitar chords and drum fills with a blinding display from Keith, culminating in an intense final crashing chord, a scream from Daltrey, and accents that the band hit again and again for emphasis. This is arguably the album's highlight; though mid-paced in tempo, it rages like a classic rock anthem.

This was also recorded on the Rolling Stones' mobile unit at Stargroves by Glyn Johns. It was originally to be included on the Lou Reizner's orchestral album version of *Tommy* in 1972. It was performed by Maggie Bell who played Tommy's mother, but the release of Reizner's album would pre-empt *Quadrophenia*'s release by a year so Pete insisted it be removed from the track listing. There were hopes that Maggie would release it as a single but to no avail.

Quadrophenia is without doubt one of the band's finest moments – a masterpiece of intelligent rock'n'roll. The record received a rapturous response from audience and media alike but Townshend saw it initially as a kind of failure. It seemed destined to always be overshadowed by *Tommy*, which Bill Curbishley observed, "in its own way, became as big as the Who."

But in time, Pete Townshend came to reappraise *Quadrophenia* and in 2007 told *Record Collector*, "I think it's the best thing I've done. In a way the Mod movement sprang from the [Baby-] Boomer fiasco... we were little warmongers – genetically programmed and predisposed to drink, fuck and kill people – who were suddenly presented with Peace in Our Time. The Mods with their uniforms, and their abstract nihilism, briefly demonstrated what was going wrong; the older generation was not communicating properly or honestly with the younger. I don't think that happens anymore." He concluded, "In *Quadrophenia* I turned our errors, and our glories, into a rock poem. It may have saved lives."

Quadrophenia would prove to be the last great album from the Who and, perhaps, somewhere deep in their collective unconscious, they all knew it. However, the band were huge rock stars now and were enjoying their notoriety and wealth to the full, but the indulgences and pressures of the last few years were slowly beginning to take their toll.

As the band rehearsed at Shepperton Studios for the forthcoming tour to promote *Quadrophenia*, tensions between Townshend and Daltrey erupted into violence. Pete and Roger argued, Pete spat at Roger, swung his guitar at the singer's head and called him a "dirty little cunt." A fight ensued and culminated in Roger punching Pete, knocking him out. Townshend was taken to hospital and later released with temporary amnesia. "He was pissed and he thought he could fight me," Roger recalled. "I thought I had killed him. No one was sorrier than I was." One's a fighter, the other a writer, Roger summed it up: "Pete should never try to be a fighter."

Keith Moon's life was also unravelling: his long-suffering wife Kim had finally left him for good and, a few weeks before the tour rehearsals, his beloved father had died suddenly. As the tour drew closer, Moon was pushing his partying to the limit and living in domestic squalor.

The bad omens proved to be correct. From the start of the tour, the new material didn't go down well with audiences – the combination of live band and backing tapes for some of the more complex arrangements was fraught with difficulty and suffered from being poorly rehearsed. One night at Newcastle, frustrated by another error with the pre-recorded material, Townshend dragged his unfortunate soundman, Bobby Pridden, on stage and started to rip up his tapes. Townshend also had regular difficulties with guitars and changed them numerous times throughout the tour.

The critics were kind to the ambitious new show, but the fans were less receptive. Townshend's friend and Mod "face", Richard Barnes, loved *Quadrophenia* and couldn't understand why the new material was flopping night after night. "They'd do 'Can't Explain' and 'Substitute'," he told Phil Sutcliffe, "then they'd say, 'And now we're going to play something from our new album,' and the whole audience went dead." Roger's attempts at explaining the story behind the new project only alienated the audience further, to Pete's horror. He revealed, "Roger thought that

Quadrophenia wouldn't stand up unless you explained the story – and he's not the most verbose character. It was done sincerely, but I found it embarrassing, and I think it showed."

Gradually, Townshend accepted the inevitable and cut back the number of songs from his precious new project. "We started off playing it all, actually," Daltrey told the audience at one show, "but it went down bloody awful. So this is what is left." By February 1974, the band had dropped nearly all of the *Quadrophenia* material. Pete confessed, "I was glad when we dropped it... The whole thing was a disaster."

The North American tour quickly descended into farce: on the first night of the US leg, November 20, Keith passed out on stage, apparently after taking some kind of veterinary tranquiliser intended for use on animals only. A member of the audience was brought up to play drums for the remainder of the show.

A couple of weeks later in Canada, the entire band was thrown into jail in Montreal after Keith and Pete wrecked a hotel room: TV in the swimming pool, glass coffee table through the French windows, food smeared over the walls. Roger, who had been asleep during the destruction, was not amused at his undeserved incarceration. Pete was chastened by the experience but, for Keith Moon, it would only serve to add more fuel to the fire of his own hell-raiser mythology.

08 Shades Of Nostalgia – 1974

The Real Me
US Single Release: 12/01/1974 (Track)
Peak Position: 92 (US)

This found an American only release early in January '74 where it barely made the Top 100. It was issued in an attempt to squeeze the last drop of life from *Quadrophenia* and support the band's tour to promote the album.

As the *Quadrophenia* tour of arenas and stadiums continued into the New Year, Townshend was increasingly looking like the fight had gone out of him. He hated shows in these huge arenas, but felt powerless to do anything about it. By the summer of 1974 he was almost catatonic with depression and self-loathing and could barely play. His disillusionment with the band's fans that had begun with their rejection of his cherished *Lifehouse* project was exacerbated by their failure to take to his latest opus.

"All I know is that when we last played Madison Square Garden," he told the *NME*, "I felt acute shades of nostalgia. All the Who freaks had crowded around the front of the stage and when I gazed out into the audience, all I could see were those very same sad faces that I'd seen at every New York Who gig. There was about a thousand of 'em and they turned up for every bloody show at the Gardens as if it were some big event – 'The Who triumph over New York.' They hadn't come to watch the Who, but to let everyone know that they were the original Who fans. They had followed us from the very beginning, so it was their night. It was dreadful."

At the ill-starred tour's end, Townshend reluctantly accepted Robert Stigwood's invitation to supervise the soundtrack to the *Tommy* movie, which he painstakingly prepared in his home studio. The process didn't help his worsening moods – he felt trapped by the apparently inescapable albatross of his first rock opera and was never happy with the sound (which he was still despairing about by the time the film was premiered the following year).

With Townshend busy on the soundtrack, Daltrey – now cast in the film's title role – on set with director Ken Russell, and Keith Moon wreaking havoc with his new drinking buddy, the actor Oliver Reed, it was left to John Entwistle to compile the Who's rarities album, *Odds & Sods*.

Ensconced in a room at Track Records, Entwistle recruited a few close friends to help him rifle through the Who archives – a mountain of unmarked tape boxes – in search of something special.

"It became my project," the bassist said. "I think the idea was to try and release everything possible to stop the bootlegs. We were probably one of the [most] bootlegged acts of all time. I mean, in 1975 there were about 250. We thought it was about time we released a bootleg of our own."

Odds & Sods is just that – bits and pieces, leftovers, outtakes, half-realised ideas and eccentric oddities that served as a stopgap between 1973's *Quadrophenia* and *The Who By Numbers*, which emerged in late '75. It also served as a good time to take stock; it had been ten years since their recorded debut as the High Numbers. And what a decade it had been.

Pete explained to the *NME* why 1974 was an opportune moment to look back: "All of these tracks have been part of bigger ideas, or at least grand dreams that didn't see the light of day. At a time when each one of us in the band is, in a sense, looking at the future wearing a blindfold, it's great to look back at a time when we were able to make mistakes without worrying too much. Prepare yourselves, people, for the Who's next mistake! Meanwhile, content yourselves with this little lot."

Upon its release, rock writer and friend to the band, Chris Welch, reviewed it for *Melody Maker*: "Normally, it is a bold, bad record company which puts out old material, usually when a group or artist has departed elsewhere, but here, for once, the artists are themselves laying bare the torturous process of their evolution... If you have an archive, this is an essential item for any Who fan."

In its original vinyl format, the eleven songs are presented as a non-chronological jumble (but the CD remastered version, issued in 1998, not only gained twelve further rarities, but sequenced the tracks in the order that they were recorded). The original packaging was rather special. The sleeve had been photographed by Graham Hughes backstage at a gig in Chicago the previous November. The group are wearing American football helmets which spell out "R-O-C-K". They each have their name on the front but Roger and Pete are wearing each other's because they're own helmets didn't fit correctly.

Townshend poured scorn on the design so Hughes ripped it up in front of him, prompting an abrupt change of heart by Townshend. They then stuck the cover back together, with Daltrey adding the *Odds & Sods* title. The actual card of the cover was die-cut, leaving gaps for some of the pictures on the inner sleeve to be visible. The back featured the song titles in Braille and a photo of the band's soundman Bobby Pridden, perhaps to make up for Pete's mistreatment of him during the tape debacle of the *Quadrophenia* tour. The packaging came with a poster of the band in the US and a lyric sheet, while some of Pete's comments in the *NME* interview about the release of the album, were used for the liner notes.

For an album of outtakes, it did well commercially, reaching number 10 in the UK charts and number 15 in the States. With *Odds & Sods*, the fans got a rare glimpse behind the scenes of their favourite group. As the reissues market is now flooded with double CD sets of rarities, it's hard to appreciate quite how remarkable a record this was back in 1974.

Odds & Sods

UK Album Release: 04/10/1974 (Track 2406 116)
US Album Release: 12/10/1974 (MCA 2126)
Peak Position: 10 (UK) 15 (US)
Postcard / Now I'm A Farmer / Put The Money Down / Little Billy / Too Much Of Anything / Glow Girl / Pure And Easy / Faith In Something Bigger / I'm The Face / Naked Eye / Long Live Rock

Odds & Sods (Remastered Edition)

UK Album Release: 03/1998 (Polydor 539 791-2)
US Album Release: 03/1998 (MCA MCAD 11718)
I'm The Face / Leaving Here / Baby Don't You Do It / Summertime Blues (Studio Version) / Under My Thumb / Mary Anne With The Shaky Hand / My Way / Faith In Something Bigger / Glow Girl / Little Billy / Young Man Blues (Studio Version) / Cousin Kevin Model Child / Love Ain't For Keeping / Time Is Passing / Pure And Easy / Too Much Of Anything / Long Live Rock / Put The Money Down / We Close Tonight / Postcard / Now I'm A Farmer / Water / Naked Eye
All songs by Pete Townshend except for where stated separately.

Nearly all the material on Odds & Sods *has been heard in one form or another before, with the real surprise being 'Glow Girl'. Two minutes of perfection, it just builds to a riveting climax.*
Anthony Oliver, *Sounds*

Postcard
(John Entwistle)
More quirky bizarreness from Entwistle in these despatches to a loved one from life on a world tour, quoting the standard holiday postcard sentiment in its chorus, "We're having a lovely time / wish you were here".

"[John] describes in luscious detail", Townshend wrote in the liner notes, "the joys and delights of such romantic venues as Australia (pause to fight off temporary attack of nausea), America (pause to count the money) and, of course, that country of the mysterious and doubting customs official, Germany...".

There are some witty couplets summing up life in particular countries – French fries and disapproving eyes in the US, for example, and "There's kangaroos / With bad news / In Australia..." The jazzy, honky-tonk arrangement matches the light-hearted mood, with a tuba sounding like an oompah band, joining in when Germany is name-checked and a springy Jew's harp prominent when the jumping Oz marsupials are mentioned. All the sound affects were, according to Pete, recorded in the relevant countries.

Though this song had been scheduled for an EP release back in 1970, this recording was produced at Eel Pie Studios in '73 with Pete as engineer – keeping one hand on the desk left him with only one hand free to play guitar which explains why he stuck to one chord throughout. Entwistle subsequently overdubbed additional horns.

Released as a single in the US – the band's first Entwistle-penned A-side – it failed to make any impression on the charts. Overall, this is an amusing, if rather unlikely, opening to the original album (Entwistle would return to similar subject matter on one of the better songs on his first solo album, the homesick "What Are We Doing Here", written after a dismal show in Houston, with no booze and nothing worth watching on TV...).

Now I'm A Farmer
More goofy comedy, this time from the pen of Peter Townshend who considered it "cut from the same bale of hay as 'Postcard'," which it duly follows on both original and remastered and expanded versions of the album.

"It's a drug song," Pete explained, "All about the good life in the fields..."

Lyrically, this rather surreal portrait of "the agricultural jungle" certainly seems substance-influenced as the narrator digs away at his crops – harvesting enough corn to keep New York in corn flakes. The chorus, sung relatively straight, leads with one of Pete's ditties: "It's alarming, how charming, it is to be farming..."

While this features all the usual Who trademarks of power chords, builds and breakdowns, it's another untypical rock song, dependent again mostly on some saloon-bar piano. The play-out features a clip-clopping horse step rhythm and a cartoon western farmer's voice – which occasionally drops into cod Cockney – who concludes in a deep drawl with a list of some of the vegetables he grows.

"This track is from the period when the Who went slightly mad," Townshend concluded in his sleeve notes, and that is certainly the impression the listener gets. Said by some sources to have been included in very early draft plans for *Tommy*, this was considered by Pete, somewhat idiosyncratically, to be one of his finest works.

Put The Money Down

A song originally intended for the *Lifehouse* project, this was produced by the band and Glyn Johns at Olympic Studios in June '72. Pete praised Johns for the "terrific sound, beautifully recorded."

Roger's aggressive vocal is full of brazen, youthful exuberance – belying his initial reluctance to get to the studio in time to do it. The archive tape of this only had a guide vocal and try as he might, Entwistle couldn't pin down Daltrey to come in and record a new vocal. Exasperated, he sent word to Roger to ask if he'd mind if John did the vocals himself. Daltrey's response was swift; he had no problem with that – as long as John had no problem with Roger doing the bass parts. Daltrey turned up at Ramport Studios the next morning.

The line "there are bands killing chickens" is a reference to Alice Cooper's supposed propensity for doing this on stage.

Little Billy

This sweet-sounding track was recorded in 1968 as an anti-smoking commercial for the American Cancer Society, though an executive there complained – in what Townshend described as a "slimy East Coast accent of the nastiest possible kind" – that it was too long to be an effective brief public service advertisement.

It was shelved, in spite of the band playing it live that summer and even mooting it as a possible single. Pete considered it to be a masterpiece and was extremely frustrated that, instead of helping to save lives, it mouldered unheard for so long. The cancer charity message is wrapped up in an adept, if dark, fable of the fattest kid in school who, unlike his cooler classmates, didn't smoke. As the smokers get to middle age, "one by one, they're passing away", while the nicotine-free Little Billy is "doing fine".

In contrast to the grim subject, it's a lovely tune with overtones of the wonderful "Tattoo". With a melodic sound driven largely by strummed acoustic guitars – with some fine hammer-on and off technique – and swooning "oooh" and "ahhh" backing vocal hooks, this is a lost classic (on the remastered 1998 CD version,

Pete's voice from the control room at the original session can be heard at the song's end, deeming the take to be "good").

Too Much Of Anything

Recorded in early '71 with Glyn Johns for the *Lifehouse* project, and premiered at the Young Vic in April, this didn't come out on vinyl until the original version of *Odds & Sods* came out in 1974.

The theme was temperance versus excess. "We felt that this summed up just what too much of anything can do to a person," Townshend explained, "too much sex, drink, drugs, even rock and roll... Realising at the last moment how totally hypocritical it would be for a load of face-stuffing, drug-addicted alcoholics like us to put this out. We didn't."

With a mellow piano, by Nicky Hopkins, and acoustic guitar intro, this quickly develops into a more up-tempo rock song with some strong electric guitar riffing. Daltrey's vocals similarly grow from sensitive to a rock star roar as the track reaches its climax.

Glow Girl

Recorded in January '68 at London's De Lane Lea Studios and produced by Kit Lambert. With a shiny opening riff, guitar scrapes and exciting sixteenth-note snare fills, the Who kick up a rumpus and the familiar raucous attitude is starting to show.

"Glow Girl" was written on a nerve-wracking flight into Chattanooga, Tennessee, in the summer of 1967, when it appears Townshend's thoughts turned to death and reincarnation. "I tried to write an archetypal rock single," Pete explained, "the Shangri-Las type thing ["The Leader Of The Pack", about the death of the leader of a motorcycle gang] the Jan and Dean-type thing ["Dead Man's Curve", about a fatal car wreck]. The car crashes, the motorcycle goes over the cliff... Well, it was a reincarnation song and it was about a plane crash and two kids on an aeroplane and they realise that the plane's crashing. The reincarnation ploy comes at the end, where you hear 'It's a girl, Mrs Walker, it's a girl...'"

When Townshend came to write *Tommy*, he picked up on this phrase and used it as the opening, taking his hero's surname from a two-year-old song, though by then Mrs Walker's baby was a boy.

"Glow Girl" was planned initially as a single in early 1968, and later as the opening track on Pete's first rock opera, before the composer rejected the idea of it having a reincarnation theme. He also wrote and rejected a similarly titled number, "Glittering Girl". He was glad they left both songs on the cutting-room floor because, as he pointed out, "better material came along." Nonetheless, he was pleasantly surprised when "Glow Girl" made it onto *Odds & Sods*. "I'm really glad and amazed that John found this one and put it on" (the original LP version fades out at the end, whereas the remastered CD has an abrupt finish).

Pure And Easy

This was the keystone track on *Lifehouse* and is discussed in detail in the *Who's Next* section. An over-the-top fill from Keith kick-starts this, the band's second recording of the song, made at Stargroves, Berkshire, in April '71 with Glyn Johns. The earlier version, recorded at the Record Plant a month earlier, is available on the *Who's Next* (deluxe edition) re-release.

In the sleeve notes, Townshend contrasted this band arrangement with his solo version: "Not all of the group's versions of my songs are as faithful to the original demo as this one, but as usual the 'Oo' make their terrible mark."

Considering that this song about the quest for the perfect note was central to Townshend's doomed concept album, it is odd it didn't surface on *Who's Next*. Townshend explained, "In the context of stuff like 'Song Is Over', 'Getting In Tune' and 'Baba O'Riley' it explains more about the general concept behind the *Lifehouse* idea than any amount of rap." He said it missed the final cut of that album because there simply wasn't room on a single disc.

Faith In Something Bigger
On this January 1968 recording, with Kit Lambert at the desk, the band follows the 60s pop formula – all soft harmony vocals and predictable chords. The music is bland and the spiritual message – "we've got to have faith in something bigger... inside ourselves" – is banal. This could be any number of groups from the era.

But its inclusion proved that, to John Entwistle at least, it had some merit – a view not shared by the song's writer. "God, this is embarrassing," Townshend winced, "I don't know where to hide." Damning his song with faint praise, he deemed it "a modest beginning to the musico-spiritual work of the irreligious Who," before dismissing the guitar solo as the worst he'd ever heard and the whole song idea as "preposterous."

I'm The Face
(Pete Meaden)
This is the High Numbers' 1964 debut single, previously unavailable on any album (discussed in further detail in the Prologue). The High Numbers had intended this for the single's A-side but Fontana opted for their intended flip-side, "Zoot Suit". Either way, the record didn't make the charts until, during the height of the *Quadrophenia*-inspired UK Mod revival, when the single was re-released in March 1980 with "I'm The Face" as the A-side. It made Number 49 in the UK chart (the remastered CD version is a slightly different mix from the initial LP and finishes by fading out, rather than with the sharp ending of the original).

Naked Eye
Thematically, this is about the difference between real truth and what can be seen merely with the naked eye, and includes another prayer invoking a higher spiritual authority: "There's only one who can really move us all". Both Roger and Pete cover lead vocal duties on this rocker, which has a standard Who arrangement of starting softly and then kicking off into sonic mayhem. Originally recorded at Eel Pie Sound, it was completed at Olympic Studios in 1971.

Townshend was a big fan of this song which was built around a riff the band used to play at the time of the early *Tommy* shows. He had planned to release a live version and so the studio cut remained in the can.

Long Live Rock

Billy Fury sang this Townshend-penned 12-bar blues ode to rock'n'roll in the film in which Keith made his acting debut, *That'll Be The Day*. Pete declared it to be "the definitive version." Appropriately for a song about the evolving rock scene, it has a classic rock'n'roll sound, all Little Richard-style piano and Chuck Berry-esque guitar licks. Pete supplies the lead vocal in the verses with Roger taking over blisteringly in the sing-along chorus. The band sound relaxed and supremely confident as they give a reverent nod to the past, but this is more than just a 50s pastiche.

The title had once given Townshend the idea for a new album about the history of the Who that would be called "Rock Is Dead – Long Live Rock". That idea later blossomed into *Quadrophenia*. "Long Live Rock" eventually appeared as a UK single in 1979, though it stalled at Number 54.

Bonus Tracks:

Leaving Here

(Edward Holland Jr-Lamont Dozier-Brian Holland)

This 1960s cover of the Motown classic was cut at Pye Studios with Shel Talmy, and features a convincing throaty vocal from Roger and some familiar frenetic moves from the teenage Moon. The guitar is a little on the pedestrian side, redeemed slightly by an enthusiastic, if naïve, clunky blues solo.

An earlier Fontana Studios recording of this would be included on the box set *Thirty Years Of Maximum R&B*. This is also now available on the deluxe CD edition of *My Generation*.

Baby Don't You Do It

(Edward Holland Jr-Lamont Dozier-Brian Holland)

Another song penned by the legendary Motown team – this one made famous first by Marvin Gaye's September '64 hit and later by the Band's live version. It was recorded as a demo at Pye Studios with Talmy at the same time as "Leaving Here". Both these Motown hits were recorded as possible follow-ups to "I Can't Explain". The sole copy of the double-sided acetate containing them went missing for years but was eventually tracked down by a loyal collector.

On this early recording the band present more bluesy moves and 60s licks with a back-to-basics, unvarnished approach to production. Pete and John provide falsetto backing vocals, which would become a major part of the band's sound in the future. The band were fond of this song and performed it during some 1971 live shows. A later "live" version was used as the B-side of the "Join Together" single in '72, while an excellent version can be found on the *Who's Next* deluxe edition where it is extended from this track's 2.27 minutes to a staggering 8.20.

Summertime Blues

(Eddie Cochran-Jerry Capehart)

This Eddie Cochran classic is another of the Who's favourites – they had been playing it in London pubs and clubs in their pre-Keith days as the Detours back in 1964, and would continue to perform it live throughout their career. This rollicking

1967 studio cut features Entwistle's chunky, treble-heavy bass sound, hand-clap percussion and all the usual Who trademarks (a scorching rendition of this can be found on all formats of *Live At Leeds*).

Under My Thumb
(Mick Jagger-Keith Richards)
B-side to the "(This Could Be) The Last Time" double-sided Jagger-Richards covers single that was put out to show solidarity with the jailed Stones (discussed in Chapter Three).

Mary Anne With The Shaky Hand
Recorded in New York City at Mirasound Studios, this relaxed alternative take is more trippy than the version on *The Who Sell Out*. This relies heavily on Dylan-cohort and Blood, Sweat and Tears mainstay Al Kooper's organ for its gentle atmosphere, and is a stereo mix of the version on the '67 B-side of "I Can See For Miles" in the States.

My Way
(Eddie Cochran-Jerry Capehart)
Another Eddie Cochran composition, not to be confused with the Sinatra standard of the same name. Recorded in 1967, this swinging rhythm and blues tune had been in the band's live act in their pre-record deal days. It has a bluesy, boogie beat but it's an unremarkable track.

Young Man Blues
(Mose Allison)
Produced by Kit in the early stages of the *Tommy* sessions, this is a more subdued studio version than the blistering performance on *Live At Leeds*, but it's a worthwhile rock'n'roll workout featuring some muscular, stinging blues guitar from Pete. This was previously included on the long-deleted 1969 Track Records sampler *House That Track Built*.

Cousin Kevin Model Child
(John Entwistle)
An embryonic alternative song for Tommy's bullying relative, this vaudevillian number, credited to John – who adds brass parts – was recorded during the *Tommy* sessions at IBC to link "Fiddle About" and "Cousin Kevin", but was cut from the final album. Vocals are shared between Roger and Pete – as Uncle Ernie – and Keith as Kevin. According to highly respected Who experts Matt Kent and Andy Neill, in spite of the publishing credits, the author of this piece was actually Townshend.

Love Ain't For Keeping
Recorded with Kit Lambert at the Record Plant in 1971 for *Lifehouse*, this exciting and energetic performance includes some inspired lead guitar licks from Pete, and features Leslie West on additional guitar. Pete takes the lead vocals here, in contrast

to the *Who's Next* version sung by Roger.

Time Is Passing
Townsend's country picking talents are to the fore, a legacy of his early banjo-playing days. Roger provides a fitting vocal for this country flavoured tune. This version was salvaged from damaged master tapes originally recorded at Olympic Studios. The song first appeared on Pete's solo record *Who Came First*.

We Close Tonight
Originally written and recorded for *Quadrophenia*, this bittersweet song about a failed romance didn't make the final cut, as Pete felt its tone simply wasn't right. John shares the vocals.

Water
This recording of the *Lifehouse* reject features a bluesy workout from the band and a guttural lead vocal from Roger. Produced by Townshend in 1973 at Eel Pie, this was released as the B-side of the first *Quadrophenia* single "5.15", and is discussed above in relation to the Young Vic sessions (Chapter Six) and in relation to the themes of *Quadrophenia* (Chapter Seven).

In both its original and expanded, remastered versions, *Odds & Sods* is a fascinating insight into the band's archives and slipped discs. There are rarities and oddities but it also serves to draw a line under the band's journey so far.

"*Odds & Sods* seems almost miraculous," reviewer Ken Barnes would enthuse, adding, "Perhaps the Who should consider releasing an *Odds & Sods*-type album as an annual event – it would make the wait between new albums a lot easier to take and would free some of the most fascinating vault material in existence. The Who have become much more conscientious about their loose ends recently, so, why not get our hopes up?"

Postcard
US Single Release: 11/1974 (Track)
Another US-only single, released to coincide with *Odds & Sods* released the same month. A John Entwistle-penned track featuring him on lead vocals, the song features heavy brass arrangements and fairly stock "Who" musical moves. This failed to chart.

When *Odds & Sods* was released, the music industry was still in the grip of Glam Rock: Sweet, Mud, Gary Glitter, Roy Wood and the magical Marc Bolan were the chart heroes of the time. Everywhere you looked, bands seemed to be smeared with glitter and eye-shadow. However, five young lads from Scotland, the Bay City Rollers, whose *Once Upon A Star* album would be played endlessly in teenage bedrooms throughout 1974, changed the rules and opted for tartan over tinsel to enormous international success. The Rollers phenomenon did not faze Townshend. Arriving at the BBC TV studios to do an interview, he saw young fans of the Rollers waiting patiently for their idols to arrive to record the weekly music show, *Top Of The Pops*. As Townshend walked past them, one of the kids recognised him and said, "Look, it's Pete Townshend!" and a couple of others chirped politely, "Hullo, Pete." The polite crowd for the Rollers was a far cry from the first time that the Who appeared at those same studios for *Top Of The Pops*: back then, a gang of girls smashed through the plate-glass front door of the building. Times had changed...

09 Tommy Blues: All Alone With A Bottle – 1975-76

The start of 1975 marked the tenth anniversary of the Who's first hit single, but instead of celebrating the success that had seen the youthful, arrogant upstarts become elder statesmen of rock, the band was riven with tensions and troubles. If ever a group started an album in a dark place, it was the Who with *By Numbers*.

As the band prepared to enter the studio to record a new album, Townshend was depressed and in crisis. His wounds from the ill-fated *Quadrophenia* tour were yet to heal. He'd had mixed feelings about playing football stadiums in the spring of '74, and the disastrous Madison Square Garden shows that summer put him off touring for the foreseeable future. He'd spent much of the previous year on the frustrating task of doing the soundtrack for the movie of *Tommy* – a project he was keen to put behind him – which had exacerbated his heavy drinking. The contradictions between his sporadic dedication to the rock'n'roll lifestyle and his devotion to the path of Meher Baba were causing a spiritual and psychological crisis. The huge box-office success of the big screen version of *Tommy*, which premiered in March 1975 – with what Pete considered to be terrible sound quality – only seemed to make him feel worse.

Tommy: The Movie

Though *Tommy* would go on to become an acclaimed stage musical – opening on Broadway in 1993 (though initially to mixed reviews) – it was sealed forever in the collective mind with the 1975 Ken Russell film. For Townshend, the movie version had been a long time coming. He was already talking motion pictures with Tony Wilson at *Melody Maker* in July 1969, a mere two months after the album's release.

There were a number of changes in transferring the source material to celluloid. Crucially, avoiding a costume-drama look, the film is set in the 1950s whereas the album was set in the 1920s. The album's song "1921" was updated to "got a feelin' '51 is gonna be a good year". The violent events that cause Tommy's condition were also changed for the movie. Additionally, in the film, Tommy's success at pinball is exploited for their own financial benefit by his mother and her lover, Frank Hobbs.

The original album doesn't form the film's soundtrack; instead of the original versions, the actors mostly sing new takes on the Who's songs. All the songs were re-recorded and the order was changed; many songs were given revised lyrics and arrangements. Several new songs were also written for the film, including "Prologue 1945", "Bernie's Holiday Camp" and "T.V. Studio".

The famously over-the-top theatrical movie director Ken Russell was a fine choice to bring the insane vision that was *Tommy* to the big screen (co-produced with impresario Robert Stigwood). Russell's CV already included grandiose movies like his legendary take on D.H. Lawrence's *Women In Love*, and biopics of the composer Gustav Mahler and the sculptor Henri Gaudier-Brzeska (*Savage Messiah*).

Russell was also a huge fan of the Who and his casting was inspired: Jack Nicholson appeared as the Doctor for no other reason than he was in town at the time of the shoot. He spent only one day on set because, given his superstar status, that was all the budget could afford. Nicholson told everybody involved that he couldn't sing very well, but Pete thought he did a fine job. Oliver Reed, however, – who played Hobbs – really did sing dreadfully. He had such a bad singing voice and no memory for retaining lyrics, that when he was cast as Bill Sykes in the multi-Oscar winning version of Lionel Bart's musical *Oliver!* he insisted that the Sykes' song "My Name" be dropped.

The Official Souvenir Brochure

Townshend was having none of this for *Tommy*. He simply placed Reed in a studio with his drinking partner Keith Moon, served up a diet of brandy and allowed the actor to record his parts line by line. Often it was Pete himself who would shout the lines into the actor's headphones and one by one, Oliver would sing them. This protracted process nearly drove Pete insane, but in the end it had the required effect and the non-singing, non-dancing actor finally earned his stripes in a musical.

Tommy's mother (Nora Walker) was played by the ultra-sexy Ann-Margret. Roger would admit much later that it was difficult to be a testosterone-filled, 29-year-old in one of the world's biggest rock'n'roll bands while playing opposite the sometimes half-naked – or at most body-stocking-clad – beauty. Daltrey said he had to remind himself constantly that she was his "mother" and he was supposed to be deaf, dumb and blind. As for Daltrey himself, he was not Townshend's immediate choice for the role, but both Roger and Ken Russell were convinced he was right for it – and he was.

On hand to play the Pinball Wizard was Elton John, even though the role had been offered at one point to a very unlikely Tiny Tim. Mick Jagger and David Bowie were also mooted at early meetings for the project, but Pete soon realised that this was nothing more than Robert Stigwood wanting some big names to boost box office takings. Much later, Stevie Wonder was suggested as a possible Pinball Wizard, but Wonder's advisers talked him out of the role. However, Pete genuinely thought Stevie would have been perfect for the part and told him so years later.

Guitar legend Eric Clapton played the Preacher while Arthur Brown filled the role of the Priest; Tina Turner's Acid Queen was a triumph, though, bizarrely, the first person suggested for this part was apparently Lou Reed. Others in the cast included renowned stage actor Robert Powell as Tommy's father (Group Captain Walker), Paul Nicholas as the evil Cousin Kevin, and Russell's own daughter Victoria as Sally Simpson, the rock star-obsessed daughter of Reverend Simpson, played by the TV actor Ben Aris.

The role of the perverted Uncle Ernie was given to surely the only man on the planet who could make the part truly his own: Keith Moon. Ironically it was Moon's lifestyle that bought him the role. Despite being the youngest member of the group, and arguably the best looking in the early days, he was now starting to look more and more ravaged from years of drugs and drink. His suitability was helped on this occasion by the addition to the cast list of fellow hell-raiser Oliver Reed. As Pete would put it years later, "Their drinking games did deliver a perfect Uncle Ernie, the worse [Keith] looked for the part the better it was!" Townshend himself and John Entwistle had very minor supporting roles.

The film's budget was originally a million pounds, but it more than doubled during production by the time the schedule had over-run by six weeks – a staggering amount in 1974. On its release, the movie was a critical and commercial success. Ann-Margret received a Golden Globe Award for her performance, and was also nominated for an Academy Award for Best Actress. Pete Townshend was also nominated for an Oscar for his work in scoring and adapting the music for the film. Pete noted, "The result was a much more literal film than I expected. It's an exaggeration in some ways, almost burlesque at times." But Daltrey raved, "I think it's a milestone in film-making... a classic, there is no doubt about it."

The ironic twist is that, before the movie was made, Townshend talked about Kit Lambert, the man largely responsible for organising the conceptually incomplete original *Tommy* and the possibility of there being a film adaptation, "It's something that I think Kit Lambert desperately wants to do before he's ready to die, and I think this is probably what keeps him alive. When I suggested to him in 1971 that we might have another bash at talking about a movie of *Tommy*, he literally jumped for joy and leapt around the room and kissed me and hugged me and took me out to dinner and started to talk to me again... I mean, when I said it might be good if he directed it, he gave up everything he owned and gave it to me, brought it round in a big truck and dumped it on me doorstep and said that he'd be my servant for life. That's how much Kit wants to make a movie." Kit Lambert did not work on the film and was barely mentioned in the final credits.

Listening To You – See Me, Feel Me
UK Single Release: 11/04/1975 (Polydor) US Single Release: 03/1975 (Polydor)

Taken from the *Tommy* soundtrack and released to coincide with the album. It failed to chart on either side of the Atlantic.

Tommy: Original Soundtrack
UK Album Release: 21/03/1975 (Polydor 2657 014)
US Album Release: 22/02/1975 (Polydor PD2-9505)
Peak Position: 30 (UK) 2 (US)

Tommy: Original Soundtrack (Remastered Edition)
UK Album Release: 12/03/2001 (Polydor 841 1212)
US Album Release: 17/04/2001 (Polydor 422 841 1212)
Disc 1: Overture From Tommy (The Who) / Prologue 1945 (Pete Townshend/John Entwistle) / Captain Walker–It's A Boy (Pete Townshend) / Bernie's Holiday Camp (The Who) / 1951–What About The Boy? (Ann-Margret/Oliver Reed) / Amazing Journey (Pete Townshend) / Christmas (Ann-Margret/ Oliver Reed/Alison Dowling) / Eyesight To The Blind (Eric Clapton) / Acid Queen (Tina Turner) / Do You Think It's Alright (I) (Ann-Margret/Oliver Reed) / Cousin Kevin (Paul Nicholas) / Do You Think It's Alright (II) (Ann-Margret/Oliver Reed) / Fiddle About (The Who) / Do You Think It's Alright (III) (Ann-Margret/Oliver Reed) / Sparks (The Who) / Extra, Extra, Extra (Simon Townshend) / Pinball Wizard (Elton John)
Disc 2: Champagne (The Who/Ann-Margret/Roger Daltrey) / There's A Doctor (Ann-Margret/Oliver Reed) / Go To The Mirror (Ann-Margaret/Oliver Reed/Jack Nicholson/Roger Daltrey) / Tommy Can You Hear Me? (Ann-Margret) / Smash The Mirror (Ann-Margret) / I'm Free (Roger Daltrey) / Mother And Son (Pete Townshend) / Sensation (Roger Daltrey) / Miracle Cure (Simon Townshend) / Sally Simpson (Pete Townshend/Roger Daltrey) / Welcome (Pete Townshend) / T.V. Studio (Pete Townshend) / Tommy's Holiday Camp (Keith Moon) / We're Not Gonna Take It (Roger Daltrey And Chorus) / Listening To You–See Me, Feel Me (The Who)

Pete had insisted that the movie would have no dialogue whatsoever and, as a result, the cast had to re-record the songs. This was a gargantuan task, especially for Pete who supervised the whole exhaustive process.

Over the years, *Tommy* has been blamed for paving the way for some of prog-rock's most pretentious conceptual ramblings, yet the original double-album mostly comprised a series of fairly lean, melodically varied, often humorous, thematically-linked short songs. *Tommy* may have come to symbolise rock excess in some ways, but it was no interminable indulgence. This cannot be said for the soundtrack, which is a well-meaning but sprawling mess, drenched in keyboards and soaring choirs. The Who's songs and performance are submerged beneath a welter of inappropriate star turns, non-singing vocalists and a surfeit of synthesizers. Jack Nicholson's and Oliver Reed's vocals are particularly tuneless and embarrassing.

The soundtrack is not without redeeming features – and not just the so-bad-it's-good kitsch appeal... Some lyrics are revised and expanded, clarifying some of the original's more obscure plot points. As well as the welter of synths, there is a harder edge to some of the guitar parts, and the soundtrack versions of "I'm Free", "We're Not Gonna Take It", "Sally Simpson" and "Sensation" are fairly impressive, while Keith takes the lead on "Fiddle About" here with some aplomb.

Also, Tina Turner and Elton John both acquit themselves rather well... and the presence of Kenney Jones on drums on some tracks was an interesting portent for the future. Nonetheless, while there are a few interesting details here, this is a rather pointless exercise that can't compete with the originals or the various Who live recordings of the opus. No wonder Pete ultimately found it such a dispiriting project to produce.

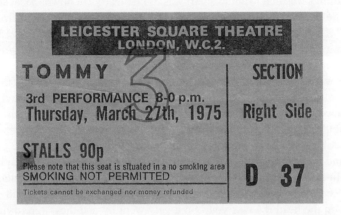

On the opening "Overture From Tommy", the Who perform with gusto: because of their total familiarity with the material, they inject a tremendous energy into the proceedings. "Prologue - 1945" is a chilling ARP synthesizer piece performed by Pete with John supplying the brass parts. "Captain Walker / It's A Boy" was recorded at the Beatles' Apple Studios in March 1974; the multi-talented Pete plays everything here, including drums, keyboards, and guitars as well as providing lead vocals. Female vocalists Vicki Brown and Margo Newman sing the nurses' parts, "It's a son".

"Bernie's Holiday Camp" is where Townshend had all the problems getting a vocal out of Oliver Reed – and it must be said that Ann-Margret's voice takes some getting used to with its untutored rasp. Female singer Alison Dowling supplies "Young Tommy's" voice while the Who provided the deliberately cheesy backing track. "1951 / What About The Boy" is where the story had to be changed and clarified; here the Wife's lover kills the Husband. "Eyesight To The Blind" features Eric Clapton singing this Sonny Boy Williamson song while his guitar tears into some funky blues-drenched licks. Clapton commented, "I think it was the song [Townshend] thought fitted me... he just thought that I could do that better than anything else, and I think he wanted me to be in it as a mate because he wanted all his mates to do it." Here John supplies bass and Kenney Jones plays drums, Pete noted that Kenney was the only drummer on the sessions where they "weren't looking round for Keith." This track is a highlight of the record that could easily have been a stand-alone single release.

"The Acid Queen" features Tina Turner, who spent just six days in the UK for the entire filming and recording process. She recorded her compelling vocal at

Ramport Studios; she gives a convincing performance as the "Acid Queen", a part she obviously relished. However Ken Russell wasn't entirely convinced at the start. He apparently said to her, "I didn't know you had that much hair." Turner countered, "And I thought you were taller."

Keith Moon gives a typically over-the-top performance as the child-molesting Uncle Ernie with "Fiddle About". Author and critic Richard Barnes says, "One of the first things was that Moonie's part was dramatically cut down, because Russell realised he couldn't act. He was always over-acting, very clumsy in front of the camera." Keith was furious when he discovered his role had been reduced and left the set outraged. He had a far more charitable view of his own acting skills: "I've always been an actor that plays the drums... I haven't been a film actor, but there are many aspects of acting. I seldom stop acting, except... well, when I'm asleep."

"Sparks" is a highlight, the band stick to the original arrangement and give the performance of their lives. Again, due to their total familiarity with the material they're able to squeeze every last drop of excitement from this intense instrumental.

Elton John gives an exceptional rendition of "Pinball Wizard". One of Elton's friends and musical rivals Rod Stewart was in line for this part, having appeared in the role in Lou Reizner's 1972 orchestral production of *Tommy* in London. Elton noted, "Rod told me they wanted him as the Pinball Wizard and I said 'I would knock it on the head if I was you.' So a year went by and they were trying to get the world and his mother to do it. I was offered loads of parts in it and I always said no. Then I found out Ken Russell was doing it, and I spoke to Pete about it, and became quite enthusiastic about the idea. To cut a long story short, I ended up doing the Pinball Wizard and, of course, Stewart, when he found out, couldn't believe it! [He said] 'You, bastard!' "

This track was the only piece on the record not produced by Pete. Elton's own Gus Dudgeon, the man responsible for the singer's run of incredibly successful albums during the 70s, assumed the producer's role. Elton and his excellent band rip into this Who classic. With Dee Murray on bass, Davey Johnstone on guitar, percussionist Ray Cooper and Nigel Olsen on drums, the band more than do this justice. They play the opening chords to "I Can't Explain" on the final breakdown as a further tribute to the Who on this most successful of covers.

Released as a single in March 1976, it reached No.7 on the UK chart and, with Elton appearing in the movie perched upon massive 10 feet high Doc Martin boots, he was forever cemented in the public's consciousness as "The Pinball Wizard".

On "Champagne", the Who provide the backing track while Roger and Ann-Margret share the lead vocals. During this scene in the movie, Ann-Margret cavorts in "Baked Beans, Fit For A Queen". Director Ken Russell revealed "*Tommy* fell nicely into my scheme of things and I was able to slip in a couple of scenes that I'd been trying to get into films for years. One being the Marilyn Monroe shrine (Eyesight To The Blind) and another was the TV set vomiting baked beans and shit." The scene had Ann-Margret's character, Tommy's mother, throwing a bottle of champagne at a TV screen leaving shards of broken glass spread across the floor. She cut herself quite badly, forcing a temporary halt to filming.

Hollywood movie star Jack Nicholson takes the lead vocal as "the Specialist", on "Go To The Mirror", with a sensibly restrained performance. Pete had no problem getting a decent, usable vocal from the star. With "I'm Free", the Who originally laid the backing track for this and "Pinball Wizard" in January '74, but Townshend said, "They came out sounding like a cliché." Featuring Kenney Jones on drums, the band gives a blistering performance. Oliver Reed is featured on lead vocals on "Welcome" – one can almost hear Townshend pulling his hair out in frustration – but is buried in the mix alongside a more prominent Ann-Margret and Roger. Townshend plays all the instruments here, guitars, drums, bass, piano and synthesizers. Recorded at Ramport Studios in May, "Tommy's Holiday Camp" features Keith on lead vocals. He gives an impressively jolly, maniacal over-the-top performance that's all too brief. The Wurlitzer organ part was played by Gerald Shaw and arranged by Martyn Ford. In the movie Keith performs this perched on a giant motorised pipe organ, and he gleefully steals the show.

The movie was a massive box-office hit; the soundtrack album reached number two on the US chart but a more modest thirty in the UK. The record somewhat confused the British audience, perhaps they had had enough of the deaf, dumb and blind boy. It was a mish-mash of performances and, although brilliantly executed by Pete, the album fell victim somewhat to poor lead vocals on many of the tracks: Elton John's version of "Pinball Wizard" being the only true musical success outside performances by the Who.

The film made Roger Daltrey a bona fide movie star in America and Ken Russell cast him in the lead role of his next movie *Lisztomania* based on the life of the composer, Franz Liszt. He co-wrote lyrics and sang three songs on the soundtrack: "Love's Dream" (Liszt's "Leibstraum"), an ode to young innocent love set to a haunting, if melodramatic Liszt melody, features some of Roger's simplest and most effective words, and is one of his most highly affecting vocals. On the more clichéd lyric of "Life is pain / Pain is loss", from "Funerailles", he sounds less convincing, raising his game only for the uplifting and quite splendid Ragtime-tinged album finale, "Peace At Last".

Meanwhile, the group's more musically talented, but comparatively anonymous, bass player was finding it more difficult to make it in his own right. Having seen his cherished *Odds & Sods* project appear the previous year, John began 1975 by touring the UK and the US with a pared-down line-up of his band, the Ox. The tour failed to capture the imagination of Who fans, though, and the Stateside leg was a box office failure which ended bitterly and tens of thousands of pounds in debt. John's fourth solo album *Mad Dog* hit the racks in March 1975, credited to John Entwistle's Ox, but was naturally overshadowed by the *Tommy* movie and again failed to light up the chart.

The king of the crazy-makers, Keith Moon had moved to California and was living it up with various Los Angeles-based celebrities; among them ex-Beatle Ringo Starr, brilliant but unpredictable singer-songwriter Harry Nilsson, shock-rocker Alice Cooper and future Dallas star Larry Hagman. They would drink together in their self-styled "Lair of the Hollywood Vampires", based at the Rainbow on Sunset Strip in Los Angeles – a notorious 70s hang out for the idle rich and famous, where Keith was often the main attraction. Alice Cooper declared him to be rock'n'roll royalty.

Without the distraction of having to play drums, drinking and partying to monstrous excess had become Moon's sole raison d'être. He was living in a house on Malibu beach next door to legendary movie star Steve McQueen, with whom he had several disputes over the noise and chaos that Moon brought to the sedate luxury colony. Keith would also spend days on end at the ultimate party house, Hugh Hefner's Playboy mansion, and was also drinking with ex-Beatle John Lennon who was in the midst of his own 18-month "lost weekend" away from Yoko.

If any of this sounds glamorous and fun, the truth was much darker. Keith's drug consumption – uppers, downers, cocaine – along with his favourite breakfast tipple of Courvoisier brandy with Dom Perignon champagne – was detaching him ever further from reality, as Dougal Butler's excellent book *Moon The Loon* details. With his health deteriorating sharply, Keith's years of excess were finally catching up with him. The avuncular Moon's hedonism had turned into a kind of nihilism. He continued to chase potential movie roles in vain and, with much of the band's royalty income suspended pending resolution of their dispute with their previous management, he was running out of money. Without even any touring income since the summer of the previous year, he continued to squander large sums of cash. He'd blow an entire royalty cheque on a vintage Rolls Royce without a second thought. Kit Lambert's early idea of treating them like rock stars and they'll act like rock stars had come to fruition.

Moon had managed to complete a solo album, *Two Sides Of The Moon*, in late 1974, but he had barely played any of the drum parts for it; instead, he wanted to sing. Preceded by a reasonable cover of the Beach Boys' "Don't Worry Baby" for a single, *Two Sides Of The Moon* – which had had a working title of Like A Rat Up A Pipe – finally reached the shops in April 1975. Old friend Roy Carr's review from the *NME* epitomised the sense of disappointment experienced by most who heard the record: "Moonie, if you didn't have the talent, I wouldn't care, but you have, which is why I'm not about to accept *Two Sides Of The Moon* – even if, after ten years, it means the end of a friendship. C'mon Moon, get your bleedin' finger out!" On his versions of "The Kids Are Alright" and the Beatles' "In My Life", Moon's charm and personality shine through, but it's hard for many to see this album as anything more than a bored, rich rock star's indulgence.

The Who By Numbers

When the time came to record what would become *The Who By Numbers*, Pete came armed with a bunch of songs that were less of an album and more of a cry for help. "[The songs] were written with me stoned out of my brain," Pete confessed, "in my living room, crying my eyes out... detached from my own work and from the whole project... I felt empty."

The Who's career had entered a whole new stratosphere; they were internationally famous, outrageously rich, and successful beyond their wildest dreams. Somehow, it wasn't enough – for Townshend, at least. "When I first started, as a kid, I didn't really want to be in a successful band," Pete would later insist. "I think it's been one of the things I've had great psycho-neurotic difficulty with, I don't really like being a star."

He had complained to *NME* in 1975, "To some extent the Who have become a golden oldies band, and that's the bloody problem that faces all successful groups at one time or another – the process of growing old." Recent touring had rendered him "thoroughly depressed. I honestly felt that the Who were going on stage every night and, for the sake of the die-hard fans, copying what the Who used to be."

Pete's vocal disgust at what the Who had become extended to a sense of dissatisfaction with rock in general. "It's not the important method of expression that it once was," he grumbled. "For many kids, rock'n'roll means absolutely nothing. It's just another form of entertainment." Fortunately, not all members of the Who took it quite so seriously.

"I never heard such a load of bullshit in all my life," Roger responded to his band mate's comments. "I don't feel that way about the Who, about our audiences, or anything in that way. He's talked himself up his own ass." Ever pragmatic, Roger recommended that Townshend "use the Who for what it is. A good rock'n'roll band."

Roger's down-to-earth approach left him and Pete on opposite sides of a cultural divide back in 1975. As John Swenson would point out in *The Who By Numbers* CD sleeve notes, by the mid-70s, rock was facing something of a mid-life crisis, "as the rabble rousers and street prophets of the 1960s were forced to adjust to their new role as middlebrow entertainers." The likes of McCartney and the Stones seemed fine with this, while Dylan and Neil Young were indulging in dark periods of introspection.

The Who By Numbers lays bare the feeling of a songwriter totally disillusioned by rock'n'roll and his position at the top of its hierarchy. The Who had become so big and successful that they really had nothing left to prove, but where did this leave Townshend? As he tried to come to terms with imminently turning thirty, it seemed like the man who wrote the ultimate teenage rebellion of "My Generation", who said he hoped he'd die before he got old, was starting to feel his age. "When I'm standing up there on stage playing rock'n'roll," Pete would say, "I often feel that I'm too old for it."

Having previously relied on adolescent bravado, teenage angst and youthful anger to fuel his work, Pete's work now seemed born out of a more world-weary bitterness, frustration and cynicism. The catharsis of writing remained vital, though, for this increasingly tortured soul. "Suicide notes tend to flush out the trouble felt by the potential ledge-jumpers," Pete explained, "revealing the fact that once the truth is out, there's no need to jump."

Having experienced tremendous pressure producing *Quadrophenia*, and having suffered some of the other band members' less than elegant reactions to the final mixes, Townshend decided to recruit Glyn Johns to produce the new album. Johns had engineered the *Who's Next* sessions, the band knew him well, and he appeared to be a good choice. But Johns himself was under stress, dealing with a marriage break-up and dealing with a band that had left him with a vast amount of work to do.

"I felt partly responsible because the Who recording schedule had, as usual, dragged on and on, sweeping all individuals and their needs aside," Pete confessed. "Glyn worked harder on *The Who By Numbers* than I've ever seen him. He had to, not because the tracks were weak or the music poor but because the group was so useless. We played cricket between takes or went to the pub. I personally had never done that before. I felt detached from my own songs, from the whole record.

"Recording the album seemed to take me nowhere. Roger was angry with the world at the time. Keith seemed as impetuous as ever, on the wagon one minute, off it the next. John was obviously gathering strength throughout the whole period; the great thing about it was he seemed to know we were going to need him more than ever before in the coming year." In the meantime, John used his talents to come up with a truly original record sleeve that fitted the title perfectly. Mimicking a children's dot-to-dot, colour-by-numbers puzzle, his artwork was a part-completed pen caricature of the four band members, with numbers showing where the incomplete lines should be extended to. Townshend is at the back, arms outstretched above the other three, in a pose that writer Simon Frith saw as aptly showing the guitarist as puppet master but without strings to control his band mates. The monochrome drawing fitted with the back-to-basics sound and initial copies of the vinyl were also individually numbered.

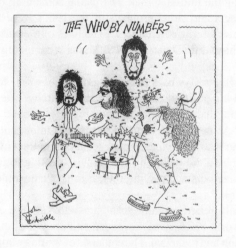

"The cover only took me an hour," Entwistle explained, "but the dots took about three hours." John would quip that while Pete's elaborate *Quadrophenia* artwork had cost around £16,000, his *By Numbers* cover cost just £32! In some ways, as with *Live At Leeds'* back-to-basics sleeve, the cover encapsulated the contents. Shorn of studio trickery, sound effects and synthesizers, and short on the usual Who trademark power chords and accented riffs, *The Who By Numbers* sounds rather rough and ready. Writer Chris Charlesworth saw it as a "non-Who sounding Who album" and certainly Townshend and Moon sound restrained when compared with previous more totemic works. Dave Marsh described the sound correctly as "brittle" but it does complement the candid nature of the lyrics perfectly, and the musical arrangements and performances are refreshingly spartan. There are some lighter moments, most notably "Squeeze Box" and "Blue, Red and Grey", but the overall atmosphere of the album is decidedly dark.

All of Pete's feelings of crisis and disillusionment found an outlet in the self-excoriation of *The Who By Numbers* material. This would be his equivalent of *Plastic Ono Band, Blood On The Tracks* or *Tonight's The Night*. "It was hard for me to admit what I knew as I was composing," Pete continued, "...that what was happening to me was an exorcism."

When the album was completed, the band themselves weren't sure what they had on their hands and neither their audience nor the critics were any clearer, though the always astute Roy Carr saw it as a reaction to *Tommy* in all its guises, not least the movie: "*The Who by Numbers* displays all the symptoms of post-*Tommy* depression," Carr concluded. "It's tainted with the decaying, bittersweet stench of enforced showbiz success wrought by the third and most commercial manifestation of that deaf, dumb and blind kid".

It isn't surprising, considering the stripped-down sound and dark subject matter, that *The Who By Numbers* would sell less than its predecessors, though it still made number seven in the UK album charts, and number eight in America. The band somehow seemed less relevant, something Townshend was starting to realise.

The press reception for the new record was also mixed. Though it wasn't hailed as a classic, and some scribes bemoaned the absence of a great single, reviewers generally praised its maturity. *Let It Rock*'s Simon Frith, who was unconvinced by *Quadrophenia*, conceded it wasn't "a triumphant return or anything like that" but did feel that, though it was devoid of hits, it was "full of hope". While Frith could see a lot that was interesting in the new record, his problem with post-*Tommy* Who was that Townshend had run out of melody – a shortcoming he didn't see as having been corrected on *The Who By Numbers*. Writer Ken Barnes conversely believed the new LP's "melodies [were] unbeatable." To him, the band weren't firing at the usual rock velocity and he regretted the number of acoustic guitars, but Barnes would conclude that *The Who By Numbers* was "a consummately-crafted record of fascinating depth and immediate surface appeal. It's a record made for repeated exposure."

Few songs of this album would make it into the band's regular live sets though, and this point marked the real beginning of the divergence between the Who's recording career and their increasingly greatest-hits based concert tours.

The Who By Numbers
UK Album Release: 03/10/1975 (Polydor 2490 129)
US Album Release: 25/10/1975 (MCA 2161)
Peak Position: 7 (UK) 8 (US)
Slip Kid / However Much I Booze / Squeeze Box / Dreaming From The Waist / Imagine A Man / Success Story / They Are All In Love / Blue Red And Grey / How Many Friends / In A Hand Or A Face

The Who By Numbers (Remastered Edition)
UK Album Release: 11/1996 (Polydor 533 844-2)
US Album Release: 11/1996 (MCA MCAD 11493)
Slip Kid / However Much I Booze / Squeeze Box / Dreaming From The Waist / Imagine A Man / Success Story / They Are All In Love / Blue, Red and Grey / How Many Friends / In A Hand Or A Face / Squeeze Box (Live) / Behind Blue Eyes (Live) / Dreaming From The Waist (Live)
All songs by Pete Townshend except where stated otherwise.

It's been a long wait but it's been worth it. The Who's talent shows up the shallowness of rock bands who have tried to emulate or even imitate them... There's no 'Pinball Wizard' here, but the Who can be said to have truly progressed.
Rosalind Russell, *Record Mirror & Disc*

Slip Kid

This cautionary tale finds Pete in world-weary mood as he outlines the problem of being a thirty-something rock star. Having been so young when the band first experienced success, the writer associates music with youth. It's as if he's trying to decide whether or not rock'n'roll is important anymore, and if it is, is he still part of it? Indeed, should he be? "Keep away old man", the young protagonist berates a more experienced contender for failing to realise his and rock's potential:

> *You won't fool me*
> *You and your history won't rule me*
> *You might have been a fighter*
> *But admit you failed*

"'Slip Kid' came across as a warning to young kids getting into music that it would hurt them," Pete explained. Ultimately then, this is a warning to any budding rock wannabe from a man who knows, although he reaches no resolution to his dilemma.

With a stop-start, mid-tempo, laid back rock rhythm, the arrangement is dominated by conventional rhythm guitar, percussion and piano. It's free from any traditional Who trademarks and, in spite of a strong vocal performance from Roger, plus a fine understated guitar solo, "Slip Kid" is a low-key opener.

However Much I Booze

After a few strummed guitar chords, there is the refreshing sound of Keith's proper entrance to the fray. But Moonie's energising and panoramic drum kit attack ushers in one of Pete's darkest songs. It finds the writer "all alone with a bottle and my head a-floating" – isolated and ashamed, haunted and hunted. Roger apparently refused to sing this due to its very personal lyrical candour, and it's not hard to see why when the protagonist concludes he is "nothing but a well-fucked sailor." Also, unsurprisingly, health-fanatic Roger didn't want the world to think he had a drink problem. Demoed as "No Way Out," Townshend's clunkier final title was chosen to stress the corrupting influence of alcohol in his life.

"Drinking around the Who is the greatest thing gutter-level life can offer," Pete would say of his love-hate liaisons with liquor. "The bawdiness of the humour, the sheer decadence of the amount put away, the incredible emotional release of violent outbursts against innocent hotel-room sofas; all these count to get a body through a lot of trouble. But at the end of the orgy, the real cancer still lies untackled deep in the heart."

"However Much I Booze" finds Pete as self-coruscating as John Lennon at his most confessional. Dave Marsh saw *The Who By Numbers* as the rock'n'roll equivalent of F. Scott Fitzgerald's *The Crack Up* and its talk of alcohol-induced "real dark nights of the soul" where you're alone and it's 3 am, and this is nowhere more true than on this track.

Self-loathing drips from every line and, though the pill is sugared with a shiny country-rock sound and breezy melody – indeed, with a different lyric this might have become a drive-time radio classic – it's almost too painful to listen to as the acclaimed songwriter and worshipped guitar hero outlines his battle with the bottle and the hollowness in his heart: "I see myself on TV, I'm a faker, a paper clown / It's clear to all my friends that I habitually lie". His moods depress his friends; he's frustrated and wallowing in brandy, but "However much I booze / There ain't no way out".

The imagery is vivid and savage as Pete describes the reality behind the façade of rock success, the insincerity of the entertainment world, the tensions between him and Daltrey, and the loneliness of his addiction – "night comes down like a cell door closing" and leaves him alone and going crazy, literally clawing the walls. The final lines address the listener directly:

You at home can easily decide what's right
By glancing very briefly at the songs I write
But you know it don't help me that you know
There ain't no easy way out

Not for the first time on the album, the rocking sound belies the bleak subject matter and Keith in particular is in fine, energetic form, adding drive with his usual manic fills, while John matches the drummer at every turn with action-packed runs and licks. This is a real high point for the rhythm section. There's also a fine melodic, more Who-sounding middle eight and some self-mocking wolf howls near the end, that all go to illustrate, ironically, that, just as Pete is most vividly self-flagellating over his own inadequacies, he is displaying his many talents.

Squeeze Box

While this song title is slang for an accordion, it is immediately clear that the particular squeeze box that mama "wears on her chest" and that ensures "Daddy never sleeps at night" is not a musical instrument. Though Townshend, who owned an accordion, confessed this was conceived as a dirty joke, he denied any double entendre: "It's not about woman's breasts, vaginal walls, or anything else of that ilk," he insisted. But lines such as: "She goes in and out / and in and out / and in and out" and "She goes, squeeze me, come on and squeeze me / Come on and tease me like you do" do not sound like accordion lessons.

"I dunno," Entwistle brooded to scribe John Ingham, "Most songs have double meanings or no meaning at all. 'Squeeze Box' isn't that dirty. It doesn't say 'tits'." Though, as Ingham pointed out, "box" does have another meaning in American street slang. Daltrey, who sang the words, was more frank about the subject matter: "Nothing wrong with a bit of 'in-and-out', mate!"

This infectious pop tune features more country picking from Pete, with acoustic guitars plus a solo on a Fender G banjo for good measure, and a skiffle influence, as it bounces along like a proper how's-your-father Cockney knees-up. With a ribald rhythm to match the suggestive lyric, this has more in common with an old music hall romp than the rock sound of the 70s.

"It's so refreshingly simple," says Daltrey, "an incredibly catchy song. It doesn't pretend to be anything other than what it is and I love it for that." A welcome relief from the dark, serious tone of much of the other material on *By Numbers*, "Squeeze Box" became the Who's first single since "Join Together" to crack the UK Top Ten – a fact that would amaze its composer who couldn't believe the band would record what he saw as a throwaway ditty, let alone that it would be a hit.

(There's a rollicking, end-of-pier, farfisa organ arrangement of "Squeeze Box" on Pete's *Scoop* demo collection, replete with *Wacky Races* bluegrass banjos, that sounds like it's going to burst into the Beatles' "Ob-la-di, Ob-la-da" at any moment. The composer may have not rated this but he sounds like he's having a ball on the demo.)

Dreaming From The Waist

Originally titled "Control Myself", after the key line "I'm dreaming of a day I can control myself", the ferocious ensemble rock'n'roll playing cannot hide the painful plea at the song's heart. Having castigated his drinking on "However Much I Booze", the writer, who is so drawn to Baba Meher's ascetic spiritual path, now struggles with his addiction to the pleasures of the flesh. His heart's pumping and his mouth tastes of sand and he fears a heart attack; he's "got the hots for the sluts in the well-thumbed pages of a magazine". It's another highly personal self-castigation as the writer criticises the sex-obsessed mind that sees him "dreaming from the waist on down". Perhaps Roger was less reluctant to be associated with lust than alcoholism as he gamely takes the lead vocal.

With a breezy intro that features the Townshend trademark of a suspended note that remains as the chords move through a progression, and some of Moon's best – and most typical – drum work on the album, Pete adds gentle backing vocals to Roger's more strident lead. Meanwhile, Entwistle's bass playing is worthy of special note; he is as nimble-fingered as ever. Name-checked by *Record Mirror* as an album highlight, this is the most Who-like track on the record so far and would be the only song from the LP that the band would regularly play in concert, but even its popularity in the group's live set apparently would not convince Townshend of its quality.

Imagine A Man

The lyrics of "Imagine A Man" lurch between insightful and tender, painful and hateful as Townshend, facing thirty in a young man's game, honestly confronts the ageing process in search of wisdom: "to see the end". He's come a long way down the road and feels a great weight on his shoulders. A broken old soul, he's "Not a child of any revolt / But a plain man tied up in life". Unlike much of the material so far, though, the voice is not bitter, but accepting and philosophical.

"It just might be a key to the way that rock could grow old," Pete explained, shortly after writing it. "It's about that feeling of being... not a failure, but over the hill... Then of course I realized the song was about me." The understated arrangement opens with a beautiful, gently-rolling, crystalline acoustic guitar motif. Townshend always admired the fine acoustic guitar sounds which producer Glyn Johns was able to get. This was the standard by which Pete would judge other producers in the future: "If somebody comes along and puts a mike on and it doesn't look like the position that Glyn would have it in, I'd move it."

Nicky Hopkins' piano is serene and the drums low-key – only entering the fray during the restrained choruses. Roger sounds compellingly vulnerable and sad while Pete adds beautiful falsetto backing vocals. The old adversaries' voices never worked better together. Keith plays a subtle rolling tom pattern while Entwistle adds flavour with a series of restrained runs in the verses plus a rumbling bass effect in the choruses. Overall, it's not Pete's most memorable tune, but the performance and arrangement make for a solid album track.

Success Story
(John Entwistle)
Pete wasn't the only Who songwriter who felt disaffected with his calling around 1975. John Entwistle was soon telling a journalist: "I hate singles. I hate the whole thing about *Top Of The Pops*," and his ironically titled "Success Story" is a cynical, darkly funny view of the music business, with its empty promises, dashed hopes and broken dreams.

But where a highly-strung Townshend found self-loathing and despair in his disillusioning experiences, the more down-to-earth Ox finds humour in a dark parody of the rock world that has a similar spirit to Pink Floyd's satire about riding the rock gravy train, "Have A Cigar", from the same year: "Come in here, dear boy, have a cigar / You're gonna go far".

While the Floyd song was spoken by a caricatured industry mogul, in Entwistle's song, the voice belongs to a jobbing part-time musician who dreams "Someday I'm gonna make it / Gonna be a super-duper-star", and wants a flash car and a house for his mum. Sure enough, his fairy godfather appears in the guise of a wideboy manager who promises the world. "Success Story" has that wonderful, black comedy feel that is so indicative of John's best writing but, ultimately, it's the cynical irony that bleeds through. Before long, rock stardom is just another job as the singer has to play extra shows to give the taxman his outrageous cut – John wrote fittingly, as someone who used to work for the Inland Revenue service. There is a real world-weariness in lines like: "Back in the studio to make our latest Number 1 / Take 276, you know this used to be fun".

While this young aspiring rock hero's story can represent the experiences of many other bands of the era, much of it does sound autobiographical – from the managerial issues to the long hard slog behind the glamour. It's also not hard to see the odd joke at his band-mate Pete's expense, in the tales of a star giving up rock for religion, and especially the line "I may go far if I smash my guitar". Musically, it's a fairly conventional bluesy rocker with a few Who trademarks that works as a pastiche to suit the parodying subject matter. Overall, it's a witty addition to the Entwistle canon and a welcome break from the dark art emanating from Pete's weary heart.

They Are All In Love

A gliding, understated drift in 6/8 time, originally titled "She Loves Everyone", musically this is one of the lighter songs on the LP. Nicky Hopkins' rolling piano riff underpins the arrangement and adds to the dreamy feel. Keith and John employ a mature reserve while Roger spits out the acrid lines and cajoles the listener, counter-pointed by wonderful harmonies.

The sweet title is repeated in each chorus but it belies the darker sentiments of the verses where an introspective, and no longer so young, Townshend struggles to see where he fits into a changing world, interrogating himself: "Just tell me right now where do you fit in? / With mud in your eye and a passion for gin." He blows a mocking raspberry at himself, as the song reaches its climax, bewilderment turns to the self-disgust of "Hand me my chequebook and I'll crawl off to die...".

"The song was about what the band had become," explained Pete. "It was about money, about law courts, about lawyers and accountants. Those things had never mattered and the band had a backlog of tax problems and unpaid royalties. We had to deal with it. I really felt like crawling off and dying." In a final coup de grace, the writer nails his perceived failings of his songs to the mast: "I've seen magic and fame now I'm recycling trash". Townshend may have felt this was an accurate reflection of where his career was at, but on the evidence of this fine, if flawed, album there was little basis for it. Nonetheless, the writer unwittingly foretells the future...

Blue, Red And Grey

Amid the despair and recrimination of so many of the album's tracks, this is a reflective celebration of taking it easy, enjoying life and being in love. Sung by Pete in conversational style, it repeats its conclusion: "I like every minute of the day".

Unsurprisingly, considering its divergence from the depression that seemed to inspire most of *The Who By Numbers*' lyrics, this was not a Townshend choice for the album's final cut – he claims Glyn Johns insisted on salvaging what he dismissed as "that fucking thing" which so failed to match his dark mood.

"[It] was a ukulele ditty," Townshend sneered, "with John Entwistle adding brass band to the misty middle distance. It was about nothing at all; it reminded me of an old *Smiley Smile* Beach Boys number." John's brass parts conjure images of a fading Salvation Army Band and add a haunted, lonely quality, but it's ultimately touchingly optimistic in its praise for the simple life. Though Keith and Roger are absent, it was apparently one of Daltrey's favourite tracks on the record. Featuring some elements reminiscent of "Sunrise" from *Sell Out*; this is an absolute gem.

A full band version was recorded but the tapes appear to have been mislaid.

How Many Friends

Having spent much of the album pointing the finger of accusation inwardly, Pete looks outward and despairs at his lack of close friends, yearning to be loved for who he really is. The title expands to the question "How many friends have I really got?" The sad answer offered is: "You can count them all on one hand!" Refusing to blame himself this time, he hits out at management – "When I first signed a contract, it was more than a handshake then" – and his fellow band members –

"we talk so much shit behind each other's back" – before finally rounding on his audience and critics:

People know nothing about their own soft gut
So how come they can sum us up
Without suffering all the hype we've known
How come they bum us up

It's reminiscent of Neil Young berating critical reviewers for being "no better than me". "How Many Friends" pushes Roger's vocal boundaries in all directions as he goes from a feminine tone in the verses to full-on rock front man for the chorus. The song's construction – powerful builds and dramatic break-downs – showcase the Who at their dynamic best. Keith plays some glorious tom triplets and Pete adds a great solo to the outro while John's high-end noodling underscores what is another great track, in spite of the gloomy subject matter.

In A Hand Or A Face

Townshend described this song as a cynical effort to "cut down the growing dependence I had on mysticism and psychic phenomena." While his material had never been more personal, the band still sounds like they were left to come up with their own way of interpreting the song – one of the best group performances on the LP. Highlights include the almighty guitar, cymbal and gong crash which kicks off the strummed electric guitar intro, Keith's signature tom and snare pattern in the verses and his final flamboyant triplet flourish, Pete's casually fired off wicked blues licks, plus more fine bass-work from Entwistle. Originally titled "Round And Round", this is a fine closer to a curious album – somewhat downbeat, but unbeaten; depressed but defiant.

Bonus Tracks:

Squeeze Box (Live) / Behind Blue Eyes (Live) / Dreaming From The Waist (Live)

All three bonus tracks were recorded live at Swansea City Football Club's Vetch Field Stadium on 16th June, 1976.

Using his "Dear boy" upper-class persona, Keith introduces a confident performance of "Squeeze Box" that features a fine Townshend guitar solo backed by incredible musical gymnastics from the faultless rhythm section. Keith interrupts Pete's spoken intro to "Behind Blue Eyes" with the words "We don't do 'Bell Boy'!" and after some more banter, there's a great live take of one of Pete's career-defining highlights. Finally, the band furnish a storming, passionate "Dreaming From The Waist". As the group raise the pressure, level upon level, accent upon accent, Pete fits quick-fingered runs in between monster power chords, Keith threatens to make sawdust of his sticks and John virtually sets alight his fret-board.

"[It was] the peak of our playing," the bassist would enthuse. "Every show we all came off and we were satisfied... that '76 tour, we were happy with every gig. We didn't want to change anything because we were playing so well."

Based on the lyrical content of *The Who By Numbers* material, observers could have been forgiven for considering the band's future uncertain. Feeling "like a standing corpse," Townshend had said after completion of the record, "I don't want to go on." How could he get back from such a self-eviscerating album to the more down-to-earth business of working in a four-piece rock band? Would the contents of that record clear the decks cathartically or drag him further into depression?

It seemed to do the former and the Who toured Britain, Europe and the US to support the album; they even broke the record for the largest indoor attendance at a show in Michigan. The band finished this successful year with three sold out UK Christmas shows at the Hammersmith Odeon.

1976:

Squeeze Box
UK Single Release: 01/1976 (Track) US Single Release: 11/1975 (MCA)
Peak Position: 10 (UK) 16 (US)

Surprisingly this was a sizeable hit on both sides of the Atlantic. The jolly ditty found the Who in a light-hearted mood, but the band were becoming disillusioned with the single format. John Entwistle told John Ingham of *Sounds* he found having a hit extremely embarrassing because of the poor competition in the charts from "Football teams, comedians, wrestlers, one-hit wonders."

Slip Kid
US Single Release: 08/1976 (MCA)

This laidback opener of *The Who By Numbers* was released as a single almost a year after the album saw the light of day. It was released in the US only, where it failed to chart. The American record company were using it as the now standard stop-gap as there was no new material to release and they needed the band to maintain a presence in the market place.

The Who were back on the road by late February '76. Financial necessity – brought on because the band's royalty income was mostly tied up in the continuing litigation with their former managers – meant the Who actually played more shows in 1976 than they had for many years. By June they'd played Switzerland, Germany, France and America, and had completed their legendary open-air festivals in British football grounds, including the seminal show at Charlton Athletic featuring the Sensational Alex Harvey Band as one of the supports.

Only two songs from the new album featured on the tour, "Dreaming From The Waist" and the very untypical "Squeeze Box". This long jaunt would see Moon's substance abuse problem worsen and his drinking escalate as he became increasingly self-destructive. He nearly bled to death in a Manhattan hotel room after slashing his foot on broken glass from a picture frame he'd just smashed. By this point, Roger and John were seriously considering the possibility of firing their increasingly unreliable drummer, but Pete couldn't let him go.

In an attempt to slow Keith's drinking, manager Bill Curbishley had him sectioned for three days in Florida. Keith's new girlfriend, Swedish model Annette Walker-

Lax, booked him into a Los Angeles rehab clinic which helped straighten him out long enough to make it to the tour's final date in Toronto, Canada on 21st October, 1976. It would be the last time Keith played on North American soil. Despite the drink and drugs, Moon was still performing at full-tilt. John commented, "That last tour with Keith was the peak of the Who's career."

Flyer for football stadium concerts

A month after the Who's tour ended, a group called the Sex Pistols released their debut single "Anarchy In The UK", on 26th November. This was the "My Generation" of a new blank generation, and rock'n'roll would never be the same.

The Story Of The Who
UK Album Release: 09/1976 (Polydor 2683 069)
Peak Position: 2 (UK)
Magic Bus / Substitute / Boris The Spider / Run Run Run / I'm A Boy / Heatwave / My Generation / Pictures Of Lily / Happy Jack / The Seeker / I Can See For Miles / Bargain / Squeeze Box / Amazing Journey / The Acid Queen / Do You Think It's Alright / Fiddle About / Pinball Wizard / I'm Free / Tommy's Holliday Camp / We're Not Gonna Take It / See Me, Feel Me / Summertime Blues / Baba O'Riley / Behind Blue Eyes / Slip Kid / Won't Get Fooled Again

This was, again, a gap-filling exercise released in the UK only while the band were on tour. They put together some of the early singles that they actually owned – they still had some contractual problems with previous producer Shel Talmy – plus excerpts from the omnipresent *Tommy*.

The front cover featured an exploding pinball machine, with the Who emblazoned on it. The exploding icon of Who history mirrored the band's own implosion. The open gate-fold inside cover featured notes from Roy Carr: "The truth can't be denied, though many have tried, no one can play rock'n'roll quite like the Who". He would find no argument from the folk who purchased the album, but were they still important? Releases by the Ramones and the Sex Pistols had galvanised a new generation: would the Who be relevant in these new musically turbulent times?

Substitute – I'm A Boy – Pictures Of Lily
UK Single Release: 10/1976 (Polydor)
Peak Position: 7 (UK)

Released to coincide approximately with *The Story Of The Who* compilation and to maintain a presence in the market, this did surprisingly well, reaching number seven on the UK chart. It was not released in the US. This hit surprised and pleased the band but possibly lulled them into a false sense of security: trouble was on its way...

10 Farewell Dear Boy – 1977-78

Almost three years passed between the release of *The Who By Numbers* and the band's next studio album, *Who Are You*. By the time the Who put out the latter, the music world was a very different place: the punk rock revolution, with the Sex Pistols, the Clash and the Damned at the helm, had well and truly arrived by 1977, and left many of the old guard looking irrelevant and sounding decidedly stale.

While punk rock had been fermenting and fulminating and then finally breaking through in all its nihilistic glory, the original hope-I-die-before-I-get-old brigade had been away from the fray. The new punk groups were supposed to blow away the old regime and usher in rock's Year Zero. Johnny Rotten wore an "I hate Pink Floyd" T-shirt, while the Clash claimed there would be no place for Elvis, the Beatles or the Rolling Stones in 1977. Initially Pete Townshend felt alienated by the new world order:

"We rushed back to England and had no new album," he bemoaned, "nothing happening, no feeling of existence, and every time we picked up a paper, there were snivelling little brats knocking us." Nonetheless, many of the new groups maintained an admiration for old lags the Who. Indeed, Pistols Paul Cook and Steve Jones would tell Townshend that the Who were their favourite group and would cover "Substitute". In return, despite themselves, the Who were drawn to the energy and attitude of the punks. John was enthusiastic about the new music, while Moon, a true punk rocker at heart, would later hang out at punk clubs like the Vortex and the Roxy. "I see a lot of myself reflected in their styles," he would tell *International Musician* magazine. "The atmosphere and the things they play. It's brash, which I love." Nonetheless, in a most un-punk style, Keith would show up at punk gigs in a Rolls Royce.

Roger declared the Stranglers and the Clash to be his particular favourites among the new pretenders, and felt, "Now it's even more important that the Who survive, because the punks are basically doing what we did years ago". Unsurprisingly, it was for the composer of "My Generation" that punk loomed particularly large. Pete Townshend, who saw shadows of the Who in the aggressive, uptight teenagers he witnessed playing in the London clubs, went so far as to claim in a 1977 article for the *NME*, "I'm sure I invented punk rock."

"When the new wave came along," he would reflect the following year, "I thought, 'aye, aye, we're not dead yet'. I felt it was the closing of a circle... The roots of practically every new wave band I saw seemed to be the Who." Certainly, Townshend felt a kinship with the working-class kids who were drawn to the destructive impulses both of his own band and these new angry young rockers. However, in some ways punk's unapologetic youthful vigour and no-frills urgency, bursting out from nowhere, while Pete was mostly tied up in meetings with lawyers and accountants, made him feel older and more irrelevant.

"Punk rock really seemed to shake Townshend up," Primal Scream's Bobby Gillespie, a punk and Who fan at the time, would reflect, "and you get the impression that he was trying to find a place for the Who in its immediate aftermath, and I'm not sure if he actually found it. Townshend had always written about how he felt inside, and just as he was trying to write about adult issues in a rock'n'roll context, along came the vibrant, youthful energy of punk, and he was like 'Fuck! We're irrelevant... How can we be relevant?'"

Townshend saw a Damned gig and felt "They reminded me of the Who in many ways... We used to have really quite heavy conversations about where music was going to go – particularly in this country – and whether we should be involved in it, and the problem of Moon living that Hollywood lifestyle and whether we should let the Who tradition just bash on until it got really boring, [or] try to force change by starting labels and working with other bands." Watching the Damned's drummer, Rat Scabies, also reminded Townshend of the extent of his own drummer's influence. "[Scabies] just looked like he was impersonating Moon," Pete insisted, "and getting pretty close to it on occasion. And I suddenly realised that Moon's drumming had affected a lot of bands and they were getting away from that tidy Ringo-style drumming which was really just an impersonation of black music."

In 1977, though Clash front-man Joe Strummer hadn't banished them to his list of acts that had no relevance for that year, the Who as a group, were nowhere to be seen. Away from the maelstrom of the band, Roger divided his time between his country estate and making a third solo album, *One Of The Boys*. Though generally eschewing ballads and representing a return to a rockier solo sound and featuring material by songwriters like Paul McCartney (though "Dizzy" isn't his most memorable tune), the Zombies' Colin Blunstone and Murray Head (the latter's "Say It Ain't So" appeared on the US version only), as well as three self-penned compositions, this was a weak record most notable for Daltrey's "The Prisoner" – a song about armed robber John McVicar who would soon loom large in the singer's life. Roger would dismiss the album as "a poxy, complete piece-of-crap album," which it wasn't, but it would be completely eclipsed on every level by his next solo work.

Meanwhile, John dabbled with ideas for a science fiction rock opera while across the pond, Keith continued going nowhere fast. Even Keith's loyal friend, personal assistant and constant companion, Pete "Dougal" Butler, realised the Hollywood highlife and high jinks could not go on forever. "I've had a great time," Butler insisted, but he had finally tired of Moonie's outrageous antics. For all their many celebrity drinking pals, real friendship was in short supply. "To be honest," Dougal confessed, "we were the loneliest guys in the world." With the offer of alternative employment, he flew back to England, leaving an angry, hurt, Keith waiting by the phone.

The year began with mixed feelings for Pete. The dragged-out litigation with Lambert and Stamp was finally resolved in January after a long meeting in a Soho office, and all the Who's rights were transferred to the band's control. However, due to some behind-the-scenes manoeuvring, Pete found that Allen Klein, who he loathed, had somehow bought shares in the company that owned his US publishing.

Settlement for American royalties owed to Pete came in the form of a huge cheque – at least six figures – but was an empty victory for him. He had control over his own material now, but he felt bad about his former managers and was appalled to find that Klein had a share of his future earnings. He adjourned with Chris Stamp to the Speakeasy club and got very drunk, before bumping into Steve Jones and Paul Cook of the Sex Pistols, who he harangued about the lamentable state of the music business. The Who were finished, Pete claimed, and it was up to bands like the Pistols to carry the flag. Pete ended up collapsed in a doorway, after apparently having torn up his publishing cheque in disgust. A policeman, who recognised Townshend, told him if he could get to his feet and walk away, he'd avoid a night in the cells. The night would inspire the keystone track on the next Who album.

Townshend subsequently threw his energies into a number of diverse projects. He finally opened his Meher Baba Oceanic Centre in Richmond, and he also laid plans to open the Magic Bus bookstore around the corner, and start his Eel Pie book publishing company. He made an underrated gem of an album, *Rough Mix*, in collaboration with fellow Baba devotee, former Small Face, Ronnie Lane. Free from the baggage of his band, Pete actually sounded like he was enjoying himself on this surprisingly upbeat, bluesy, folky set, and the quality of his writing boded well for the future. Unless, of course, he had already used up his best new songs on this solo project.

For John and Roger to use solo albums as an outlet made sense, but if even Townshend wasn't keeping his premier compositions for the Who, what hope was there for the group? Great runs of group albums from the likes of the Beatles, Stones and, even say, Pink Floyd, or later, the Clash, tended to come when all the band members' creative impulses were focused on the good of the main agenda. Once groups allowed this to get diluted by spin-off projects, the central band's albums would inevitably suffer. Would that happen to the Who?

With live shows off the agenda for the year, work commenced on a Who documentary project, *The Kids Are Alright*, much of which would be shot at Shepperton Film Studios, in which the band had recently taken a large stake. While other big acts of the era had their money in offshore tax shells, there was something rather admirable about the Who investing in their homeland. Townshend also looked to salvage and update his *Lifehouse* project, moving the events 200 years into the future. As well as working on a new script, he composed a number of new songs for the piece, some of which, in revised form, would see their way on to the next Who album. The *Lifehouse* revival was soon dropped, but Pete continued working on demos for a new group record, and studio time was scheduled at Ramport for that autumn, with Glyn Johns at the desk. By late '77, Pete had some 40 songs prepared for the new record and Keith had already, finally, received the phone call he had wanted and needed. Moonie had returned from the US that September with Annette to take up residence in Harry Nilsson's Mayfair flat. The Who were about to return to work.

1978:

Who Are You

"[Keith] probably thought LA was wonderful for about a year," said Entwistle, "but for two years after that, he had been waiting for us to tell him to come back. When we told him, 'We need you over here, we've got stuff to do, it's no use you living over there,' that was the only excuse he needed. Whoosh! He was back."

"I had a lot of fun in California," Keith said on his return, "but it was superficial fun... I got bored and lost sight of myself... I feel more excited, more enthusiastic about work and life than I have for years."

The sessions got off to a shaky start as Pete, John and Keith seemed happier shooting the breeze over a few brandies than settling to work. Alienated by this wastrel wantonness, health fanatic Roger would often not bother to turn up at all. When the group did knuckle down, it was clear that, in spite of Keith's optimism and his admirable desire to return to the fray, the drink and drugs had taken a heavy toll. Keith was out of practice and out of shape and his performance in the studio suffered enormously – he often needed visual cues from Johns or engineer Jon Astley to let him know where to come in or stop.

"He could play a drum solo for five minutes," John Entwistle observed, "but we were worried that he wouldn't be able to do an hour and three-quarters. There was no way. He was too overweight, too heavy. And he knew that. He was disgusted with himself." Townshend was keen to help Keith, and called in Freddy Clayton, a senior figure in Alcoholics Anonymous. Clayton spoke to Moon, and reported back to Pete that, "Keith has 'survivor' written all over him. He's not the kind of guy that fits in at AA, but I could help you!" A dismayed Townshend suddenly realised he was in denial, and that he too had a massive drink problem.

The difficulties in the studio weren't just down to lifestyle issues, though. Musical differences were a problem from the start. Townshend's demos took a very different direction from the previous Who album. Perhaps oddly, considering his enthusiasm for the new angry mob of punks, there was precious little sign of any punk references; instead, Glyn Johns told Who biographer Dave Marsh, Pete's new material was synth-heavy, jazz influenced and more art-rock in nature – mature music that was not easily played live. It was certainly a more studio-bound sound. Engineer on the initial sessions, Jon Astley – who also happened to be Pete's brother-in-law – would describe the material as tailored for US radio – a long way from punk or new wave. Johns liked the direction and was pushing the band for a new sound but Moon struggled with a format more suited to session drummers than a maverick musical mayhem-maker.

The band were using Pete's pristine demos to work to. These were the basis of the tracks so Moon was playing along to drum machines and strict arrangements – it was all too much for the out-of-practice drummer. He did get frustrated and play a manic solo declaring "I'm still the best Keith Moon type drummer in the world." But as Townshend remarked, "Unless you wanted that, you were fucked!"

Producer Johns grew more frustrated with Keith: "By that time, he'd lost the ability to do it." Johns told Dave Marsh. "The more he kept fucking up takes... the more insecure he got, like anybody would get, and of course, then it just got worse and worse." Johns had been unwisely trying to simplify Keith's demonic drumming as far back as the *Who By Numbers* sessions. According to Matt Resnicoff's sleeve notes, "Part of the concern was that the day's other insurgent musical movement, disco, had compelled record producers to aim for a more mechanical, less complex rhythmic feel, which was a potential stake through Keith Moon's heart." Keith's drumming was expressive and emotional and he didn't play well when outside forces tried to control him. When Keith was eventually given a free rein on the album's title track, he found his form again.

Roger also had problems with Johns' new approach – and may have felt some general hostility towards him due to the producer's closeness to, and extreme admiration for Townshend. Johns was keen to get the vocalist to try different singing styles, but Roger stuck to his guns. The disputes between singer and producer culminated during a playback of one song that featured dubbed-on strings, which Roger considered to be overproduced. "There are things you can do with strings that can be really good and exciting but what he'd done on this I didn't like," Daltrey recalled. "I don't like slushy strings. [Johns] said, 'What do you think?' And I said, 'Don't like it much.' He went up the fucking wall. So I think he smacked me, and I smacked him, and that's how we were in those days. No big deal."

The producer had finally had enough and decided to leave the project. He'd run out of time and patience. Johns had committed to work on Joan Armatrading's *To The Limit* album – having enjoyed some hit success with her previous record – and left the Who sessions in early spring confessing afterwards that by now he was "bored rotten." The band could have chosen to wait for him, but instead they promoted engineer Jon Astley to the producer's chair. Having worked on the successful *Rough Mix* recordings, Astley seemed a good choice.

"I still don't think Glyn was the right producer for that album," Roger reflected. "He was the right one for *Who's Next*, because we had already done all that kind of pre-production work, and all he had to do was mike it up and get it down on record and mix it. I do like the record, but basically the mixes are down to Jon Astley, they weren't down to Glyn Johns at all."

Astley would tell *Generations* fanzine, "They were at an all-time low when I took over." Pete was working in the daytime and Roger would only come to the studio at night, feeling that his voice wasn't warmed up enough until the evening – Pete would remind the engineer as he left the studio to "Make sure he (Roger) sings the melody." Incredibly the two band members saw virtually nothing of each other during the entire recording process. "Things had been going very slowly," Astley continued, "and Keith was in no shape."

By early 1978, after a spell at a health farm, Moon was seemingly in a much better state to record. With a new-found optimism, and encouraged by Jon, he was ready to turn in some good performances, but recording was further delayed in the first part of '78 when Pete cut his hand badly – preventing him from playing any guitar – during a family argument at his parents' home. Recording resumed with Glyn Johns back on board at RAK Studios (owned by music impresario Mickie Most), late in March.

Keith wasn't the only one Glyn Johns was dissatisfied with: Entwistle and Townshend were both drinking heavily; Roger and Pete were barely speaking. Much of the material was uncharacteristic of the band and Glyn was trying to make a record the band seemed incapable of delivering. Johns decided that Entwistle's bass needed more bottom-end to augment and anchor the bassist's fast techno-flash style. He brought in bass player Dave Marquee who'd worked previously with Pete on the album *Rough Mix*. The idea was not a success.

The troubled sessions came to a crashing halt after a single week. Keith still wasn't cutting it and, at dinner one night, Astley recalls, the other members of the band rounded on the drummer saying, "If you don't get your shit together, you're out of the band." This outburst worked. Keith stopped clubbing and later in May, with the band back in Ramport Studios, he laid the final drum tracks. The last overdubs were finished and with recording completed, mixing took place in May and June. The album hit the stores in August.

By this time, the band had already had to absorb news of the death of their original publicist, Pete Meaden, who was found dead after an overdose of alcohol and barbiturates on 30th July. Though an open verdict was recorded, close friends felt it was probably suicide. Meaden had been the first person ever to put any real faith or hard cash into the Who, but his career had not met with the same success as the musicians he had mentored. Though Kit and Chris hadn't treated Meaden especially fairly back when they "bought" out his contract, the Who had stayed loyal to their original Mod maestro.

"The last time I saw Pete Meaden, which was about five months before he died," Andrew Loog Oldham told the BBC, "he was basically being [financially] supported by people from the Who." The news of Meaden's death understandably shattered the Who.

In spite of his various drying-out periods, Keith continued to battle with alcohol and drugs, believing himself immortal. He had promised again and again to clean up and get his act together, but his real problems were deeply embedded. He really believed that he wouldn't have to pay any price for his hard-living. "If I feel like doing something I go ahead and do it," Keith had told the *NME* years earlier. "If I had some kind of morbid death wish, I never would have survived any of those times when I've crashed my cars. I suppose it's luck and the fact that I never think anything could happen to me."

On 6 September, 1978, Moon – accompanied by his girlfriend Annette Walter-Lax – attended Paul McCartney's premiere party at the Peppermint Park in Upper Saint Martin's Lane, for the film *The Buddy Holly Story*. McCartney owned Holly's publishing rights and regularly held parties in the singer's honour. At the lavish do Keith and Annette were seated at the top table, with Paul and Linda and journalist David Frost. Keith was in fine form and held court as usual despite the revered company. Some of the best-known pictures from the party are of Keith chatting with Small Faces drummer Kenney Jones – another Mod icon who would go on to play a much larger role in this story.

Keith Moon was found dead in his bed at Harry Nilsson's top floor apartment, number 12 Curzon Place, at 3.40 pm the following afternoon. In a painful irony,

Keith's friend Mama Cass had died in the same flat back in 1974.

"I knew he was dead before I went into the bedroom," his girlfriend said. "There was a very quiet quietness. Like the air stood still." The cause of death was an overdose of Herminevrin, a drug that had been prescribed to help Keith's alcohol withdrawal. The coroner's report concluded that there were a total of 32 Herminevrin tablets in his stomach, 26 of which had not dissolved. It was described as "a vast overdose" although considered at the time to be only twice the medical danger level; there was minimal alcohol and no cocaine in Keith's system.

When Pete received the news he exclaimed, "Oh God, he's bloody gone and done it." In an official statement he declared, "Now we cry the tears that can't be held back... We want the spirit of the group to which Keith contributed so much to go on, although no human being can ever take his place." Roger Daltrey declared it to be the end of an era. "He was the most original drummer in rock", he said. "We could never replace him because we've never met anyone like him. He was like a younger brother." It was less than a month after the release of *Who Are You*, with its cover photo of the band amid a jumble of electric PA equipment and cabling, and Keith Moon sitting astride a director's chair marked with the words "Not to be taken away".

Most of the newspapers were filled with eulogies for the passing of the wild man of rock. Some pundits, however, would not mourn Moon's demise. "We're better off without him," ranted Tony Parsons in the *NME*. "Decadent cunt driving Rolls Royces into swimming pools; if that's what rock'n'roll's about, who needs it?" Townshend would not forget this insult and would castigate Parsons, and his punk partner in crime Julie Burchill, in the abrasive put-down "Jools And Jim", on his 1980 *Empty Glass* solo album.

But Keith wasn't just the maniac the *NME*'s young Stalinist bucks wanted to see gone. For all his reputation as a hell-raiser, Moon was a truly original, creative artist. He may not have been the greatest technical drummer but he had a brash spontaneity, a creative imagination and a heartfelt passion. Just as he partied to the ultimate limit, Moon played as if his life depended on it. Away from the drums, boredom got the better of him. "He'd get up in the morning and decide to be Hitler for the day," his wife Kim would say. "He did do horrible things," Roger would concede, in 2005, when wrestling with the dilemmas of portraying all sides of the Moon in a proposed biopic, "like dress up as a Nazi but he could get away with it because he had such charisma."

Moon's demise surprised few of those who knew him best: "With Keith, it was a phone call that we knew was going to happen one day", said Daltrey. "He lived nine lives and I'd seen him nearly die several times. When people talk about living on the edge, they don't know what [that's like] until they had seen how Keith Moon used to live."

"His playing hadn't really deteriorated," John would insist. "Basically he was overweight, he couldn't keep up the pace in a proper show. I heard him play some of the best fucking drums I'd ever heard him play when we did the 'Who Are You' thing with Jeff Stein for the [*The Kids Are Alright*] movie... He played a drum solo after one of the takes that was absolutely fucking phenomenal."

The Who would carry on, but things could never be the same. "Here ends the story of the Who," biographer Dave Marsh concluded at Moon's death. "In its wake, a new one began, and even though it involved all but one of the central figures in the other story, it is a very different story indeed – ultimately, it's the story of a different band." It remained to be seen what format this new story would take. Would their drummer's demise liberate the Who from the shackles of their past and the burden of Keith's emotional instability, or would they forever be toiling to reclaim former glories? Though Keith's death was a tragedy keenly felt by the band and their inner circle, there was also a sense of release.

"When Keith was alive, there was a time when I just didn't know what we were gonna do," Townshend would reflect the following year. "It consumed me. I spent most of me time worryin' about the group; worryin' about my role in the group; worryin' about whether we should tour or not; worryin' if we did tour, it would kill Keith or me; worryin' if we should try and crack through all of the old stuff we've been doing. I became terribly self-conscious and self-obsessed with the band and the band's past. It's all gone now. In a way it's quite weird, because I feel it's gone to the extent that we can actually go out and do a lot of stuff without worryin' about it too much.

"It's something like a great expunging of problems has occurred with Keith's death. Obviously, we all need to see a purpose in his death or use a positive result from it. But... we seem to have a clean break, and I feel I can just go on the stage and do what the fuck I like. Still a little tied down by the old stuff, but I think we can get over that, get past it, getting past the history."

Who Are You was the final legacy of the original "'Orrible Oo". It made number six in the UK and number two in the US and the title track would become one of their better-known songs, but the album's overall reception would be muted. In his conclusion that "With the honourable exception of the single 'Who Are You,' I get the distinct impression that the Who could well be washed up", critic Pete Silverton was not alone. Other reviewers were generally unimpressed, either considering it hollow or merely uninspired. Writing in *Crawdaddy*, respected US writer Ira Robbins felt all the synths and strings were there to disguise a lack of inspiration in Townshend's writing and took no pleasure in summarising "*Who Are You* [as] a tired and old album, one that scarcely does them justice".

Pete would insist *Who Are You* was one of his favourite albums, admiring its cynicism and venom. For the majority though, this was a downbeat note to exit on.

Who Are You
UK Single Release: 14/07/1978 (Polydor) US Single Release: 05/09/1978 (MCA)
Peak Position: 18 (UK) 14 (US)

Released ahead of the album, this was a return to form for the band. It was not indicative of the rest of the album, but this more than proved that the Who were a musical force to be reckoned with. "When I listen back to 'Who Are You'," Townshend would muse, "I can hear that [punk] made me incredibly aggressive. But that's what that song was about. Being pissed and aggressive and a cunt!"

Who Are You
UK Album Release: 18/08/1978 (Polydor 2490 147)
US Album Release: 21/08/1978 (MCA 3050)
Peak Position: 6 (UK) 2 (US)
New Song / Had Enough / 905 / Sister Disco / Music Must Change / Trick Of The Light / Guitar And Pen / Love Is Coming Down / Who Are You

Who Are You (Remastered Edition)
UK Album Release: 11/1996 (Polydor 533 845-2)
US Album Release: 11/1996 (MCA MCAD 11492)
New Song / Had Enough / 905 / Sister Disco / Music Must Change / Trick Of The Light / Guitar And Pen / Love Is Coming Down / Who Are You / No Road Romance / Empty Glass (Demo) / Guitar And Pen (Olympic 78 Remix) / Love Is Coming Down (Work In Progress Mix) / Who Are You (Lost Verse)
All songs by Pete Townshend, except where stated.

It is back to the optimistic, gutsy Who, and not at all pessimistic like The Who By Numbers.
Roger Daltrey

Musically, it's impeccable, middle-of-the-road hard rock with a surfeit of synthesizers (used I must stress, with only a fraction of the imagination that the Bee Gees displayed on 'Stayin' Alive'). But, beyond that, there's an empty core.
Pete Silverton, *Sounds*

New Song
Townshend kicks off this sarcastically-titled, sardonic diatribe against the blandness of FM radio with a huge scrape down the neck of his edgy-sounding Les Paul guitar. His power chords have rarely sounded better but his lyrics are drenched in the disillusionment of someone who seems to have lost faith in his calling, considering himself to be singing "the same old song just like a vintage car". He is also uncharacteristically mocking of the listener with lines such as "I write the same old song with a few new lines / And everybody wants to cheer it / I write the same old song you've heard a good few times / Admit you really want to hear it". Still, the refrain that the same song is always playing on the radio is ironic considering Jon Astley felt these songs were made with US radio in mind.

As on much of *The Who By Numbers*, Townshend's lyrical honesty has curdled into hostility and cynicism towards the audience, while he once again agonises over the possibility that he may be merely reheating old ideas. It was a fear that would continue to plague him: "I think my musical vocabulary is unbelievably limited," he confessed. "It astonishes me. I'll sit at a piano or work on a guitar and think I've hit on something new, and then a couple of weeks later I'll go back and analyze it and realise that I'm drawing on a very limited 'goodie bag' of ideas."

Moments of inspired guitar work can be perceived through the glossy production, but the drums are standard rock fare, plodding along after, rather than directing things forward, meanwhile synths dominate. Townshend said "New Song" was the first song he wrote on a polyphonic synthesizer and this is evident. "Pete is into keyboards now, yeah," Roger would sneer to music writer Sylvie Simmons. "Well that's just a phase..."

Glyn Johns' production is crystal-clear and the music almost sparkles, but with the superficial sheen of AOR million-sellers like Boston or Journey – or even Phil Collins-era Genesis – rather than the tough edge of the Who's platinum back catalogue. None of the finished tracks on this album would feature the entire band recorded playing together. It was all built up from individual parts and overdubs – and it sounds like it.

From the opening track, it is clear that the sonic quality is certainly slicker than on *Numbers*, but, is this the route the band should have opted for at the height of punk rock? A stripped-down, more back-to-basics approach might have been more advisable, but the producer's eye was apparently focused on the USA's million-selling AOR scene, rather than where it should have been, on the noisy boys of the London new wave.

Had Enough

(Entwistle)

Unusually for a John Entwistle composition, the first of three on the album, Roger sings lead vocal here. John claimed that writing for Roger was the only way of getting more of his songs on a Who record, and the approach seems to have worked. This song, along with "905", dated back to John's mooted sci-fi rock opera.

"I had started a concept album along the same lines as *Lifehouse*," he explained. "My story was set in the future. The hero's name was 905 and he lives with this guy named 503 and they're absolutely identical. There aren't any women around because that's what they're eating." The bassist submitted this and "905" to the group when there was talk of a *Lifehouse* revival.

On synthesizer, was former Zombies keyboard wizard Rod Argent (who had also had a huge hit with his eponymous band, with the single, "Hold Your Head Up"). Argent had helped out on Roger's *One Of The Boys* LP. As well as the strings Daltrey loathed, Entwistle adds brass to the mix, while ex-Amen Corner singer Andy Fairweather-Low helps Pete on some pleasing harmony backing vocals. Underneath all the synths and symphonic sturm und drang, there lurks a simple, rather uninspired song whose only message is that "life is boredom, living boredom".

"I used an old Who trick," John explained of the tune's composition, "which is playing that sort of dum dum dum dum beat like 'Bell Boy'. I put that kind of beat to it and I used a suspended chord where you play just a C bass note and stay on the C and write chords around it that fit in. And presto! Instant Who song!" But not an instant classic. The result – in terms of composition, performance and arrangement – is well-made, but lacks passion.

Pete Silverton's *Sounds* review described the album as "middle-of-the-road", and this particular track is definitely one of the main offenders. It passes the time pleasantly enough, but it's simply not good enough; there's a complete absence of fire and guts. Released as a double A-side with "Who Are You", this was rightly consigned to B-side status.

905
(Entwistle)

John's second sci-fi opera relic here, "905" is narrated by the project's hero and features his own vocals this time. This follows a more obvious science-fiction narrative – perhaps influenced by Aldous Huxley's *Brave New World*'s vision of a futuristic, futile, factory-farmed existence – as the singer talks of his test-tube birth and incubated life. It shares a world-weariness with "Had Enough" – which ended by heralding the end of the world – as 905 searches for a meaning in his empty existence. Everything, he says, has been said before – we're all living a lie.

For once, Entwistle wasn't tempted to add brass parts to one of his songs, and Townshend's guitar also takes a back seat. Instead, an effective bubbling and bleeping Polymoog dominates the track's texture, rather than synths for synths' sake this adds a suitable futuristic space-aged tinge. "905" avoids the over-glossy keyboards and strings of some of the album's more overtly commercial songs, and with a laconic laid-back rock rhythm and a languid melody, this is one of the album's highlights.

Sister Disco

"Sister Disco" finds the protagonist walking out of a hospital into the biting wind, but is he saying goodbye to a ward Sister, or does Sister Disco and her "clubs" and "tramps" represent a lover or a whole scene? Townshend would swear he had nothing against "disco" per se, though he was keen to distance himself from the group and musical movement that had swept the nation in the wake of the success of the previous year's *Saturday Night Fever* movie.

"With 'Sister Disco', I felt the need to say that the group would never, ever, in any way do anything like the Bee Gees," Townshend told Barbara Charone. "We stand over here and what we stand with is alright. They might say we're boring old farts but we still feel more at home with the boring old farts than any of that crowd."

The lyrics hint at a kind of resonance in "cold, stormy seas" and "grief and disease", as the narrator declares, "I go where the music, where the music fits my soul, And I, I will never let go, I'll never let go..." Lyrically, there is sound and fury, but it seems to signify nothing much at all. Roger wasn't alone when he said that he didn't "necessarily understand what [Pete] was saying [here]."

Musically, "Sister Disco" relies heavily on frenetic synthesizer parts, replicating busily bowed strings and frantic fanfares. Pete had spent hours working on this with his ARP synth and was apparently looking for a threatening sense of pomposity. "This is a perfect example of the progression I was making towards theatrical music writing," Townshend explained. "I was trying to evoke absurd Baron Munchausen musical textures." Munchausen was an arch fantasist whose outlandish stories of his adventures were pure fiction. The parallel is fitting here, as behind all the bluster something feels hollow. There are some trademark Moon fills in the breakdown, some deft guitar-picking and a melodic-enough middle-eight, but it's neither a meaningful lyric nor a memorable melody. On "Sister Disco" the craftsmanship is there to see; unfortunately so are the joins and false starts. It all sounds too much like hard work – and, not enough inspiration...

The arrangement would be re-worked for live performance where it fared much better but this would never become a concert favourite.

Music Must Change

"Music Must Change" sees the narrator looking for inspiration and a return to former glories in a business that was reduced to just a matter of money-making. Though, when he bemoans that we're stuck chewing on the same old bone, and regrets that "we soared like the sparrow hawk flied / Then we dropped like a stone," it's not clear if the "we" refers to the Who or the music scene in general, or something even more nebulous. Either way, the Baba-influenced lyric looks for life in death and a natural creative rebirth to break out of a tired mechanical cycle, and is quite optimistic in its hope and faith that musical expression will rise from the ashes and triumph. Nonetheless, while the angry young bucks of punk were still pushing for rock'n'roll revolution, the change Townshend was looking for in music appeared to be something far more spiritual and organic.

Musically and melodically, "Music Must Change" has a muted jazz-blues atmosphere, ushered in without explanation by the ominous sound of a coin landing on the ground. "Visually I could see a kid walking down the street kicking a tin can," Roger would say. "We put footsteps on it so if you listen with cans on you've got this geezer walking down the middle of your head! It's eerie." Pete claimed that while he was recording the demo for this, he recorded the rhythm track by walking up and down in his tiled studio; he actually tossed a coin to demonstrate that as far as he was concerned, "The word 'music' had transmogrified into 'money' for most of the musicians in my age group."

Occasionally, the organ veers into show tune territory – and later there is a choirboy-style diversion from Pete – but the sound of tinkling and breaking glass, and some urgent understated guitar stabs, drag us back to the blues as the genre's staple lyrical themes find the singer waking up at night in an ice-cold sweat.

Instead of drums, there are accented organ strikes and some brief staccato slabs of electronic sound – as punctuation rather than rhythm. It has been claimed that Keith Moon's virtual absence from "Music Must Change" – save for a sparing contribution on cymbals – is a consequence of his not being able to cope with its 6/8 time signature. At one point, Moon is said to have confessed that he knew that what he was playing on this was "shit," however, Keith had no trouble with the same time signature of "They Are All In Love" on *The Who By Numbers* three years earlier – but he was in better shape back then. Band members' opinions on the matter differ.

"He just couldn't get it together," Daltrey claimed. "That was just when he was really bad on the alcohol. He'd just started to go for a cure." Entwistle was more guarded and loyal, "He literally couldn't think of anything to play," the bassist insisted.

In spite of what Pete would call "quite a weary backing track," some critics thought of this as one of the more effective tracks on the record, and perhaps Roger's passionate performance represents the album's finest vocal – trying to sing like Mose Allison, according to Pete. "Townshend wasn't even going to put that on the album," Daltrey told Barbara Charone in disbelief. "That's the nearest Pete's been to the street in a long time so it had to be on the album. The song was so good that I asked if I could stick a vocal on it."

Pete featured his new favourite toy, the Yamaha CS80 with a touch sensitive keyboard, on this and the resulting arrangement doesn't sound like any previous Who recording. Pete Silverton dismissed the LP as having "an empty core", a description that could well be applied to this multi-layered triumph of form over substance.

Trick Of The Light
(Entwistle)
In his third song on the album, Entwistle brings to dramatic life that age-old cliché, "What's a nice girl like you doing in a place like this?" as he vividly portrays a client looking for more than just sex from an encounter with a prostitute. Or is the insecure punter just worried that he hasn't performed satisfactorily? "Was I all right? Did I take you to the heights of ecstasy?" Was the prostitute really moved, or was it just a trick of the light? The besotted romantic wants this girl to run away with him, believing her to be the classic tart with a heart that only he can save. Wisely, and perhaps not for the first time, the girl takes the money, checks her watch and shows this dreaming punter the door. Lyrically, it's a witty take on a familiar male delusion.

Musically, this is a testosterone-fuelled, turbo-charged rock assault, which surges out of the speakers and nails you to the floor. Pete described the sound as "brutal" and the aggression is a welcome relief from the often mushy songs it nestles amongst. Eschewing John's traditional quirkiness, this heavy-rock bulldozer powers along on some tough riffs and a monster solo played on his Alembic 8-string bass. This may be John's most accomplished composition for the band to date; it's undoubtedly a powerful few minutes and gives a synth-drenched album a well-needed rock'n'roll adrenalin injection. This would see the beginning of John's leanings towards a much heavier feel – an almost "metal" approach to songwriting – leaving behind his more quirky musical traits.

Guitar And Pen
"A deliberate attempt to cynically evoke Gilbert and Sullivan," Pete would call this. And, duly, it does capture the theatrical feel of those arch-purveyors of Victorian comic light opera, William S. Gilbert and Sir Arthur Sullivan, though by incorporating a 4/4 rock rhythm, the overall effect is more reminiscent of one of Andrew Lloyd Webber's West End shows than *The Mikado*.

What's a poor songwriter to do? However bad things get, never give up your guitar or pen – an oddly incongruous pairing that brings to mind the better-known coupling of "wig" and "pen" that would better suit this musical arrangement. The protagonist claims that if the song is struggling to emerge, it must be all the more worthwhile, so stick at it – ironic for a writer who often claimed his best songs had been written very quickly. Yet it's a double-edged sword, as Townshend well knew, and the reference to smashed guitars underlines the song's personal relevance. It may seem worth the bleeding fingers and white knuckles if your "music proclaims", but what if all this effort and heartache leaves you angry and alone, with only the guitar and pen for company? As with much of Pete's songwriting around the time, the message is simply, is it bleedin' worth it? Yet a message quite suited to a *Who By Numbers*-setting is here subjected to an – albeit, tongue-in-cheek – genre experiment that would alienate many fans and critics.

After a low-key enough guitar and keys intro, staccato piano takes over as the group head towards Freddie Mercury territory. Gilbert and Sullivan-style choruses are soon joining our solo vocalist from both theatrical wings. Underneath all the rippling keys and show-tune bluster, Roger is in fine voice, and was a fan of this song in spite of its detractors. Indeed, in 2007 he would consider it the lesser-known Who song most deserving of rediscovery. "Something about it resounds strongly with me," he told Ken Sharp.

John was less convinced by Pete's musical experiment, but in spite of this and even though fans did not take to the song, the players do sound like they are having a ball. Keith even adds some tuneful backing vocals, Pete plays some mean, occasionally ragtime flavoured piano, and Rod Argent again adds keyboards.

Love Is Coming Down

With its title and chorus imagery reminiscent of the Baba-inspired desire for redemption, encapsulated in "Love, Reign O'er Me", Pete set out here to write a song about the inevitable triumph of the spiritual life. Later, however, he felt that the real inspiration for "Love Is Coming Down" came when he "sensed the end coming for the band – for me as its creative engine and for Keith as its physical heartbeat." Seen in this context, the song does take on a new eerily prescient meaning. Though it begins with the narrator feeling all alone in a crowd, reflecting on past failures and feeling like he is sinking, it finishes on a bittersweet mood tinged with an optimistic belief in second chances:

I'm not a loser
But did I really win?
I'm lookin' forward to doin' it all again

Musically, this is less interesting as the band fully embrace a US-friendly ballad sound more reminiscent of satin-jacketed, multi-platinum AOR giants like Foreigner and Chicago. We are as far from punk rock as it's possible to be and the lightweight tune is soon submerged under the grandiose arrangement. A beautiful string part, scored by producer John Astley's father Ted – overdubbed two months after the main recordings were completed – adds a melancholy depth that this song doesn't really merit. Keith proves here he can play sensitively when required, adding tasteful fills and fine cymbal work. Entwistle's playing is lithe and fluid, while Roger's vocal performance displays a level of tenderness for which he is all too often overlooked. The band certainly stray here towards the musical middle of the road, but fortunately they don't quite settle there. All in all, it's an accomplished generic drivetime rock ballad, but it is far from memorable.

Who Are You

The roots of this track lie in a synth instrumental that dates back to 1971, entitled "Meher Baba M4 (Signal Box)". Musically, there is a lot going on here as the main swirling, buzzing avant-garde synth riff and the beatific circular Sufi-chant of the choruses clash with the angry snarl of the verses. It's like all Pete's concerns of the day, lyrically, musically and spiritually, have converged on one final multi-faceted piece. In these six action-packed minutes, Townshend asserts his authority with inspired bluesy licks, and slabs of rhythm guitar, while Roger's furious vocal brings Townshend's heartfelt autobiographical lyrics to life. John adds flamboyant octaves in the choruses and Keith proves that there's still fire in his blood and energy in his tired bones. Rod Argent's piano seeps through in the quieter moments, as stereo-panned synthesizer lines pulsate vibrantly between each speaker. Through the convoluted arrangement of unexpected stops, crashed accents and breakdowns, the band build the tension, finishing on a final crash chord climax with Roger's devastating final demand.

Ending the LP with a bang and not a whimper, "Who Are You" is the album's one song that can genuinely be described as worth the wait. It's also perhaps the last truly great Who song.

The aggression and power of the band here is intoxicating. It's a pity the attitude behind this strident finale wasn't replicated on most of the LP's preceding tracks.

Bonus Tracks:

No Road Romance

"No Road Romance" is Pete's demo of a song that he submitted for the album but that was rejected. He plays piano, fretless bass and drums on this session recorded at Goring Studios. While not a classic, this is actually stronger than many of the tracks that did make the final cut. There is an urgency lacking from some of the other compositions and the theme is familiarly Townshend territory: the gulf between the attractions of stardom and the bleak reality:

> *When you look through the lights to the stage*
> *You see the man of your dreams*
> *You think his life's full of parties and love*
> *But it's not what it seems*

The protagonist rock star may seem like a hero, but his brow is creased with worry, he bites his nails and fidgets in his room in front of the TV, drunkenly phoning home, missing his family – he can't trust anyone who seems to fall in love with him; they are probably just riding his coat-tails. The song's sad conclusion: "There's never romance on the road... Just frustration and overload". It's another heartbreaking piece of autobiography that didn't bode well for its writer's peace of mind.

Empty Glass (Demo Version)

"Empty Glass" was originally called "Choirboy" and is best known as the title track of Pete's hugely successful 1980 album, which was widely considered the finest of his solo LPs, though Pete would claim it was a "cry for help" at a time when his life was in extreme crisis.

This is Pete's demo with overdubs from Keith and John, the latter adding some interesting bass harmonics in the intro, but the result, for all the lyrical candour, is a rather lumpy, bass-heavy plodder that is far inferior to the whirring synth-driven, heavenly-voiced, harmonious solo album version, which featured some particularly energetic lead guitar (and is discussed in more detail in Chapter Twelve).

Guitar And Pen (Olympic 78 Mix)
This early Olympic Studios version features a more aggressive guitar track.

Love Is Coming Down (Work In Progress Mix)
This unfinished mix features alternative parts for piano and bass.

Who Are You (Lost Verse Mix)
The "lost verse" version of "Who Are You" doesn't sound too many miles away from the finished master. Maybe the extra verse does ramble a little, and doesn't quite fit with Pete's account of his experience in Soho. It does, however, continue his questioning of rock's sense of complacency: "I used to jack my reflection / And jump in with my cheap guitar / I must have lost my direction / 'Cause I ended up a superstar."

There is, incidentally, also a superb bootleg of sessions and Pete's home recordings for this album available under the title, *You Are Who?* (Who Records WHO 78). Among the demo versions are unreleased gems like the fooling-around studio take of "Barbara Ann" from Shepperton Studios in 1977, which would be seen in *The Kids Are Alright* film, as well as "Peppermint Lump" – Pete's home demo of a single which was released by Stiff Records in 1979 under the pseudonym of female singer Angie.

The album reached a respectable sixth position in the UK but was kept off the number one spot on the US *Billboard* chart by the soundtrack to *Grease*, another John Travolta movie blockbuster. Its double platinum success was overshadowed by Keith Moon's death. His celebrity-studded funeral was at Golders Green Crematorium, in North London, in September.

Three months later, it was announced that the former Small Faces drummer, Kenney Jones, would join the Who. It appeared to be a good choice: Jones had shared the Who's formative experiences in the 60s Mod scene, had played on the *Tommy* movie soundtrack and was an accomplished musician. Townshend described him as "a tremendous blood transfusion. Not just as a player 'cause he's different from Keith, very much a backbone drummer. Kenney fits in very well as a person with the other guys in the band."

Roger has claimed that a supernatural experience at a séance was critical in the decision to recruit Jones and continue as the Who. "We were going to break up the group," he told US TV host Robin Leach. "There didn't seem much point in going on without him. But then, at the séance, I heard Keith's spirit talking loud and clear. It was just like being on the phone with him... I told him we couldn't replace him if we had a hundred drummers. He told me there was only one choice to make. And I made it. The group decided we had to go on and Kenney Jones was the only choice to take his place. It was what Keith wanted. We followed his decision."

Trick Of The Light
US Single Release: 12/1978 (MCA)
Entwistle's "Trick Of The Light" was released in the US only, late in December. John's "905" was on the flipside but did not chart.

Book Two

11   Are The Kids Alright? – 1979

Perhaps wisely, there would be no new Who album in 1979. Instead the group would concentrate on the stage and silver screen, touring with a new line-up and releasing two movies, the documentary of their career, *The Kids Are Alright*, and a film based on their 1973 album *Quadrophenia*. Work also took place on another Who Films production, the Roger Daltrey vehicle, *McVicar*. Spring would also see a West End outing for Townshend's opus, *Tommy*.

Kenney Jones made his live debut with the Who on 2nd May, 1979, at a well-received show at London's Rainbow Theatre, and the band then set off on tour. Now freed from the need to restrict their touring band to the original four Who members, they also hired a brass section for the shows and recruited John "Rabbit" Bundrick (recently of band Crawler and formerly of Free) on keyboards to augment the group's sound. He had also played on *Rough Mix*.

The Kids Are Alright

As the Who moved forward into this year of transition, it was perhaps a fitting time to re-examine their past. Two years earlier, the band had teamed up with a 22-year-old New York filmmaker and avid fan Jeff Stein, who set about tirelessly compiling footage shot throughout the band's career. Pre-production work on what would become *The Kids Are Alright* film had begun in May 1977, and filming of new material started two months later.

From the start, it was clear that the group would take a different approach to the typical rock movie. They were keen to retain a sense of humour and to avoid the pitfalls of po-faced movies like Led Zeppelin's oft-ridiculed *The Song Remains The Same*. "Most rock films are pretentious," Daltrey told *Creem*'s Barbara Charone. "They're made for the sole purpose of making Robert Plant's dick look big. This is totally the opposite. Within the first half hour we're made to look complete idiots. You need pretentious films but you also need the Who."

Stein had no footage of the band playing "Won't Get Fooled Again" and "Baba O'Riley", so a couple of gigs were planned to rectify this. By now the band was in rather bad shape – and the straightforward matter of playing two shows was far from the simple task it seemed. Unknown to anyone present, these would be the last performances on stage by Keith Moon. The first show to be filmed was a 75-minute set at Kilburn's Gaumont State cinema in December 1977, but because the band's performance was so poor, little of the film was usable. A second gig, at Shepperton Studios, was scheduled five months later. For continuity's sake, the band were told to wear the same clothes as the first show. Pete, Roger and John duly complied, but for Keith, typically it was impossible to find what he'd been wearing so many months earlier. The second gig proved to be a far superior affair and footage from this show was used in the final edit.

"It was Moon's film," Roger would conclude. And indeed it was. The movie turned out to be an apt tribute to Keith, although the work-in-progress screenings he attended had been sad affairs. The first saw him break down into floods of tears as he watched a rough-cut with Roger. Moon, who at 32 was the youngest member of the group, watched a 95-minute film which showed just how much of a toll the years of drink and drugs had taken on him. He saw himself go from a beautiful young boy to a bloated old man. At a second screening, Moon turned up so out of it that after watching a few scenes, he told John that he was "sure he knew the guy up there on screen." The guy on the screen was Pete Townshend.

Moon's travails aside, Stein and the band did a great job in creating a gripping celluloid collage of some of the Who's highpoints; the result is one of the most compelling rock documentaries of all time. And, in spite of the dark times, it had plenty of light relief. "First and foremost, the film is very funny," *NME*'s Steve Clark would insist, "and Keith Moon's untimely death in no way muffles the laughs."

Yet as the Who pundit John Atkins points out, "the film contains no footage from the definitive 1970-74 era," a flaw for which the new live performances of *Who's Next* highlights were no compensation. And the double soundtrack album omits much material from the movie, including the "Barbara Ann" rehearsal and the electrifying "My Generation" from Monterey – perhaps the inferior Vox amps used at that festival in place of the group's trademark Marshalls meant the guitar sound simply wasn't up to scratch.

More confusingly, the record includes different versions of songs featured in the film, and some material not featured at all. The soundtrack unsurprisingly veers towards the better-known songs in the film. Standard studio versions of a few songs would even take the place of more interesting live footage from the movie, and a TV studio recording of "I Can See For Miles" is included, even though the song didn't appear in the film at all, likewise the Kilburn live take of "My Wife".

The double album would chart well considering it was an expensive set of old material, making the number 26 spot in the UK and number 8 in the US. The critics were divided, though, many considering that in spite of the undoubted quality of some of the recordings, the exercise was pointless when the definitive versions of many of the songs were available elsewhere.

Long Live Rock
UK Single Release: 04/1979 (Polydor) US Single Release: 04/1979 (MCA)
Peak Position: 48 (UK) 54 (US)

Released to help promote *The Kids Are Alright*. This forgotten gem made little impact on either the US or UK chart.

The Kids Are Alright
UK Album Release: 08/06/1979 (Polydor 2675 179)
US Album Release: 23/06/1979 (MCA 2-11005)
Peak Position: 26 (UK) 8 (US)
My Generation / I Can't Explain / Happy Jack / I Can See For Miles / Magic Bus / Long Live Rock

/ Anyway, Anyhow, Anywhere / Young Man Blues / My Wife / Baba O'Riley / A Quick One, While He's Away / Tommy, Can You Hear Me? / Sparks / Pinball Wizard / See Me, Feel Me / Join Together-Roadrunner-My Generation Blues / Won't Get Fooled Again

The Kids Are Alright (Remastered Edition)

UK Album Release: 03/2001 (Polydor 543 694-2)
US Album Release: 04/2001 (MCA 314 543 6942)
My Generation / I Can't Explain / Happy Jack / I Can See For Miles / Magic Bus / Long Live Rock / Anyway, Anyhow, Anywhere / Young Man Blues / My Wife / Baba O'Riley / A Quick One, While He's Away / Tommy, Can You Hear Me? / Sparks / Pinball Wizard / See Me, Feel Me / Join Together–Roadrunner–My Generation Blues / Won't Get Fooled Again

Just give me a stack of Who singles and I can hear my whole damn life there... An open postcard to the Who then, with just three sentences: 'Keep on walkin' and don't look back. Be of good strengths'. And 'Thanks'.
Charles Shaar Murray, *New Musical Express*

My Generation

Like the movie, the soundtrack begins with an explosive re-recording of the group's third hit, performed specially for the American television variety series *The Smothers Brothers Comedy Hour*, and originally broadcast by the CBS Network in September 1967. Roger sang live while his band-mates mimed along to a specially recorded, initially more restrained, backing track. This version kicks into the outro section earlier than usual, solely for the group to smash their instruments for the cameras. Amid the destruction, the audio cuts to live sound for some feedback and cymbals.

This track is straight from the movie, where on screen, Pete smashes his guitar and Keith kicks over his Premier "Pictures Of Lily" drum kit while smoke billows from behind the guitar amp stack. After a brief drum solo, a huge explosion emanates from Moon's bass drum, which had been crammed with his favourite "cherry bombs" (this is the blast that would cause permanent damage to Townshend's hearing).

Roger has claimed that the preparation for the performance involved Keith getting a stagehand drunk: "He paid him a few hundred dollars and the guy put four or five times the amount of charge that should have been there. It went off like a grenade. It was a huge explosion, huge! I mean, the Smothers Brothers nearly got sacked for that. They got into a lot of trouble for that."

When the smoke had settled, Pete grabbed an acoustic guitar from one of the Smothers Brothers and smashed it to pieces. American primetime TV had never seen anything quite like this.

I Can't Explain

Another early Who hit re-recorded for US television, though filmed at Twickenham Studios in the UK, this time for the ABC weekly music series *Shindig* in 1965. This is a snotty, stripped-back version, more R&B than pop, that in spite of a muddy sound and the audience's excited wails, captures the primal stomp of "Louie Louie" and the raw energy of "You Really Got Me".

Happy Jack

The movie features a madcap safe-breaking caper sequence, with the original single version of "Happy Jack" as the accompanying music. The soundtrack album replaces this with a live version from the Valentine's Day 1970, Leeds University show immortalised in *Live At Leeds*. Previously unreleased at the time of *The Kids Are Alright*, this has since been included on the expanded CD versions of *Live At Leeds*.

I Can See For Miles

As with the opening "My Generation", this was performed on *The Smothers Brothers Comedy Hour* in 1967, and was another re-recorded backing track with a live vocal from Daltrey. Like the preceding "Happy Jack" live version, this did not actually appear in the film, but it's worthy of inclusion here. The new shimmering, shuddering garage backing track, all grunge guitar chords and searing lead notes, isn't the equal of the original, but it does add another dimension to the slicker single.

Magic Bus

Pete punches out the Bo Diddley beat on an acoustic guitar, while Keith supplies the familiar clave part. The throbbing groove provides a fitting backdrop for this raucous rhythm and blues workout of call and response vocals. In the film version, we see the group miming this original recording on the German television show *Beat Club* in October 1968.

Long Live Rock

Recorded on May 5th, 1972 at Olympic Studios, this featured effectively during the closing credits to the movie. In the light of Keith's untimely death, the lines, "We were the first band to vomit in the bar / and find the distance to the stage too far" have an added poignancy (for more see *Odds & Sods* Chapter 8).

Anyway, Anyhow, Anywhere

Although the Who made no less than sixteen appearances on ITV's *Ready, Steady, Go!*, this great, uninhibited performance is thought to be their only known surviving clip. Broadcast live on 1st July, 1965, it showcases Roger bellowing for all he's worth while Pete tortures his guitar with glee. Crucially, it gave Keith the opportunity to show off in front of a mass audience. Keith's outrageous showmanship was perfectly timed for the coming fashion of putting pop on television.

"When I started showing off a bit, the directors would notice," Keith later recalled. "There were two great directors, Mike Lindsay-Hogg (who directed *The Rolling Stones' Rock'N'Roll Circus* TV show) and Mike Mansfield (who directed 70s pop show *Supersonic* among others) and they started getting the camera on the drums. *Ready, Steady, Go!* and *Top Of The Pops* really treated the band as a whole, and up until then, it was just Billy Fury and his group or Adam Faith and his group. Most of the TV in those days was only a couple of cameras, one trained on the front of the singer and the other getting a side shot of the singer and they never bothered with the rest of the group. They were always there as part of the furniture. It wasn't until Townshend started smashing guitars and I started smashing up the drums that the producers of the shows began to realize that there was more than the singer in the band. They'd actually line up a camera for the drums, which was a first. People started to actually notice the drummer."

Young Man Blues
Recorded at the Coliseum in London's Covent Garden – traditionally the home of the English National Opera – in December 1969, this is a raw and brutal rendition of the blues classic.

My Wife
This is an excellent live version of one of John Entwistle's most enduring songs. It's one of the few moments of the ill-fated Kilburn State cinema gig that was salvaged, although it doesn't actually appear in the big-screen version. With John in fine voice, the band head off into an inspired extended power jam in the middle section, which resolves by twisting satisfactorily back into the outro choruses and a further rock workout as a coda.

Baba O'Riley
This was recorded especially for the movie, in front of a select audience at Shepperton Studios in May 1978. Pete's on top form as he punches the chords out of his custom Les Paul, and Roger glows with fitness as he rasps his way through this *Who's Next* highlight. Although Keith's health is failing – and this would be his last concert – he still delivers a solid enough performance, although the baggy drum sound doesn't help.

A Quick One, While He's Away
The Who turn in an energetic performance of their mini-opera for *The Rolling Stones' Rock'N'Roll Circus* TV special in 1968. Though the show would remain unavailable in full for more than 30 years – Mick Jagger was reported to be dissatisfied with the Stones' performance – Pete persuaded him to allow use of the Who material.

The Who display an infectious sense of fun in their segment. Keith bawls his way throughout most of the seven and a half minutes, and even strikes his sticks on the side of a floor tom which he had tossed over his shoulder. In the climactic section of "Forgiven", viewers of the movie can see droplets fly off the drumheads as Keith has covered his drums in water – or beer.

Tommy, Can You Hear Me?
Recorded at IBC Studios in London at the end of August 1969 for German TV's *Beat Club*, this appears as a mimed performance in the film version, although there's a surprise contribution from Keith at the close of its slightly extended coda.

Sparks – Pinball Wizard – See Me, Feel Me
All are taken from the Woodstock set which culminated in the 'See Me, Feel Me' finale at sunrise. It thrust *Tommy* back on to the *Billboard* chart.

Join Together – Roadrunner – My Generation Blues

This ten-minute medley was recorded at the Pontiac Stadium in Michigan at the end of 1975. Most notable is the concluding take of "My Generation" played as a slow blues – in the style of Mose Allison – the way Townshend had originally written it.

It's surprising how mean and hard this whole section sounds. The volume is not the only ingredient that makes these songs sound so powerful: it's pure, unadulterated, rock'n'roll.

Won't Get Fooled Again

Like "Baba O'Riley", this was recorded especially for the movie at Shepperton Studios in May '78, and features more brash, boisterous, full-on rock'n'roll. John Entwistle's fingers are a blur as they race up and down his fret-board, whilst Pete grinds power chords out of his Les Paul. Roger gives an aggressive, microphone-spinning, performance while a breathless Keith is wide-eyed and angelic.

In the final scenes, this *Who's Next* classic climaxes as Townshend smashes his Les Paul custom, bouncing one of Keith's discarded cymbals off the pick-ups. Keith climbs atop his massive rack of toms and jumps somewhat shakily into Pete's arms before the whole band take a well-earned bow. It's a poignant finale – the band's last live performance with Keith Moon.

Quadrophenia: The Movie

For five years, Pete Townshend cherished the idea of seeing his second rock opera, *Quadrophenia*, transformed into a film. Scripts were drafted and redrafted but, somehow, the time never seemed right. The October 1973 release of the album stretched further into the past – until British popular culture finally caught up with Townshend's dream.

When a young working-class Mod-influenced three-piece band called the Jam emerged from the '77 punk rock pack, with Rickenbacker guitars, Who-inspired target T-shirts, sharp suits, and angry soundbites, it seemed like the spirit of "My Generation" was reborn. "In The City", the Jam's Top 40 single (and Top 20 album) stole the title – and melody – from a rare Who track. The lead singer Paul Weller worshipped Townshend and, as his band became increasingly more successful, Weller's influences in turn inspired the Jam's fans – more and more young men were donning parkas, riding scooters, and rediscovering R&B. In October 1978 the Jam released "Down In The Tube Station At Midnight", which made it to number 15 on the UK chart, and had a cover of Townshend's "So Sad About Us" as a tribute to Keith Moon, on the B-side.

Though a few minor hit singles would not persuade the money-men to fund a major movie (and other Mod-revival groups like Secret Affair and the Lambrettas were yet to hit the charts), the climate suddenly seemed as right as it might ever be for a celluloid take on *Quadrophenia*. The acclaimed newcomer, Franc Roddam was recruited as director. Best-known for his pioneering reality documentary *The Family*, Roddam's reputation was cemented with his 1977 docu-drama, *Dummy*, about a deaf-mute Bradford girl, played by Geraldine James, who descended into a spiral of poverty and prostitution. In spite of the bleak subject matter, *Dummy* was watched by 14 million viewers.

Martin Stellman and Dave Humphries were brought in to develop the script. Humphries had cut his teeth on gritty TV cop shows like *The Professionals* and *Target*, as well as contributing dialogue for Slade's 1975 movie, *Flame*. Pete, Roger and John were co-executive producers of *Quadrophenia*. Though none would act in the film, there were some crafty glimpses of them inserted into the film: the cover of *Who's Next* is visible in a party scene, a poster of Townshend adorns Jimmy's bedroom and Jimmy is shown watching a fine early Who performance of "Anyway, Anyhow, Anywhere" on *Ready, Steady, Go!* Eschewing band members and big stars, the cast would be drawn from a bunch of virtual unknowns, though TV actor Michael Elphick would take the role of Jimmy's father and many a young star would emerge from the casting sessions.

Press ad for Quadrophenia, *1979*

For the central role of Jimmy Cooper, Roddam had his heart set on the former Sex Pistol Johnny Rotten, who'd reverted to his real name, John Lydon. If the controversial, former tabloid pariah Lydon got the role, the producers could count on plenty of media coverage. Lydon was certainly angry enough and smart enough to play Jim. But he didn't have enough physical presence to play the Mod Everyman – he was skinny, unhealthily pale, suffering from acne and decaying teeth. Besides, Lydon was preoccupied: between suing his ex-manager and working with his new band Public Image Limited, he had little time to spare. In any case, it later transpired the film's insurers would have blocked his involvement. He did however audition for Roddam in August 1978, showing up with greased-back hair and sporting a skinny black suit, white shirt, black tie and green army parka. He had even learned his lines. Townshend happened to be at the auditions that day – a classic encounter between the sullen young icon of the new guard and the Mod Godfather. Townshend, Lydon and Roddam adjourned to the Ship pub nearby.

"Johnny was downing lagers," Roddam recalls, "and Townshend was determined to prove he was as cool as Rotten, so he started drinking vodka, and in the end he was drinking it from the bottle. So I was in the middle [with] Johnny being very cool and surly, and Townshend trying to be magnanimous but at the same time, some of his old anger was coming out." Eventually, they headed for a punk gig in Camden, North London, in Townshend's large Volvo which, Roddam remembers, "Rotten thought was absolutely crass. Townshend by this time was massively drunk and still intent on showing off to Rotten, which was the funniest thing."

Roddam explains how, at one point on their journey, Townshend braked suddenly forcing the car behind – a Ford Escort with a family inside – to slightly bump the back of the Volvo. An enraged Townshend accelerated forward and then reversed into the Escort, repeatedly. As Townshend finally sped away, he almost hit a woman on a bicycle, missing her only because Roddam grabbed the wheel just in time. "Rotten just sits there," Roddam sighed, "completely impassive, all pale skin and spotty, saying, 'Daft bastard!'"

The role of Jimmy went to 19-year-old Phil Daniels who overcame a mysterious illness, contracted shooting *Zulu Dawn* in Africa, to win through at his second audition. A singer in an unknown London band called Renoir, Daniels had already appeared in several small TV roles, and his first major role was as Richards in the brutal television play about appalling borstal conditions, *Scum*. It was banned by the BBC for its uncompromising violence. Although he was to shine in a 1979 cinematic remake of the play, it was *Quadrophenia* that would make Daniels a star. Daniels' friend Trevor Laird had accompanied him to the audition, which turned out to be a happy accident. Laird instantly reminded Pete Townshend of an old drugs dealer he'd known named Winston, and he cast Trevor as Ferdy, the smart-dressing pill-pusher.

The first choice for the role of Ace Face was Garry Cooper, but he was recast as poseur Pete when Roddam clapped eyes on the rising star of the Police, Sting. The minute Sting put on the suit, the Ace Face role was his, though the director would later say that the movie's flashiest mover was actually a pretty hopeless dancer in real life. Gary Shail, who auditioned for the role of Spider, almost fell at the first hurdle when Roddam felt he didn't look tough enough. To prove his credentials, Shail invited the director to attack him. When Roddam lunged forward, the young actor performed a backwards somersault, kung-fu style, and landed some ten feet away. He passed the audition.

The female lead role of Steph was taken by future household name, Leslie Ash. Her key scene, a quick knee-trembler with Jimmy in a Brighton alleyway, almost never happened. Her real-life boyfriend didn't think she should do it, and negotiations held up filming for half a day. Talented 16-year-old actor Mark Wingett, later a regular on *The Bill*, was cast as Jimmy's friend Dave. After one too many bollockings from the filmmakers for misbehaving on set, Wingett threatened to quit mid-shoot. In another reference to the young punks that were making Pete Townshend feel obsolete, the only way Roddam managed to persuade him to stay was by gifting him a shirt that used to belong to Sid Vicious and apparently was still stained with Sid's vomit.

Phil Davis – another cast member of *Scum* – having failed to secure the lead role, got the part of Chalky, and Toyah Wilcox (whose big break had come two years earlier in Derek Jarman's *Jubilee*) landed the part of Monkey after repeatedly pestering the director – apparently Roger Daltrey later considered her the spitting image of his sister back in the 60s. Certainly, her then-plumper shape suited the look of the period more accurately than Ash's sylph-like figure. Just after the film was premiered, Wilcox released the first of many successful indie singles under the name Toyah and a successful mainstream pop career – best-known for lisping hits "It's A Mystery" and "I Want To Be Free" – would follow. The beach fight scenes in *Quadrophenia*, though, were all-too realistic for her; she broke an arm in the midst of one shoot.

Roddam cleverly insisted that his young cast hang out together and immerse themselves in the Mod lifestyle. The fact that the kids did like each other, partied together and adopted the Mod lifestyle they were portraying, helped create a strong ensemble and was an important factor in ensuring the effectiveness of the many improvisations that helped make the film so realistic.

As well as mostly favouring young new faces instead of established stars, the big-screen version of Townshend's second rock opera also took a very different approach from Ken Russell's *Tommy* in the way it took a concept album to the big screen. Instead of bringing *Quadrophenia* dramatically to life, line-by-line, Roddam took a more liberal approach to portraying the Mod spirit documented in the record, as evidenced by the fact that most of the roles mentioned don't feature in the original album at all.

The film also has some major divergences from the album's plot – Steph is a much larger presence in the film than the fleeting glimpse of her as the unnamed love interest in the album and its liner notes (where the scene of their quickie sex moves to a sleeping bag on the beach). Also, Jimmy works as a junior clerk in an advertising agency – as Franc Roddam had – rather than ending up as a dustman and instead of stealing a boat and heading for the Rock off Brighton beach in the final act, he steals the Ace Face's scooter and rides to the top of the cliffs up the coast at Beachy Head, a notorious suicide blackspot, before pushing the bike off the edge.

Instead of replicating the album's action, the filmmaker concentrates on vividly capturing the original Mod scene the Who would have known from their early days – what their manager Pete Meaden perceptively called "clean living under difficult circumstances". Roddam stays true to Jimmy's emotional journey, but instead of the flamboyant fantasy of *Tommy*, we get a naturalistic portrait of a working-class Britain that was already vanishing – the public bath-houses and outdoor toilets, stodgy staple food like pie and mash, grubby kitchens and grainy black and white TVs. If *Tommy* was fantasy, *Quadrophenia* is social history.

"It's making films in the British tradition," Townshend would tell Charles Shaar Murray. "Which is the only kind of film that I think we can make well, which is the kind of *Saturday Night And Sunday Morning* thing. I know it's depressing, but that's our cinema verite, if we ever had one."

The way the Who's music is presented in the movie is very different from Ken Russell's *Tommy*. The actors do not sing the multiple voices featured in Townshend's songs; no flamboyant rock stars litter the cast. Instead, the music comes in mainly as a motion picture soundtrack and mixes flashes of Pete's opus with a few new incidental fragments and some Mod favourites like "Green Onions", "Louie, Louie", and "Be My Baby". In fact after the opening credits sequence – which features Jimmy riding his scooter around West London at night to the sound of the Who singing "The Real Me" – music is conspicuously absent from many extended sequences. It is only when Jimmy starts to go off the rails that the album takes on a more literal screen incarnation as the original version of "5.15" scores Jimmy's celluloid train ride to Brighton, while "Bellboy" voices both sides of his otherwise silent encounter with the Ace Face, now in his hotel porter's uniform – confusingly, the singer says of the Face, "I used to follow you back in '63", when Jimmy has only just met him, in the summer of '64.

WORLD-NORTHAL   and   THE WHO FILMS
CORPORATION   LIMITED

invite you to a sneak preview
of the film

QUADROPHENIA

DATE: OCTOBER 30, 1979
TIME: 7:30 pm
PLACE: 8TH STREET PLAYHOUSE
ADDRESS: 52 WEST 8TH STREET
             (off Avenue of the Americas)
RSVP: (212) 223-8181

The American film premiere of QUADROPHENIA will be November 2
in New York City. Soundtrack to be released on Polydor
Records. Motion picture released by World-Northal Corporation

Interfering with the album chronology, the movie skips "Dr Jimmy" and "The Rock", and switches back to the side two closer "I've Had Enough" to articulate Jimmy's growing despair as he rides off on the stolen scooter, interspersed with flashes of the album's closing track "Love, Reign O'er Me" – which he punctuates once to shout "Me!" As the movie culminates with Jimmy, in the ultimate repudiation of his Mod identity, throwing Ace Face's scooter off a cliff, we hear the familiar train special effect from the record before the final sung line "He stopped dancing" reinforces the message that Jimmy is moving on. When the credits finally roll and the album version of "Dr Jimmy" dramatically crashes in, for the first time the music seems bigger than the images on screen.

This is a film which, for all its flaws, both dramatically brings to life some of the key themes and musical motifs of Townshend's rock opera, and stands alone as an exciting work of cinema – albeit, one powered by a classic soundtrack. Something neither *Tommy*, nor other ill-starred rock movies such as *The Wall* could claim even if they stayed truer to those original double albums.

But Townshend would soon distance himself from the movie. It wasn't that he didn't like Roddam's work, insisting "it was a good film," while pointing out that it was very different from the source work. "It's not true to my story," he told John Robinson in 2007, "which was more of a poem, I suppose. *Quadrophenia* is a story that must be told as a musical poem, a series of songs."

Posterity has also been much kinder to Roddam's *Quadrophenia* than Ken Russell's *Tommy*; it remains a staple of Best British Movie lists and has taken on a new life both on VHS and DVD. And it has had a new incarnation on the stage: in February 2007, the Royal Welsh College of Music and Drama staged the first official "workshop" production. Pete Townshend attended the premiere in Cardiff. In May 2009, a production of *Quadrophenia* began a six-month UK tour at the Theatre Royal in Plymouth. Using Townshend's lyrics, music and concept, it was adapted for the stage by Jeff Young, John O'Hara and Tom Critchley, and produced by Ina Meibach – a Broadway producer and former entertainment industry lawyer, whose clients had once included... the Who.

Quadrophenia Soundtrack

The soundtrack album of a movie based on an album does seem a rather inessential offering – especially when the movie is set in 1964 and the source music dates from 1973. Nobody would choose the quite bizarre, star-studded *Tommy* movie soundtrack over the Who's first rock opera, just as few would prefer this release to the Who's original *Quadrophenia*. But, that's not to say that this isn't a good listen.

Though it is sequenced rather oddly, much of the best of Pete's original Mod opera is here, remixed, and augmented by three previously unreleased Who songs. The track listing is rounded out with some fantastic original 45s from the early 60s by artists as diverse as James Brown and the Ronettes, and there is even room for both sides of the High Numbers' original single. But, nearly all the strong material here is easily available elsewhere and, though the film's popularity ensured this was a commercial success, the feeling remains that this soundtrack album exists because movies, especially musical ones, have soundtrack albums.

There is no escaping the incongruous mixture of original 60s R&B that Jimmy and his peers would have danced to, and the synth-driven 70s prog rock that Pete chose to score his story of Mod. Frankly, Jimmy Cooper would have hated much of *Quadrophenia*. Critics were quick to pick up on this anachronism and were generally hostile to the mix of Who music and originals. "As an album, it is a failure", concluded the *NME*.

Quadrophenia Original Soundtrack
UK Album Release: 05/10/1979 (Polydor 2625 037)
US Album Release: 06/10/1979 (Polydor PD2-6235)
Peak Position: 23 (UK) 46 (US)

Quadrophenia Original Soundtrack (Remastered Edition)
UK Album Release: 03/2001 (Polydor 543 691-2)
US Album Release: 04/2001 (Polydor 314 543 691-2)
I Am The Sea (The Who) / Real Me (The Who) / I'm One (The Who) / 5.15 (The Who) / Love, Reign
O'er Me (The Who) / Bell Boy (The Who) / I've Had Enough (The Who) / Helpless Dancer (The Who)
/ Doctor Jimmy (The Who) / Zoot Suit (The High Numbers) / Hi Heel Sneakers (Cross Section) / Get
Out And Stay Out (The Who) / Four Faces (The Who) / Joker James (The Who) / The Punk And The
Godfather (The Who) / Night Train (James Brown) / Louie Louie (The Kingsmen) / Green Onions
(Booker T & The MG's) / Rhythm Of The Rain (Cascades) / He's So Fine (Chiffons) / Be My Baby
(Ronettes) / Da Do Ron Ron (Crystals) / I'm The Face (The High Numbers)

Tracks 1-9 and track 15, "The Punk And The Godfather", curiously included and
sequenced though it does not feature in the movie – comprise recordings from
the double album, remixed by John Entwistle, who also added a number of new
overdubs, including a raw bass sound on most tracks, occasional piano and extra
guitar, and a flute on "Love, Reign O'er Me".

Roger's vocals were made more prominent – a previous bone of contention for
the singer – and John added some 7-string bass to "Dr Jimmy". Though critic Dave
Marsh would consider the new mix gave the songs "the punch they've always
missed", and John Svenson praised the new version, having felt the original
did sound a bit too much like a Townshend solo album, there was, in truth, no
improvement. The originals remain the definitive cuts. The remixed "Real Me" has
a completely new bass part, more upfront vocals and a proper ending, but it was
"5.15" – perhaps the song to most benefit from Entwistle's overhaul – which would
be released as the A-side single, though it wouldn't trouble the higher reaches of
the charts in the UK and limped to number 45 on *Billboard*.

Tracks 10 and 23 are the original two sides of the High Numbers' Fontana single,
"Zoot Suit" and "I'm The Face" respectively (see Chapter One), the latter omitted
from the original vinyl and from the Japanese CD. Track 11 is a throwaway new
number by a young Mod-revival combo, while tracks 16-22 comprise a selection
of fine original soul and R&B recordings that may or may not be appropriate to
the setting, depending on how much of a Mod purist the listener is. The covers
comprised the fourth side of the original double record set, but were dropped from
the first compact disc edition before being restored on subsequent CD reissues. As
Ed Hanel has commented, it's curious that, considering Jimmy disrupts a house
party by getting his Mod crew to jump around to "My Generation", this most iconic
of Who tracks doesn't feature on the soundtrack.

This leaves three previously unreleased tunes, written or recorded for the original
concept, resurrected with the movie in mind, and recorded or completed at Ramport
Studios in January 1979 with Entwistle as producer. Kenney Jones drums on "Get
Out And Stay Out" and "Joker James", while Keith's drum track is salvaged from
the 1973 recording of "Four Faces". Though interesting, there is nothing here to

question Pete's judgement in cutting these three from the original album, and their inclusion on the soundtrack was presumably an inducement for Who completists to buy another version of *Quadrophenia*.

Get Out And Stay Out
(Townshend)
On a rolling piano-driven rock'n'roll rhythm, this rather basic stop-start song lyrically just reiterates a variation on its name – "Get out and don't come back", rather than the title line – again and again. Ramming home the point alluded to in the original album's lyrics, but only actually stated in the sleeve notes, that Jimmy's parents have finally thrown him out of the family home, this was written to accompany the movie scene that illustrates this event. The instrumental track to this would be used in the film for a scene showing Jimmy and his Mod cohorts riding their scooters through the English countryside on their way to Brighton. Nice enough, but underdeveloped, this was written for the original album but soon dropped as unsuitable.

Four Faces
(Townshend)
Beginning by reiterating the point that Jimmy is now homeless, this rather unmemorable tune stresses the "quadraphonic" nature of his neurosis, "four heads in my mind"; "four faces in the mirror and I don't know which one is me". This originally had the working title of "Quadrophenia", before being re-titled "Four Hang-ups". While this track makes clear something vital to *Quadrophenia*'s conception – often only alluded to in the lyrics of the far more subtle songs on the original album – its simple first-person clarification is vastly inferior to the many-layered subtleties and dramatic expositions of Townshend's source work. Trying to pin down the multiple dimensions of Jimmy's fractured psyche so succinctly here, when previously it took four sides of long-playing vinyl to explain, was bound to end up sounding rather glib. Certainly, it's hard to imagine Franc Roddam finding a place for this in the movie's score.

Sung by Pete and musically propelled by simple piano arpeggios and featuring the odd vocal hook and an amiable refrain, this is pleasant enough but there is none of the ire, energy, or complexity of the original album recordings and the overall mood is whingeing rather than wistful. It's a reasonable addition to the soundtrack for Who fans, especially for the presence of Moon, but it's far from compelling and, again, this would have simply failed to make the grade on the original double record. Pete was right to cut it.

Joker James
(Townshend)
"Joker James" is an anomaly: a light-hearted throwaway ditty about how James (or "Jimmy"?) seems to alienate a series of girlfriends due to his penchant for playing practical jokes on them. All whoopee cushions and itching powder, this Townshend composition seems more likely to have come from Entwistle's pen. After a brief

opening flash of George Harrison-style guitar, this mid-tempo, piano-and-drums-driven track actually does sound like the Who. But, though it features a strong Kenney Jones drum track, trademark harmonies and a lilting middle-eight, it's hard to see what this pleasant song has to do with the *Quadrophenia* album or movie – the Jimmy of both projects seems far from a practical joker.

"'Joker James' was the first song I wrote for *Quad'*," Pete has claimed, and he told *Record Mirror* in 1972 that he'd written it around the same time as "I'm A Boy" back in 1966, and, indeed, the lyrics were published in a magazine in 1968. It shows that Pete had a very different idea of the character who would become Jimmy way back then.

"I took that song as the basis for the image of the kid," Pete explained, "the way he saw himself – as this kind of reasonable joker whose life doesn't come off but, in fact, on the outside he didn't appear that way at all and he was very far from being a joker."

In fact, Pete was still planning to include this song in the *Quadrophenia* running order when the band entered the studio. But then the material took, what Pete described as, a very different turn. "As soon as the band started laying down backing tracks at Battersea," Pete continued, "it didn't feel like the *Quad* that I thought was going to come out. It was much heavier, much more brutal, and so I dropped it." It was the right decision.

5.15 – I'm One
UK Single Release: 09/1979 (Polydor) US Single Release: 09/1979 (MCA)
Peak Position: 45 (US)
Released to help promote *Quadrophenia*.

The Who went back on the road, but the US tour was to become infamous because of one tragic night in Ohio. On 3rd December, 1979, at the Riverfront Coliseum in Cincinnati, eleven fans were trampled to death as the doors were opened, and a stampede ensued. The band played on – oblivious; they weren't informed until after they'd finished their performance and were soon facing criticism from all quarters.

"The stampede could have happened at any rock concert," Townshend insisted. And, indeed, Dave Marsh put the blame on the venue for its festival-seating arrangements – a lack of seats on the venue's main floor. "But that doesn't mean you don't feel guilty," Townshend added. "It was a symbolic moment and we could have handled it right, but we didn't."

12 Can't Face It – 1980-81

If the tail end of the 1970s seemed a bleak and violent time in the UK, 1980 brought the dawn of what would become an arguably more brutal decade. These years would become synonymous with Margaret "there's no such thing as community" Thatcher's Tory party, union-bashing, nuclear proliferation, the Falklands war and the rise of the unabashed new "greed is good" breed of millionaire.

Yet, Pete Townshend was too busy sinking into dissolution and joyless promiscuity to notice, never mind speak out. His wife had finally tired of his drinking and he was living out of hotels and above a shoe shop on London's Kings Road, strung out on cocaine and partying hard in the city's pubs and clubs with a celebrity social-set whom he both loved and loathed. Haunted by the ghosts and guilt of the Cincinnati tragedy, and by his own demons, Townshend would later claim to have been drunk for the entire year.

"I was just so socially demented," he reflects, "that I didn't know what I was doing." But in April, he released an acclaimed and commercially successful solo album, *Empty Glass*, from which he notched up a US number nine single with "Let My Love Open The Door". The LP would make it to 11 in the UK chart and five in the US, where it would eventually go platinum. It was as if Pete had found a purpose, and he wanted to keep on working. The album was packed with energy and ideas and Townshend sounded creatively reinvigorated. Throughout the solo album, the arrangements are creative, the lyrics adept and heartfelt, keyboards sparingly effective, while bluesy harmonica flashes in just the right places, and the guitars are never overdone. Even where a more US-radio friendly touch endows "A Little Is Enough", it doesn't sound crass; it actually works. Townshend's voice has rarely sounded more moving.

This album showed that he had taken just enough from punk's back-to-basics approach to avoid becoming a copyist or a parody. There is not a weak song out of the ten, and the title track, in particular, is electrifying: hammering, slashing guitar riffs and roared vocals. But, underneath the apparent rock'n'roll posturing of this razor edge rocker, is a real world-weariness, from the days of "Hope I die before I get old" to "Why was I born to die? Life is useless ". Pete would insist that *Empty Glass* was "a cry for stability... a cry for an empty glass, for sobriety and a return to values that I held above everything else. But," he would insist, "the reason the cry was authentic was that I was in real trouble."

"My life's a mess", Pete would sing in the haunting slow middle section of the title track, "...I stand here at the bar, I hold an empty glass". It was ironic that the success of *Empty Glass* coincided with Pete's drug and drink-fuelled decline. His career was on the rise while his personal life continued to collapse.

By the time *Empty Glass* was released, the Who's production company, Who Films, was preparing to release its new project – a gritty biopic of the now-reformed armed robber John McVicar. Roger Daltrey was cast as Britain's former Public Enemy Number One, who'd been released on parole after serving 11 years of a 26-year sentence and was now making a living as a writer. Roger had been gripped by the story ever since hearing McVicar described by police as "the most dangerous man in Britain".

"From the time I first met John McVicar, I was struck by the idea of making a film about him," Daltrey said. He bought the film rights to the autobiography that McVicar had written while in jail, seeing in the former criminal, a dark mirror image of his own macho alpha-male self. "I identify with him because his life is so similar to mine," Daltrey explained. "When you're on the street there's only so many ways out. I've got a big machismo, that whole fuckin' male thing. And he's the same. But he can't sing. So he's gotta have a fast car and flash suits and you don't get that workin' at Ford's in Dagenham.

"So he robs a bank. I understand the rush he got from it. I was lucky. I found rock'n'roll, otherwise I would have ended up the same way." Shorn of his golden curls, and looking lean and mean, Roger gave the performance of his career in a gritty Brit crime flick that has stood the test of time better than any other Who film. The action is split between a convincing jail setting and McVicar's post-prison life in London. The excellent supporting cast included Roger's friend Adam Faith and arch thespian Stephen Berkoff.

There had been initial talk of Townshend scoring the film but, instead, a team of highly accomplished and commercially-proven songsmiths was assembled including Russ Ballard (ex-Argent), the writer of a string of hit singles including Colin Blunstone's "I Don't Believe In Miracles", Three Dog Night's "Liar", Hot Chocolate's "So You Win Again", and Rainbow's "Since You've Been Gone". He'd also produced and written three songs for Daltrey's *Ride A Rock Horse* album. Joining him was Billy Nicholls, a close friend of Townshend's, who'd had a hit single with the Leo Sayer song "Can't Stop Loving You" in 1977. A fellow Baba devotee and native West Londoner, Nicholls had helped Townshend arrange the choir for the *Tommy* movie soundtrack and the two would later collaborate on Baba-related projects. In a musical relationship spanning 30 years, Billy would later join various live line-ups of the Who (in 1989, 1993, 1996 and 2000).

Jeff Wayne produced the album at Advision Studios in London; Daltrey's vocals were recorded separately at Air Studios on the island of Montserrat. To do justice to the first-class songwriting, a fine band was assembled comprising Pete, John, Kenney and John "Rabbit" Bundrick supplemented by bass virtuoso Herbie Flowers ("Walk On The Wild Side", "Space Oddity", founder of Sky), drummer Dave Mattacks (Fairport Convention) and guitarist Jo Partridge (*War Of The Worlds*). Of the original eight songs – later CDs would add two Jeff Wayne tracks of incidental music – there is not a moment of filler here: a rare state of affairs for a soundtrack album. The highlights are many, including piano-ballad "Just A Dream Away" which shimmers with guitar hooks; the slow McCartney-esque swing of "White City Lights" – perhaps adding to the song's authenticity, composer Billy

Nicholls was born on the White City estate in West London – and "Waiting For A Friend". Russ Ballard's bass-driven revenge rocker "My Time Is Gonna Come" adds a whole new sense of menace to the template of the *Batman* theme to come up with a classic rock anthem that shares the spirit and energy of AC/DC's "A Touch Too Much" with Ballard's hits for Rainbow. Ballard does as good a job as Pete ever did in giving Roger something suitably macho and belligerent to sing here:

> *Load up your bullets*
> *Shot me through the head*
> *Gasp from where you're standing*
> *You might think I'm dead*
> *When I hit the ground*
> *Look at me bleed*
> *Old man your sympathy*
> *Is something I don't need*

The album was released on Polydor in June, 1980. It gave Daltrey his biggest singles success in years with Nicholls' ballad "Without Your Love", which made it to number 20 on the US chart.

With a dramatic role to play, quality songs of bitterness and resentment to sing, and backed by his old sparring partners and the cream of session players, Roger finds form and direction here that he would struggle to recapture on other solo albums, where his choices of collaborators and material would often be found wanting. This album had the edge, the anger, and the musical hooks, that the next two Who studio albums would lack.

Townshend had also been busy with another musical project – making demos for a forthcoming Who album. When he played the tapes to the rest of the band, no-one said a word; nothing. Pete grabbed his tapes and walked out.

Insiders had long been muttering that Pete may have been tempted to save his best material for his own projects. Contractually, he had to deliver plenty of new material both for his solo records and his group's. But with more than one outlet now, would Pete ever turn up to a Who rehearsal with a dozen of his absolute best songs? Daltrey had admired Townshend's previous solo album *Empty Glass*, but felt that the songs on it could have made the basis for an even better record: "It could have been a great, great [Who] album," he'd insist and he was right. There would be very little on the next Who album to match the ire and energy of *Empty Glass*.

The band went back into the studio. For a group so impressed by punk's raw energy – and who would invite the Clash to support them on a US tour – they opted to use producer, Bill Szymczyk, best-known for his multi-platinum success with the California-based 70s soft-rock hedonists the Eagles. Pete's friend Joe Walsh was now an Eagle, and Townshend had known Bill socially for ten years. Perhaps, as Szymczyk felt, Pete was looking for a new beginning for the Who's first original post-Keith album. But recording was beset by tensions and delays: it was a slow process fraught with personality clashes. Szymczyk's painstaking approach to constructing tracks was very different to the Who's fast and furious way of recording live.

"We'd do three backing tracks and then take a break," Entwistle complained, "and then do three more of the same thing. I think that the backing tracks took us ages for that album. Then [Bill] would take a group of three of the best ones and cut them to little pieces and stick them back together again. And we were doing stuff like, 'I prefer that bit because of the bass and there's a good drum break there. I want that bit.' It just seemed an incomplete way of recording."

When the sessions were finally complete, the producer adjourned to his own Florida studio with the tapes and mixed them himself. Pete flew in to make some suggestions but it was Szymczyk's mix, and the results would not be popular with the band.

1981:

Face Dances

The Who went back on the road with a UK tour that kicked off in Leicester on 25th January. Townshend was in bad shape and hit a new low at a 4th February show at London's Finsbury Park. He allegedly knocked back four bottles of brandy on stage and deliberately played badly – long drawn-out solos packed with bum notes.

"I knew that everybody's friends and family were there and I deliberately picked that day to fuck up the show," Pete would confess. "I just ceased to care. I threw my dignity away." The others were incensed by his bad behaviour and the public humiliation. Roger was particularly disillusioned: "It ended it all for me." The shows that followed were lacklustre; the band were trading on past glories and appeared to have nothing new to offer. Audience responses were mixed and the group members continued to drift further apart. Not even a Top 10 single in March – "You Better You Bet" – could inject life into the band or their tour. By the time the UK dates were completed on March 16th, the atmosphere was so bad that the Who cancelled the scheduled US shows. It appeared like the end was in sight.

"The Who were sleepwalking along the edge of a cliff," Pete would reflect. "The band had become a celebration of itself and was slowly grinding to a halt. But no one would make a decision to call it a day." In spite of it all, by 28th March, 1981, the release of the new Who album was eagerly awaited – it had been well over two years since *Who Are You* and expectations were high.

The original intention had been to name the new record, simply the Who. This would signify that though the band name remained the same, this was a new beginning. At the last minute, Townshend decided to call it *Face Dances*. He'd coined the phrase while observing a girl he knew, move a match between her teeth in time to the beat of a song.

"It was only later," he explained, "that someone pointed out to me that in [Frank Herbert's science-fiction] *Dune* trilogy there are a group of characters called 'face dancers,' sort of like chameleons; they can change completely for special purposes." It's easy to see why such an image would appeal to the continually-shifting songwriter. Ironically, the song "Face Dances" was omitted from the album's final running order. The band had rejected it, making the title concept a tad meaningless. Townshend would later release the song as "Face Dances Part Two" on a solo album. As *Rolling Stone*'s reviewer pointed out, the new album's moniker sounded more reminiscent of 80s Genesis than the Who.

Tour programme, 1981

The album sleeve, however, was quite extraordinary. Directed by *Sgt Pepper* cover designer and Pop Art leading light Peter Blake, it features a grid of 16 portraits – four each, of the band members, painted from photographs on 6" by 6" canvas by some of the finest contemporary artists of the day – Richard Hamilton [Pete], David Hockney [Roger], RB Kitaj [John], and Blake himself [Kenney]. The results were beautiful, inspiring, challenging, striking and haunting. For once the cover really was art. The music would struggle to live up to such superb packaging.

Bill Szymczyk genuinely seemed to believe that it did; he was convinced he had a classic on his hands. He believed that Kenney was the perfect replacement for Keith Moon and Pete's writing had never been better. "The songs that Pete Townshend wrote are just amazing," Szymczyk insisted before its release, "and when I can stand back from it and listen to it as a whole, the album is brilliant... I really love the record."

Szymczyk told *Creem* magazine that the band were "tighter personally and musically than they have been for a time. I think the punk thing really stirred Pete's juices and his material now just explodes on the tracks. I think he's back to writing the kind of material there was on *Who's Next*." He conceded, "It was such a big deal to me that I can't be certain that I'm being completely objective about it."

This was something of an understatement. To see *Face Dances* as on a par with *Who's Next* shows a staggering level of delusion. Townshend, himself, was more realistic: "I did a lot of demos at Sigma Studios in LA, and Rickie Lee Jones was in one studio and the Doobie Brothers were in another studio and the atmosphere was just absolutely extraordinary," Pete reflected. "I did some really good songs, but then we went home and came up with one of the most insipid albums that we ever produced. I don't know what went wrong; I think I was just working too hard."

The results of Pete's labours were certainly an odd mixture: the songs are drenched in keyboards, and submerged in the glossy West Coast radio-friendly sheen of Eagles-producer Szymczyk. Yet, though often unmemorable, some of Pete's new material does retain a certain cachet. Entwistle would blame the album's woes on the dominance of the keyboards and a lack of Townshend guitar solos, maintaining his own tracks were the only "two strong guitar songs" on the record. Certainly, John's two compositions are more energetic and raw than any of Pete's new tunes, but they get stuck in an unremarkable, mainstream heavy rock cul-de-sac.

Kenney Jones was sure the problem was the choice of Szymczyk: "I liked the songs, but I just thought the chemistry of the band and producer wasn't right," the drummer would say. "The sound was too laid-back, like rubber. It simply wasn't right."

Daltrey, for his part, would place much of the blame on the hapless Kenney. Initially, perhaps relieved at no longer having to deal with all of Keith's excesses, Roger had optimistically claimed: "The band is now different, but I think it's better." Still, he probably didn't even believe it when he said it, and before long he was telling anyone who would listen that Kenney's "drumming stinks."

"Listen to the drums on that album," Roger begged a journalist, "and you tell me if they're any fucking good." This was unfair: Kenney was a good player – professional and highly proficient, skilled and committed. It simply confirms that it had been Keith Moon whose inspired madcap magic had completed Townshend's musical vision. "Kenney was harshly treated by the Who," the group's PR Keith Altham maintains, "when... they decided that perhaps [he was] not the right man to fill Moon's boots; as though anyone could."

Jones's years of holding his own against the likes of Steve Marriott had left him with a thick skin, and he could cope with levels of abuse that might have scared off other musicians. Roger would curb his criticism of Kenney over time, but he would maintain that the drummer just wasn't what the Who needed: "I'm not saying he's a bad drummer," Roger insisted. "I'm not saying he's a bad guy... but I just felt he wasn't the right drummer for the Who. It's like having a wheel off a Cadillac stuck onto a Rolls Royce. It's a great wheel but it's the wrong one."

Daltrey too would mellow over his initial dislike of *Face Dances*: "It was a little overproduced," he would conclude in 2007, "but the songs are great." The problem with this and subsequent records, he would insist, was that they had such a hard act to follow: "You come out of *Who's Next* and *Quadrophenia* and *Who Are You*, it's a tough call to follow that and have almost every track perfect." While the latter perhaps doesn't deserve to be linked with the former two, Daltrey does have a point. The Who were no longer the same group and yet they would be forever judged against the highpoints of their previous incarnation. But, the problem wasn't just by comparison. Judged purely in isolation, *Face Dances* would still be found wanting.

"It didn't seem to do anything or go anywhere," Pete concluded. "And I couldn't work out why." Although the record sold well at the time, propelled up the charts by the success of the catchy single, most critics were not overly impressed – though the *Boston Globe*'s reviewer considered it the Who's best since *Quadrophenia*. Instead of an event, a new Who album was now just a collection of well-recorded songs: not unwelcome, but not essential. "Neither triumph nor failure", concluded *Rolling Stone*'s Tom Carson, giving it a fence-sitting two-and-a-half stars out of five. To Carson it was interesting as another instalment in the Who's musical journey but, by any measure, he felt it to be a slight piece of work.

Ira Robbins summed things up by damning with faint praise: *"Face Dances* is an excellently produced and performed collection of well-written and up-to-date sounding songs by a band of legendary status... In context with the Who's enormous and illustrious body of work, *Face Dances* is a pleasant and rather meaningless album that proves, not the Who's continuing genius, but rather their ability to churn out 'product', watered down from their days of glory". The "product" would indeed shift units, reaching number one in the UK and number four in the US. Yet, it did appear to confirm that the band were unlikely to regain their past musical heights. Worse, the catalogue of tragedies which accompanied the album's genesis, completion and promotion, cast a shadow over the group's artistic future. Within a year, Pete Townshend's life would be teetering on the brink of disaster.

You Better You Bet
UK Single Release: 02/1981 (Polydor) US Single Release: 09/1981 (Warner Bros)
Peak Position: 9 (UK) 18 (US)
The song was good, the band sounded on form and Kenney played tastefully. It was accompanied by a strikingly stark black and white video that found Pete looking a little rough round the edges but the band looked "together" nonetheless. The record was a hit on both sides of the Atlantic and to fans, all looked reasonably well in the new Who camp.

Face Dances
UK Album Release: 16/03/1981 (Polydor 2302 106 WHOD 5037)
US Album Release: 03/1981 (Warner Bros WB HS 3516)
Peak Position: 2 (UK) 4 (US)
You Better You Bet / Don't Let Go The Coat / Cache Cache / The Quiet One / Did You Steal My Money / How Can You Do It Alone / Daily Records / You / Another Tricky Day

Face Dances (Remastered Edition)
Remixed by Jon Astley
UK Album Release: 05/1997 (Polydor 537 695-2)
US Album Release: 06/1997 (MCA MCAD 11634)
You Better You Bet / Don't Let Go The Coat / Cache Cache / The Quiet One / Did You Steal My Money / How Can You Do It Alone / Daily Records / You / Another Tricky Day / I Like Nightmares / It's In You / Somebody Saved Me / How Can You Do It Alone (Live) / The Quiet One (Live)
All songs by Pete Townshend except where stated.

The biggest surprise on Face Dances *is producer Bill Szymczyk. It's unexpected because Townshend would still appear to be more at home in a public bar than the Hotel California. The result is to smooth out a lot of the Who's harsh edges... I've*

got used to both the Who's strengths and weaknesses and I don't like seeing them
glossed over.
Hugh Fielder, *Sounds*

You Better You Bet

In a curious symmetry, while the last original Who album finished with its best
and best-known title cut, the new Who line-up began their recorded debut with
its strongest track: a twisted Townshend love song that takes in lust and longing,
heartbreak and booze.

"I developed the song over several weeks of clubbing and partying," Townshend
explained. "I had gone through a lean period in my marriage and was seeing the
daughter of a friend of mine. I wanted it to be a good song because the girl I wrote
it for is one of the best people on the planet." It's touchingly honest and extremely
convincing in its autobiographical nature – few rock stars admit to listening to their
own records, never mind courting a girlfriend to them. But it's also tainted by the
self-disgust of "Who Are You", as the protagonist sings of embracing his lover
while blind drunk, "to the sound of old T-Rex and *Who's Next*". There's a very
plausible spirit of banter between an older man and his younger lover in the central
image, "When I say I love you / You say, You'd better", and the song, for all its dark
moments, does end on a high note about the power of love – or sex:

I know I been wearing crazy clothes
And I look pretty crappy sometimes
But my body feels so good
And I still see the rays of light every time

Like so many of the great pop and rock singles, this leads with all of its main
hooks – piano crash, bleeping synth, arpeggiated acoustic guitars, the repeated "You
Better You Bet" – an instant anthem to stir the hearts of those longing to recapture
the fists-in-the-air rage of howling along to "It's a teenage wasteland". Szymczyk's
production has given the group a clear and commercial sound; from the opening
bars, it's certain to sound great on radio. There's a myriad of looping keyboards,
bright, shiny acoustic guitars and strong vocal harmonies; in fact, something new
is taking place nearly every few bars. Kenney Jones makes a solid start behind
the kit, but follows where once Keith would have led. Roger meanwhile roars in a
powerful performance, his barks of "You better" in the choruses not a million miles
away from how John Lydon might have sneered them.

"You Better You Bet" was *Face Dances'* most obvious candidate for single
release. After all, it was just a pop song, Pete would insist. Wisely selected as the
lead-off 45, this attained a very respectable top ten placing (their last) in the UK.
They performed it on *Top Of The Pops*, their first appearance since promoting
Quadrophenia's "5.15" in 1973. It would be the band's final major hit.

In the US, the Who's main market since *Tommy*, the chart situation was a little
more complicated. As Fred Dannen documented in *Hitmen*, his fine study of payola
in the US record industry, Warners had decided to take a stand against a shadowy

network of independent record promoters, known as the Network, who had US radio sewn up and charged even the biggest labels, large fees for airplay. Surely such a great song by a legendary group, would be a hit without having to pay a shady middleman for radio coverage?

Certainly "You Better You Bet" got off to a good start, entering the *Billboard* Hot 100 at number 63 in the week ending 21st March. *Billboard* marked the record with a superstar, rather than a star, signifying the "greatest upward movement". *Radio and Records* marked the song with its own equivalent symbol, a bullet. "The Who single", Dannen wrote, "rose in *Billboard* to 48, then 35, then 28, then 26, 24, 21. The week ending May 9, it peaked at 18, then with a star. For two weeks, it hovered at 18. Then... it went into free-fall: 31, 36, 73, 90, 100, gone".

Warners executive and close friend of Daltrey's, Fred Haayan, simply couldn't believe it, telling Dannen: "It was at least a top five record. It was shooting up the charts, then bang, it was stopped." It appeared that Warners' experiment in not paying the Network had had disastrous results for the Who. There were no other potential hits on *Face Dances* and, though the album made it to number four on the US chart, it was not the commercial success it could have been there. Considering the choice of producer and sound was aimed at US radio, to have been effectively cut off from this outlet, for whatever reason, was ill-timed to say the least.

"'You Better You Bet' is still one of my favourite songs of all," Roger would insist. It's an oddly partisan choice for the singer, but this certainly is the best of the Kenney Jones years. If it wasn't going to be a hit in the US, nothing the Who had in reserve would stand a chance.

Don't Let Go The Coat
In this plainly autobiographical song, Pete sums up his recent turmoil: "I can't be held responsible for blown behaviour / I lost all contact with my only saviour".

"At the heart of all my work is the fear of abandonment," Townshend would confess, as this moving paean to loss, fear and keeping the faith, makes clear. There is a desperate sense of strife as the protagonist vows to return to and cling to the ways of a guru, as a child would cling to the coat of his father. Though, it should be remembered that it was Pete's mum and dad who would get him out of his drink and drugs spiral, this presumably refers to Meher Baba, who was fond of the image of holding on to the hem of the master's garments.

Musically, the bitter pill of Pete's spiritual torment is sweetened by a full coating of Californian country-rock sugar. Pete's angular guitar sound is reminiscent of the Pretenders at their most melodic, and he contributes an outstanding Spanish-inflected guitar solo, but in spite of pristine production – this rolling, laid-back acoustic sound is pure Bill Szymczyk – it never really gets out of first gear. It's a reasonable song, but perhaps it simply isn't strong enough to be placed so early in the album's running order, and is something of an anti-climax after the set's powerful opener. Released as the second 45 from *Face Dances* later in 1981, this failed to make the higher reaches of the charts.

Cache Cache

"Cache Cache" is another dark little slice of autobiography as Roger voices Pete's lament of searching for a safe hideaway. He's slept in a bear pit, on a hard wooden bench or bed of stone: lost, suicidal, hoping even the police might take him in. Pete had been exiled from his family home, but the point of this song is to reiterate the need for a spiritual, rather than physical, haven where he can find respite. This song was based on an actual experience when, in March 1980, Pete experimented with living like a tramp for a couple of days in Switzerland, and ended up literally sleeping in an old disused bear pit in Berne.

Kenney plays some strong triplets in the intro section, while Roger's enthusiastic vocal has its moments, but though he displays some deft finger work, Townshend's "search and destroy" guitar of old is missing. In spite of some fine organ flourishes and regular half-time to double-time changes, this is ultimately an ordinary four-on-the-floor rocker that, regardless of the fairly furious pace, still sounds rather plodding. Pete's *Scoop* demo of "Cache Cache," for once, sounds superior to the finished take, but even that more raw, rambunctious take can't create a classic from a cast-off.

The Quiet One

(Entwistle)

"I ain't quiet", John rasps, "Everybody else is too loud". Being in a band with three huge personalities like Townshend, Daltrey and Moon, must have been quite overwhelming at times. "He doesn't demand attention," Pete would say of Entwistle. "For years nobody even noticed he was there." Competing with his fellow band members in terms of pure volume would have always been a challenge, so Entwistle's self-myth-making about the depths of still waters is wry and apposite. But other than in the central image, his trademark humour is absent.

"John felt that somehow his early media reputation of being 'The Quiet One' had to be confronted," Keith Altham would later muse, "and challenged by turning up his amp to a deafening level that would have impressed Spinal Tap!"

This triplet-based rocker, written and roared by John in a standard hard-rocking yowl, motors along boisterously, testing Kenney's boundaries, while Townshend's guitar sounds tougher than on either of the previous two tracks. With some muscular rhythm work and Thin-Lizzy-style lead breaks, Pete acquits himself admirably. Nonetheless, on another level, this is rather ordinary heavy fare – sludgy and short on the hooks that make great rock so memorable. The Who are now following an established template – albeit one that was heavily influenced by their own golden years – rather than inventing a new one.

Did You Steal My Money?

This self-explanatory complaint is set to a futuristic, funky, keyboard-driven arrangement that sees the Who sounding not unlike Phil Collins-era Genesis. It's an ignominious sound to match a cliché-ridden and hectoring lyric, detailing rip-offs, lies and deceit via a relentless series of questions and recriminations, as the protagonist finds a wide variety of phrases to reiterate the title: "Did you turn me over while I cold-turkeyed on the sofa?... Did you pinch my brasso / Nick my gelt, you asshole?".

This is subject matter clearly rooted in autobiography, as Townshend vents his anger and frustration at the shabby way his group have been tricked and cheated along the way, and the spirit of his nemesis Allen Klein hovers above. Then again, everyone in this business has been ripped off at one time or another, in what Keith Richards called "the price of an education." It's hard for the average listener to feel too much sympathy for millionaires bemoaning their lot. While Pete and his cohorts had suffered badly in business, not least from the terrible Talmy royalty rates and terms (and his galling five-year 5% override), and later the missing US publishing, others such as the Small Faces had suffered far worse. Pete bemoaned, "How can we forgive a grievance?" But the music business is littered with exploitation far more severe than anything Pete and his band-mates had endured. While Townshend used to write for his audience, and give voice to emotions they felt but couldn't articulate, here he is simply pouring out his own personal angst, largely unstructured and unfiltered, and sounding a bit spoilt. If there is a great anthem to be written about wealthy rock stars being financially hard-done-by, this isn't it. At least the Beatles' "Taxman" had a great riff...

Under the early 80s production gloss, this is a musically unoriginal, melodically unmemorable, millionaire's moan about money matters. In a few years it seems we've gone from *Who's Next* to Who Cares?

How Can You Do It Alone?

The ever-guilt-wracked Pete presents a series of vignettes about "feelings of shame", and isolation, featuring encounters with a set of characters that include a lonely old man "of fifty or so" who beneath his coat is "naked and wet", a school kid in the paper shop who gets caught having "stuffed girlie mags down into his jeans", and a casual girlfriend who "seems to have the knack of attaining the stars of her dreams". The first of these meetings was based on an actual encounter Townshend had on Holland Park Road in West London, which left him to ruminate on the isolated way in which some people get their kicks. However, while "Eleanor Rigby"-style he is wondering at these people's loneliness, this still sounds like a personal cry for help as he concludes by asking: "How can you do it without any help? / How can you do it all by yourself?".

Originating from a band jam session back in 1979, musically, this alternates between the Paul McCartney-esque jaunty eighth-note bounce of the verses and the rock ballad chorus refrain. It also showcases excellent bass runs from John in the choruses.

Daily Records

Pete gives voice to the pleasure and pain and downright addictive compulsion of making records, or more specifically songwriting. Unsurprisingly, for someone with two demanding contractual schedules requiring new material for both solo work and the Who hanging over him, Townshend was conscious, daily, of the need to write and record. But as he explained, songwriting for him was like a drug and he wouldn't have it any other way – lost in private worlds, oblivious to normal life.

Musically, after a pleasant opening guitar figure, this slowly drifts towards the light opera territory of "Guitar And Pen". *Rolling Stone* rather unkindly accused Daltrey of sounding "as fatuously preening as an aria from *Pirates Of Penzance*". This does see the Who sounding a little too much like Queen, but there is plenty of melody here and it is a pleasing diversion from the album's synth norm.

Roger's performance is impressive, and other highlights include a dextrous country-rock style, finger-picking solo from Pete and some tasteful fills from Kenney. All in all, this is a likeable cut, even if it does suffer from a disjointed, stitched-together feel.

You
(Entwistle)
This contains possibly the worst lyrics John ever penned, not least the cringe-making: "One Look / and I'm hooked / one touch and my goose is cooked", followed by the equally poor "You lead me on / like a lamb to the slaughter / then you act like a fish out of water". These lyrics are way below his usual standard of dark humour and highlight just how desperate for material the band were.

This ill-conceived cliché-ridden tale of a treacherous, poison-eyed temptress is stock material for many 80s melodic rockers – Whitesnake practically made a career from this one theme alone – and from its opening slamming guitar power chords, this dual-riffing rock assault is an unfortunate Entwistle excursion into mainstream metal. Worked out at Shepperton between the bassist and the new drummer, it was Kenney Jones that convinced his new cohort that this was a Who song rather than one for an Entwistle solo project.

Another Tricky Day
In an echo of the famous Stones song "You Can't Always Get What You Want", Townshend tells us "You can't always get it / When you really want it". After the self-excoriation and various laments that have dominated this record's lyrics, Pete is finally saying that this isn't a crisis, just another tricky day, get over yourself and get on with it. Though Pete is something of an expert at brooding, worrying and generally making a drama out of a crisis, this is still a pragmatic and optimistic note on which to end the album, as the song references itself in its final lines:

The world seems in a spiral
Life seems such a worthless title
But break out and start a fire y'all
It's all here on the vinyl

Despite the lead-in track's "single" status, this is the real high point of *Face Dances*. Townshend's guitar is more animated and the arrangement has a relaxed, cruising funky feel. The chorus is glorious, and the song is full of harmony cascades and counterpoint vocals. The band have regained much of the swagger of old... just in time.

Bonus Tracks:

I Like Nightmares

Pete sings lead on this seemingly light-hearted unfinished bluesy, boogie-woogie, *Face Dances* sessions outtake. The musical mood is jovial but at odds with the lyrics, "Gotta be a fucking fool to blame TV" and "There's a simple way to die, they call it news" Pete states. This song fails to gel and it's no surprise it was omitted from the original track listing.

It's In You

Framed as a response to an angry letter from a fan called Virginia – in fact, prior to this official release, bootlegs used to refer to this under that title – though the narrator refers to her as "Tich", this angry track seems an excuse for Pete to vent his spleen at his audience in general, who he complains still want to live their lives vicariously through the Who. Pete also feels constricted by fans' expectations that the Who will continue to do the same old thing, year in year out:

> *I read your letter*
> *You said that power chords are all that we should play*
> *If you depend on me to make you rock'n'roll*
> *You better look out Tich, 'cause we're getting old*

For Townshend, the time has long passed since he wanted to be a spokesman for a generation and he certainly doesn't feel he should take advice, especially when it's not even politely put. He can live the rock'n'roll lifestyle if he wants, hanging out with VIPs at the cool clubs, but fans shouldn't live their lives through him:

> *As for you, the place to look for rock'n'roll, is in you*
> *You got it in you... You know you got it in you*

Worse, the rude fan letter – accusing Pete of being "a fake," among other sins – had arrived around the anniversary of Keith Moon's death. Taking a cue from the fan's name, real or imagined, Pete addresses his correspondent as "Sweet Virginia", which seems an excuse for offering up this dull sub-Stones sound-alike. In direct opposition to Pete's finest work, the anger of the lyric – wherein loathing for his fans drips from line after line – is not matched by the music. This is a boring groove, in spite of some reasonable honky-tonk piano and brushes of organ, that is only held together by some funky frenetic Entwistle bass runs and a reasonably fat Kenney beat. Roger, singing without backing support, tries to muster Pete's required level of spite, but only convinces in the outro where he mutters that the fan is a "toe rag" and a "tosser".

"It's In You" was recorded and mixed as part of the main *Face Dances* album sessions, but was wisely considered too weak and rejected at the last minute. Initial copies of the remastered CD had a defect on this track, a good excuse for skipping this weak filler, though MCA quickly fixed the glitch. "It's terrible," Roger conceded. "It's so clichéd isn't it? I quite like it but I don't think it's exceptional. It could be a Rolling Stones song... it's just an ordinary song as far as I'm concerned." And so this dull track encapsulates the problem with *Face Dances* – in all its incarnations – too many ordinary songs and a sense of contempt for the audience.

Somebody Saved Me

Townshend takes over lead vocal on this half-time ballad, which was also recorded as part of the *Face Dances* sessions but rejected from the final cut. It's an extremely personal song that Pete would re-record for his 1982 solo record, *All The Best Cowboys Have Chinese Eyes*, about being rescued from his own worst excesses – though it's not clear if his saviour is a beloved woman or a spiritual guru like Meher Baba. After some storming rock'n'roll, the song ends on a calm note as Pete counts himself lucky to have survived:

> *And when I finally woke up clean*
> *My friend was dead, stone dead*
> *But somebody saved me*

How Can You Do It Alone (Live)

A recording from a concert at Chicago International Amphitheatre in December 1979, months before *Face Dances* was recorded. This is almost a completely different track; raw, more aggressive and more effective than the LP version. Townshend's performance is breathtaking. His guitar bites your head off and his vocal is slurred and aggressive as he asks accusingly. "How can you do it alone?" he immediately retorts, "You can't!". The album version finds him sympathetic, but here he's on the attack. Townshend launches into a nimble-fingered solo and ends with crash chords, as Jones storms into some tough snare drum work. The two of them start to jam with the whole track, ending with the guitar player leading the band through an improvised rock'n'roll thrash ending. This is what the album version should have sounded like.

The Quiet One (Live)

(Entwistle)

Taken from a gig at Shea Stadium in New York, October 1982, here's another example of why the Who still mattered as a live band. John belts out the lyric that stretches him vocally and there is an urgency in the group's performance that is sadly lacking from the studio version. With more inspired soloing from Pete that harks back to *Live At Leeds* days, this proves that there really was still fire in their collective belly.

Face Dances went on to sell a million copies. It was kept off the top UK album spot by Adam and the Ants' *Kings Of The Wild Frontier*. Despite those sales, the Who would have a lot of work to do on the next album to show that, post-Keith, they weren't a spent force. Just weeks after the album's release, on 7th April, 1981, the group's former manager Kit Lambert died from a brain haemorrhage caused by a fall down the stairs at his mother's home. He was just 45 years old. Despite his estrangement from the group since the early 70s, Kit had had an enormous influence over every aspect of their early career, and was a personal inspiration to each individual member.

The years had not been kind to Kit. Despite apparently holding millions of pounds in a number of different bank accounts, his alcoholism and heroin addiction had seen him declared bankrupt. Even this didn't curb his addictions, and he continued to spend any money he could access on alcohol and drugs. Nor did Lambert's death act as a cautionary tale for Pete Townshend. "I just took anything I could lay my hands on as a way of passing the time," Pete would confess, "because I hated the sensation of not being drunk."

Townshend collapsed after taking heroin and alcohol, while partying at Covent Garden's Club for Heroes, in September. He was rushed to hospital; his heart stopped and it was only quick medical attention that revived him. Pete had often been sorrowfully critical of Keith Moon's lifestyle, but he was now indulging himself to a similarly dangerous degree. After his release from hospital, Pete finally returned to the studio in November, to resume work on a solo album project that he'd previously put on hold.

Other band members had their problems too. Entwistle's marriage collapsed and Kenney's was in turmoil. But it was Pete whose life Roger feared was in danger. Townshend was freebasing between two and three grammes of cocaine, smoking heroin and taking his Ativan tablets at a rate of eight or ten a day. This was a deadly combination, and by the time his wife Karen invited him back to the family home that Christmas, he was a walking wreck. His excessive reliance on drink and drugs had also put him £1million in debt. At one point, he'd nearly lost the house. After a temporary bail-out by his management, two huge recording contracts – with Warners for the Who, and Atlantic for his solo work – would solve his financial problems, but Townshend's life was spiralling out of control all the same. He would soon have to face the added pressure of having to deliver commercial material for two separate outlets and in line with strict contractual schedules.

Over the Christmas holiday, his parents convinced him to seek help and he headed for California and checked into rehab.

Don't Let Go The Coat
UK Single Release: 05/1981 (Polydor) US Single Release: 05/1981 (Warner Bros)
Peak Position: 47 (UK) 84 (US)

The second single to be taken from the *Face Dances* record this fared relatively poorly on both the British and US charts.

The year was topped and tailed by two further compilation albums, new repackaged collections containing mostly the usual early tracks including yet again, "I Can't Explain", "I Can See For Miles" et al. In February *My Generation* was released on Polydor in the UK but it failed to chart. *Hooligans* came out eight months later on MCA in the US where it made number 52 on the *Billboard* Top 100. This featured more tracks from the 70s period, but nothing that wasn't abundantly available elsewhere. It would serve as little more than a good introduction for anyone unfamiliar with the band's back catalogue.

13 Trying Harder – 1982-84

When work began on the Who's tenth studio album in early 1982, Pete Townshend was in a rehabilitation centre in Los Angeles, cleaning up after many well-documented years of drink and drug abuse. With Pete in no fit state to write or perform new material, guitarist Andy Fairweather-Low (formerly of Amen Corner) joined Roger, John and Kenney at Glyn Johns' home studio in Sussex, to start writing for the new album. It was a desperate attempt on the band's part to actually get something moving. But trying to make a start without Pete, though well-intentioned, was wildly optimistic.

It took much persuasion to get Pete to California, but Dr Meg Patterson's celebrated NET (also known as "Black Box") cure seemed to work. On his return to the UK, he rebuilt family ties and sorted out his finances, determined to get his life back on track. Pete also had plenty of new songs to offer and set to work on recording demos. But his need to write about his own experiences, to make sense of his addictions by examining them through songwriting, received a cool response from the rest of the band. They felt much of his new material was too highly personal; they didn't want yet more songs about his excesses or his experiences in rehab. Townshend was incensed but perhaps also defensive, because, as he later acknowledged, he knew even then that he wasn't delivering the kind of material that the Who needed.

"What do you want to sing about?" he demanded of the others. "Tell me and I'll write the songs." After establishing quite quickly that there was very little common ground between them, Townshend recalled, "We did find that we all cared very deeply about the planet, the people on it, about the threat to our children from nuclear war, of the increasing instability of our own country's politics."

Considering how apolitical Roger and John had always seemed to be, these concerns do seem surprising, but this was the early 80s of Thatcher and Reagan, the fears surrounding nuclear proliferation and the last remaining geopolitical divisions between East and West, CND marches and the Greenham Common women's peace camp, slogans like "Protect and Survive", "Mutually Assured Destruction", dole queues and race riots in British cities. Politics seemed to imbue every area of life. Groups like the Clash proudly wore their political credentials on their sleeves.

Having often eschewed the radical politics of the 60s, it seemed the Who now wanted to write their own polemical works; they had decided to become relevant. But Townshend's strengths were in articulating his audience's unvoiced feelings, telling stories with a quirky Englishness and baring his soul. He was neither political sloganeer nor celebrity activist.

It's Hard

A truce of sorts had been declared between Townshend and the others but, soon after the recording sessions began at Glyn Johns' Turn Up-Down Studios in Surrey in June 1982, they were finding the adopted title *It's Hard* all too apt. Despite his time in rehab, Townshend was still grappling with his life-threatening addictions.

"[We were] trying to support a man we thought we were going to lose," Roger later reflected. "This wasn't just an alcoholic binge. This was someone who was kind of nodding out on the big one [heroin]. You try and pull together."

Before the record was even completed, an extensive US tour was lined up to follow a couple of UK dates in Birmingham on 9th and 10th of September. As soon as it was billed officially as the Who's Farewell Tour, there was an unprecedented demand for tickets. That intensified the pressure to have the album released ahead of the tour. Ideally, Townshend should have been given time to write more material, but big money was now at stake. The final tour had to go ahead so *It's Hard* was bulldozed through. Kenney Jones saw something positive from this tight deadline.

"It was amazing what we came out with," he insisted, with an admirable, if unconvincing, optimism, "because we only had two songs [at first]. The rest were a bunch of riffs. And, because we approached it more like a workshop thing, it brought us all back together." With Townshend far from firing on all cylinders, the Who did their utmost, but the results were half-finished at best. The results sadly didn't really back-up Kenney's claims of unity and he would go on to be more candid, conceding, "Everyone seemed confused about which way the band should be going and it showed on the record."

Roger Daltrey was even more blunt: "As usual we were being manipulated at that time to be other things," he complained. "The record company wanted a record out and they wanted us to do a tour. What I said to Pete was, 'If we'd tried to get any of these songs onto *Face Dances*, or any of the albums that we've done since our first fucking album, we would not allow these songs to be on an album! Why are we releasing them?' I hated it", he said in 1994.

With a highly-polished studio production, *It's Hard* arrived in the shops in September 1982 and, in spite of its flaws and ugly packaging (a derivative sleeve depicting a kid playing a video arcade game, rather than pinball), sold surprisingly well.

"The music on *It's Hard* is worse than the record's cheapo cover", *Sounds'* Garry Bushell complained. "Most of it sounds like the watered-down bits of other Who LPs. It's sort of like a 60s footballer who's got old and fat and out of condition but keeps kicking a ball about".

The album has its moments. Sparks fly occasionally with welcome glimpses of the Townshend power chord that was practically invisible on *Face Dances*. Roger is in fine voice, while John anchors the band and Kenney enthusiastically does his best. All the same, even Jones was to concede the magic was missing: "There is no right drummer for the Who once Keith isn't there. You can't keep searching for what doesn't exist."

Rolling Stone considered *It's Hard* the band's best album since *Who's Next*. *Rolling Stone* critic Parke Puterbaugh saw it as "fitting that this is such a great record... [because] it's what you were least expecting...". He described the album as "a strong affirmation of the band's ability to reach millions with powerful rock'n'roll and trenchant, galvanizing politics". It's hard to believe Puterbaugh was listening to the same record, and most commentators took the opposite view – scathing of the political posturing and dismissive of, what they believed was a contractual obligation exercise, hastily fulfilled.

By contrast, the subsequent stadium world tour (the US leg of which was supported by more revolutionary firebrands, the Clash) which began on 22nd September at Capital Centre, Largo, Maryland, was a success, breaking box office records. In New York, Shea Stadium's 72,000 seats sold out in under two hours. The Who turned in some strong performances on these dates, although most of the songs on the new LP were conspicuous by their absence from the set lists. The tour wasn't immune to criticism though. Underwriting the cost of major rock tours with corporate sponsorship had become commonplace by now, but when the Who went out under the Schlitz beer banner, it led to inevitable "The Who Sell Out" jibes. The group's choice of sponsor was also ironic, considering Pete's much-publicised battle with the bottle.

Twenty-five years after the album was released, Roger Daltrey would concede, "Some of the songs on *It's Hard* are great... but there was kind of a dark cloud hanging over the band... We were tiptoeing on landmines around Pete, he was so fragile."

Athena
UK Single Release: 02/10/1982 (Polydor) US Single Release: 12/09/1982 (Warner Bros)
Peak Position: 40 (UK) 28 (US)

If the record has a minor saving grace, it's the first single "Athena" but even that, by the Who's standards, is little more than soup from bones. Released ahead of the LP as a single in the US, "Athena" appeared later in the UK with the album cut of "A Man Is A Man" on the flipside; always a sign of an inspiration shortage.

It's Hard
UK Album Release: 04/09/1982 (Polydor WHOD 5066)
US Album Release: 04/09/1982 (Warner Bros WB 23731)
Peak Position: 11 (UK) 8 (US)
Athena / It's Your Turn / Cooks County / It's Hard / Dangerous / Eminence Front / I've Known No War / One Life's Enough / One At A Time / Why Did I Fall For That / A Man Is A Man / Cry If You Want

It's Hard (Remastered Edition)
UK Album Release: 05/1997 (Polydor 537 696-2)
US Album Release: 06/1997 (MCA MCAD 11635)
Athena / It's Your Turn / Cooks County / It's Hard / Dangerous / Eminence Front / I've Known No War / One Life's Enough / One At A Time / Why Did I Fall For That / A Man Is A Man / Cry If You Want / It's Hard (Live) / Eminence Front (Live) / Dangerous (Live) / Cry If You Want (Live)
All songs by Pete Townshend, except for where stated.

For me, what's interesting about the latter stages of the Who was not just that we failed, it was that we failed and I was trying really hard.
Pete Townshend, *The Sunday Times*, **1999**

Athena

For all the talk of politics, the album begins with a heartfelt love song of unrequited longing that is tinged with doubt and fear: "Athena, I had no idea how much I'd need her / Athena, all I ever want to do is please her".

The only "bomb" here is "just a girl". Inspired by Pete's unreciprocated infatuation with actress Theresa Russell (who married film director Nic Roeg in 1982), this was originally entitled "Teresa." The palpitations Pete sings of may be down to coke usage rather than love-struck anxiety, but his suicidal feelings of rejection are vividly presented:

> *Athena, my heart felt like a shattered glass in an acid bath*
> *I felt like one of those flattened ants you find on a crazy path*

Even with the name-change from "Teresa", Pete regretted airing something quite so transparently personal: "It was just too revealing." The song had been around for some time; Pete had demoed it in Hollywood back in February 1980, so it's no surprise it isn't representative of the rest of the record. Nonetheless, this is a bright enough start to side one. It breezes in with a few identifiable Who musical trademarks – a wheeling, strummed guitar, distinctive Entwistle horns, a driving acoustic rhythm and a haunting instrumental break. But this is rather lightweight and even a little complacent, and the vocals sound unconvincing.

It's Your Turn

(Entwistle)

This tongue-in-cheek Entwistle song sees an old hand "up on the ledge" passing on the rock'n'roll stardom baton to a young new pretender, ready "to step into my shoes". The tone mixes regret and defiance: the veteran won't miss all aspects of his rock'n'roll life – though he can still stay up drinking all night with the best of them. The sardonic diatribe features some of Entwistle's most perceptive lyrics:

> *I was a face in a magazine*
> *When you were still playin' with your plasticine*

It shows he's back on writing form after the comparatively dire "You" from *Face Dances*. Musically, this is another Entwistle full-on hard rock track with added 80s sheen. "I think John was in the wrong band," Pete would later wryly tell *Uncut*'s Simon Goddard, "John wanted to be in, I dunno, Whitesnake." Nonetheless, here, the crash chords, fills, and chiming lead guitar help this sound a little like the Who of old, if a bit self-conscious and overwrought. Andy Fairweather-Low's rhythm guitar adds an extra dimension while Daltrey clearly relishes some of John's best lines.

Cooks County

It's the third track before *It's Hard*'s vaunted political themes kick in. This was inspired by a documentary Pete saw about the Cook County hospital in Chicago. Based in a ghetto and mostly treating black people and drug addicts, Cook County offered free medical care to all who needed it, but cutbacks in federal government funding meant that the hospital would be forced to close.

"I just felt so moved by this," said Pete, "that I had to scribble out a few lines about it... I just went in with the poem I'd written 'people are suffering' and we turned it into this particular track." Unfortunately, he seemed unable to draw any broader insight from this moving microcosm of an uncaring age, content to simply point out that: "People are suffering... People are hungry... People are lonely...". This is neither news, nor enlightening. Roger does his best to imbue a sense of anger that is absent from the insipid lyric, as he roars through the half-paced verse into the up-tempo choruses, where Pete's Fender power chords hark back to classic windmilling days.

It's Hard

The album title track sounds initially like it might be making points about the difficulties faced by the less well-off in life, but it turns out to be a self-pitying, repetitive lament about the protagonist's own bad luck:

> *Anyone can do anything if they hold the right card*
> *So I'm thinking about my life now*
> *I'm thinking very hard*
> *Deal me another hand Lord, this one's very hard*

This does have a certain rocking energy and, musically, it's one of the album highlights. Sadly, for all its passionate playing and blue-collar bluster, this is a mannered Bruce Springsteen copy that shamelessly steals the main riff from the Boss's epic "Badlands", note for note, while adding none of Bruce's lyrical insight. Whereas previously, like Springsteen, Pete gave voice to the inarticulate young working class, now he is simply moaning about how tough it is at the top. Released as a single in the USA, this failed to chart.

Dangerous

(Entwistle)

The second John composition on *It's Hard*, "Dangerous" focuses on a vague sense of impending menace but, while "It's Your Turn" was packed with witty couplets, this is po-faced and clunky; pretentious rather than portentous: "This is a jungle, not an illusion / Jungle city, in confusion".

Perhaps "jungle" is referring to Vietnam, and the later lyrical references to the stone age [refer to] a US General's stated aim of bombing the North Vietnamese back to that prehistoric age. But it's too vague really to work out what John really sees as the source of danger and, after avoiding the conflict in South East Asia while it escalated in the 60s and 70s, it seems odd now for him to address it, even so obscurely, while other wars raged around the world.

The keyboards here were played by John and Tim Gorman, the latter formerly of Glyn Johns-produced San Francisco cult band, Lazy Racer, and a future member of Jefferson Starship. Gorman, who also added organ to the track, was recruited to fill a gap after the Who's usual keyboard player "Rabbit" Bundrick had been fired over a drunken violent incident the previous summer, though he would later return to play with Townshend on a solo project and, ultimately, be welcomed back into the Who fold.

In rock'n'roll terms, the Who could often rely on sheer bombast to get them through a less inspired composition but, without Keith Moon's energy and virtuosity, they struggle here. "Dangerous" – the B-side of the "It's Hard" single – was Entwistle's favourite of his three songwriting contributions to the album, but it never really gets out of second gear.

With a carbon-datable early 80s guitar and shiny synth sound that owes a lot to US band the Cars, this is very much of its time. Townshend and Entwistle chug along while Roger rips through the vocal, giving everything he's got, but to no avail.

Eminence Front

The affluent materialist trappings of 80s success, Pete complains – the speedboats, the glamorous girls, dress-to-kill parties and ski holidays – are all just a shiny façade: an eminence front: "People forget / Forget they're hiding /... It's a put-on". The yuppie 80s were clearly not to the liking of spiritual-seeker and Baba-follower Townshend, though perhaps this is more based on Pete's spell of pre-rehab coke-fuelled partying with the glitterati while estranged from his wife.

Like the best songs from Bernard Edwards and Nile Rodgers' Chic, this expression of modern malaise takes the musical form of a minimalist, tight funk track that could fill dance floors with the beautiful people, while sounding uptight enough to convey the menacing undercurrents of the lyrics. The sound is pure early 1980s, but the rhythm and vocal explore the new terrain of funk-rock. After a taut intro comprising Tim Gorman's flickering electric piano, Pete's noodling synths and spare lead guitar work, this snakes along as Pete's blues-inflected solo sets the song up perfectly for his intermittently vitriolic vocal. This is one of Pete's finest singing performances, largely because the melody sits comfortably within his range. However, the fact that he sings lead vocals on this only goes to reinforce the feeling that this is a Townshend solo track that sounds nothing like the Who.

This insidiously ice-cool outing may be the LP's best track; it's certainly the catchiest thing the Who had come up with since "You Better You Bet". The song attracted considerable praise from an unexpected quarter: the controversial post-feminist intellectual and radical critic, Camille Puglia – not known as a Who fan – who commented, as quoted by Brian Cady on *thewho.net*, "I would cite the Who's magnificent, rumbling 'Eminence Front', with its penetrating insights into psychology and politics, as an example of what an evolved punk can and should achieve".

Praise indeed, if a little like discovering that radical feminist Andrea Dworkin was a huge Led Zeppelin fan...

I've Known No War

For this anti-war plea, Townshend's starting-point for what he called "the key song on the new album" was apparently a ticking clock, a throbbing rhythm and the word "war". Having grown up in post-war austerity, and become a hero to the pampered baby-boomer generation that came of age in the swinging 60s, Townshend reflects on how his peers have complacently wasted their parents' hard-fought legacy: too busy enjoying their blessed lives in "victorious clover" to listen to the older generation's stories of wartime tragedies and privations.

"It's really just about the fact that we're a privileged generation," he elaborated, "in the fact that our fathers and grandfathers did go through two world wars and we didn't... I think to a great extent we've abused that. We've allowed ourselves to make our own wars and allowed life to get a bit violent. I think basically we're a bunch of spoilt brats."

The key at the heart of the lyric is that, while Pete has never experienced warfare himself, he feels the world is drifting back to war. Though, even if this time he is around for the next world conflict, he won't "know war" because humankind will be blown to pieces by nuclear weapons in an instant: "The glimpse will be short / Fireball in the sky / No front line battle cries".

Packed with vivid imagery and fired by righteous anger, this is the album's strongest lyric and perhaps the only song where the politics ring true – perhaps because they are driven by a personal experience of fear for the future rather than general observations on the state of the world. Sadly the uninspired music does not match the fury of the message. The overall effect is one of posturing bluster that fails to persuade or engage, even in the more delicate keyboard coda. Roger does his best to breathe life into the plodding rock relentlessness, while the band crank out some standard rock riffs, but with few audible Who trademarks, this is far from memorable. Townshend considered this "possibly one of the best Who tracks we've ever done." Few others did.

One Life's Enough

Thematically, a huge shift from the war protest of the previous song, this slight reverie drifts back to a fondly remembered, intoxicating teenage sexual encounter, conjured in a few vivid images, including how the protagonist's lover threw back her head and pulled him "into the long grass of the bed / Pull me down into your hair". More of a poem than a song, this short, curious ballad sung with understatement by Daltrey, is another untypical Who track. It's set to a delicately tinkling piano and a swathe of John and Tim Gorman's synth string parts; Jones adds a brief cameo midway through, but this delicate fragment remains conspicuously guitar-free.

"One Life's Enough" is a pretty piece, nicely arranged and played, but it's not melodically memorable and quietly meanders in and out without leaving much of an impression.

One At A Time
(Entwistle)
Another down-and-dirty Entwistle rocker with a typical heavy metal subject: a woman who's mad, bad and unfaithful. Faced with a choice between this cheating shrew and a supposed better prospect, he explains he can only handle "one at a time". More chauvinistically, he says to a friend: "If you want her, you can keep her / ... Call her up right away...". Entwistle says he only completed the lyrics to the

final verse an hour or so before singing them for the recording.

After the previous low-key keyboard piece, the opening horn deluge and electric guitar does feel like a return to business. Jones asserts his authority quickly, he seizes the bulldozing beat in its tracks, anchors the rhythm and drives it relentlessly forward. John supplies one of his best lead vocals plus the distinctive horn parts. John and Tim add soaring keyboards and Pete churns out chiming chords, blistering lead guitar and aggressive close harmonies. John has pulled out all the stops, but the track's no-nonsense riffing and basic rock'n'roll belligerence can't turn back the inexorable tide of an album that has struggled to get up a head of steam.

Another Entwistle hard-rock song only emphasises the disjointed nature of *It's Hard* – this is by now turning into a rather random collection of ill-matched themes and disparate musical styles. Also, while this is an energetic heads-down rocker, it is not especially original, and displays few of the Who's real strengths. "One At A Time" would form the B-side of the ill-fated "Eminence Front" US single in December, and suffers by comparison to that untypical album highlight.

Why Did I Fall For That?

This articulates both a cry of disappointment at being tricked by broken promises and shattered dreams, and, on another level, drifting blindly towards some kind of nuclear holocaust, hoping for the best and believing what the authorities tell us – we're "four minutes from midnight", soon the streets would be full of "scattered remains". Somewhat dispiritingly, rather than engage with the difficulties of the world, Pete withdraws with resignation, under the safety of his metaphorical umbrella. "Won't Get Fooled Again", this ain't. What's more, Townshend knew it. In 1980, he had told *Oui* magazine: "When I was nineteen or twenty, I really felt I had something to say. Now, to be quite frank, I don't give a shit. I just wanna be happy and enjoy the people around me and try to enjoy life." Pete is being overly harsh, but he does seem to be repeating himself here, albeit in the shadow of the bomb, rather than in the twilight of the radical 60s dream.

As the cumulative effect of this album builds, it's clear by track 10 that the performances are growing tired and the songs more hackneyed. Again, there is nothing really wrong with this track – it breezes along at mid-tempo with some fine ringing guitar and the odd snappy couplet. It's a strong vocal and Kenney Jones is on particularly good form, but for all the ooh-ing harmonies and plaintive horns and keyboards, this never transcends the ordinary. It appears as if the artistic core of the band has sadly collapsed.

A Man Is A Man

An attack on machismo, "A Man Is A Man" derides a series of macho stereotypes, from bragging, bottle-smashing street fighters and hard-drinkers to strong, silent types and John Wayne B-movie heroes. Instead, according to Pete, a real man is sensitive and spontaneous, acting from the heart and offering a helping hand. The acidic self-scrutiny of *The Who By Numbers* seven years earlier, has been transmuted into something critical but somehow simultaneously self-celebratory. Townshend's sincere, but he's said similar things less smugly to greater effect many times before. "When a man is a man / he don't act to a plan", might scan, but it's clunky and meaningless.

Unlike Pete's solo triumph *Empty Glass*, where the shiny synth fanfares of "A Little Is Enough" lifted a strong pop song into a great contemporary track, this is a rather dismal dirge dominated by 80s keyboards. This could be any AOR band of the age and simply isn't worthy of the Who.

Cry If You Want

The final track on the album was assumed by many at the time to signal the end of the band's recording career. With a martial drum and some frantic guitar work, the closing piece crashes in all bluster and little charm, but lyrically Pete has raised his game here. It's as if there is time for one final exorcism as he tries to come to terms with his own rock'n'roll past now that times have changed. As he revisits his own back pages, it's as if he is writing his own epitaph, documenting the highs and lows, the sins and salvations, on his long journey from "innocence / brash ideas and insolence", to where he is today. Older, wiser, more sanguine – the righteous anger of youth is replaced by the accommodation of experience.

"Don't you get embarrassed", he asks of himself, "when you read the precious things you said?". But, Pete won't commit to an answer. He knows now he simply has to accept where he has been and where he is now: "you can cry if you want", but it won't make any difference. "Let your tears flow, let your past go".

"The song that most captures what the Who feel at the moment is a song called 'Cry If You Want'," Roger would insist. "I think it should have been the single... I think that really does state how it feels to be 38 years old and singing in a rock band called the Who!" This wouldn't have actually made a great single, but it is a fitting close to an uneven LP that seems to pre-empt the criticism which would soon rain down on the band.

Bonus Tracks:

It's Hard (Live) / Dangerous (Live) / Eminence Front (Live) / Cry If You Want (Live)

The quartet of live additions to the remastered edition was recorded at Maple Leaf Gardens in Toronto, Canada, on December 16-17th, 1982. These were the last shows on their "farewell" tour. Many critics felt the Who breathed new life into the *It's Hard* material at these shows, and it would have been almost impossible to deliver anything less than an improvement on the studio versions. Without the glossy production sheen, "It's Hard" in particular, and "Dangerous" do sound more energised, but "Eminence Front" loses its ice-cool urgency and ends up sounding ragged and diminished, though it would remain the only one of this quartet of *It's Hard* recordings to become a regular live fixture. The other three would be quickly dropped. Even with the additional four live cuts, the expanded CD still ends on the final state-of-the-Who reflections of "Cry If You Want".

Eminence Front
US Single Release: 12/1982 (Warner Bros)
Peak Position: 68 (US)

This was wisely chosen as another US single, though it surprisingly got no higher than number 68. There were plans to put this out in the UK too, and a striking sleeve depicting a suitably glacial art-deco fronted mansion was even printed up, but the idea was shelved. Nonetheless, "Eminence Front" would get regular outings on the 1982 live dates and would be revived on the 25th anniversary tour in 1989.

1983:

The Official Split

After the Farewell Tour ended, the intention remained to record another studio album. Townshend faced the prospect of going off to write some new material. "After finishing the 1982 tour," he recalled, "and being confronted with going to the studio yet again with the band, which I thought was really bereft, I had the courage to say, 'Fuck it, it's over'." In the summer of 1983, Pete told the band that it was over.

"The last two albums for the Who were incredibly painful affairs," Pete would later reflect, "because we were fucking up and it was quite clear, and there was nothing we could do to stop the process. We all looked around for someone to blame but it was quite clear there wasn't much we could do about it." Indeed, the blame lay firmly with the group themselves. There had been an overwhelming sense of artistic inertia with *It's Hard*. The band had never lost their magic in the live arena, but their studio work had deteriorated dramatically. It was a pity that a band as influential and imaginative as the Who should appear to finish their studio recording career with such a patchy and underwhelming album.

Perhaps with hindsight, the Who should have split up immediately after Keith's death. Pete had voiced this view on a number of occasions. Or, the three survivors should have taken a few years off to lick their wounds and regroup, as Daltrey has suggested he wanted them to do. Instead, Keith's replacement, Kenney Jones, was brought in with almost indecent haste and used as a scapegoat for later problems that went directly to the heart of the group. "The first tour Kenney did with us, he was absolutely fucking brilliant," Daltrey conceded. "But after that he settled in to what he knew, which was his Faces-type drumming, which doesn't work with the Who."

Townshend found that he could no longer muster the energy to even convince the rest of the band that his heart was still in it. "I love the group," he insisted. "What I couldn't stand was the tension of not knowing when it was going to end. I just had to know when it would finish. I couldn't stand the indecision." On 16th December, 1983, the Who issued a statement saying that they had called it a day. The group that had changed so much in the world of rock'n'roll, both in the studio and on the live stage, were no more.

"I wanted to get on with my solo career," Entwistle reflected, "I thought there were much greater heights to go on to. You'd always get dragged back and have the Who thrown at you." Yet, in spite of the announcement, would the Who be able to resist the lure of a later reunion? Pete, Roger and John's solo projects had been often interesting, but rarely reached the artistic or commercial heights of the group.

"I was full of grandiose ideas when the Who broke up for the first time," Entwistle conceded, "but it doesn't take long to spend five million dollars!" Entwistle's words would cast a shadow over the band members' future. The Who would be back, but arguably the motivation would be financial rather than artistic. A sad come-down for such a driven creative force. As if to reinforce this, there was a live album on the horizon.

The Who's Greatest Hits
US Album Release: 05/1983 (MCA 5408)
Peak Position: 94 (US)
Yet another compilation of tracks already available. Another cash-in effort by the record company.

Rarities Vol. 1 (1966 -68)
Rarities Vol. 2 (1970-73)
UK Album Release: 08/1983 (Polydor)
US Album Release: 05/1982 (Warner Bros)
A re-cap of the group's early career for any collector who missed out first time round: a collection of originals, covers, B-sides and obscure tracks – some Townshend compositions but many by other band members or outside writers. *Rarities* failed to chart in the US or UK.

1984:

Under the terms of the Who's original Polydor contract, they still owed the label one more album so an agreement was reached where the band could release one of the live shows on their final US tour as a live LP. So it was that *Who's Last* crept out in late 1984, almost exactly 20 years after "I Can't Explain".

Who's Last
UK Album Release: 11/1984 (MCA WHO1)
US Album Release: 11/1984 (MCA MCA2-8018)
Peak Position: 48 (UK) 81 (US)
My Generation / I Can't Explain / Substitute / Behind Blue Eyes / Baba O'Riley / Boris The Spider / Who Are You / Pinball Wizard / See Me Feel Me / Love, Reign O'er Me / Long Live Rock / Long Live Rock (Reprise) / Won't Get Fooled Again / Dr Jimmy / Magic Bus / Summertime Blues / Twist and Shout

Apparently this was squeezed onto one disc by editing out much of the crowd applause, giving shorter track running lengths. MCA US CD reissue 1990 on two discs – disc one finishing on "See Me Feel Me" – features an even worse cover with gold lettering on black, spelling out the title and no picture.

Who's Last, aka *The Who Live* in some territories, was the final release from the Who before the various reunions and regroupings; before the reissues and rarities and endless concert and compilation compact discs would flood the market. Though it is no longer easily available and has been superseded by many superior releases, *Who's Last* is part of the band's musical story, though the tale it tells is not entirely complimentary.

This was a chance for the fans to get a full concert of material but, for the band, it was a lost opportunity: it was symptomatic of their declining standards and deteriorating quality control, and perhaps indicative of the huge gulf that had been allowed to grow between the musicians and their audience.

Shoddily packaged and featuring a desultory, solipsistic cover shot of a burning Union Jack in the UK, this was in many ways a shabby offering. Even the sleeve notes, packed with overdone praise for the 1982 shows – "some of the most awesome, electrifying performances delivered on any stage in the world" – and self-aggrandising statistics about smashing box-office records, had an inappropriate ring, as the record was patronisingly painted as a gift to fans in gratitude of their years of support. Keyboardist Tim Gorman is oddly credited as Jim, and worse, in some European territories – where the album was lazily entitled *The Who Live* – the cover misleadingly featured a 1975 shot of the band. French and German fans expecting a 1975 set would be very disappointed...

The contents of the discs were even worse. The track selection is fine and it's good to have the Who's version of "Twist And Shout", but these are, at best, run-of-the-mill performances from the uninspiring '82 world tour with competent vocals and a play-safe drum approach; there's plenty of crowd noise but no real electricity. Only sporadically, during "Who Are You" and "Won't Get Fooled Again" in particular, does the band hark back to former glories. Some of the tracks had already been made available on a concert VHS released the previous year, and many were already available in better live versions, either on *Live At Leeds*, *The Kids Are Alright* or the *Woodstock* soundtrack.

Sales were deservedly less than glorious: the live LP didn't progress further than number 48 in Britain and number 81 in the US. "Keith would have rolled over in his grave if he'd heard it," Chris Charlesworth later bemoaned.

"As a document of the [dubious money-making] tour, *Who's Last* is an appropriately crass artefact", *Rolling Stone*'s Kurt Loder would conclude. Loder was a Who fan, and had enjoyed the '82 tour at the time, praising the band's energy and the audience's rapturous enthusiasm. He'd clearly cooled now; in the cold light of day these mundane recordings didn't bear up under repeated listening.

"To put it bluntly", Loder continued, "The Who never sounded worse – more impotent and eviscerated – than on this dismal double album. Even the most casual comparison with those previous LPs exposes *Who's Last* as the disgraceful cash-in that it is... I can't think of another band as committed and allegedly idealistic as the Who that has ended its career on so sour and sickening a note".

14   The Long Road: Farewell, The Ox – 1985-2004

The Who extricated themselves from their Warners recording commitments by repaying a chunk of their huge advance but, though no studio album would be forthcoming, there was no shortage of new Who-related product. A succession of compilations would capture the public imagination to varying degrees while live albums and rarities collections would cater for the diehard fans.

There were also plenty more solo albums from Pete, John and Roger, but they made precious little impact and the most interesting of these works were Townshend's *Scoop* volumes of archive demos from 1983 and 1987. Two collections of covers and originals – *Who's Missing* and the follow-up *Two's Missing* – were released in 1985 and 1987 respectively.

Two years after their "final" tour, the Who regrouped to play Bob Geldof's huge *Live Aid* African famine relief charity gig on 13th July, 1985. Subsequently, they would continue to reform intermittently for another twenty years and beyond. Sometimes, these reunions were clearly spurred on by financial imperatives, but there would be other motivations too. More surprising would be the fact that *It's Hard* would not, eventually, turn out to be the Who's final studio album. In the meantime, the musicians continued work on a succession of solo projects while their back pages got another outing with 1988's TV-advertised UK compilation, *Who's Better, Who's Best* making it to number 10 on the UK album charts. A reissue of "My Generation" even made it to number 68 on the UK singles chart around the same time.

Pete, Roger and John reconvened in 1988 to work as the Who on a couple of tracks for Pete's star-studded *The Iron Man* concept solo record, based on a children's book by poet Ted Hughes. Simon Phillips was brought in on drums after Kenney was passed over for any regroupings at Roger's insistence. Other quality guest turns on the project include legends John Lee Hooker and Nina Simone, as well as Pete's old friend and fellow Meher Baba devotee, Billy Nicholls, who'd written some of the highlights of the *McVicar* soundtrack. Pity there was nothing on *The Iron Man* to match that level of songwriting quality. *The Iron Man*, which premiered the following spring, proved to be an unremarkable set and met with a patchy response, in spite of some good performances and occasionally inspired guitar playing. The pair of "Who" tracks were arguably the highlights of an ambitious but uneven affair.

In the liner notes, Pete described his intention as having been to write "a modern song-cycle musical in the manner of *Tommy*". But as *Rolling Stone*'s David Fricke pointed out, "Hardcore Who disciples listening to the choral parts and rather sleek arrangements that make up much of the album can be forgiven for thinking Townshend actually wrote *The Iron Man* in the manner of a highbrow

Cats". Nonetheless, Fricke found the project enjoyable if inessential, and gave it a generous three-and-a-half stars out of five, concluding that this child-oriented project was "Townshend's 'My Generation' for the next generation". While it may have appealed to children, it did not appeal to their parents. Even with the publicity of a large Who reunion tour, the album was a commercial flop.

Pete Townshend
The Iron Man: The Musical
UK Album Release: 03/1989 (Virgin V 2592)
US Album Release: 1989 (Atlantic 81996)
Peak Position: 58 (UK)
I Won't Run Anymore / Over the Top / Man Machines / Dig* / A Friend Is A Friend / I Eat Heavy Metal / All Shall Be Well / Was There Life / Fast Food / A Fool Says / Fire* / New Life (Reprise)
2006 remastered CD on SPV Records; digi-pack sleeve featuring a new booklet. Digitally balanced and remastered by Jon Astley. Bonus tracks: Dig (Simons Vocal) / Man Machines (Long Version) / I Eat Heavy Metal (Demo) * Credited to the Who

Fire
(Arthur Brown, Vincent Crane, Mike Finesilver, Peter Ker)
A grinding, bulldozing synth-drenched heavy metal reconstruction of the Who's old Track label-mate, Arthur Brown's Townshend-produced UK number one hit enters on a cascade of white noise. Where the original was Hammer House of Horror pop-schlock, this menacing piece manages to be both tribal and industrial. Roger does battle with coruscating slabs of metallic guitar against some thundering drumming. While not a patch on Arthur's original, this is a thrilling reinvention. There are plenty of ideas on display with an intriguing understated bells and wind-chimes outro.

Dig
(Townshend)
After a brief chain-gang chant, "Dig" emerges as a rootsy rocker. Daltrey's vocals, the trademark synths, haunting harmonies, pounding rhythm section, and chiming guitars do make this sound like a modern Who record, and its plaintive coda is curiously moving. The Who would play this live during their coming tour, while resisting Pete's attempts to extensively showcase *Iron Man* material.

By the time the *Iron Man* CD hit the shops, the Who's full-scale 25th anniversary 1989 reunion tour was already underway. Townshend, complaining of deafness, would restrict himself to acoustic guitar, and chose to perform inside a perspex box. The fans turned out in force, but the dominant presence of session musicians resulted in shows that were too clean, too polished – this was showbiz, not Maximum R&B.

The tour culminated in a Hollywood gala all-star production of *Tommy*, which many observers dismissed as a purely money-making exercise, motivated in part, perhaps, by a large tax demand for the former Inland Revenue employee, John Entwistle. There was precious little new material, the group having vetoed Townshend's plan to feature more than a few songs from *Iron Man*, so it was something of a nostalgia trip, albeit a commercially successful one. The four New Jersey stadium shows grossed over $5million alone. John would claim, rather implausibly considering the statistics in the *Who's Last* liner notes, that this was the only tour the Who ever made money on, adding, "We should have charged $140 a ticket." More tours and live albums would follow.

1990-94:

The only real pleasures for Who fans were now in revisiting the past. Certainly, it was with former glories in mind that the Who were inducted into the Rock'N'Roll Hall Of Fame in 1990, and a year later, when Townshend was crowned a "Living Legend" at the International Rock Awards.

Away from the awards galas, life beyond music was starting to become rather more settled: Pete had bought a yacht and Roger was concentrating on acting and trout farming. In March 1991, Daltrey announced he was quitting the music business, tired of struggling to forge a successful solo career. He missed the Who, though, and found the film world very frustrating. But his pet project, *Buddy's Song*, was acclaimed in 1991, and he found plenty of work in lesser movies like *Cold Justice* and Paul Hogan's *Lightning Jack*.

Nineteen ninety-three saw a new Broadway production of *Tommy*, now named *The Who's Tommy*, pick up five Tony awards. The following February, Roger was returning to the Who's back pages himself, when he played a couple of "Daltrey Sings Townshend" shows at New York's Carnegie Hall, with a 70-piece band and orchestra, to celebrate his 50th birthday. Also known as "A Celebration: The Music of Pete Townshend and the Who", this memorable pair of nights was produced by Roger and arranged for orchestra by Michael Kamen, who directed the Juilliard Orchestra for the event. As well as a fantastic band, that included past – and future – Who members, Rabbit on keyboards, Pino Palladino on bass and Simon Phillips on drums, guests included Eddie Vedder, Sinéad O'Connor, Lou Reed, David Sanborn, Alice Cooper, Linda Perry, the Chieftains and John and Pete. A 1994 Bob Ezrin-produced CD recording was a fitting tribute to the shows, which would also get a VHS and DVD release.

Perhaps surprising was the amount of *Quadrophenia* material aired both at the shows and on the album. Linda Perry's demolition of "Dr Jimmy" was pure dynamite, while, after bemoaning the original mixes, Roger reclaimed "The Real Me" and "5.15" with a vintage rock star roar. It was on these nights that the foundations were laid for the 1996-97 reinvention of *Quadrophenia* in concert.

In the meantime, when Roger took his show on the road – with John Entwistle on bass, Ringo Starr's son Zak Starkey on drums and Simon Townshend on guitar – though it lost money, its critical success seemed to drive a wedge between the singer and composer, who was still licking his wounds after the relative failure of *The Iron Man*. Ironic, considering that in every way, the project was a tribute to Pete's songwriting genius.

"He was out there doing his thing," Pete confessed, "and I was going through probably one of the worst chapters of my life, having just messed up in London with *Iron Man*. Although it was a success in its way, I was emotionally fucked up by it. I couldn't work out what had gone on. I knew that *Tommy* was hugely successful and I knew that *Iron Man* had somehow failed and it didn't have to do with the disparity in their budgets, it was something else... I went away to review my life and think about what I was going to do next. Meanwhile, Roger's tour was rolling and I was somehow expected to be a happy-go-lucky part of it all. I couldn't do it."

Pete also felt Roger's manager was trying to expand the show into a fully-fledged Who reunion, which he knew Roger was also keen on. Pete would adamantly resist these entreaties feeling that he, Roger and John wouldn't be able to come up with any new Who recordings to justify a regrouping. There would be no new Who studio album, of that Townshend was absolutely adamant.

Basking in the admiration of successful Britpop bands like Oasis and Blur, who bore their influence and sang their praises, the Who were enjoying a resurgence in popularity. That would intensify with the release in July 1994, of the CD box-set *30 Years Of Maximum R&B*, an ambitious project driven by Who expert Chris Charlesworth which would help detract from the group's more recent failings and focus on their finest hours.

The Who: 30 Years Of Maximum R&B
UK Album Release: 07/1994 (Polydor 521751-2)
US Album Release: 05/1994 (MCA MCAD4-11020)
Peak Position: 48 (UK) 170 (US)
Disc 1: Pete Townshend Dialogue / I'm The Face / Here 'Tis / Zoot Suit / Leaving Here / I Can't Explain / Anyway, Anyhow, Anywhere / Daddy Rolling Stone / My Generation / The Kids Are Alright / The Ox / A Legal Matter / Pete Dialogue / Substitute (Live) / I'm A Boy / Disguises (Stereo Mix) / Happy Jack Jingle / Happy Jack / Boris The Spider / So Sad About Us / A Quick One / Pictures Of Lily / Early Morning Cold Taxi / Coke 2 / The Last Time / I Can't Reach You / Girl's Eyes / Bag O'Nails / Call Me Lightning
Disc 2: Rotosound Strings / I Can See For Miles / Mary Anne With The Shaky Hand / Armenia, City In The Sky / Tattoo / Our Love Was / Rael 1 / Rael 2 / Track Records / Premier Drums / Sunrise / Russell Harty Dialogue / Jaguar (Edited) / Melancholia / Fortune Teller / Magic Bus / Little Billy / Dogs (Stereo Mix) / Overture / Acid Queen / Abbie Hoffman Incident / Underture / Pinball Wizard / I'm Free / See Me, Feel Me (Live) / Heaven And Hell / Pete Townshend Dialogue / Young Man Blues / Summertime Blues
Disc 3: Shakin' All Over (Live) / Baba O'Riley / Bargain (Live) (Edited) / Pure And Easy / Song Is Over / Studio Dialogue / Behind Blue Eyes / Won't Get Fooled Again / The Seeker / Bony Moronie (Live) / Let's See Action / Join Together / Relay / The Real Me / 5.15 / Bellboy / Love, Reign O'er Me
Disc 4: Long Live Rock / Life With The Moons / Naked Eye (Live) / University Challenge / Slip Kid / Poetry Cornered / Dreaming From The Waist (Live) / Guitar And Pen / You Better You Bet / Eminence Front / Twist And Shout (Live) / I'm A Man (Live) / Pete Townshend Dialogue / Saturday Night's Alright For Fighting

Well, this set does the business. There's no way round it.
Jon Savage

One of Britain's most influential music magazines, *Q*, called this the "best box-set ever". It featured a fine combination of hits and album highlights – mostly remixed here – with some blistering live versions and rarities, including some enlightening recordings of dialogue but, most importantly, some tracks which up until this point had remained unreleased.

A selected number of these gems included "Here Tis", recorded in 1964 as the High Numbers. This was part of the recording sessions that led EMI to reject the band. Produced by Chris Parmeinter and Pete Meaden, this naive cover of the Ellas McDaniel song features a jolly-up 60s backing track with Roger on lead harmonica.

They sound quaint and eager to please – it's a snap-shot of the band at their most unguarded. Leftovers from *The Who Sell Out* are also included: "Early Morning Cold Taxi", "Coke 2", "Girl's Eyes", "Bag O'Nails", "Track Records", "Jaguar", "Melancholia" and "Fortune Teller".

A previously unheard track recorded for *Quadrophenia* appears, a half-time version of "The Real Me"; it's much closer to Pete's original demo version, but in no way does it measure up to the turbo-charged track eventually used. There's storming live renditions of "I'm A Man" from NYC in '89, "Dreaming From The Waist" from the '76 tour plus "Twist And Shout" from Shea Stadium in 1982. There's also a fantastic cover version of Elton John's "Saturday Night's Alright For Fighting" recorded for the 1991 tribute album *Two Rooms: Celebrating The Songs Of Elton John & Bernie Taupin*. The street-tough lyrics sound far more convincing on Roger's lips than they ever did from Elton John's. In a breakdown close to the end of the track the Who segue into "Take Me To The Pilot", a track from Elton's 1970 eponymous LP. Pete revealed that this was a nod to Elton's version of "Pinball Wizard", where he segued briefly into the Who's first single, "I Can't Explain".

Also included are the dialogue tracks which feature Pete at turns; entertaining a live audience with jovial banter ("Substitute" live at Leeds University 1970) and then berating them (live at Long Beach Arena in 1971). From the Woodstock festival you hear Pete shouting at Abbie Hoffman, "Fuck off! Fuck off my fucking stage!" But relaxed good humour prevails in the recording studio as the intro to "Behind Blue Eyes" is abandoned among coughs and laughter from the band. Collectively, these dialogue tracks are an entertaining and telling insight into a different aspect of the band. And then there is Keith's interludes and brief comedy sketches where he mocks the popular UK TV show *University Challenge*, poetry with "Poetry Corner" and contemplates, during "Life With The Moons", the idea of staging a rock opera version of *Pilgrims Progress*, where Keith purports, "I could play the part of Chaucer me-self... Daltrey could help me with the hard bits!"

This monumental collection is a must for all Who fans and well worth the still substantial purchase price. Chris Charlesworth excelled himself with this exhaustive look back at the band's varied and illustrious career to date. He gave listeners a candid and unique insight into the band's output.

1995-2002:

A fine campaign of remastered and expanded, and sometimes deluxe, editions of the Who's classic albums would follow. One, the 1995 remastered *Live At Leeds* even made it to number 59 on the UK album charts.

Later in 1995, Roger expanded his acting roles with the part of the Tin Man in an all-star charity performance of *The Wizard Of Oz* in New York. Meanwhile, John confirmed the love of heavy metal that had infiltrated his songwriting contributions to Who albums once and for all, by recording an album, *Edge Of The World*, with Judas Priest guitarist Glen Tipton – who wrote and sang all the songs – and legendary hard rock drummer Cozy Powell. Rainbow alumni Don Airey added keyboards. It didn't get any more metal than this. There were plans for Tipton, Powell and Entwistle to tour, but Tipton's record label dismissed the album as too "old school", suggested he worked with some younger musicians and *Edge Of The World* was shelved. It's a shame because, even though this is generic and cliché-strewn heavy metal, it's solidly energetic, with some highpoints and Entwistle's playing is remarkable throughout. It would eventually gain a 2006 release on Rhino.

In 1996, the Who would regroup for some landmark shows. Credit card giant, MasterCard, were sponsoring a Prince's Trust charity show at London's Hyde Park on 29th June, to feature a line-up that would include Bob Dylan and Eric Clapton. Promoter Harvey Goldsmith invited Pete to take part and, spurred on by *Tommy*'s recent resurgence, Townshend suggested resurrecting *Quadrophenia*. He'd been thinking about reviving the piece for some time, and had even drafted a rough treatment. First thoughts were for a very ambitious staging along the lines of U2's *Zoo TV*. Pete's initial idea soon gathered momentum, spurred on by interest in the Italian scooter manufacturer Piaggio using his work as a focus for a 50-year celebration of, Mod icon, the Vespa scooter.

Townshend may have also been influenced by the fact that US band Phish had been playing an authentic version of the entire *Quadrophenia* album during their marathon Grateful Dead-influenced live sets. It brought the Who's music to a new generation of young American music fans. Phish would even release their live version of the material, recorded at the Rosemont Horizon on 31st October, 1995, *Livephish 14*.

For Hyde Park, Pete would later say that, initially, he thought of just performing a selection of the material single-handedly with an acoustic guitar, but he quickly realised he needed more. "I suddenly thought that obviously the path that would be the easiest to go and the most straightforward to go," he explained, "would be exactly the path that I went on with *Tommy*, which would be to do a bunch of concerts in which we had celebrity performers, and to see whether it would work."

The key would be to convince Roger and John to come on board. Though Daltrey wasn't keen initially, Pete persevered and Roger finally conceded he was willing to give it a chance. A lot of the material was still fresh for Townshend and Entwistle; they'd recently performed at a Who fans convention where their two-hour set had included several *Quadrophenia* songs. The band would take part in the Hyde Park gig not as the Who, but upon John's suggestion, billed as TED (Townshend, Entwistle, Daltrey). Phil Daniels, who'd acted in *Quadrophenia*, would be the narrator, and Gary Glitter – later disgraced as a convicted paedophile – was cast as the Godfather character.

"It's a much more cohesive, dramatic work, than anything I've ever done," Pete maintained, but he was aware of the difficulties in bringing his masterpiece to the stage. "The problem with it, is it's an inside view. It's an internal story. So it's quite difficult to realise without quite a lot of suspension of disbelief on the audience's part." To help overcome this, as well as Daniels' on-stage narration, the story would be illustrated by a screen backdrop showing specially-shot film footage. Roger Daltrey collaborated on the script.

Drummer Zak Starkey, son of Ringo Starr, had joined the band, after a stint as Roger's drummer on his solo projects. "He does a garage band imitation of Keith which is probably unbeatable," Pete would tell Ira Robbins. "Keith used to be a kind of musical godfather to [Zak]... Ringo may have actually given him his first drum kit, but I think Keith gave him the first drum kit that he really wanted. It had nude women on it."

"Keith taught Zak to drum and his style is very similar to Keith's," Roger would insist. "For the first time since Keith died, we had a drummer who was on the same level as the other three in the band, and the music came to life for the first time since Keith was in the band. Basically, that was reforming the Who."

Pete's brother Simon was drafted in to play additional guitar. An expanded line-up of musicians – featuring guests including Pink Floyd's David Gilmour – and better technology meant the original challenges of malfunctioning backing tapes were overcome and the show was well-received. Also, in spite of Pete's much-publicised hearing difficulties that usually restricted him to strumming an acoustic guitar, he decided to play some electric guitar, and would even contribute the occasional solo. Following the acclaim for their appearance at the Prince's Trust gig, the Who took the show to New York a month later, for a six-night run at Madison Square Garden. After honing the script, dropping the on-stage narration and shooting additional screen footage, the Who would continue to tour *Quadrophenia* in the US, Britain and Europe over the next year or so. For some of the shows, Billy Idol came in as the Ace Face and PJ Proby replaced Gary Glitter.

"In-between the songs we took a piece from the record sleeve and inserted it into the script," Pete explained. Roger wanted to deal with a couple of grey areas in the original story, giving the piece more form without undermining the dreamlike quality, and – according to Townshend – to compensate for the fact that "the narrative falls to pieces once Jimmy is on drugs."

With the aid of the big screen backdrop – a combination of vintage footage, both of Mods and early High Numbers shows, specially filmed location-shot vignettes featuring Jimmy as narrator, and clips from the movie – the live performance was able to follow the plotline of Townshend's original music and liner notes more closely than Franc Roddam's movie had attempted to. Unlike the sometimes jarring mixture of source material and new plotlines in the film, the live show had greater musical and narrative cohesion. The shot footage can't compete on quality terms with Franc Roddam's evocative naturalism, but does succeed in bringing to life Jimmy's internal struggles. So unlike in the film, here Jimmy does work as a dustman, become politicised and try to persuade his war veteran work colleagues to organise and rebel against their bosses.

The symbol of the rock jutting from the sea off Brighton beach, which was so important to the source album, returns here as plot element and metaphorical device. The Meher Baba-inspired oceanic imagery which dominated the album's lyrics, sound effects and booklet artwork is even more prominent here. On the big-screen backdrop, Jimmy makes explicit before the "Love, Reign O'er Me" thundering climax, that he is both older and wiser. Though clips from the film version's ambiguous finale flash on the screen, there is no question at all of the 90s Jimmy choosing suicide. Also, as the US was the main market, the screen footage was much more explanatory about the nature of the Mod phenomenon in Britain than was necessary in the original film, with its British cultural and historical references that were immediately understood at home.

"Everything I write will always have the post-war thing running through it," Pete would comment, "because that's my period." So there is grainy black and white footage of the Blitz and people sleeping in Tube stations, war evacuees, the food queues, and the terrifying mushroom clouds of the nuclear bomb blasts over Nagasaki and Hiroshima. There are scenes of the victory homecoming celebrations and the end of rationing in the 50s, through the news events of the early 60s – the obscenity trial over D.H. Lawrence's novel, *Lady Chatterley's Lover*; the assassination of President Kennedy; Beatlemania; the war in Vietnam, and the Mods and rockers of *Quadrophenia*. It's a timeline that vividly illustrates the change in society from the war years to the birth of the "teenager" and the youth culture that would heighten the sense of a generation gap, with parents who had experienced the war and now just wanted safety, security and quiet domesticity, and their post-war offspring who were looking for excitement, self-expression and meaning.

"All our parents wanted was a peaceful life," Roger would explain. "Nine-to-five, pipe and slippers... they'd had enough excitement for 10 lifetimes... we couldn't understand it... they came across to us as incredibly boring."

As Pete would explain years later, Jimmy suffered from "misdirected anger that can't be channelled in a post-war situation, where the established practices of looking after difficulties in life couldn't help you; you had to work this one out yourself." The finished script made it clear that, for all the talk of Mods and rockers, and fractured psyches, *Quadrophenia* really was the story of an angry, frustrated post-war kid's adolescent identity crisis, of failing to find a connection with the previous generation, or to find meaning as part of a tribe of his own age, and ultimately, having to work it out for himself.

As for the music, it really did work this time. Once they had honed the set after a few shows, the performances were electrifying, with Entwistle particularly on ferocious form on tracks like "5.15" and "The Punk And The Godfather", and Zak almost making Moon's position his own. Where the source album was more mid-paced and dominated by synths, the live revival shows were more guitar-driven with a harder edge. Billy Idol and PJ Proby put in good star turns and Pete and his brother Simon also ably took some of the lead vocals, though Roger leads the way here, sounding confident and mature. Pete may be mostly playing acoustic rhythm, but he bashes the hell out of his instrument and when he does pick up an electric guitar, he goes for a blistering solo at the climax of "Love, Reign O'er Me". The live songs have additional musical colour aided by a five-piece horn section that enhanced John's original arrangements; unlike the '89 reunion tour, where they ruined the songs. And, though the source album versions of all the *Quadrophenia* songs remain the definitive ones, the horn-drenched, electric guitar-powered "Love, Reign O'er Me" comes very close to surpassing its illustrious predecessor.

The original *Quadrophenia* album benefited from all of the attention and briefly returned to the UK album chart, peaking at 47; "My Generation" returned to the UK singles chart yet again, peaking this time at 31. Yet, *Quadrophenia* again failed to quite capture the imagination in the way that the various incarnations of *Tommy* did. Pete continued to harbour further plans for the work, though, hoping for a proper theatrical presentation. "What I think *Quadrophenia* lends itself to," he told Ira Robbins, "and what I might be able to pull off where others have failed in the long term, is to create a rock'n'roll event of great integrity and authenticity which can sit down somewhere in an installation."

Nineteen ninety-nine would also see further fruits of the long-delayed *Lifehouse* project that had played such a huge part in the Who's musical journey. A version of the piece premiered on BBC Radio 3 on 5th December and, later the same month, a six-CD box set was made available from Pete's own Eel Pie label. And he was still talking about making it into a film.

Roger, meanwhile, continued his varied acting career, appearing as a former drug dealer in an episode of long-running British TV crime drama *The Bill* and as a washed-up alcoholic rock star in US sitcom, *Rude Awakenings*. He also took a small part in a new movie of *Oliver* and hit Broadway as Ebenezer Scrooge in a production of Dickens' *A Christmas Carol*. "Until I can come up with something that sounds completely different, I don't want to make an album," Roger insisted. "I'd hate to make a record that made people ask 'Why?' I'm a singer who acts when I'm out of work and an actor who sings when I can't get a gig. I can't just sit around doing nothing…"

The Who marked the end of the century with two fine shows at the Shepherd's Bush Empire, in a West London homecoming that brought them only a short walk from their old 60s stomping ground. At the dawn of a new millennium, the group were still touring and enjoying some of their best live notices in years.

Two thousand and one saw a final resolution to the ongoing wrangle over the CD release of *The Who Sings My Generation*. After setting an outrageous price for the master tapes on Ebay, Shel Talmy saw reason and the rights were cleared, though some parts seemed to have been wiped along the way. A CD version of this rock landmark was long overdue and it was given a warm welcome.

The Ox Dies In Las Vegas

Playing with renewed energy and vigour and to more acclaim than they'd had in years, it seemed like the indomitable Who would go on forever. Then tragedy struck.

On 27th June, 2002, just before the band were about to embark on a US tour, John Entwistle was found dead in a hotel room at the Hard Rock Hotel in Las Vegas. He was 57. The medical explanation was a heart attack brought on by cocaine use. While the media made much of the coke aspect, and the presence in his hotel room of a mystery female, Entwistle only had a small amount of the drug in his system and had long suffered from a heart condition. He'd rarely indulged to the level of his more extreme contemporaries, and as Keith Altham put it, "The Ox was seemingly indestructible."

Tributes poured in from fans, fellow musicians and friends. Pete and Roger were devastated. "We knew he had blood pressure problems," Roger commented at the time. "But no one thought to ask him to get his heart checked. But if we had, he would have told us to fuck off and mind our own business. Or just grunt and ask for another brandy…"

Unmoved by the more sordid angles of some of the reporting, Roger insisted Entwistle wouldn't have wanted his demise to have been any other way: "Ask most blokes how they would like to go," Roger told one reporter, "on the seafront in Eastbourne in a bath chair or in Las Vegas after a line of coke and a good bang with a hooker?"

The Who's poignant official statement read "The Ox has left the building. We've lost another great friend...". Entwistle's body was returned to England and buried near his Stow-on-the-Wold home in Gloucestershire. On a memorial card, Roger wrote "It seems ridiculous to tell you to rest in peace, my friend, so Rave On." Roger remarked later that it should have said "Rest in Noise".

As the quiet stoic, Entwistle's contributions to the band were less obvious than the world's most flamboyant drummer's had been – certainly, John was less of a visual focal point than Keith Moon. Perhaps the stolid bassist wouldn't be missed in the same way as the ultimate rock showman. When Bill Wyman quit the Stones, Mick Jagger acidly quipped that he'd play bass himself, adding "how hard can it be?" Yet Entwistle was far more than a beat-hugging four-stringer. A multi-instrumentalist with a dexterity and imagination that was far superior to any of his peers, John was arguably the finest technical musician in the Who. He was the anchor that held all of the Who's disparate musical forces together, but his playing was also packed with hooks, riffs and melodic runs. John played bass like the lead guitarist he'd always wanted to be, just with added maximum bottom-end resonance.

"He was the best," Roger commented in tribute to his friend. "As Bill Wyman said, he did for the bass guitar what Jim Hendrix did for the lead guitar. He made the bass do things it was never meant to do – extraordinary."

"What's interesting in our group is that the roles are reversed," Pete had earlier insisted. "John's the lead guitar, and although I'm not the bass player, he produces a hell of a lot of lead work." But, for all his power and virtuosity – he wasn't known as "Thunderfingers" for nothing – John wasn't unnecessarily flashy. Away from his main instrument, John's haunting horn parts and sophisticated brass arrangements were vital to works as diverse as "Pictures Of Lily" and *Quadrophenia*. Possessing a wide vocal range, he could go from way-down-in-your-boots tenor rumblings to the highest falsetto shriek. Though no compositional genius like Pete, Entwistle was a clever, witty, songwriter equally at home with the whimsical or sardonic, the darkly twisted or knock-about humour.

The surviving members of the Who were faced with the same predicament as they'd been in after Keith Moon's death. How to replace the irreplaceable? And yet, a US tour was upon them and difficult decisions had to be made. Pete told Who biographer Dave Marsh in 2006 that Roger said he'd do whatever Townshend thought best. Pete decided that the tour must go ahead and Roger concurred. Pino Palladino was brought in on bass – learning the set with minimal rehearsal time – to line up alongside Zak Starkey, Simon Townshend and Rabbit Bundrick, and the tour went ahead in spite of the tragedy. In fact, Townshend seemed to play with a renewed sense of fury. It was surely what the Ox would have wanted...

"As soon as we started playing it was like John was back," Roger commented at the time. "He's in that music, just like Keith Moon is. That really helped with the grieving."

In September 2002 *Q* magazine included the Who in its poll of 50 Bands To See Before You Die.

2003-4:

Who 2

Roger Daltrey spent part of 2003 fronting the History Channel's *Extreme History* series. He interrupted this work to appear in Alan Jay Lerner and Frederick Loewe's classic Broadway musical, *My Fair Lady*, a show Roger had loved since childhood, relishing the blue-collar fecklessness of his role as Alfred P. Doolittle.

During the winter of 2003 a line-up of the Who, these days referred to as "Millennium" Who or Who 2 (Pete's favourite), convened at Pete's own Eel Pie Studios in Twickenham. The group were now finally working on a brand new Who album, a selection of songs said to be jointly written by Townshend and Daltrey, though which would turn out to be Pete's material. Pete had been composing and recording material for a new Who record as far back as the previous year.

The line-up that started recording was the one that had finished the last USA tour – Pete, Roger, Zak and Pino Palladino, Rabbit Bundrick on piano and Pete's brother Simon adding guitar and keyboards. Simon also took over as producer. However, after completing only one song, "Old Red Wine" Pino had to leave to join a previously planned tour with Simon & Garfunkel. He was replaced by Greg Lake (formerly of King Crimson and Emerson, Lake and Palmer) and another song was completed, "Real Good Looking Boy". The two finished songs were then released as a single in the UK. They became the final disc of *The 1st Singles Box*, a classy and stylish Polydor collection of 12 CD singles comprising facsimile sleeves and featuring the A- and B-sides of a selection of classic 45s. The box set was Townshend's idea, and the tracks were selected with the help of Who experts George McManus and Matt Kent. In the USA, the two new Who tracks made up the final two songs of a new Who compilation, *Then And Now: 1964 - 2004*.

The 1st Singles Box

UK Singles Release: 26/04/2004 (Polydor 9866338) 12 Individual CD singles in facsimile sleeves:
I Can't Explain / Bald Headed Woman
My Generation / Shout And Shimmy
Substitute / Circles
I'm A Boy / In The City
Happy Jack / I've Been Away
Pictures Of Lily / Doctor, Doctor
I Can See For Miles / Someone's Coming
Pinball Wizard / Dogs (Part 2)
Won't Get Fooled Again / Don't Know Myself
5.15 / Water
Who Are You / Had Enough
Real Good Looking Boy / Old Red Wine

Then And Now 1964-2004

US Album Release: 30/03/2004 (Universal/Geffen B0001836-02)
I Can't Explain / My Generation / The Kids Are Alright / Substitute / I'm A Boy / Happy Jack / I Can See For Miles / Magic Bus / Pinball Wizard / See Me, Feel Me / Summertime Blues (Live) / Behind Blue Eyes / Won't Get Fooled Again / 5.15 / Love, Reign O'er Me / Squeeze Box / Who Are You / You Better You Bet / Real Good Looking Boy / Old Red Wine

We were part of a machine. A pop-record churning-out machine, a big package.
Pete Townshend

I'm still angry about a lot of things. So many things we thought would get better when we were young have not. Pete is the old person who can articulate this and drag rock'n'roll into old age. He is still writing great songs about things we all feel and can identify with. We owe it to our audience and the talent we were given to carry on.
Roger Daltrey

Real Good Looking Boy

(Pete Townshend, Luigi Creatore, Hugo E. Peretti, George David Weiss)
The extended writing credits are because the song incorporates, right from the offset, the melody to Elvis's "Can't Help Falling In Love" in a beautiful piano intro – and later quotes directly from its chorus. But this was written as more than just an Elvis tribute; instead it's a meditation on appearances in general, as the protagonist wonders if he is considered handsome. His mum tells him he's "an ugly boy" and blames the family's odd genes.

"'Real Good Looking Boy' is a song I wrote quite a few years ago about two young men who worry about their looks," Pete would explain. "One of them, based on me, hopes and believes he might look like his best friend who is a conventionally handsome fellow (he is disabused of this notion by his mother). The second, based on Roger, hopes and believes he will one day turn out to be like the young Elvis (he, more happily, sees part of his dream come true)."

While every post-war rock'n'roller was influenced by Elvis to some degree, seeing Presley on television had changed Roger's life: "I was gobsmacked," he would relate in 2007. "Suddenly the world made sense. That was when I knew what I was going to be when I grew up."

Dreams of beauty and stardom aside, Pete's consolation in the song for the two boys is that "they both find love in later life". Indeed, this is a survivor's tale. The protagonist realises he has been given far more than mere physical beauty – he was given a gift and has grown to appreciate it with grace. And he has known love.

The arrangement and tune has a real maturity to match the mood. This is an ebbing and flowing rock ballad, that gathers momentum and grows. While piano, strings and guitar dominate, Zak Starkey sounds inspired here, as the band truly take off in the Springsteen-esque play-out. Crucially, "Real Good Looking Boy" has something that was missing from the last new Who number, "Dig", and that is a memorable melody. Even without the steal from Elvis's composers, this is a great tune. It's not surprising that the US label were so excited and willing to hold back their compilation album to incorporate this.

When Pete and Roger came to perform "Real Good Looking Boy" at a charity concert, Roger sang, accompanying himself on an acoustic guitar with very restrained backing from the band. Treating it almost as a solo folk performance, Roger truly inhabited Pete's song, turning it into a meditation about Elvis's effect on his life. That performance helped to convince Townshend that they could make another Who album, fired by his compositions and Daltrey's interpretations: "I make the widgets and [Roger] takes it to the public."

Old Red Wine
(Townshend)
This tribute to John Entwistle takes its title from the bass player's wine obsession. He fancied himself as something of an oenophile, so Pete would give him a bottle of cheap plonk pretending it was an expensive vintage to test him out, or be shocked to find John knocking back a bottle that was clearly corked.

"John loved expensive claret," Pete reflected, "and often drank it past its prime. There is an irony there somehow: John never seemed to realise how perfectly mature he had really become as a rock musician. He didn't need the trappings he thought essential, and that – in my opinion – led directly to his premature death."

This is a soaring rock ballad with a hard edge; somehow the group avoid slipping into sentimentality, but the lyrics are moving as Pete's words dwell on when he may well see his old friend again:

Old red wine
Well past its prime
May have to finish it with you
After crossing the line...
Old red wine
Gonna have to drink it with you
Some other time...

"Old red wine well past its prime", of course, could easily refer to the band themselves, but on this form, especially the full-on rocking "Let it breathe" coda, they sound in rude good health.

After the declining standards of the last two studio albums and a few false starts, the Who were back in the studio and sounding fresher than they had in years. No gimmicks, no in-vogue producers or fashionable sounds here, these were two pretty timeless recordings that revealed a band that had come to terms with their place in the scheme of things. There is no attempt here to be at rock's cutting edge, and yet, both in the shameless Presley appropriation and the lyrical maturity and, not least, the moving Entwistle tribute, here is the sound of a group that has, against all the odds, grown older with wisdom and good grace.

Five years earlier, reflecting on the band's demise, Pete had imagined Daltrey's view on a reunion: "We got a few things wrong, [Roger would] say, but if we picked up from where we were before, we could go on and everything would be great." Perhaps he was right; certainly, these two tracks would bode well for a forthcoming Who studio album.

The first ten singles in the box were discussed earlier when they originally appeared – including comments on the B-sides, where relevant. The facsimile UK original single inner artwork for "Substitute", here, has the correct Townshend production credit, "A New Action Production", for the original B-side, "Circles" ("Instant Party"), but the box set liner booklet states that the recording on the CD single is the Talmy production, which sounds like it is the case. The two authorised versions of this Who single, prior to the litigation-inspired change of flipside to the non-Who instrumental "Waltz For A Pig", featured Townshend's production. Talmy's version only appeared on the flip of his label's "A Legal Matter" 45. Disc twelve formed the Who 2 material. Disc eleven is the original single edit of "Who Are You" with the original B-side, John's "Had Enough" drawn straight from the album.

The coupling of "Real Good Looking Boy" with "Old Red Wine" would require mock single cover artwork unavailable outside this set. For the other facsimile 45s, rather than simply featuring the original UK 7" sleeves and inners, a variety of interesting and colourful covers were reproduced in this beautiful box, along with a fine set of lavishly illustrated liner notes. The CDs themselves are also printed as replica mini 45s. "I Can't Explain" features the original Decca US artwork, "My Generation" features the 1965 German single cover while "Substitute" has the original 1966 UK sleeve. "I'm A Boy" is in the 1966 German picture sleeve while "Happy Jack" features the Norwegian sleeve with a stunning ink pen caricature of the band by cartoonist Ralph Steadman. "Pictures Of Lily" comes in a 1967 French promotional sleeve while "I Can See For Miles" is wrapped in its Japanese picture cover. "Pinball Wizard" features the US "pinball" sleeve, "Won't Get Fooled Again" comes in its 1971 Yugoslavian picture sleeve, "5.15" in the French picture sleeve while "Who Are You" features the 1978 UK sleeve.

Rolling Stone magazine place the Who at a very healthy number 29 on their 100 Greatest Artists Of All Time list; 2004 would also be memorable for another revisit to the Who's illustrious history, when the group returned to play as headliners on the Isle of Wight. This time the sun shone. It was a more sober affair than the legendary 1970 festival, where Roger shared bottles of Southern Comfort with the Doors' Jim Morrison, and Keith Moon's madcap spirit reigned supreme. But the Who were proven survivors and put in a great performance to the acclaim of fans and critics alike.

The *Daily Telegraph* critic concluded, "Roger Daltrey and Pete Townshend of the Who delivered a masterclass in mind-crushingly intense power rock".

15 Endless Wires And Honours – 2005-08

I'm trying to write songs for two old fucks from Acton who should be dead.
Pete Townshend

As long as Pete's there on guitar, and I'm there to sing the lead, then the sound's still there and you're going to have the Who. We're not going to give up now. We're going to keep playing until we're dead.
Roger Daltrey

In a performance that was only slightly overshadowed by a full Pink Floyd reunion, the Who were one of the highlights at the massive *Live 8* gig in London's Hyde Park, London on Saturday July 2nd, 2005. Zak and Pino had previous engagements and couldn't make the gig, so drummer Steve White and bass player Damon Minchella stepped in at the last minute. They were the rhythm section for the Godfather of Brit Pop, ex-Jam frontman and lifelong Who fan, Paul Weller.

In the meantime, there was another trawl through the back pages. On 7th November, 2005, Warners put out a three-disc DVD box set comprising an all-star live 1996 performance of *Tommy* and an equally star-studded live performance of *Quadrophenia* from 1998 (both had been previously available on VHS, but this box featured additional back-stage interviews and commentary).

Two thousand and five also saw Roger made a Commander of the Order of the British Empire (CBE for short), for his work for the Teenage Cancer Trust. Inspired by the tragic premature death of his beloved younger sister Carol from breast cancer, Roger has devoted a vast amount of time to charity fundraising. Events he organised for the charity have included Who gigs at London's Royal Albert Hall in London. He has admirably used his stardom to the great benefit of others, but without ever seeking credit himself.

Townshend had been busy with several writing projects: he'd sent a series of songs to Roger for possible inclusion on a new Who album and, in September, he published on his website the first chapter of 25 weekly instalments of his novella *The Boy Who Heard Music*. This tale took direct influence from a previous Townshend unpublished novel *Ray High & The Glass Household*. Both narratives could be traced back to the ubiquitous *Lifehouse* and Pete's solo piece *Psychoderelict*; gradually he began to use this narrative as the basis for a mini-opera.

Townshend was also inspired by appearances on his partner Rachel Fuller's website broadcasts *In The Attic*. These informal shows had a limited audience but Pete found them liberating, artistically. This led to more tracks for the forthcoming Who record. He talked to the *Salt Lake Tribune* about the new material: "I use concepts mainly to keep myself inspired", but would this be a concept too far? Did the world want or need another rock opera from the Who? The fans wanted new songs – but a new opera?

Endless Wire

When the singles box appeared, it seemed likely to many Who watchers that those two new songs would be the nearest anyone would get to hearing a new Who album. The Who's final studio album had been *It's Hard* – but more than 20 years after that creative nadir, the musical history books would have to be rewritten.

Townshend had been working on a new album as far back as 2002. By that point he already had "In The Ether" and "Black Widow's Eyes" and was relying on more light-hearted material from John, who always seemed to be writing, and even Roger had promised a song or two. This left Pete to focus on songs that were, in his words "arch, dark and extreme." Pete revealed that Roger wanted to make a more traditional rock album, but that he felt it should be more about himself and Roger.

The work had sprung to life as *Wire And Glass* and, although Pete would deny that it was entirely autobiographical, in places it paralleled many aspects of the band's career and his life. In addition to Pete and Roger, this Who line-up would feature the regular touring musicians Pino Palladino on bass, Rabbit Bundrick on organ and Pete's brother Simon on backing vocals. Zak Starkey had started to play with Oasis and could only work with the Who sporadically. He did feature on one track on the new album, "Black Widow's Eyes". Pete played most of the other instruments himself, including mandolin, banjo, violin and even drums on one track.

Recording took place at Pete's home studio and his Eel Pie recording studio in Twickenham. He produced the sessions, with help from a number of engineers, including old ally Bob Pridden (who also produced Roger's vocals). Pete mixed the tracks in the summer of 2006 in-between Who live shows, taking portable equipment on the road with them. The disc was mastered in August.

Anticipation was high for a new album of original Who songs, though Pete seemed to warn against excessively high expectations when, in an interview with *Reuters* news agency, he remarked that the new record was "the same old stuff." Unfortunately, this was not to be the case.

Wire And Glass

UK EP Release: (As iTunes Download) 17/07/2006 Maxi CD 24/07/2006 (Polydor)
Sound Round / Pick Up The Peace / Endless Wire / We Got A Hit / They Made My Dream Come True / Mirror Door

Released well ahead of the album, this featured six new tracks presented as one complete piece of music. Four more tracks were added to the final opera for inclusion on the album. There was confusion among fans, some of whom thought this was actually a new album. The band failed to secure a release date in the States to coincide with the UK issue.

It's Not Enough

UK Single Release: (As iTunes Download) 03/10/2006 (Polydor)
US Single Release: (As iTunes Download) 03/10/2006 (Universal)

Peak Position: 37 (US)

Tea And Theatre
UK Single Release: (As iTunes Download) 03/10/2006 (Polydor)
US Single Release: (As iTunes Download) 03/10/2006 (Universal)
Peak Position: 47 (UK)

Both tracks were taken from the album and embraced the brave new world of internet music distribution, when they were made available on iTunes simultaneously ahead of the album release.

Endless Wire
UK Album Release: 30/10/2006 (Polydor 1709519)
US Album Release: 30/10/2006 (Universal Republic B0007967-10)
Peak Position: 9 (UK) 7 (US)
Fragments / Man In A Purple Dress / Mike Post Theme / In The Ether / Black Widow's Eyes / Two Thousand Years / God Speaks Of Marty Robbins / It's Not Enough / You Stand By Me
Wire & Glass: A Mini-Opera: Sound Round / Pick Up The Peace / Unholy Trinity / Trilby's Piano / Endless Wire / Fragments Of Fragments / We Got A Hit / They Make My Dream Come True / Mirror Door / Tea And Theatre
Bonus Tracks: We Got A Hit (Extended Version) / Endless Wire (Extended Version)
All songs by Pete Townshend except where stated.

The unfinished business of the Who is the friendship... We did such a lot of great work together and we should have enjoyed our friendship more, and we didn't. And now we do. I think that we're finishing that, and what may come out of that might be very profound, I think.
Pete Townshend, 2000

We haven't got the glamour or all the stuff that goes along with it anymore, but in some ways that makes the music more significant than ever before.
Roger Daltrey, 2007

Ultimately, it's about our audience...
Roger Daltrey to Ken Sharp, 2007

Fragments
(Townshend-Ball)
And so, after twenty-four years, a new Who studio album opens promisingly with a swirling synthesizer that instantly conjures the spirit of the epochal album *Who's Next*. Pete's electronic collaborator here, Lawrence Ball, was also a big fan of Terry Riley's minimalist music that had so influenced "Baba O'Riley".

Within seconds of the opening synth part, the track segues into a frustrating mid-tempo groove accompanied by a rather downbeat guitar motif. Daltrey's voice rings out crystal clear, but the backing track sounds as if it were recorded by a bunch of pony-tailed LA session musicians with one eye on the mirror and the other on the clock. But this is all Pete here – he is responsible for every instrument plus all the thick harmony backing vocals, with Ball providing the electronics and Roger the lead vocal. The band are immediately missed, there's virtually no energy, musical tension or intensity that a Who fan would expect, especially when compared to *Quadrophenia*'s opener, "The Real Me" or "Baba O'Riley".

It's an inauspicious start to their first album in more than two decades – it sounds nothing like the Who of old; but then, how could it? Pete and Roger were both in their 60s, and had their own personal artistic values and goals for the band that differed hugely from what their seemingly insatiable audience desired and demanded. The internet reviews and chat room conversations confirmed this at the time of release, with fans voicing their disapproval vociferously, but this record is, as Townshend commented, about himself and Roger. This opening track states firmly that what you want is not what you will get. The two artists have their own agenda and they're most definitely not playing to the gallery, writing "the same old song".

For Townshend, "Fragments" was a throwback to his pre-*Who's Next* project. "[It was] based on the continuation of the 'Method' music way," Pete explained, "of creating individual pieces of music dictated by parameters and information from individuals, which I first explored in the *Lifehouse* project." This idea to have your own tailor-made piece of music was developed further by Lawrence Ball in conjunction with software designer Dave Snowdon with his "Harmonic Maths" computer programme. This same programme was also used to create the album's cover. Richard Evans utilised it and came up with the strikingly colourful computerised landscape of wires, birds, blocks, diamonds, hearts and spades disappearing into the horizon, somewhat reminiscent of *Tommy*'s cover.

Man In A Purple Dress

Inspired by an angry sense of injustice after seeing Mel Gibson's film *The Passion Of The Christ*, Pete wrote three songs. Here, the man in a purple dress is symbolic of a pope or a cardinal and Pete rages at their hypocrisy and cowardice. Roger spits out the heartfelt Townshend lines of contempt at religious leaders' imperious stance, "How dare you wear a robe to preside / How dare you cover your head to hide / your face from God".

The lines "How dare you be the one to assess me / in this God-forsaken mess" are Townshend's response to the allegations that he had accessed indecent images of children on websites in 2003. Pete talked of the "unbelievable fucking humiliation" he endured when he was arrested, describing the media frenzy that ensued as a witch hunt. In a press statement, he said unequivocally that he was not a paedophile. He later explained that he had simply been researching the subject for a book that would include an exploration of his own experience of sexual abuse as a child (Mark Wilkerson's fine Townshend biography *Who Are You* deals with this subject sensitively and at length).

Musically, "Purple Dress" is an improvement on the first track's glossy sheen, as Roger sings to a simple acoustic guitar backing, the arrangement possibly influenced by Pete's love of Dylan's *The Freewheelin' Bob Dylan* released in 1963. Townshend acknowledged that it was similar to a Bob Dylan song "from the early days." He referred to this song as a breakthrough, where he was no longer afraid to just leave the arrangement simple with no unnecessary musical ornamentation.

The lyrical diatribe rips incisively into various religious leaders, "You Priest, you mullah so high / You Pope, you wise rabbi / You are invisible to me / Like vapour from the sea". It does however include the embarrassing lyrical couplet, "Men above / Or prats? / With your high hats".

This would be a showcase solo spot for Roger in concert, and shows the singer and writer finding a mature sound and style that suits their years. It's melodic, tuneful and tasteful, if a tad over-long. Townshend remarked in *Billboard* that the simple arrangement focused the listener's attention where it should be, "on the song".

Mike Post Theme
A trademark Daltrey roar ushers in some frantically strummed mandolins and powerful accented playing from Townshend on drums. Though the verses are subtle, there are some strong musical hooks and memorable melodic flourishes. This, crucially, does sound like the Who – albeit in semi-unplugged mode.

It's named in homage to Mike Post, who composed memorable theme tunes to classic US TV shows like *Hill Street Blues*, which Pete would say, "created a kind of regular sparkle in my life." He saw such long-running TV crime series and soap operas as something of a constant in an ever-changing world, allowing the viewers to often live their own lives and experience emotions vicariously through the characters on the screen. There may also be a hankering from Townshend for a loving relationship to retain its allure in the way that a beloved old tune endures. But the lyrical thrust here is obscure, conjuring images and snippets from crime dramas, without really saying anything specific about anything. For an erudite spiritual seeker like Pete, even if joking here, a line like "If there really is a God, we should get laid today", can hardly be said to rank with his best.

The song was also Townshend's response to criticism over the use of Who songs on TV Shows – for instance, "Baba O'Riley" and "Won't Get Fooled Again" had opened episodes of the popular US crime series, *CSI*. Here he harks back nostalgically, reminiscing about cop show themes he'd loved in an earlier time. "Mike Post's theme from *Hill Street Blues* reminds me that, once, I associated the sound with a cop who couldn't deal with his drink problem," Pete lamented. "Now I hear it and I remember a brother, for pretty soon I was facing the same problem."

In The Ether
On the surface, this is the Who-do-Tom-Waits circa *Blue Valentine*. Roger's well-worn larynx couldn't stretch to match anything like the old Bourbon Street growler's nicotine-stained, whiskery vocals. Pete had to take the lead vocal, because Roger dismissed this as "a bit music-theatre." In the spirit of mature collaboration, Roger suggested a change of instrumentation; he felt the song would benefit from a more "Young Man Blues" approach. A piqued Pete resolved to sing it himself. Later he admitted he was trying to write in the style of Stephen Sondheim, one of the greatest theatrical writers, whose enduring works include *Sweeney Todd*. At least Pete wasn't harking back to Gilbert and Sullivan a la "Guitar And Pen". It does, however beg the question, why wasn't he trying to write in the style of Pete Townshend?

Less convincingly, he denied he was imitating Waits, instead claiming he was just trying to sound older than his years. "I'm 60 years old pretending to be 80," he told *Mercury News*. "My voice is an instrument I can't always control. I love Tom Waits, but listen to him, he sounds like gravel being hauled through an oil can. I just sound a teensy bit gruff." Perhaps he doth protest too much – though considering Waits was known to sue imitators for millions of dollars, perhaps he was just being discreet. Either way, Pete conjures a suitably laconic, mid-period late-night piano bar Waits-ian atmosphere and arrangement. It's all mist and moonshine as Pete peers through a dreamy haze of booze – ether is, of course, an alcohol-based anaesthetic – to pledge his love... "drunk with his love". Pete took inspiration from his own novella, *The Boy Who Heard Music*, which featured a washed-up rock star, cleaning up in rehab and trying to follow a lonely spiritual path which seemed to appear, like radio waves, out of the ether.

Townshend's initial gruff vocal delivery early on in the track obscures a beautiful heart-melting melody which is revealed later, as he sings in his "regular" voice, but ultimately, this is unrecognisable as the Who.

Black Widow's Eyes

Lyrically, "Black Widow's Eyes" is complex. Pete called it, "A love song," adding "We sometimes fall in love when we do not want to, and when we do not expect to; suddenly, foolishly." Nothing surprising about that really, but circumstances here are unusual.

"Black Widow's Eyes" was inspired by the bloody siege of a school in the Russian town of Beslan in September, 2004. Chechen separatist fighters had occupied the school and threatened to blow it up, with all 1200 hostages inside – many of them, children. Russian troops eventually stormed the building but more than 300 civilians were killed by the terrorists' bombs or Russian guns.

One survivor explained later how he'd watched a woman terrorist detonate explosives in a suicide attack and, as Townshend told *Mojo*, he had written the song from the man's perspective: "They said to him, 'We hear that you saw the Black Widow', and he said 'Yeah, I saw her just before she blew herself up but I only saw her eyes'. And then he goes on to talk about the fact that she had the most beautiful eyes, and that he was just noticing how beautiful her eyes were when she looked at him and pressed the button. And she had two little girls next to her... And I've amplified that into a thing where we become so obsessed with terrorism and our destroyer, that we kind of fall in love with them and we embrace them."

It's an interesting idea, but one can't help wondering if Pete was up to the task, with tasteless couplets like: "I fell right in love with you / Into a thousand parts I blew" and "As the blood come blowing through / I fell right in love with you". There is perhaps a great song of moral outrage to be written about Beslan, but this isn't Pete's equivalent of U2's "Sunday Bloody Sunday", while in Bono's disclaimer "this is not a rebel song", it is a powerful condemnation of the killing of civilians. Pete has always strayed into politics at his peril in the past, and this shows that, at times, the political really should remain personal.

This is the only track that features Zak Starkey on drums, but you don't notice the difference because, throughout the record, the drums are never a feature, always seeming low in the mix – unlike in Moon's day or for that matter Kenney Jones's. Roger croons "I fell right in love with you...". He delivers other dramatic lines with aplomb between the melodic hooks. "Black Widow's Eyes" really lifts off in a haunting, multi-layered middle-section, packed with taut backing vocals. The pace change is reminiscent of the Who in their heyday, and when Roger retakes the lead, slowing things briefly down further, the spirit of previous victories is there to see. Though far from a Who classic, there are enough reminders here of how great Pete and Roger can be when they really collaborate.

Two Thousand Years

This is another of the songs Pete wrote after watching *The Passion Of The Christ*. Reviewer Andy Gill referred to this in *The Independent* as "a weedy alliance of cello and mandolin", and with a few lame handclaps thrown in, he's not entirely wrong. The protagonist tells of a two thousand year wait for the "new Christ". Pete wrote in a press release that, "Judas may not have been acting to betray Christ at all, but precisely following his instructions". The lyrical concept is somewhat lost amid a dull musical back-drop, and this acoustic track just hasn't got the gentle, heartbreak quality of "Sunrise" from *Sell Out* or the quaint nostalgia of "Blue Red And Grey" from *By Numbers*. There are no dynamics to inspire, no beguiling atmospheres to intrigue, and there's none of the dexterous finger-picking that one would expect from an acoustic Townshend arrangement. Ultimately, this is a well-meaning non-event. Pete played all the instruments here including violin and viols.

God Speaks Of Marty Robbins

Townshend had previously recorded a demo titled "Marty Robbins" in June 1984; this instrumental piece was finally released on his 2001 *Scoop 3* album. The song made its live debut on *The Basement Jam*, an internet-only streaming concert on 4 December, 2005.

Here God sleeps, before time has begun – pre-Big Bang – and dreams up the veteran country and western singer, Marty Robbins (whom Pete has always admired). God decides it's worth waking up to create Marty so he can hear some beautiful music.

This song features an inspired melody and a classic acoustic guitar workout; Pete also provides the lead vocal where his voice sounds at ease with the key. The stripped down no-frills approach of a single acoustic guitar works well on this pretty and infectious tune – another example of Pete's "breakthrough" in simple arrangements. It sounds like a Pete Townshend solo record.

It's Not Enough

(Townshend-Fuller)

This track originally began life as a Rachel Fuller song; Pete thought it had potential and asked her if he could use it for the new album.

This echoes the Who circa *Face Dances* and features Stuart Ross on bass, Peter Huntington on drums, Jolyon Dixon on acoustic guitar and Rachel Fuller on keyboards.

A solid backing-track from the band, thick multi-tracked backing vocals from Pete, and a muscular, pushed-to-the-max lead from Roger elevate this to one of the finest pieces on the entire record.

"I found myself wondering why it is that we choose people to partner, who we feel aren't quite right", Pete wrote, and his torment rings loud and clear:

> *I work so hard*
> *It gets so tough*
> *Whatever I give*
> *Never feels like enough*

Townshend's guitar sound is tough and edgy, but nowhere near the rip-roaring power of "Baba O'Riley" or even "New Song" from *Who Are You*, which is exactly what this cries out for. This lends itself to a full-on rock'n'roll workout and there's no doubt it would have benefited further had the live band been used. Pino and Zak would have ripped it up and taken the song to a whole new level. As it stands, the musicians do a professional job but it just hasn't got the bite and aggression it needs. It is a glimpse of some of the old spark of the Who but, ultimately, Pete and Roger miss the power and musical understanding of their live band.

You Stand By Me

Pete wrote this just minutes before a live webcast on Rachel Fuller's *In the Attic* show: "I had nothing new to play, and decided to write a song," Pete explained.

This song of gratitude to family, friends and bandmates for believing in him when he was "out of order", is yet another acoustic track with Pete on lead vocal – while Roger's vocal may have been more powerful, it's the autobiographical nature of the lyrics that make it Townshend's own.

Wire And Glass: A Mini-Opera:

Extracts from the novella *The Boy Who Heard Music* from Pete's weblog appear in italics.

Sound Round

This first emerged around the *Lifehouse* period in 1971; Pete rediscovered it while reading through some old notes. This, he said, began the collection. The track flies by in a frenetic flurry of drums and guitars as Pete writes *"My friends are all dead now"*, but Roger sounds supremely optimistic here nonetheless. This has a classic Who feel to it but is way too short at 1.21. You want it to continue, to go somewhere, but it finishes all too soon; a trend that continues frustratingly throughout the entire collection.

This story of *"old 60s rocker"* Ray High (this character also appeared as the protagonist of Townshend's solo album *Psychoderelict*) begins with him looking back on his life. At the start, he's a young man driving around in a large camper bus with *"extreme air-con"*. Close to a power station at the edge of an estuary, he sees a huge number of jellyfish drawn in by the *"over-heated"* water. According to Pete's weblog, this is based on actual events in Essex, 1971. Ray sees the *"future in the sky... nothing ecological or apocalyptic, more a vision of a society strangled by wire and communications"*.

Reportedly, not only this track but the following song "Pick Up The Peace", and an unreleased track titled "Ambition" (see below) were all written back in 1971.

Pick Up The Peace

Power chords introduce this pounding mid-paced rocker as Roger roars out loud and proud, straining somewhat, but delivering the vocal with a gutsy conviction. Choppy guitars and an undeniably catchy chorus scream out to be extended, but this piece also ends prematurely and, as a result, feels woefully unfinished. There is so much potential here, it really does feel like the opportunity to create a major Who track has been lost. What they *do* deliver is simply magnificent.

Here the protagonist, Ray, is in deep thought in what appears to be a *"cell in a secure hospital"*. He initially envisions three characters, teenage kids: Gabriel, Josh and Leila. They are all from his local area and get a group together called the Glass Household. He sees them becoming stars but he thinks back to his own childhood in the same area and recalls only *"bombed buildings and old soldiers"*. This is reminiscent of Pete's own beginnings and there is already the whiff of autobiography about the whole proceedings. There are obvious parallels between Pete and the character Ray – and the Glass Household and his early band, the Detours.

Unholy Trinity

Bass, drums, piano and a beautifully rhythmic banjo accompany Roger's clear vocal delivery, as we discover that the three kids in the story are from completely different backgrounds. These three characters could easily be seen as Daltrey, Entwistle and Townshend – who were all from roughly the same area but from very different backgrounds.

In the narrative, Gabriel comes from showbiz stock who are *"lapsed Christians"*; Josh's folks are Jewish, his father died *"in an incident in Israel"*. Leila's Muslim kin have too suffered a tragic loss, *"her beautiful and charismatic mother"* died when she was just a child. They all become close friends and share the same dreams and fantasies. *"Like urchin-angels they share their secrets"* it becomes apparent that, *"Gabriel hears music; Josh voices; Leila can fly"*.

Trilby's Piano

Pete orchestrated the strings on this piece, a brave step for the writer but he did benefit from Rachel Fuller's expert advice. She watched over the session in an advisory capacity, Pete revealed: "Without her help I would have lost control." There is true melodic beauty here, but Pete's limited vocal range is exposed as his voice is pushed to its outer limits. However, his delivery has a haunting quality that beguiles.

The story deepens and stretches out, becoming unnecessarily complex as *"Josh's widowed mother vests all her hopes in her brother Hymie becoming a great man"*. He falls in love with Trilby, *"Gabriel's goofy blonde aunt"*. Aunt Trilby has encouraged Gabriel's musical talent which has been overlooked by his heartbroken mother. The band decides to stage a musical play at Leila's father's studio and this song is featured, sung by Gabriel. This is the catalyst that *"finally breaks Josh's mother's resistance to the love match"* between the characters Hymie and Trilby.

Endless Wire

Pete explained "Endless Wire" refers to the internet: "All the lines of communication that envelope the globe." The plot develops as the teenagers find old papers belonging to Ray High who was once Leila's father's business partner: *"The documents refer to a crazy scheme to use the global wire network Ray saw as a young man to spread unifying music to everyone"*. The kids think they can make Ray's vision a reality. This is very similar to the basic theme of *Lifehouse*. Pete added in his weblog, *"This matches my own vision for the Lifehouse Method, a computer-driven website through which people can commission their unique musical portrait"*.

Pete performed this song solo on an *In The Attic* broadcast at Joe's Pub on 14 September, 2006. The Who had also performed it on-stage in full in Berlin on 12 July, 2006, separate from the mini-opera, which wasn't performed that night. An extended version appears on special editions of the record.

Fragments Of Fragments
(Townshend-Ball)

A brief interlude reprise of the intro to this album features here where Pete enquires, "Are we breathing out or breathing in?". Brilliant vocal effects surge and swirl around, more audible here than in the opening version. This further demonstrates the "Method" music which Pete first outlined in *Lifehouse*.

We Got A Hit

As the narrative unfolds, the kids become media experts and have huge global success with the song "Fragments" which is the "hit" referred to here. Again there are parallels to the Who's own career; Pete writes, *"We got rich and famous / Papers at our door / We talked a load of crap / They just wanted more"*. Roger belts out the lyric with gusto as Pete adds the vocal canon response effectively in the chorus refrains. The feel is bouncy and once again it concludes all too soon, but the piece has a bright and shiny sheen that distracts.

They Made My Dream Come True

From his cell while *"meditating"*, Ray High watches the massive success of the Glass Household. He predicts a tragedy during the band's last and biggest gig: someone's going to die. Again, this has an autobiographical feel from Pete; in interviews he referred to the Stones gig in Altamont where a man was killed and the Who's own Cincinnati show where 11 audience members died tragically in a stampede.

The opening line declares, *"People died where I performed"* and Pete sings the lyric with heart-felt sincerity over laidback acoustic guitars in a lazy 6/8 time signature. Again, this is all too brief, over just as it's begun and, conceptually, the confusion continues. A casual listen would lead one to believe that Pete is singing about his own dreams/nightmares coming true but, in the context of the story, it's the imaginings of Ray High. Pete explained in his weblog, *"What is never clear is whether the concert he foresees ever takes place in reality, or actually remains a dream forever".*

Mirror Door

Familiar Townshend rhythm guitar heralds the opening on this, as the band heads off into a mid-paced rock work-out. Here is where, undoubtedly, the band, with Zak on drums, could have delivered a much needed muscular backing-track; unfortunately the band sound more mushy than muscular.

The story approaches its apocalyptic climax as the Glass Household put on their own huge charity show based on the childish musical they performed at Leila's father's studio many years before. Staged in Central Park, in the heart of Manhattan, they bring to life Ray's idea to *"turn everyone into music"*. Terrorists try to disrupt the celebratory concert – the tension mounts – but the band continues to play. Deceased legends of popular music appear at the top of a huge staircase on the stage. Roger sings of a *"Golden stairway to a Zeppelin heaven"*. Again, a casual listen would suggest Pete is simply listing his many influences down through the years; Howling Wolf, Link Wray, Elvis (Presley), Buddy (Holly), Eddie (Cochran), Frank (Sinatra), Ella (Fitzgerald).

Tragedy suddenly strikes the concert – just as Ray High predicted. Josh, who is revealed as a paranoid schizophrenic, shoots band-mate Gabriel dead, after not taking his medication. *"He ascends the stairway to join the dead. Even now, it is not clear whether this particular series of events actually takes place".*

In his weblog, Pete added, *"It will be noted that one of the listed names of deceased singing geniuses (Doris Day) is still alive. In show-biz heaven, behind the "Mirror Door" no one ever really dies (it is rather like an after-show pub gathering). "Fragments", the kids' biggest hit, becomes a moment to look back and celebrate life, death, breath, creation, science, physics, maths, literature and growth".*

This song was released to radio stations ahead of the mini-opera in June 2006, but was remixed for the *Wire & Glass* release later in July.

Tea & Theatre

As the tale concludes, the ageing characters Leila and Josh meet up to *"take tea"* and reminisce together. It is revealed that Josh and Ray High are now in the same sanatorium and have, together with fellow inmates, acted out the kids' musical that the Glass Household had once performed. Pete suggests here that perhaps Ray has confused everything; that the play performed in the sanatorium was possibly *"the one they all hoped to see happen one day in New York, in the sky, and up into the universe".*

Fans have interpreted this song as being about the death of John Entwistle, and Pete's and Roger's decision to carry on as the Who, though Pete refuted this in interviews, saying that it was the concluding track of the Glass Household, but that he was pleased that people interpreted it differently.

Roger and Pete would often finish Who shows with this song throughout their US 2006 tour, and on numerous concerts from thereon, with Pete (on acoustic guitar) and Roger at the front of the stage. These performances confused audiences at first, but gradually the fans began to feel the undoubted power of the song.

Roger delivered emotional reflective renditions as Pete excelled with stunning finger-picking atmospheres. The studio version utilizes a simple drum machine part, accompanied by an effectively subtle bass guitar.

Roger felt, "It's something that's kind of taking it back to square one. It's where we started, acoustic guitars and singing. We're troubadours, that's what we do."

Bonus Tracks:

We Got A Hit (Extended Version)
This extended version features an additional verse not heard on the mini-opera version.

Endless Wire (Extended Version)
Though just less than two minutes long in the original rock-opera version, this rolling country-rock track is one of Pete's finest songs in years. A deceptively simple verse leads into a beautifully harmonised, sing-a-long chorus. For anyone who thought Pete's melodic gifts had deserted him, this is as good as anything he has come up with since the glory days. Roger does his old sparring partner proud with an affecting vocal.

There are two special edition versions of *Endless Wire*: one contains a bonus DVD with five live songs: "Mike Post Theme", "Baba O'Riley", "Who Are You", "Behind Blue Eyes", and "Won't Get Fooled Again". The second version contains a live CD from Lyon 2006: "The Seeker", "Who Are You", "Mike Post Theme", "Relay", "Greyhound Girl", "Naked Eye", and "Won't Get Fooled Again".

So is *Wire And Glass* just the ravings of some mad old rocker locked up in a cell to protect himself and others? We're left to make up our own minds but without many clues, who knows? Reading the weblog helps, but as a stand-alone piece it is the most confusing, convoluted and complex storyline of all the Townshend operas. The overwhelming feeling is that this is completely autobiographical – the story simply serves as an elaborate smokescreen.

Roger admitted that he was initially unsure of the songs that Pete played him when they first began the process of recording *Endless Wire*, but said that, once the album was finished, he believed that, "there's tracks on there that are really right up there. They've got that Townshend magic." With a media barrage, *Endless Wire* made the Top Ten on both sides of the Atlantic but reviews were mixed: Bob Stanley wrote in *The Times* newspaper, "*Endless Wire* does sound undernourished alongside *The Who Sell Out* or *Who's Next*". He criticised Roger's voice, saying "Age has not added to its charm". But he conceded, "If Coldplay didn't make an album for 20 years, I wonder if we'd care as much?". John Metzger, writing in *Music Box*, described the album as flawed.

Some fans felt betrayed; others virtually ignored the album altogether. Writing on a Who website, devoted fan John Wright voiced a common doubt, "The mini-opera is neither coherent nor satisfying and, again, the lasting impression is of fragments of ideas that might have come to something had Townshend been challenged more in the studio". This dedicated fan concluded by saying candidly, "It saddens me to write this because the Who remains my favourite band; it's just that we all need to realize that the Who ended in 1978. None more so than Pete and Roger". Pete had commented himself back in 1989, "I think the Who stopped two albums too late." Perhaps now it was three?

It wasn't all doom and gloom from the fans, Ian Woolstencroft wrote on *Blogcritics* online, "I fell in love with this new album". Journalist David Fricke wrote in *Rolling Stone* that this was as "right for it's day as *The Who Sell Out* or *Tommy* were in theirs". Dave Marsh wrote in the December issue of *Mojo* after getting a preview of the album in Pete's hotel room, "*Endless Wire* sounds more like the classic version of the band than any record they've made since 1975's *The Who By Numbers*". He countered many a "Townshend solo album" jibe by stating that this was not a glorified Townshend solo album but rather "a true Who album". Many fans disagreed and critic Andy Gill claimed in *The Independent* this was "half a Who album" scathingly referring to the mini opera as "a preposterous fantasy".

The end-of-year-polls were muted; *Endless Wire* reached number 17 in *Mojo*'s list, but was pretty much eclipsed on all fronts by Dylan's new record *Modern Times*. Tom Waits and Morrissey even left it for dead in the end of year lists with *Wire* not making the Top 20 in *The Guardian*, *NME* or *Uncut*. *Q* magazine however did bestow on Daltrey and Townshend their "Legend" award that year. But the album didn't make the top 75 best-selling albums in the UK and it also failed to be mentioned in the US round-up of 2006.

As many website critics and fans noted, there is the feel of a Pete Townshend solo album here with Daltrey appearing almost like a special guest. It's worth considering that if there is a flaw with these recordings, the problem could possibly be traced to the fact that the Who didn't record with the touring band. In 2000, John Entwistle praised Zak Starkey stating that he had put the "fire" back into the band. Zak should have played on the whole album – not just a single track. Pete Huntington did a great job under difficult circumstances but the chemistry is lost. The "fire" Entwistle talked of so enthusiastically, is noticeably absent. Where it should rampage, it rambles. Where it should fly, it falters – flapping but never getting off the ground. You could subscribe to an argument that says the songs would have benefited greatly from the band waiting until Zak was available and then playing the ideas over and over in a rehearsal room, thrashing out songs until Pete was totally happy with them. "Old Red Wine" and "Real Good Looking Boy" featured Zak and both had a great feel. It is fair to say that that feel is sadly lacking from this record.

In 2006, Pete said he felt it wasn't about "who played the drums," claiming that what he did need was to find "a mindset that was almost Zen-like." In 1981, in the song "It's In You" from *Face Dances*, Pete wrote, "You said that power chords are all that we should play / If you depend on me to make you rock'n'roll / You better look out Tich, 'cause we're getting old ". Those lines were even more relevant now than they were then.

There were more songs that didn't make it onto the final version of the album. "Ambition" which was written in the *Lifehouse* era plus a song entitled "Uncertain

Girl" which featured Zak on drums, but this piece didn't see the light of day until the Vassar College workshop performance of *The Boy Who Heard Music*. On another new song "How Can I Help You, Sir?" Pete preferred his acoustic take, writing in his online diary that, "The rock version seems altogether more jolly, almost throwaway". Journalist Dave Marsh revealed in *Mojo* that there were three more outstanding songs: "Cinderella", about an abused friend; "There's No Doubt", inspired by a comment to Townshend from manager Bill Curbishley about his new wife who was most definitely "the one"; and "He Said, She Said", a song which told the story of a relationship from both the male and female perspective.

The Who's new album went out into a market that was unrecognisable to the rock dinosaurs of old. The internet had an immensely influential role in how music was made and consumed. Gnarls Barkley's "Crazy" was the first single ever to top the charts on downloads alone. It stayed there for nine weeks until the band deleted the track. Lily Allen's use of MySpace to promote her debut single "Smile" sent it to number one.

The longest-running music programme on British television, the BBC's *Top Of The Pops* had been axed after more than forty years. Television music programming was now dominated by *X Factor*, an immensely commercial talent show created by music mogul Simon Cowell. The show had produced three number one-selling artists, Leona Lewis, Shayne Ward and Chico Slimani and changed the way many young people viewed the music business and fame in general.

2007:

Time At Home

Two thousand and seven was a less frenetic year but highlights included a triumphant headlining set at the Glastonbury festival in the summer, playing to a whole new generation of Who fans. A rough version of the proposed Pete Townshend musical *The Boy Who Heard Music* debuted on 13 July, 2007 as part of Vassar College's Powerhouse Summer Theatre workshop series in the United States. Ethan Silverman adapted and directed the performance and the cast included John Hickok as Ray High, Jon Patrick Walker as Josh, Matt McGrath as Gabriel, and Bree Sharp as Leila.

November would see the release of a Who documentary that, for many, would supersede the legendary *The Kids Are Alright*. The new movie *Amazing Journey* came as a two-DVD set and garnered plenty of media coverage and much critical acclaim. An impeccable, comprehensive biography of the band, it featured some amazing lost footage of the High Numbers shot by Kit and Chris back in 1964, as well as interviews with famous fans such as Noel Gallagher and The Edge. Pete would call this "Roger's story of the Who," and claim he had never watched it.

Roger Daltrey continued to try to get his Keith Moon biopic off the ground. He hoped to cast Mike Myers of *Austin Powers* fame in the lead role – an inspired piece of casting. "When the idea started, someone was trying to make a film which was akin to Carry On Moon," Roger complained to *Uncut*'s John Robinson in 2007. "And that would be a disaster, because he was a very unique talent in a number of different areas – but he had this enormous vulnerability. He had so many psychological wounds, and it's really a film about that... Some of it will be funny.

But there's an awful lot of stuff that's not funny... It'll all have to be there, but it's got to carry the audience – they can't ever hate him. They could never hate him as much as he hated himself."

Provisionally titled, *See Me Feel Me: Keith Moon Naked For Your Pleasure*, Roger felt the movie needed to be made because Keith is "an important character in rock'n'roll." Unfortunately the plans failed to come to fruition and, at the time of writing, the project still languishes.

In addition to his charity work, Roger spent the majority of his time on his Sussex estate, raising cattle and farming trout, admirably never seeking to make a profit from his farm and eschewing tax exile in favour of ploughing his own money into preserving centuries of local tradition. His clean-living lifestyle has paid dividends; Roger looks at least a decade younger than his 60-plus years.

Townshend still harboured plans for *Quadrophenia* to become a stage musical just like *Tommy* before it. There have been theatrical performances since the turn of the century, with an acclaimed Hampshire youth theatre version in 2001 and a later production on the US East Coast, but for Pete it remained a work-in-progress. "I have high hopes for it as a musical theatre piece," Pete insisted in December 2007, "now that technology has caught up with the theatre. It might work at last."

Pete had two other projects close to his heart. First, a full-length animated version of *Lifehouse* and his autobiography, a process that has dragged on for years. Back in 1996, when he felt the book would take about two years, Pete gave tantalising intimations as to the project's scale. "What I'm really doing," he told Ira Robbins, "is writing about my life and my music, about life and music in general. It's going to be an artist's view of the last fifty years and what's been going on with music in that time."

With Mick Jagger having returned his publisher's advance and Keith Richards' memory notoriously hazy, Pete Townshend's autobiography is likely to be the most interesting autobiographical account of rock'n'roll's glory days.

2008:

Rock Honours

The Who is not Pete and it's not me. We talk of it as a third person; it's weird. And I think it touches an audience as a third person.
Roger Daltrey, 2006

In April 2008, *Rolling Stone* reported that the Who was planning to record another new album, this time with T-Bone Burnett in the producer's chair. This would be a collection of classic R&B songs. Burnett commented they were "digging through lots of material" and added that Pete may well be writing some completely new tracks stating "It might be a combination of both... We're still turning it over." Later, however on the band's website Pete wrote that he was working on material for a new Who album and that the covers album idea had been shelved.

On the 12th July, 2008, VH1 honoured the Who by filming a TV special from the UCLA Pauley Pavilion in Los Angeles. Broadcast a week later, the show saw a series of bands pay tribute to Pete and Roger – including the Flaming Lips, Incubus, Tenacious D, Pearl Jam and the Foo Fighters. The gig was a huge success; highlights included "Young Man Blues" and "Behind Blue Eyes" by the Foo Fighters who opened the show. There was concern that the band would have to pull out at the last minute because Dave Grohl had lost his voice, but he soldiered on and delivered a ferocious performance. Pearl Jam, fronted by Who fanatic and Townshend's friend Eddie Vedder, performed with a ten-piece orchestra and gamely played key tracks from *Quadrophenia*. The effect was stunning – their versions of "The Real Me" and "Love, Reign O'er Me" seriously rivalled those of the Who's.

When Pete and Roger finally took to the stage accompanied by Zak, Simon, Rabbit and Pino, the expectation was palpable. The Who stormed through their hits including, "My Generation", "Who Are You" and "Won't Get Fooled Again", giving the performance of their lives. They closed the show with "Tea And Theatre", giving possibly the best filmed rendition of this now regular finale of Who gigs. Pete told *Rolling Stone*, "In the end I enjoyed it," saying that he was grateful to have "three great bands like the Foo Fighters, Pearl Jam and the Flaming Lips on the show." He described his own performance as a little rusty because he hadn't played the guitar for a while, musing that "electric guitar and arm-swinging is not what I do between dog walks."

At the end of the show, both Roger Daltrey and Pete Townshend were visibly moved by the whole evening and rightly so. They had been honoured by media, fans and younger musicians alike – they invented blistering rock'n'roll and here their undoubted stature was incontestably confirmed: "Meet the new boss! Same as the old boss!"

A week later, the band played at the 2008 E3 Media business summit. Embracing the burgeoning new technology, they launched the 12-track play-along "best of" for the video game *Rock Band*. In August, Roger Daltrey appeared on the front cover of the respected music magazine *Q* with young Scottish rockers the Fratellis. Presided over by Who aficionado Pat Gilbert, the piece was a general knockabout between Daltrey and the fledgling rock stars. Roger asked questions, considered their responses and meted out sound, hard-earned advice – the most poignant being, "Learn to appreciate each other's difference. The more different you are as individuals the better the band will be."

I'm most effective with my guitar, on stage acting.
Pete Townshend, 2006

Afterword

The original Who were a rock'n'roll blueprint. Diverging from the multiple guitar line-ups of classic groups like the Beatles and the Stones, the Who stripped things down to voice, guitar, bass and drums. The sound was in the performance – of a flamboyant front-man, a theatrical, ground-breaking guitarist, a virtuoso bassist and an incredible drummer who played more like an inspired jazz improv genius than a four-to-the-floor beat-keeper.

To capture the impact and appeal of the band throughout their classic era, on record and on stage, you would have to combine the Rolling Stones of the 1960s with Led Zeppelin in the 1970s, and perhaps even the Clash at the tail end of that decade. They had the songs, the albums, the musical chops, the look and the theatrics to match any of the great rock acts at their peak. And they remained at the top, critically and commercially, for longer than almost any other active band. When the Beatles retired from playing concerts, the Who invented the live rock performance as we know it today. And when the Stones were resting on their laurels in tax exile, the Who were making some of the greatest albums in the rock canon, in England and at facilities they had often funded themselves.

Which other band could combine the angry punk snarl of early 45s like "Substitute" and "My Generation" with the complexity of a mature concept piece like the psychological rock opera *Quadrophenia*? All the truly disparate strengths of the Sex Pistols and Pink Floyd were rolled into one four-piece group. Led Zeppelin looked great and made towering blues-rock, on record and on stage, but they didn't have jukebox classics like "I Can See For Miles" or "Pinball Wizard" in their repertoire. Where Zep had the risible *Song Remains The Same*, the Who had *The Kids Are Alright*!

You can't *do* rock'n'roll without stealing something from them, even if it was second- or third-hand. From Springsteen to the Pistols; the Clash to U2; Van Halen to the Jam, the Who helped lay the foundations of modern rock music, both as a group and as individual players... and along the way, they made some of the most timeless rock'n'roll albums of all time. They are originals – real stars in a world of instant-fame seekers and talentless wannabes.

Through all the tragedy, pain, arguments, addictions and scandals, weaker post-Moon albums, Townshend's hearing problems, and various solo tangents, the Who remain a first class live act. They have continued to thrill and captivate audiences around the world, despite the passing of Keith and John, possibly the greatest rock rhythm section, and the consequent various line-up augmentations.

There may well be another Who studio album, but it's clear that, for all *Endless Wire*'s merits, the depleted core of the band will never create a work to match their greatest records. Then again, which other 60s survivors will? In the meantime, the rock'n'roll heart that lives and breathes in the Who's live shows is there in the groundbreaking albums they made with Keith; flashes of it are still there in the inconsistent post-Moon works, but the story of the ultimate rock'n'roll band is there on those 1965 to 1978 discs.

Pete and Roger, the two survivors of the band that sang of hoping to die before they got old, have aged, but far more gracefully than many of their peers and are still competing in an arena that, even 30 years ago, Pete feared was a young man's game. "The reason rock is still around is that it's not youth's music," Townshend mused. "It's the music of the frustrated and the dissatisfied." Roger reflected in 2007, "Yes, we're too old for most things but we still make great music."

"The definition of rock'n'roll lies here for me," Townshend would conclude. "If it screams for truth rather than help, if it commits itself with a courage it can't be sure it has, if it stands up and admits something is wrong but doesn't insist on blood, then it's rock'n'roll. We shed our own blood. We don't need to shed anyone else's."

In looking at the Who's back catalogue of life-changing music, an old Dylan title was never more apposite: there is blood on these tracks...

Appendix I – Instant Access Tracks

This is an attempt at an objective list of representative tracks that any new Who fan should have on their MP3 player as an absolute minimum. You can purchase these tracks as downloads from the web or simply cherry pick them from original albums and compilations. Then again, you might just want to load your iPod with the entirety of the Who's back catalogue, it's up to you.

The Who Sings My Generation
I Can't Explain
My Generation
The Kid's Are Alright

A Quick One
Run, Run, Run
Boris The Spider
So Sad About Us

The Who Sell Out
Armenia City In The Sky
Tattoo
I Can See For Miles

Tommy
Pinball Wizard
I'm Free
See Me, Feel Me (*Tommy* Finale)

Live At Leeds
Young Man Blues
Shakin' All Over
Magic Bus

Who's Next
Baba O'Riley
Bargain
Won't Get Fooled Again

Quadrophenia
The Real Me
5.15
Bell Boy

Odds & Sods
Summertime Blues
Mary Anne With The Shaky Hand
Long Live Rock

The Who By Numbers
Slip Kid
However Much I Booze
How Many Friends

Who Are You
Who Are You
Trick Of The Light
905

The Kids Are Alright
A Quick One, While He's Away
My Wife
Join Together – Roadrunner – My Generation Blues

Face Dances
You Better You Bet
Tricky Day
Do It Alone (Live)

It's Hard
Eminence Front
Athena
I've Known No War

Appendix II – Authors' Notes

When I was first asked to co-write a book about my favourite band the Who, I declined, not feeling worthy of the task. The late Sean Body (from whom I learned much), then owner of Helter Skelter, finally convinced me to take part in the project when he explained exactly what he wanted from me. I was to collect facts, reviews, opinions, chart positions and conduct interviews to give an objective overview of the group's musical life. Having spent the last four years writing and researching the Who's career for this book, I've learned more than I ever thought possible. I believed I had a good comprehensive knowledge of the band but I was mistaken – there was much to learn. So, contained herein are not Alan's or my opinions, they are an objective view of the band's music according to the research carried out in retrospect. I would never, ever deem myself worthy of judging the Who!

One of my personal goals for this book was, not only to inform, but to inspire long-term Who fans to revisit old albums they may have neglected for a while and to help new Who converts navigate their way through the enormous back catalogue the band have amassed over the years. I do hope all readers; fans new and old, find inspiration here to listen to the Who's music.

I was honoured to be asked to contribute to this book because, as a teenager, the Who gave me a direction in life. At that point, they were my life! I was inspired further when the punk rock revolution exploded in late 1976, but it was obvious to me and many others; the Who had been prototype punks all along!

Being a drummer myself, Keith Moon is God and no one can tell me otherwise. He was the greatest showman to sit behind a drum kit ever and the one "famous" person I really wish I had met.

John Entwistle's death in 2002 was, of course, a shock to us all. I assumed that he would continue touring with the Who and live to a ripe-old age – Keith was always, sadly, a candidate for an early demise but with John it was so tragically unexpected.

All this time, after first seeing the Who at Charlton, I'm still a huge fan and proud of it. The music always sounds so fresh when I return to their records and I'm exhilarated by film of their live performances and TV appearances, even though I've seen the footage many times over.

For me, Townshend, Daltrey, Entwistle and Moon really are "the greatest rock'n'roll band in the world." For these boys have seen and done it all. From smashed guitars and drums to drugs, groupies and fights. They've trashed hotel rooms and broken box office records, had a million laughs, loved, and then loathed each other. There's been madness and genius in equal amounts and they've given exhilarating concert performances the world over, year after year. They've made movies, recorded rock operas, produced musicals and, let's not forget, that they have been responsible for some of the finest pop songs and greatest rabble-rousing rock anthems ever committed to tape.

So, long may they Reign O'er us all! Long Live Rock! Long Live the "Orible Oo"! I love 'em.
Steve Grantley, 2008

I remember the first time I ever saw, or for that matter, heard, the Who like it was yesterday. It was on *Top Of The Pops*, the BBC TV chart show that I would watch every Thursday night, to decide which singles to buy on Saturday afternoon. It was the late summer of 1978, because I had a paper round by then, and was in a position to buy four singles a week, should the fancy take me. I'd been a very early starter music-wise, borrowing albums, buying singles (well my dad bought them for me, but you get my drift) and even attending gigs from the ripe old age of eight in 1973. My first was Slade with the Alex Harvey Band in support, as "starts" go, you'd be hard pressed to name a better one!

By 1978, my attention was fully fixed on punk, though glam still got a look in as I felt I could never seriously leave the Slade or Sweet camp behind! But punk certainly had a grip over me and any money I would ever make. That night, however, I saw the video for "Who Are You?" and I loved it – if only because of that funny man with the headphones gaffer-taped to his head, the one that looked like Robert Newton in *Treasure Island*. Years later, I would discover that this strange looking man was, perhaps, the greatest rock'n'roll drummer ever to sit behind a kit... Also, as the years passed, I became aware that the very song I'd loved on *Top Of The Pops* was inspired by Pete Townshend's first encounter with two of the Sex Pistols (Steve Jones & Paul Cook). Had I known this at the time, I would have convinced enough people to buy it to keep it in the number one spot for months!

Beyond that one single, the Who didn't trouble my life again for a few more years. These were punk's golden years and I needed nothing more. By 1981, however, punk appeared to be reaching the end of the line. The Pistols were long gone, the Clash were busy in America, and the best that the music press could come up with to fill the punk void were the likes of Crass, Discharge and GBH – a scene I just didn't want to be part of. And so I found myself in a Blackburn record store on a Saturday afternoon, with enough money to buy two albums burning a hole in my pocket, and nothing I wanted in sight. Then I noticed the sleeve of *The Who By Numbers* – like ice cream on a summer's day it seemed to wave at me. Wasn't this that group from *Top Of The Pops* with the drummer who had made me laugh? Without further thought I bought it, along with the same group's brand new album, *Face Dances*. To this day, I love *Face Dances*, although attending Who conventions has made me realise this puts me in a minority. I just wish I knew which ex-girlfriend still has the poster that came with it!

In fact, my mates and I had already witnessed the Who live at the Empire Stadium in Wembley on August 18th, 1979. The Stranglers were on the bill too, which was reason enough to attend, but it was the headliners who blew me away. Roger was the perfect front-man, swinging the microphone so high I thought its cable would do someone a serious injury. Pete was a pent-up windmill of fury, a million ideas fighting with their creator for space on his stage. John never moved an inch, but he kept the bass beating like solid thunder and Kenney played out of his skin. I had, after all, no Keith in my life to compare him to. That would come later, first in a cinema, and much later on DVD. Since then, I've seen the Who live on more occasions than I care to remember.

On a personal note, I'd like to add that my dad did at least get to see the advance press release for this book, so he knew what we were up to. I just wish he'd had the chance to see the finished article, because I know he was always proud of my work... Finally, if you're wondering whether the Who led this die-hard punk to any other classic rock bands, the honest answer is that, I guess in a roundabout way, it opened a door marked metal, which led me further away from those awful third division punk bands that I had no time for in the first place! I know things got louder in the Parker household following the arrival of the early eighties. I like the Who for their own distinctive qualities and for the way that Pete Townshend is willing to share his very soul with us.

Alan G. Parker (boy in a bubble called W9), 2008

Appendix III – Selective Discographies

This discography has been complied from a number of resources, including the official Track Records website, the authors' collections, plus best estimates based on the various discographies in many of the most reliable books on the Who listed in the bibliography below. It is not meant to be absolutely exhaustive for either the group or its solo members but is as comprehensive as possible at the time of writing.

Singles

I'm The Face / Zoot Suit [as the High Numbers]
UK Release: 13/07/1964 (Fontana TF 480)
NB: Reissued on Back Door Records in March 1980, and peaked at 49 on the UK charts.

I Can't Explain / Bald Headed Woman
UK Release: 15/01/1965 (Brunswick 05926) Peak Position: 8
US Release: 13/02/1965 (Decca 31725) Peak Position: 93

Anyway Anyhow Anywhere / Daddy Rolling Stone
UK Release: 21/05/1965 (Brunswick 05935) Peak Position: 10

Anyway Anyhow Anywhere / Anytime You Want Me
US Release: 05/06/1965 (Decca 31801)

My Generation / Shout And Shimmy
UK Release: 05/11/1965 (Brunswick 05944) Peak Position: 2

My Generation / Out In The Street
US Release: 20/11/1965 (Decca 31877) Peak Position: 74

Substitute / Circles
Substitute / Instant Party
UK Releases: 04/03/1966 (Reaction 591001)

Substitute / Waltz For A Pig
UK Release: 15/03/1966 (Reaction 591001) Peak Position: 5

Substitute / Waltz For A Pig
US Release: 02/04/1966 (Atco 6409)

A Legal Matter / Instant Party
UK Release: 11/03/1966 (Brunswick 05956) Peak Position: 32

The Kids Are Alright / A Legal Matter
US Release: 07/1966 (Decca 31988) Peak Position: 85

The Kids Are Alright / The Ox
UK Release: 12/08/1966 (Brunswick 05965) Peak Position: 41

I'm A Boy / In The City
UK Release: 26/08/1966 (Reaction 591004) Peak Position: 2
US Release: 10/12/1966 (Decca 32058)

La La La Lies / The Good's Gone
UK Release: 11/11/1966 (Brunswick 05968)

Ready Steady Who EP
Disguises / Circles / Batman / Bucket T / Barbara Ann
UK Release: 11/11/1966 (Reaction 592001)

Happy Jack / I've Been Away
UK Release: 03/12/1966 (Reaction 591010) Peak Position: 3

Happy Jack / Whiskey Man
US Release: 18/03/1967 (Decca 32114) Peak Position: 24

Pictures Of Lily / Doctor Doctor
UK Release: 22/04/1967 (Track 604002) Peak Position: 4
US Release: 24/06/1967 (Decca 32156) Peak Position: 51

The Last Time / Under My Thumb
UK Release: 30/06/1967 (Track 604006) Peak Position: 44

Substitute / Waltz For A Pig
US Reissue: 08/1967 (Atco 6509)

I Can See For Miles / Someone's Coming
UK Release: 07/10/1967 (Track 604011) Peak Position: 10

I Can See For Miles / Mary-Anne With The Shaky Hands
US Release: 14/10/1967 (Decca 3206) Peak Position: 9

Call Me Lightning / Doctor Jekyll And Mister Hyde
US Release: 16/03/1968 (Decca 32288) Peak Position: 40

Dogs / Call Me Lightning
UK Release: 15/06/1968 (Track 604023) Peak Position: 25

Magic Bus / Someone's Coming
US Release: 27/07/1968 (Decca 32362) Peak Position: 25

Magic Bus / Doctor Jekyll And Mister Hyde
UK Release: 18/09/1968 (Track 604024) Peak Position: 26

Pinball Wizard / Dogs Part Two
UK Release: 07/03/1969 (Track 604027) Peak Position: 4
US Release: 22/03/1969 (Decca 32465) Peak Position: 19

I'm Free / We're Not Gonna Take It
US Release: 05/07/1969 (Decca 32519) Peak Position: 37

The Seeker / Here For More
UK Release: 21/03/1970 (Track 604036) Peak Position: 19
US Release: 11/04/1970 (Decca 32670) Peak Position: 44

Summertime Blues / Heaven And Hell
UK Release: 10/07/1970 (Track 2094 002) Peak Position: 38
US Release: 11/07/1970 (Decca 32708) Peak Position: 27

See Me Feel Me / Overture From Tommy
US Release: 23/09/1970 (Decca 32729) Peak Position: 12
UK Release: 10/10/1970 (Track 2094 004)

Tommy EP
Overture / Christmas / I'm Free / See Me Feel Me
UK Release: 07/11/970 (Track 2252 001)

Won't Get Fooled Again / Don't Know Myself
UK Release: 25/06/1971 (Track 2094 009) Peak Position: 9

Won't Get Fooled Again / I Don't Even Know Myself
US Release: 17/07/1971 (Decca 32846) Peak Position: 15

Let's See Action / When I Was A Boy
UK Release: 15/10/1971 (Track 2094 012) Peak Position: 16

Behind Blue Eyes / My Wife
US Release: 06/11/1971 (Decca 32888) Peak Position: 34

Join Together / Baby Don't You Do It
UK Release: 17/06/1972 (Track 2094 102) Peak Position: 9
US Release: 08/07/1972 (Decca 32983) Peak Position: 17

Relay / Waspman
US Release: 25/11/1972 (Track 33041) Peak Position: 39
UK Release: 23/12/1972 (Track 2094 106) Peak Position: 21

5.15 / Water
UK Release: 09/1973 (Track 2094 115) Peak Position: 20

5.15 / Love, Reign O'er Me
US Release: 10/1973 (MCA 40152)

Love, Reign O'er Me / Water
US Release: 23/10/1973 (MCA 40152) Peak Position: 76

The Real Me / I'm One
US Release: 12/01/1974 (MCA 40182) Peak Position: 92

Postcard / Put The Money Down
US Release: 11/1974 (Track 40330)

Squeeze Box / Success Story
US Release: 22/11/1975 (MCA 40475) Peak Position: 16
UK Release: 24/01/1976 (Polydor 2121 275) Peak Position: 10

Slip Kid / Dreaming From The Waist
US Release: 07/08/1976 (MCA 40603)

Substitute / I'm A Boy (Stereo Version) / Pictures Of Lily
UK Reissue: 10/1976 (Polydor 2058 803) Peak Position: 7

Who Are You / Had Enough
UK Release: 14/07/1978 (Polydor WHO 1) Peak Position: 18
US Release: 08/1978 (MCA 40948) Peak Position: 14

905 / Trick Of The Light
US Release: 02/12/1978 (MCA 40978)

Long Live Rock / I'm The Face / My Wife
UK Release: 01/04/1979 (Polydor WHO 2) Peak Position: 48

Long Live Rock / My Wife
US Release: 01/04/1979 (MCA 41053) Peak Position: 54

I'm One / 5.15 (Soundtrack Version)
US Release: 09/1979 (MCA 2022) Peak Position: 45

You Better You Bet / The Quiet One
UK Release: 27/02/1981 (Polydor WHO 4) Peak Position: 9
US Release: 03/1981 (Warner Bros 49698) Peak Position: 18

Don't Let Go The Coat / You
UK Release: 01/05/1981 (Polydor WHO 5) Peak Position: 47
US Release: 05/1981 (Warner Bros 49743) Peak Position: 84

Athena / It's Your Turn
US Release: 04/09/1982 (Warner Bros 29905) Peak Position: 28

Athena / A Man Is A Man
UK Release: 25/09/1982 (Polydor WHO 6)

Athena / Won't Get Fooled Again / A Man Is A Man (12" Single)
UK Release: 06/10/1982 (Polydor WHOX 6) Peak Position: 40

Eminence Front / One At A Time
US Release: 12/1982 (Warner Bros 29814) Peak Position: 68

It's Hard / Dangerous
US Release: 02/1983 (Warner Bros 29731)

Twist And Shout / I Can't Explain
UK Release: 11/1984 (MCA 927)

Real Good Looking Boy / Old Red Wine
UK Release: 02/05/2004 (Polydor 986 6338)

Wire And Glass EP
Sound Round / Pick Up The Peace / Endless Wire / We Got A Hit / They Made My Dreams Come True / Mirror Door
UK Release: 24/07/2006 (Polydor 1702801)

It's Not Enough
US Release:31/10 /2006 (Universal) Peak Position: 37

Albums

My Generation
UK Release: 03/12/1965 (Brunswick LAT 8616) Peak Position: 5

The Who Sings My Generation
US Release: 04/1966 (Decca 74664)

A Quick One
UK Release: 09/12/1966 (Reaction 593002) Peak Position: 4

Happy Jack
US Release: 05/1967 (Decca 74892) Peak Position: 67

The Who Sell Out
UK Release: 15/12/1967 (Track 612/613 002) Peak Position: 13
US Release: 01/1968 (Decca 74950) Peak Position: 48

Tommy
UK Release: 23/05/1969 (Track 613 013-014) Peak Position: 2
US Release: 05/1969 (Decca DXSW 7205) Peak Position: 4

Live At Leeds
UK Release: 16/05/1970 (Track 2406 001) Peak Position: 3
US Release: 05/1970 (Decca 79175) Peak Position: 4

Who's Next
US Release: 31/07/1971 (Decca 79182) Peak Position: 4
UK Release: 25/08/1971 (Track 2408 102) Peak Position: 1

Quadrophenia
UK Release: 19/10/1973 (Track 2657 013) Peak Position: 2
US Release: 10/1973 (MCA2 10004) Peak Position: 2

Odds & Sods
UK Release: 28/09/1974 (Track 2406 116) Peak Position: 10
US Release: 10/1974 (MCA 2126) Peak Position: 15

The Who By Numbers
UK Release: 18/10/1975 (Polydor 2490 129) Peak Position: 7
US Release: 25/10/1975 (MCA 2161) Peak Position: 8

Who Are You
UK Release: 18/08/1978 (Polydor 2490 147) Peak Position: 6
US Release: 08/1978 (MCA 3050) Peak Position: 2

Face Dances
UK Release: 16/03/1981 (Polydor 2302 106 WHOD 5037) Peak Position: 2
US Release: 03/1981 (Warner Bros HS 3516) Peak Position: 4

It's Hard
UK Release: 04/09/1982 (Polydor WHOD 5066) Peak Position: 11
US Release: 09/1982 (Warner Bros 23731) Peak Position: 8

Endless Wire
UK Release: 30/10/2006 (Polydor 1709519) Peak Position: 9
US Release: 30/10/2006 (Universal Republic B0007967-10) Peak Position: 7

Soundtracks

Tommy
US Release: 03/1975 (Polydor PD2 9505) Peak Position: 2
UK Release: 02/1975 (Polydor 2657 014) Peak Position: 30

The Kids Are Alright
UK Release: 08/06/1979 (Polydor 2675 179) Peak Position: 26
US Release: 23/06/1979 (MCA 11005) Peak Position: 8

Quadrophenia
UK Release: 05/10/1979 (Polydor 2625 037) Peak Position: 23
US Release: 06/10/1979 (Polydor PD2-6235) Peak Position: 46

Compilations

Meaty, Beaty, Big And Bouncy
UK Release: 10/1971 (Track 1406 006) Peak Position: 9
US Release: 11/1971 (Decca 79184) Peak Position: 11

Join Together
UK Release: 03/1990 (Virgin CD VDT 102) Peak Position: 59
US Release: 03/1990 (MCA MCAD2 19501)
Overture / It's A Boy / 1921 / Sparks / Eyesight To The Blind / Christmas / Cousin Kevin / Acid Queen / Do You Think It's Alright? / Fiddle About / Pinball Wizard / There's A Doctor / Go To The Mirror / Tommy, Can You Hear Me? / Smash The Mirror / Sensation / Miracle Cure / Sally Simpson / I'm Free / Tommy's Holiday Camp / We're Not Gonna Take It / 5.15 / Join Together / I Can See For Miles / Face The Face / Eminence Front / Dig / Behind Blue Eyes / A Little Is Enough / Love, Reign O'er Me / Rough Boys / Trick Of The Light / You Better You Bet / Won't Get Fooled Again

30 Years Of Maximum R&B (Box Set)
UK Release: 07/1994 (Polydor 521751-2) Peak Position: 48
US Release: 07/1994 (MCA MCAD4 11020)

My Generation – The Very Best Of The Who
UK Release: 08/1996 (Polydor CD 533150-2) Peak Position: 11
US Release: 08/1996 (MCA MCAD 11462)
I Can't Explain / Anyway, Anyhow, Anywhere / My Generation / Substitute / I'm A Boy / Boris The Spider / Happy Jack / Pictures Of Lily / I Can See For Miles / Magic Bus / Pinball Wizard / The Seeker / Baba O'Riley / Won't Get Fooled Again / Let's See Action / 5.15 / Join Together / Squeeze Box / Who Are You / You Better You Bet

The Who: BBC Sessions
UK Release: 02/2000 (Polydor 547727-2) Peak Position: 24
US Release: 02/2000 (MCA 088111960-2)
My Generation (Radio 1 Jingle) / Anyway, Anyhow, Anywhere / Good Lovin' / Just You And Me, Darling / Leaving Here / My Generation / The Good's Gone / La La La Lies / Substitute / Man With Money / Dancing In The Street / Disguises / I'm A Boy / Run Run Run / Boris The Spider / Happy Jack / See My Way / Pictures Of Lily / A Quick One, While He's Away / Substitute (Version 2) / The Seeker / I'm Free / Shakin' All Over – Spoonful / Relay / Long Live Rock / Boris The Spider (Radio 1 Jingle)

Then And Now
UK Release: 30/03/2004 (Polydor 9866577)
US Release: 03/2004 (Universal B0001836-02)
I Can't Explain / My Generation / The Kids Are Alright / Substitute / I'm A Boy / Happy Jack / I Can See For Miles / Magic Bus / Pinball Wizard / See Me, Feel Me / Summertime Blues (Live) / Behind Blue Eyes / Won't Get Fooled Again / 5.15 / Love, Reign O'er Me / Squeeze Box / Who Are You / You

Better You Bet / Real Good-Looking Boy / Old Red Wine

Rarities

Who's Missing

US Release: 30/11/1985 (MCA 5641) CD Reissue 2003 MCAD-31221
Shout And Shimmy (1965) / Leaving Here (1965) / Anytime You Want Me (1965) / Lubie (Come Back
Home) (1965) / Barbara Ann (1966) / I'm A Boy (Original Version) (1966) / Mary Anne With The Shaky
Hands (Original Version) (1967) / Heaven And Hell (1970) / Here For More (1970) / I Don't Even
Know Myself (1971) / When I Was A Boy (1971) / Bargain (1972)

Two's Missing

US Release: 1987 (MCA 5712) CD Reissue 2003 MCAD-31222
Bald Headed Woman / Under My Thumb / My Wife (Live-1971) / I'm A Man (Stereo Version) / Dogs
/ Dogs Part Two / Circles / The Last Time / Water / Daddy Rolling Stone (Stereo Version) / Heatwave
(Shel Talmy-Produced Version) / Going Down (Live-1971) / Motoring / Waspman

Other Live Albums

Who's Last

UK Release: 12/1984 (MCA MCAD WHO 1) Peak Position: 48
US Release: 11/1984 (MCA 8018) Peak Position: 81

Live At The Isle Of Wight Festival 1970

UK Release: 03/1996 (Castle EDF 326)
Disc 1: Heaven And Hell / I Can't Explain / Young Man Blues / I Don't Even Know Myself / Water /
Overture / It's A Boy / 1921 / Amazing Journey / Sparks / Eyesight To The Blind (The Hawker) / Christmas
Disc 2: The Acid Queen / Pinball Wizard / Do You Think It's Alright? / Fiddle About / Tommy, Can
You Hear Me? / There's A Doctor / Go To The Mirror / Smash The Mirror / Miracle Cure / I'm Free /
Tommy's Holiday Camp / We're Not Gonna Take It / Summertime Blues / Shakin' All Over / Spoonful
/ Twist And Shout / Substitute / My Generation / Naked Eye / Magic Bus

Live At The Royal Albert Hall

UK Release: 22/07/2003 (Steamhammer SPV 093-74882)
I Can't Explain /Anyway, Anyhow, Anywhere (Townshend, Daltrey) / Pinball Wizard / Relay / My Wife
(John Entwistle) / The Kids Are Alright / Mary Anne With The Shaky Hand / Bargain / Magic Bus /
Who Are You / Baba O'Riley (ft. Nigel Kennedy) / Drowned / Heart To Hang Onto / So Sad About Us
(ft. Paul Weller) / I'm One (ft. Eddie Vedder) / Gettin' In Tune (ft. Eddie Vedder) / Behind Blue Eyes (ft.
Bryan Adams) / You Better You Bet / The Real Me / 5.15 / Won't Get Fooled Again (ft. Noel Gallagher)
/ Substitute (ft. Kelly Jones) / Let's See Action (ft. Eddie Vedder) / My Generation / See Me, Feel Me
(ft. Bryan Adams & Eddie Vedder) / I'm Free / I Don't Even Know Myself / Summertime Blues / Young
Man Blues

Selected Solo Material

Pete Townshend
Singles

Forever's No Time At All / This Song Is Green

UK Release: 10/1972 (Track)

My Baby Gives It Away / Lane Track

US Release: 09/1977 (MCA 40818)

Street In The City / Annie [by Ronnie Lane]

UK Release: 11/1977 (Polydor 2058 944)

Nowhere To Run / Keep On Turning

US Release: 04/1978 (MCA 40878)

Rough Boys / And I Moved
UK Release: 03/1980 (Atco K 11460)

Rough Boys / Jools & Jim
US Release: 11/1980 (Atco 7318) Peak Position: 89

Let My Love Open The Door / Classified / Greyhound Girl
UK Release: 06/1980 (Atco K 11486) Peak Position: 46

Let My Love Open The Door / And I Moved
US Release: 06/1980 (Atco 7217) Peak Position: 9

A Little Is Enough / Cat's In The Cupboard
US Release: 09/1980 (Atco 7312) Peak Position: 72

Keep On Working / Jools & Jim
UK Release: 11/1980 (Atco K 11609)

Face Dances (Part 2) / Manwatching
UK Release: 05/1982 (Atco K 11734)
US Release: 05/1982 (Atco 99989)

Uniforms (Corps d'Esprit) / Slit Skirts
UK Release: 08/1982 (Atco K 11751)

Uniforms (Corps d'Esprit) / Stop Hurting People
UK Release: 08/1982 (Atco K 11751T) 12" Single Peak Position: 48

Uniforms (Corps d'Esprit) / Slit Skirts
US Release: 08/1982 (Atco 99973)

Bargain / Dirty Water
US Release: 04/1983 (Atco 99884)

Face The Face / Hiding Out
US Release: 10/1985 (Atco U 8859) Peak Position: 26

Give Blood / Magic Bus (Live)
UK Release: 02/1986 (Atco U 8744)

Secondhand Love / White City Fighting
US Release: 01/1986 (Atco 99553)

Behind Blue Eyes / Barefootin'
US Release: 05/1986 (Atco 99499)

A Friend Is A Friend / Man Machines
UK Release: 07/1989 (Virgin VS 1198)
US Release: 07/1989 (Atlantic)

I Won't Run Anymore / A Fool Says...
UK Release: 11/1989 (Virgin VS 1209)

English Boy / English Boy (A Dialogue Mix)

UK Release: 07/1993 (Atlantic A7370)

Pete Townshend
Albums

Who Came First
UK Release: 10/1972 (Track 2408 201) Peak Position: 30
US Release: 10/1972 (Decca 79189) Peak Position: 69
Pure And Easy / Evolution / Forever's No Time At All / Let's See Action / Time Is Passing / There's A Heartache Following Me / Sheraton Gibson / Content / Parvardigar
Though marketed as the first Townshend solo album, this was essentially a collection of demos. Reissued 1992 on Ryko with bonus tracks: His Hands / The Seeker / Day Of Silence / Sleeping Dog / The Love Man. Reissued 2006 on Imperial (Japan) with bonus tracks: Mary Jane / I Always Say / Begin The Beguine

Rough Mix (With Ronnie Lane)
UK Release: 09/1977 (Polydor 2442 147) Peak Position: 44
US Release: 09/1977 (MCA 2295) Peak Position: 45
My Baby Gives It Away / Nowhere To Run / Rough Mix / Annie / Keep Me Turning / Catmelody / Misunderstood / April Fool / Street In The City / Heart To Hang Onto / Till The Rivers All Run Dry
Various CD editions, including Atlantic release. Remixed by Bob Pridden in 2005 for European edition issued in 2006 by SPV (GMBH 304852) in digipack with booklet, with the following bonus tracks: Only You / Good Question / Silly Little Man

Empty Glass
UK Release: 04/1980 (Atco K 450699) Peak Position: 11
US Release: 05/1980 (Atco 32100) Peak Position: 5
Rough Boys / I Am An Animal / And I Moved / Let My Love Open The Door / Jools And Jim / Keep On Working / Cat's In The Cupboard / A Little Is Enough / Empty Glass / Gonna Get Ya
Various CD editions; 2006 Revisited CD, deluxe edition, features the following bonus tracks: I Am An Animal (Demo Alternate Vocal Version) / Keep On Working (Demo Alternate Vocal Version) / And I Moved (Demo Alternate Vocal Version) / Gonna Get Ya (Work-in-Progress Long Version)

All The Best Cowboys Have Chinese Eyes
UK Release: 06/1982 (Atco K 450889) Peak Position: 32
US Release: 06/1982 (Atco 38149) Peak Position: 26
Stop Hurting People / The Sea Refuses No River / Prelude / Face Dances Part 2 / Exquisitely Bored / Communication / Stardom In Action / Uniforms (Corp d'Esprit) / North Country Girl / Somebody Saved Me / Slit Skirts
2006 CD remastered by Jon Astley, issued with bonus tracks: Vivienne / Man Watching / Dance It Away. European edition: SPK GMBH SPV 97742 2CD in luxury disc digipack with booklet – available from www.eelpie.com. Japanese edition Imperial, 2006

Scoop
UK Release: 03/1983 (Atco 7900631)
US Release: 03/1983 (Atco 900631 F)
So Sad About Us-Brrr / Squeeze Box / Zelda / Politician / Dirty Water / Circles / Piano: Tipperary / Unused Piano: Quadrophenia / Melancholia / Bargain / Things Have Changed / Popular / Behind Blue Eyes / Magic Bus / Cache Cache / Cookin' / You're So Clever / Body Language / Initial Machine Experiments / Mary / Recorders / Goin' Fishin' / To Barney Kessell / You Came Back / Love Reign O'er Me
Various CD editions; remastered by Jon Astley in 2000. European edition issued in 2006 by SPK GMBH in 2-disc digipack with booklet

White City – A Novel
UK Release: 11/1985 (Atco 252392-1) Peak Position: 70
US Release: 11/1985 (Atco 90473) Peak Position: 26

Give Blood / Brilliant Blues / Face The Face / Hiding Out / Secondhand Love / Crashing By Design / I Am Secure / White City Fighting / Come to Mama
Reissued on Hip-O-USA, 2006, with bonus tracks: Night School / Save It For Later / Hiding Out (12" Mix). Reissued on Imperial (Japan), 2006, with bonus tracks: Secondhand Love (Live In Brixton) / Face The Face (Live In Brixton)

Deep End Live
US Release: 10/1986 (Atco 90553-1) Peak Position: 98
Barefootin' / After The Fire / Behind Blue Eyes / Stop Hurting People / I'm One / I Put A Spell On You / Save It For Later / Pinball Wizard / Little Is Enough / Eyesight To The Blind
CD Release 1999, Yellow; CD Release 2006 SPV with bonus tracks: Magic Bus / Won't Get Fooled Again

Another Scoop
UK Release: 03/1987 (Atco 7905391)
US Release: 03/1987 (Atco 7905391 G)
You Better You Bet / Girl In A Suitcase / Brooklyn Kids / Pinball Wizard / Football Fugue / Happy Jack / Substitute / Long Live Rock / Call Me Lightning / Holly Like Ivy / Begin The Beguine / Vicious Interlude / La La La Lies / Cat Snatch / Prelude #556 / Baroque Ippenese / Praying The Game / Drifting Blues / Christmas / Pictures Of Lily / Don't Let Go The Coat / The Kids Are Alright / Prelude, The Right To Write / Never Ask Me / Ask Yourself / The Ferryman / The Shout
Various CD editions, including Japanese CD Teichiku CD. Remastered by Jon Astley in 2000. European edition issued in 2006 by SPK GMBH SPV 97712 2CD in 2-disc digipack with booklet

The Iron Man – A Musical
UK Release: 03/1989 (Virgin V 2592) Peak Position: 58
US Release: 1989 (Atlantic 81996)
I Won't Run Anymore / Over The Top / Man Machines / Dig* / A Friend Is A Friend / I Eat Heavy Metal / All Shall Be Well / Was There Life / Fast Food / A Fool Says… / Fire* / New Life – Reprise
(*Credited to the Who)

Psychoderelict
US Release: 06/1993 (Atlantic 82494-2)
Dialogue Version: English Boy / Meher Baba M3 / Let's Get Pretentious / Meher Baba M4 (Signal Box) / Early Morning Dreams / I Want That Thing / Dialogue Introduction To Outlive The Dinosaur / Outlive The Dinosaur / Flame (Demo Version) / Now And Then / I Am Afraid / Don't Try To Make Me Real / Dialogue Introduction To Predictable / Predictable / Flame / Meher Baba M5 / Fake It / Dialogue Introduction To Now And Then (Reprise) / Now And Then (Reprise) / Baba O'Riley (Reprise) / English Boy (Reprise)
Music Only Version: English Boy / Meher Baba M3 / Let's Get Pretentious / Meher Baba M4 (Signal Box) / Early Morning Dreams / I Want That Thing / Outlive The Dinosaur / Now And Then / I Am Afraid / Don't Try To Make Me Real / Predictable / Flame / Meher Baba M5 / Fake It / English Boy (Reprise)

The Oceanic Concerts (Pete Townshend & Raphael Rudd)
UK Release: 10/2001 (Rhino R2 72489)
Raga / Drowned / Seeker / Magic Grace / Who Is Meher Baba / Ferryman / Kitty's Theme / Little Is Enough / Contact In Solitude / Sleeping Dog / Sound Barrier / Bargain / Longing For The Beloved / Tattoo / Let My Love Open The Door / Awakening / Western (American) Arti / O Parvardigar

Scoop 3
UK Release: 11/2001 (Eel Pie EPR013)
Can You See The Real Me / Dirty Water / Commonwealth Boys / Theme 015 / Marty Robbins / I Like It The Way It Is / Theme 016 / No Way Out (However Much I Booze) / Collings / Parvardigar / Sea And Sand / 971104 Arpeggio Piano / Theme 017 / I Am Afraid / Maxims For Lunch / Wistful / Eminence Front / Lonely Words / Prelude 970519 / Iron Man Recitative / Tough Boys / Did You Steal My Money? / Can You Really Dance? / Variations On Dirty Jobs / All Lovers Are Deranged / Elephants / Wired To The Moon, Pt 2 / How Can You Do It Alone / Poem Disturbed / Squirm Squirm / Outlive The Dinosaur

/ Teresa / Man And Machines / It's In Ya
Various CD editions; remastered by Jon Astley in 2000. European edition issued in 2006 by SPV GMBH
SPV 97742 2CD in 2-disc digipack with booklet – available from www.eelpie.com

Pete Townshend Live: Live At The House Of Blues Chicago /
A Benefit For Maryville Academy
US Release: 03/2005 (Platinum 9555)
Disc 1: On The Road Again / Anyway, Anyhow, Anywhere / Little Is Enough / Drowned / You Better
You Bet / Now and Then / North Country Girl / Let My Love Open The Door / Won't Get Fooled Again
/ Magic Bus / I'm One
Disc 2: Magic Bus / Heart To Hang Onto
Highlights from the benefit concert. Disc one features Townshend backed by a quintet, though no live
drummer, on a mixture of Who and solo classics, some more obscure originals, plus Canned Heat's
droning "On The Road Again" and Dylan's "Girl From The North Country". Disc 2 features reworked
extended versions of "Magic Bus" and "Heat To Hang Onto" with Pearl Jam's Eddie Vedder. All
proceeds to charity.

Anthology
European Release: 10/2005 (Spv 089 304292)
Disc 1: English Boy / Secondhand Love / Little Is Enough / Heart To Hang Onto / Sheraton Gibson / Sea
Refuses No River / Brilliant Blues / Now And Then / I Won't Run Anymore / Keep Me Turning / Let My
Love Open The Door / Slit Skirts / Friend Is A Friend / Street In The City / Empty Glass
Disc 2: Rough Boys / Give Blood / Exquisitely Bored / Jools And Jim / Crashing By Design / Don't Try
To Make Me Real / Face The Face / Uniforms / My Baby Gives It Away / Outlive The Dinosaur / Keep
On Working / White City Fighting / All Shall Be Well / Time Is Passing / I Am Afraid / Misunderstood
/ Pure And Easy / Parvardigar

John Entwistle
Singles

I Believe In Everything / My Size
UK Release: 04/1971 (Track 2049 008)
US Release: 05/1971 (Decca 32896)

I Wonder / Who Cares
US Release: 11/1972 (Track 33052)

Made In Japan / Hound Dog
UK Release: 01/1973 (Track 2049 107)

Made In Japan / Roller Skate Kate
US Release: 06/1973 (MCA 40066)

Mad Dog / Cell No. 7
UK Release: 02/1975 (Decca FR 13567)

Too Late The Hero / I'm Coming Back
UK Release: 09/1981 (WEA K 79249)

Too Late The Hero / Dancing Master
US Release: 09/1981 (Atco)

Talk Dirty / Try Me
US Release: 11/1981 (Atco)

John Entwistle
Albums

Smash Your Head Against The Wall
UK Release: 05/1971 (Track 2406 005)
US Release: 10/1971 (Decca 9183)
My Size / Pick Me Up (Big Chicken) / What Are We Doing Here? / What Kind Of People Are They? / Heaven And Hell / Ted End / You're Mine / No. 29 (Eternal Youth) / I Believe In Everything
2000 CD Reissue on Repertoire; 2005 Sanctuary CD reissued with the following bonus tracks: Cinnamon Girl (Previously Released Outtake) / It's Hard To Write A Love Song (Previously Unreleased Demo) / The Haunted Can Be Free (Previously Unreleased Demo) / World Behind My Face (Previously Unreleased Demo) / My Size (Previously Unreleased Early Take) / What Kind Of People Are They? (Previously Unreleased Demo) / Pick Me Up (Big Chicken) (Previously Unreleased Demo) / No. 29 (Eternal Youth) (Previously Unreleased Demo) / Ted End (Previously Unreleased Demo)

Whistle Rymes
UK Release: 11/1972 (Track 2406 104)
US Release: 11/1972 (Decca 79190)
Ten Little Friends / Apron Strings / I Feel Better / Thinkin' It Over / Who Cares? / I Wonder / I Was Just Being Friendly / The Window Shopper / I Found Out / Nightmare (Please Wake Me Up)
1996 CD reissue Repertoire REP-4618-WY; 2005 Castle CD reissue with the following bonus tracks: I Wonder (Demo Version) / All Dressed Up (Demo Version) / Back On The Road (Demo Version) / Countryside Boogie (Demo Version)

Rigor Mortis Sets In
UK Release: 05/1973 (Track 2406 106)
US Release: 06/1973 (MCA 321)
Gimme That Rock'N'Roll / Mr Bass Man / Do The Dangle / Hound Dog / Made In Japan / My Wife / Roller Skate Kate / Peg Leg Peggy / Lucille / Big Black Cadillac
2002 CD reissue Repertoire; 2005 Castle CD reissue with the following bonus tracks: BP Big Gallon Jingle ("100 Miles Of Motorway") (Demo Version) / BP Big Gallon Jingle ("100 Miles Of Motorway") (Demo With...) / Made In Japan (Early Take) / Peg Leg Peggy (Early Take)

Mad Dog (Credited To John Entwistle's Ox)
UK Release: 02/1975 (Decca TXS 114)
I Fall To Pieces / Cell Number 7 / You Can Be So Mean / Lady Killer / Who In The Hell? / Mad Dog / Jungle Bunny / I'm So Scared / Drowning
1997 CD reissue Repertoire; 2005 Castle/Sanctuary CD reissue features the following bonus tracks: Mad Dog (Single Mix) / Cell Number 7 (Single Mix)

Too Late The Hero
UK Release: 11/1981 (WEA K99179)
US Release: 09/1981 (Atco 38142)
Try Me / Talk Dirty / Lovebird / Sleeping Man / I'm Coming Back / Dancing Master / Fallen Angel / Love Is A Heart Attack / Too Late The Hero
1997 CD reissue Repertoire; 2005 Castle/Sanctuary CD reissue features the following bonus tracks: Sleeping Man (Demo) / Dancing Master (Demo) / I'm Coming Back (Demo) / Love Is A Heart Attack (Demo) / Overture (Outtake)

The Rock
UK/US Release: 08/1996 (Recorded 1986) (Griffin Music GCD 6152)
Stranger In A Strange Land / Love Doesn't Last / Suzie / Bridges Under The Water / Heartache / Billy / Life After Love / Hurricane / Too Much Too Soon / Last Song / Country Hurricane
Due to the poor reception of *Too Late The Hero*, though this was originally recorded in 1986, it was only released privately by WEA Records at the time, and did not get an official release until 1996. Reissued on CD in 2005 and on import with the following bonus tracks: Casualty (Outtake) / Light In The Dark

(Outtake) / Break Your Heart (Outtake) / Love Doesn't Last (Demo) / Heartache (Early Version)

Music From Van-pires (Credited To The John Entwistle Band)
US Release: 2000 (Pulsar ROC 30012)
Horror Rock / Darker Side Of Night / Sometimes / Bogey Man / Good And Evil / When You See The Light / Back On The Road / Left For Dead / When The Sun Comes Up / Rebel Without A Car / Don't Be A Sucker / Endless Vacation / I'll Try Again Today / Face The Fear
The soundtrack to a children's CGI TV series. Unlike the rest of Entwistle's solo work, this was not reissued in 2005 and is now generally unavailable, though a few copies seem to be for sale at www. johnentwistle.com with all proceeds to the John Entwistle Foundation.

Boris The Spider Live
Release: 2001 (King Biscuit)
Boris The Spider / My Size / Whiskey Man / Who Cares / Give Me That Rock'N'Roll / Cell Number Seven / Not Fade Away / My Wife / Heaven And Hell

Left For Live (Credited To The John Entwistle Band)
Release: 2002 (Eastworld / Plastic Head EWO014CD)
Horror Rock / The Real Me / Darker Side Of Night / Success Story / 905 / I'll Try Again Today / Under A Raging Moon / Endless Vacation / Too Late The Hero / Had Enough / Shakin' All Over / Young Man Blues

So Who's The Bass Player?: The Ox Anthology
Release: 02/2005 (Sanctuary Midline)
Disc 1: My Size / Pick Me Up (Big Chicken) / What Are We Doing Here / Heaven And Hell / Ted End / Ten Little Friends /Apron Strings / Thinkin' It Over / Who Cares / I Wonder / I Was Just Being Friendly / Do The Dangle / Made In Japan / Roller Skate Kate / Peg Leg Leggy / Lady Killer / Mad Dog / Cell Number Seven / Whisky Man / Boris The Spider
Disc 2: My Wife / I'm Flash / Space Pirates / Let's Go To The Chop / Blast Off / Try Me / Talk Dirty / Too Late The Hero / Love Doesn't Last / Life After Love / Real Me / Success Story / 905 / Had Enough / Bogeyman / Back On The Road / When The Sun Comes Up / Don't Be A Sucker

Edge Of The World (Tipton, Entwistle & Powell)
Release: 2006 (Rhino/WEA 8122 73352 2)
Unknown Soldier / Friendly Fire / The Holy Man / Never Say Die / Resolution / Searching / Give Blood / Crime Of Passion / Walls Cave In / Edge Of The World / Stronger Than The Drug
Essentially a Glen Tipton (Judas Priest) solo album – it was written, produced and sung by him – this was recorded in 1996, but rejected by Tipton's record label, Atlantic. Tipton had it finally released as a tribute to Entwistle, but it is likely if it had surfaced in 1996, it would have been credited solely to the Judas Priest man.

Roger Daltrey
Singles

Giving It All Away / The Way Of The World
UK Release: 05/1973 (Track 2094 110) Peak Position: 5
US Release: 1973 (Track 40053) Peak Position: 83

I'm Free / (Overture)
UK Release: 06/1973 (Ode ODS 66302) Peak Position: 13

Thinking / There Is Love
UK Release: 05/1973 (Track 2094 014)
US Release: 05/1973 (MCA 40084)

It's A Hard Life / One Man Band
UK Release: 07/1973 (Track 2094 016)

One Man Band / The Story So Far
UK Release: 08/1973 (Track)

Come And Get Your Love / Hearts Right
UK Release: 06/1975 (Polydor)

Get Your Love / World Over
UK Release: 07/1975 (Polydor 2058 593)

Walking The Dog / Proud
UK Release: 08/1975 (Polydor 2058 628)

Ocean's Away / Feeling
US Release: 01/1976 (MCA 40512)

Orpheus Song / Love's Dream
UK Release: 06/1975 (A&M AMS 7206)

Love's Dream / Orpheus Song
US Release: 06/1975 (A&M)

Written On The Wind / Dear John
UK Release: 03/1977 (Polydor 2121 319)

One Of The Boys / You Put Something Better Inside Me
UK Release: 06/1977 (Polydor 2058 896)

Say It Ain't So, Joe / Satin & Lace
UK Release: 09/1977 (Polydor 2058 948)

Leon / The Prisoner
US Release: 04/1978 (MCA 40862)

Free Me / McVicar
UK Release: 06/1980 (Polydor 2001 980) Peak Position: 39
US Release: 08/1980 (Polydor)

Without Your Love / Escape (Part 1)
US Release: 10/1980 (Polydor) Peak Position: 20

Waiting For A Friend / Bitter & Twisted
US Release: 11/1980 (Polydor)

Avenging Annie / Martyrs And Madmen
US Release: 04/1982 (MCA)

Walking In My Sleep / Somebody Told Me
UK Release: 02/1984 (WEA)
US Release: 02/1984 (Atlantic)

Parting Would Be Painless / Is There Anybody Out There?
UK Release: 06/1984 (WEA)
US Release: 06/1984 (Atlantic)

After The Fire / It Doesn't Satisfy Me
UK Release: 09/1985 (10 Records)

US Release: 09/1985 (Atlantic)

Let Me Down Easy / Fallen Angel
US Release: 11/1985 (Atlantic)

Under A Raging Moon / The Pride You Hide
US Release: 04/1986 (Atlantic)

Quicksilver Lightning / Love like You Do
US Release: 04/1986 (Atlantic)

Hearts Of Fire / Lover's Storm
UK Release: 06/1987 (10 Records)
US Release: 06/1987 (Atlantic)

Take Me Home / Balance On Wires
US Release: 08/1987 (Atlantic)

Don't Let The Sun Go Down On Me / Lost Boys
US Release: 09/1987 (Atlantic)

Roger Daltrey
Albums

Daltrey
UK Release: 04/1973 (Track 2406 107)
US Release: 05/1973 (MCA 328) Peak Position: 45
One Man Band / The Way Of The World (Adam Faith, David Courtney) / You Are Yourself / Thinking / You And Me (Adam Faith, David Courtney) / It's A Hard Life / Giving It All Away / The Story So Far / When The Music Stops / Reasons / One Man Band (Reprise)
Produced by David Courtney and Adam Faith. All songs written by David Courtney and Leo Sayer except where noted. CD 2002; remastered CD 2005 (Hip-O-Records) features bonus track: There Is Love (original B-side of "Thinking")

Ride A Rock Horse
UK Release: 06/1975 (Polydor 2442 135) Peak Position: 15
US Release: 07/1975 (MCA 2147) Peak Position: 28
Come And Get Your Love (Ballard) / Hearts Right (Korda) / Oceans Away (Goodhand-Tait) / Proud (Ballard) / World Over (Korda) / Near To Surrender (Ballard) / Feeling (Korda) / Walking The Dog (Thomas) / Milk Train (Bugatti/Musker) / I Was Born To Sing Your Song (Neal/Marchand)
Produced by Russ Ballard. CD 2002; remastered CD 2005 (Hip-O-Records) features bonus tracks: Dear John (Dave Courtney) (B-side of the 1977 single "Written On The Wind") / Oceans Away (Alternate Version)

Lisztomania Original Soundtrack (Credited To Rick Wakeman)
UK Release: 06/1975 (A&M AMLH 64546)
US Release: 06/1975 (A&M SP 4546)
Rienzi (Chopsticks Fantasia) / Love's Dream*@ / Dante Period / Orpheus Song*# / Hell / Hibernation / Excelsior Song / Master Race / Rape, Pillage And Clap / Funerailles* / Free Song (Hungarian Rhapsody) / Peace At Last*#
*Features Roger's vocals; @entire lyric by Roger; #lyrics collaborated on by Roger.
CD (A&M D32Y 3550) (Japan); 2006 limited edition CD, (Japan) 2006, (UICY-9294), mini cardboard sleeve, with bonus track "Peace At Last (Movie Version)"*. Though Roger, as the star of the movie, dominates the cover art, he is really the guest on a Rick Wakeman solo album. However, this is worthy of a place in Roger's solo discography as some of his vocal contributions are of the highest order.

The Real Lisztomania (Credited To Rick Wakeman)
UK Release: 2002 (Voiceprint VPTCCD1)
The Scene / The Metronome / The Country Sword Dance / Free Song / The Freudian Dream / Dante Period / Orpheus Song* / For The Chop / Hell / Wagner's Dream / The Dream Of Hell / The Inferno Ride / Master Race / The Ride Of Thor / Excelsior Song / The Guardian Virgins / Rape, Pillage And Clap / Love's Dream* / The Suffering / Peace At Last* / Love's Dream (Previously Unreleased)*
Anyone interested in *Lisztomania*, should check out this Rick Wakeman-authorised version of the soundtrack. While this much longer, idiosyncratic, often-humorous, collection cuts the weakest Roger vocal from the original, "Funerailles", it adds a previously unreleased and quite spine-tingling Roger, solo voice and piano take on "Love's Dream" at the end.

One Of The Boys
UK Release: 05/1977 (Polydor 2442 146) Peak Position: 45
US Release: 06/1977 (MCA 2271) Peak Position: 46
Parade / Single Man's Dilemma / Avenging Annie / The Prisoner / Leon / One Of The Boys / Giddy / Written On The Wind / Satin And Lace / Doing It All Again
US LP version replaced "Written On The Wind" with a fine version of Murray Head's "Say It Ain't So, Joe". CD 2002; remastered CD 2005 (Hip-O-Records), features bonus tracks: Say It Ain't So, Joe / You Put Something Better Inside Me / Martyrs And Madmen (Session Outtake) / Treachery

McVicar (Original Soundtrack)
UK Release: 06/1980 (Polydor POLD 5034) Peak Position: 39
US Release: 06/1980 (Polydor 1-6284) Peak Position: 22
Bitter And Twisted (Steve Swindells) / Just A Dream Away (Russ Ballard) / White City Lights (Billy Nicholls & Jon Lind) / Free Me (Russ Ballard) / My Time Is Gonna Come (Russ Ballard) / Waiting For A Friend (Billy Nicholls) / Without Your Love (Billy Nicholls) / McVicar (Billy Nicholls)
Produced, arranged and conducted by Jeff Wayne. CD 1996 (Polygram 527 341-2), features bonus tracks "Escape Part One" (Jeff Wayne) / "Escape Part Two" (Jeff Wayne)

Best Bits
US Release: 03/1982 (MCA 5301)
Martyrs And Madmen / Say It Ain't So, Joe / Oceans Away / Treachery / Free Me / Without Your Love / Hard Life / Giving It All Away / Avenging Annie / Proud / You Put Something Better Inside Me

Parting Should Be Painless
UK Release: 02/1984 (WEA 2052 981)
US Release: 02/1984 (Atlantic 80128)
Walking In My Sleep / Parting Should Be Painless / Is There Anybody Out There? / Would A Stranger Do? / Going Strong / Looking For You / Somebody Told Me / One Day / How Does The Cold Wind Cry / Don't Wait On The Stairs
CD 2004 (Wounded Bird Records)

Under A Raging Moon
UK Release: 10/1985 (10/Virgin DIX 17) Peak Position: 52
US Release: 10/1985 (Atlantic 81269) Peak Position: 42
After The Fire / Don't Talk To Strangers / Breaking Down Paradise / The Pride You Hide / Move Better In The Night / Let Me Down Easy / Fallen Angel / It Don't Satisfy Me / Rebel / Under A Raging Moon
CD 1990 (WEA)

Can't Wait To See The Movie
UK Release: 06/1987 (10/Virgin DIX 54)
US Release: 06/1987 (Atlantic 81759)
Hearts Of Fire / When The Thunder Comes / Ready For Love / Balance On Wires / Miracle Of Love / The Price Of Love / The Heart Has Its Reasons / Alone In The Night / Lover's Storm / Take Me Home
CD 2004 (Wounded Bird Records)

Best Of Rockers And Ballads
UK Release: 04/1991 (Polydor 8478552)
It's A Hard Life / Giving It All Away / Without Your Love / Say It Ain't So, Joe / Leon / Prisoner / Parade / White City Lights / Oceans Away / One Man Band / Avenging Annie / Walking The Dog / One Of The Boys / Thinking / Free Me / Proud / Reprise – One Man Band

Rocks In The Head
US Release: 04/1992 (Atlantic 782359-2)
Who's Gonna Walk On Water / Before My Time Is Up / Time's Changed / You Can't Call It Love / Mirror Mirror / Perfect World / Love Is / Blues Man's Road / Everything A Heart Could Ever Want (Willow) / Days Of Light / Unforgettable Opera
CD 2004 (Wounded Bird Records)

A Celebration: The Music Of Pete Townshend And The Who
US Release: 1994 (Continuum CD 19402)
Overture / Pinball Wizard / Imagine A Man / Doctor Jimmy / Song Is Over / The Real Me / Baba O'Riley / After The Fire / 5.15 / Sea Refuses No River / Who Are You / Won't Get Fooled Again

Martyrs & Madmen: The Best Of Roger Daltrey
US Release: 1997 (Rhino R2 72846)
One Man Band / It's A Hard Life / Giving It All Away / Thinking / World Over / Oceans Away / One Of The Boys / Avenging Annie / Say It Ain't So, Joe / Parade / Free Me / Without Your Love / Waiting For A Friend / Walking In My Sleep / Parting Would Be Painless / After The Fire / Let Me Down Easy / The Pride You Hide / Under A Raging Moon (Single Version) / Lover's Storm

Moonlighting: The Anthology
UK Release: 02/2005 (Sanctuary SMEDO 013)
Disc 1: One Man Band / The Way Of The World / Thinking / There Is Love / Giving It All Away / (Come And) Get Your Love / The World Over / Proud / Dear John / Avenging Annie / One Of The Boys / Martyrs And Madmen / Say It Ain't So, Joe / Bitter And Twisted / Free Me / Without Your Love / Waiting For A Friend / Parting Would Be Painless / After The Fire / Under A Raging Moon
Disc 2: Behind Blue Eyes / Won't Get Fooled Again / Quicksilver Lightning / Lover's Storm / Mack The Knife / The Pig Must Die / Don't Let the Sun Go Down On Me / Rock And Roll / Who's Gonna Walk On Water / Love Is / Blues Man's Road / Baba O'Riley / Pinball Wizard / The Real Me / Child Of Mine / Born To Run / A Second Out (Previously Unreleased)

Gold (Compilation)
US Release: 2006 (Hip-O Records)
Disc 1: One Man Band / Way Of The World / Thinking / There Is Love / Giving It All Away / (Come And) Get Your Love / World Over / Proud / Dear John / Avenging Annie / One Of The Boys / Martyrs And Madmen / Say It Ain't So, Joe / Bitter And Twisted / Free Me / Without Your Love / Waiting For A Friend / Parting Would Be Painless
Disc 2: After The Fire / Under A Raging Moon / Pride You Hide / Behind Blue Eyes / Won't Get Fooled Again / Lover's Storm / Pig Must Die / Who's Gonna Walk On Water / Love Is / Blues Man Road / Baba O'Riley / Pinball Wizard / Real Me / Child Of Mine / Born To Run (Live) / Second Out

Keith Moon
Singles

Don't Worry Baby / Together
UK Release: 09/1974 (Polydor 2058 584)

Don't Worry Baby / Teenage Idol
US Release: 10/1974 (MCA 40316)

Solid Gold / Move Over Ms L

US Release: 04/1975 (MCA 40387)

Crazy Like A Fox / In My Life
US Release: 07/1975 (MCA 40433)

Keith Moon
Albums

Two Sides Of The Moon
UK Release: 04/1975 (Polydor 2442 134)
US Release: 03/1975 (MCA 2136)
Crazy Like A Fox / Solid Gold / Don't Worry Baby / One Night Stand / The Kids Are Alright / Move Over Ms L / Teenage Idol / Back Door Sally / In My Life / Together
1997 CD reissue (Repertoire) features bonus tracks: US Radio Spot / I Don't Suppose / Naked Man / Do Me Good / Real Emotion / Don't Worry Baby (US single A-side) / Teenage Idol (US single B-side) / Together "Rap"
2006 Castle/Sanctuary deluxe 2-CD edition, features a staggering 41 bonus tracks:
Disc 1: Crazy Like A Fox / Solid Gold / Don't Worry Baby / One Night Stand / The Kids Are Alright / Move Over Ms L / Teenage Idol / Back Door Sally / In My Life / Together / Lies (Album Outtake) / I Don't Suppose (Album Outtake) / Hot Rod Queen (Album Outtake) / Don't Worry Baby (Original 1974 US single) / Teenage Idol (Original 1974 US single) / Back Door Sally (Mal Evans Mix) / One Night Stand (Mal Evans Mix) / Crazy Like A Fox (Mal Evans Mix) / In My Life (Mal Evans Mix) / Move Over Ms L (Mal Evans Mix) / Solid Gold (Mal Evans Mix) / We Wish You A Merry Xmas (Unreleased '74 Christmas Single) / Do Me Good (1975 Clover Master) / Real Emotion (1975 Clover Master) / Naked Man (1975 Clover Master)
Disc 2: Keith & Ringo "Together" (Session Dialogue) / Don't Worry Baby (John Sebastian Guide Vocal) / Don't Worry Baby (Keith Lead Vocal) / Teenage Idol / Crazy Like A Fox / Solid Gold / A Touch Of Moon Madness / Move Over Ms L / Lies / My Generation / The Kids Are Alright / Keith & Ringo "Together" (Session Dialogue) / Together / Together (Keith & Ringo Vocals) / Together (Harry Nilsson Ending Tag) / I'm Not Angry / Hot Rod Queen (Backing Tracks) / Solid Gold (Ad-libs) / Teenage Idol (Dick Dale Overdubbing) / Solid Gold / Real Emotion (Clover Recordings) / "Ok Mr. Starkey" (Clover Recordings, False Start And Chat) / Do Me Good (Clover Recordings) / Keith & Ringo "Together (Again)" (Record Plant) / In My Life (Record Plant)

Kenney Jones
Singles

Ready Or Not / Woman Trouble
UK Release: 10/1974 (GM Records)

The Jones Gang
Angel (1-Track Only)
US Release: 08/2005 (Reality/Aao Music)

Kenney Jones
Albums

The Jones Gang
Any Day Now
US Release: 08/2005 (Reality/Aao Music 40501)
UK Release: 09/2006 (But Records)
Time Of Your Life / Mr Brown / Angel / She'll Never Know / With You / Gypsy Lane / Lucy / Six To Midnight / Hole In My Sole / Where Are You? / Red Hot
Only solo projects; Kenney's discography with the Small Faces, the Faces and many other artists is, of course, extensive.

Appendix IV – Selective DVD Listing

DVDs are UK PAL region unless stated otherwise. Dates are release dates for these editions.

Movies

Tommy
(Odyssey Quest ODX20290) 2-DVD Set
(Single disc DVD 2004, budget single DVD edition, 2007)
The whole movie, plus director's commentary; Ken Russell on *Tommy*; Pete Townshend interview; Roger Daltrey interview; Ann-Margret spills the beans; the story of sound; film trailer; press promo and colour booklet.

The Kids Are Alright
(Pioneer 12103) 2-DVD Set 2004
(Single disc DVD 2005 and 2004, without additional features)
The two-disc set contains original movie, plus additional features: interviews with Roger Daltrey and Jeff Stein; full length audio commentary; previously unseen footage; multiple camera angles; isolated John Entwistle audio track; a documentary about the movie's restoration; video/audio showdown: a warm-up for the casual fan; the Who's London: interactive tour; a quiz; slide show; a 5.1 mix of the album version of *Who Are You*; and a collectable 32-page booklet.

Quadrophenia
(Universal DVD 051 835 2) 2-DVD Set 2006
The original movie, plus a fine making-of feature and an 8-minute montage of stills and off-screen cast photos. Previously released on DVD in 1999 on a single disc.

Live

Listening to You: The Who Live At The Isle Of Wight Festival 1970
(Eagle Vision EV30054-9) 2000 (Warner 0630-14360-2) 1996
The Who's second performance at the legendary festival, 30 August, 1970, in front of a crowd of 600,000. Previously released on VHS, the DVD also features an exclusive new Pete Townshend interview.
Introduction / Heaven & Hell / I Can't Explain / Young Man Blues / I Don't Even Know Myself / Water / Shakin' All Over–Spoonful–Twist And Shout / Summertime Blues / My Generation / Magic Bus / Overture–It's A Boy–Eyesight To The Blind (The Hawker)–Christmas / The Acid Queen / Pinball Wizard / Do You Think It's Alright? / Fiddle About / Go To The Mirror / Miracle Cure / I'm Free / We're Not Gonna Take It–See Me, Feel Me–Listening To You / Tommy Can You Hear Me?

30 Years Of Maximum R&B Live
(Universal 820 742 7) 2001
Awesome video version of the fantastic box set of the same name that collects some of the best live footage of the band, first released on VHS in 1994. Though there is a shortage of footage of the '71-75 glory era, there is no duplication of *The Kids Are Alright* material and this makes a nice complimentary work to that collection. Also includes unseen early documentary footage plus exclusive new interviews with Pete Townshend, Roger Daltrey and John Entwistle. Unfortunately, this is currently out of print.
Anyway Anyhow Anywhere / So Sad About Us / A Quick One, While He's Away / Happy Jack / Heaven & Hell / I Can't Explain / Water / Young Man Blues / I Don't Even Know Myself / My Generation / Substitute / Drowned / Bell Boy / My Generation Blues / Dreaming From The Waist / Sister Disco / Who Are You / 5.15 / My Wife / Music Must Change / Pinball Wizard / Behind Blue Eyes / Love Reign

O'er Me / Boris The Spider / I Can See For Miles / See Me, Feel Me

The Vegas Job
(United Energy Entertainment DVDL001D) 2003; reissued with different artwork, 2006
The Who reunion concert live in Vegas. Live footage:
I Can't Explain / Substitute / Anyway Anyhow Anywhere / Pinball Wizard / See Me, Feel Me, Touch Me, Heal Me / Baba O'Riley / My Wife / 5.15 / Behind Blue Eyes / Who Are You / Magic Bus / Won't Get Fooled Again / The Kids Are Alright / My Generation
Previously released on VHS in 1999, the DVD special features include interviews with Roger Daltrey and John Entwistle, interactive motion menus, a 35-minute making-of featurette, and fan interviews.

The Who & Special Guests Live At The Royal Albert Hall
(MCY 1X0834MYUKD) 2003
Live show from November 27th 2000, featuring; Bryan Adams, Noel Gallagher, Kelly Jones, Nigel Kennedy, Eddie Vedder and Paul Weller.
I Can't Explain / Anyway, Anyhow, Anywhere (Townshend, Daltrey) / Pinball Wizard / Relay / My Wife (John Entwistle) / The Kids Are Alright / Mary Anne With The Shaky Hand / Bargain / Magic Bus / Who Are You / Baba O'Riley (Featuring Nigel Kennedy) / Drowned / Heart To Hang Onto / So Sad About Us (Featuring Paul Weller) / I'm One (Featuring Eddie Vedder) / Gettin' In Tune (Featuring Eddie Vedder) / Behind Blue Eyes (Featuring Bryan Adams) / You Better You Bet / The Real Me / 5.15 / Won't Get Fooled Again (Featuring Noel Gallagher) / Substitute (Featuring Kelly Jones) / Let's See Action (Featuring Eddie Vedder) / My Generation / See Me, Feel Me (Featuring Bryan Adams & Eddie Vedder) / I'm Free / I Don't Even Know Myself / Summertime Blues / Young Man Blues
Additional features include: rehearsal and backstage footage; Roger Daltrey interview and multi-angle sequences on "Pinball Wizard".

Live & Alive
(Falcon Neue Medien 0248) 2004
A substandard transfer of the 1988 VHS *Who's Better Who's Best* ragbag of live footage, plus "Relay" from the Russell Harty TV show and a clip from the *Quadrophenia* movie for "5.15". Caveat emptor!
My Generation / I Can't Explain / Substitute / The Kids Are Alright / I'm A Boy / Happy Jack / Pictures Of Lily / You Better, You Bet / Anyway Anyhow Anywhere / I Can See For Miles / Magic Bus / Pinball Wizard / I'm Free / See Me, Feel Me / Baba O'Riley / Join Together / Relay / 5.15 / Who Are You / Won't Get Fooled Again

Live In Boston
(Warner Music Vision 2564 61764-2) 2004
This 24th September, 2002, Boston show features Pino Palladino on bass in place of the sadly missed Ox who had died just before the US tour had begun...
I Can't Explain / Substitute / Anyway Anyhow Anywhere / Who Are You / Another Tricky Day / Relay / Bargain / Baba O'Riley / Sea And Sand / 5.15 / Love, Reign O'er Me / Eminence Front / Behind Blue Eyes / You Better You Bet / The Kids Are Alright / My Generation / Won't Get Fooled Again / Pinball Wizard / Amazing Journey / Sparks / See Me, Feel Me–Listening To You

Tommy And Quadrophenia Live With Special Guests
(Warner Music Vision [Rhino] 0349 70500) 3-DVD Set 2005
Disc 1 features *Quadrophenia* live from the 1996-97 tour and mixes live performance footage with the specially shot footage which was originally shown on the concerts' big screen backdrop. Guests include Billy Idol and PJ Proby. Bonus features include a documentary about the 96-97 *Quadrophenia* tour, and a commentary from Roger and Pete.
Disc 2 features a 1989 live Performance of *Tommy* at the LA Universal Amphitheatre. Guests include Phil Collins, Billy Idol and Elton John. Bonus features include an interview with Billy Idol, a photo gallery and a commentary from Roger and Pete.
Disc 3 features a selection of classic Who hits played live from the second set from the *Tommy* shows, the encore from the *Quadrophenia* shows and another 1989 New York stadium gig.
NB: both *Tommy* and *Quadrophenia* available separately on DVD.

Who's Better, Who's Best: The Videos
(Universal) 2006
My Generation / I Can't Explain / Substitute / The Kids Are Alright / I'm A Boy / Happy Jack / Pictures Of Lily / You Better You Bet / Anyway Anyhow Anywhere / I Can See For Miles / Magic Bus / Pinball Wizard / I'm Free / See Me, Feel Me / Baba O'Riley / Join Together / Who Are You / Won't Get Fooled Again / Don't Let Go The Coat / Another Tricky Day / Eminence Front
This is basically the VHS *Who's Better Who's Best* with the addition of three videos from the Kenney Jones era – 1981's "Don't Let Go The Coat" and "Another Tricky Day", plus the 1982 soundcheck video for "Eminence Front".

Other

Who's Next: Classic Albums
(Eagle Rock DVD2011) 2001
Previously broadcast on TV and available on VHS, this well-told story of the classic album features rare footage and new interviews with Roger Daltrey, Pete Townshend and John Entwistle, as well as others involved in the making of *Who's Next*.

Special Edition EP
(Classic Pictures DVD6068X) 2002
Eleven minutes of good quality early archive footage of the band shot for German TV released as part of a series of budget DVD-EPs. The Pop-Up DVD features the same tracks but with added on-screen facts along the lines of *TOTP2*. Apparently, though recorded and listed, "I'm Free" is actually missing from the footage on this DVD.
See Me, Feel Me (Tommy Can You Hear Me?) / I'm A Boy / Pinball Wizard / I'm Free / Pop-Up DVD

The Who: Under Review 1964-68
(Chrome Dreams CVIS393) 2005
A 62-minute unauthorised documentary about the group's early years. There's some good commentary from Chris Welch, Paolo Hewitt, Alan Clayson, Shel Talmy and Malcolm Dome, among others. Essentially a cut-price collection of talking heads, this does have some nice early TV and promo clips, but it severely suffers from a shortage of footage of the glory days, though it may be the only place you'll find film of Keith singing "Bucket T" – if you want it. One for completists only.

The Who – Videobiography
(Classic Rock Legends) 2007
Two rambling discs of previously seen footage and talking heads make for a pointless substandard documentary. Rendered entirely superfluous even for the most obsessive fan by the appearance of *Amazing Journey*.

Amazing Journey: The Story Of The Who
(Universal) 2-DVD Set 2007
Simply one of the greatest rock DVDs ever released with an embarrassingly rich selection of bonus features. Drawing on all-new interviews with Roger Daltrey and Pete Townshend and famous fans like Sting, The Edge of U2, Noel Gallagher and Pearl Jam's Eddie Vedder, Murray Lerner and Paul Crowder's acclaimed two-hour documentary features rare and unreleased concert footage in 5.1 surround sound.
Disc 1: The Story of The Who
Disc 2: Six Quick Ones: Films 1-4 are fine mini-documentaries on Roger, John, Pete and Keith; Film 5: *Who Art You?* is a study of the Who's relationship with Pop Art; Film 6: *Who's Back* is the legendary DA Pennebaker's short about the recording of the Millennium Who's "Real Good Looking Boy". Bonus features include a fine scrapbook and Kit and Chris's amazing early footage, previously presumed lost, of the High Numbers at the Railway Hotel.

Bibliography & Selected Sources

Web Resources – Official Sites
www.thewho.com
Fantastic official group subscription site.
www.eelpie.com
Pete's solo site; a great resource and great place to obtain various less-well known solo CDs, demo collections and books.
www.johnentwistle.com
Tributes, archive articles and a selection of merchandise, plus plenty of focus on the John Entwistle Band.
www.johnentwistle.org
Charitable foundation in John's name.
www.jonesgangmusic.com
News on Kenney Jones' latest group.

Unofficial Sites
www.thewho.net
An unofficial but fantastic website packed with discographical details, perceptive and informative liner notes by Brian Cady, quotes and an excellent band biography, as well as numerous other features, including an on-line forum.
www.quadrophenia.net
By the makes of thewho.net, all you need to know about Pete's mod masterpiece.
www.thewho.info
WhiteFang's Who site, packed with over 5,000 colour images of records, CDs, books and memorabilia. Virtually every Who release is pictured here.
www.keithmoon.co.uk
Biography, great gallery of photos and more.

General Sites
www.allmusic.com
The best online rock music resource.
www.connollyco.com/discography/
Dave Connolly's idiosyncratic site with discographical – Mr Connolly calls it a pornography - details and informed opinion on a variety of classic rock records, with an emphasis on the progressive end of the spectrum.
www.rocksbackpages.com
Barney Hoskyns and co.'s online subscription rock library; a fantastic, easily searchable collection of classic rock articles and interviews by some of the finest music journalists across the globe.
www.rockdetector.com
Gary Sharpe-Young's invaluable on-line rock resource claims to be the world's biggest rock music database; it is certainly the definitive site for the heavier end of the rock spectrum.

Books – General
Altham, Keith, *The PR Strikes Back* (Blake, London, 2001)
Clapton, Eric, *Eric Clapton: The Autobiography* (Orion, London, 2007)
Dannen, Frederic, *Hit Men* (Times Books, Random House, New York, 1990) (Helter Skelter edition, 2002)
Des Barres, Pamela, *I'm With The Band* (Beech Tree, New York, 1987) (Revised edition, Helter Skelter, London, 2005)
Des Barres, Pamela, *Let's Spend The Night Together* (Helter Skelter, London, 2007)

Doggett, Peter, *There's A Riot Going On* (Canongate, Edinburgh, 2007)
Hewitt, Paolo, Ed, *The Sharper Word: A Mod Reader* (Helter Skelter, London, 2002)
Hewitt, Paolo and Hellier, John, *Steve Marriott: All Too Beautiful* (Helter Skelter, London, 2004)
Kurlanksy, Mark, *1968: The Year That Rocked The World* (Jonathan Cape, London, 2004)
Various, *Mojo Classics: The Who And The Story of the 70s* (Emap, London, 2006)
Bogdanov, Vladimir; Woodstra, Chris and Erlewine, Thomas, *All Music Guide To Rock*, 3rd Revised Edition (Backbeat, USA, 2002)

Books – The Who

Particularly essential titles are noted with an asterisk*

Atkins, John, *The Who On Record: A Critical History, 1963-1998* (McFarland & Co, Inc., USA, 2000)
Barnes, Richard, *The Who, Maximum R&B* (Eel Pie Publishing, Twickenham, 1982) (Revised edition, Plexus, London, 1996 & 2000)*
Black, Johnny, *Eyewitness: The Who: The Day-By-Day Story* (Carlton, London, 2001)
Bogovich, Richard & Posner, Cheryl, *The Who's Who* (McFarland & Co, Inc., USA, 2002)
Butler, Peter "Dougal", *Moon The Loon* (Star Books, London, 1981); US edition titled *Full Moon* (William Morrow & Co, New York, 1981)
Cawthorne, Nigel, *The Who And The Making Of Tommy* (Unanimous, London, 2005)
Champ, Hamish, *The 100 Best-Selling Albums Of The 70s* (Igloo 2005)
Charlesworth, Chris & Hanel, Ed, *The Complete Guide To Their Music* (Omnibus Press, 1995, Revised edition 2004)
Clayson, Alan, *Keith Moon: Instant Party* (Chrome Dreams, London, 2005)
Dougan, John, *The Who Sell Out* (Continuum, London, 2006)
Entwistle, John, *Bass Culture: The John Entwistle Bass Collection* (Sanctuary, London, 2004 – NB: in spite of the Entwistle author credit, this is a posthumous collection, published after many interesting pieces had been sold)
Ewbank, Tim and Hildred, Stafford, *Roger Daltrey: The Biography* (Portrait, London, 2004)
Fletcher, Tony, *Dear Boy: The Life Of Keith Moon* (Omnibus Press, London, 1995)*
Giuliano, Geoffrey, *Behind Blue Eyes: A Life Of Pete Townshend* (Hodder & Stoughton, London, 1996)
Hanel, Ed, *The Who Illustrated Discography* (Omnibus, London, 1981)
Kent, Matt & Neill, Andy, *Anyway, Anyhow, Anywhere: The Complete Chronicle Of The Who* (Virgin Books, London 2002) (US edition, Friedman/Fairfax Publishing, New York, 2002, appeared first)*
Colin Larkin, Ed, *The Guinness Encyclopaedia Of Popular Music* (Concise Edition, Guinness, 1993)
McKnight, Connor and Silver, Caroline, *The Who... Through The Eyes Of Pete Townshend* (Scholastic, New York, 1974)
McMichael, Joe & Lyons, "Irish" Jack, *The Who Concert File* (Omnibus Press, London, 1997)
Marsh, Dave, *Before I Get Old: The Story Of The Who* (Plexus, London, 1983) (US edition, St Martins Press, New York, 1983)*
Perry, John, *Meaty, Beaty, Big And Bouncy* (Schirmer, New York, 1998)
Rolling Stone, editors of, *The Who: Ten Great Years* (Straight Arrow, US, 1975)
Sculatti, Gene, *The 100 Best Selling Albums Of The 80s* (Igloo, 2004)
Strong, Martin C, *The Great Rock Discography* (Mojo Books, London, 2000)
Townshend, Pete, *Horse's Neck* (Faber, London, 1985)
Townshend, Pete, *Lifehouse* (Simon & Schuster, New York, 1997) (Pocket, London, 1999)
Wilkerson, Mark, *Amazing Journey: The Life Of Pete Townshend* (www.lulu.com, 2006)
Wilkerson, Mark, *Who Are You* (Omnibus, London, 2008) [an updated version of Wilkerson's previous work]

Articles

Altham, Keith, "Drummer Moon On Who LP," *NME*, 7 October, 1966
Altham, Keith, "Thunderfingers' Last Stand: Remembering John Entwistle," *Rock's Backpages*, 5 July, 2002
Appleyard, Steve, "Before They Got Old", *Rolling Stone*, Issue 718, 5 October, 1995
Black, Johnny, "The Greatest Songs Ever - 'Won't Get Fooled Again'", *Blender*, Aug/Sept 2001
Blake, Mark, "The Who: Roger Daltrey Interview", *Q*, March 2008
Brown, Mark, "A Brief Conversation With Pete Townshend", *Addicted To Noise*, June 1996
Carson, Tom, "Who Are These Guys?" *Face Dances* review, *Rolling Stone*, Issue 343, 14 May, 1981
Charone, Barbara, "Who's Who?" *Creem*, November 1978

Cohn, Nik, *Live At Leeds* album review, *The New York Times*, May, 1970
Drums And Drumming, 1980 - 2008
Daltrey, Roger, "Roger Answers Back", *Classic Rock*, February, 2008
Eliscu, Jenny, "Pearl Jam, Foo Fighters Pay Tribute To The Who", *Rolling Stone*, 7 August 2008
Fricke, David, The *Iron Man* LP review, *Rolling Stone*, Issue 558, 10 August, 1989
Gilbert, Pat, "Roger Daltrey And The Fratellis", Q , August, 2008
Gillespie, Bobby, *Amazing Journey* review, *Classic Rock*, February, 2008
Goldberg, Michael, "Monterey Pop: Dawning Of A New Era", *Rolling Stone*, Issue 501, 4 June, 1987
Hughes, Rob, "The Who", *Uncut*, October, 2001
Ingham, John, "John Entwistle: Is This The Right Man For Mayor Of Acton?" *Sounds*, 28 February, 1976
Jisi, Chris, "Partners In Time", *Drums And Drumming*, October, 1989
Kaye, Lenny, "Quadrophenia: The Who's Essay On Mod", *Rolling Stone*, Issue 150, 20 Dec, 1973
Loder, Kurt, *Who's Last* album review, *Rolling Stone*, Issue 440, 28 February, 1985
Makowski, Pete, "Jimmy Page: Living Legend Interview Pt 2", *Classic Rock*, January, 2008
Marcus, Greil, Pete Townshend interview, *Rolling Stone*, June 26, 1980
Marsh, Dave, "Who Are We?" *Mojo*, December, 2006
Murray, Charles Shaar, "Lets See Action", *Mojo Classic*, June, 2006
O'Hagen, Sean, "Everyone To The Barricades", *The Observer*, 20 January, 2008
Prior, Clive, "Long Live Rock", *Mojo*, September, 2006
Puterbaugh, Parke, "It's Hard", *Rolling Stone*, 30 September, 1982
Robbins, Ira, "The Who: Who Are You", *Crawdaddy!*, October, 1978
Robbins, Ira, "The Who: *Face Dances* Album Review", *Trouser Press*, June, 1981
Robbins, Ira, "Pete Townshend Interview", *Cleveland Live*, November, 1996
Robinson, John, "Fights, Camera, Action", *Uncut*, December, 2007
Rolling Stone, "The Who Prep Covers Album", *Rolling Stone*, 17 April, 2008
Salewicz, Chris, "Pete Townshend Stops Hurting People; Stops Hurting Himself", *Creem*, November, 1982
Savage, Jon, "The Who: 30 Years Of Maximum R&B", *Mojo*, July, 1994
Shaar Murray, Charles, "Conversations With Pete", *NME*, 19 April, 1980
Sharp, Ken, "We Were Always At The Top Of Our Game", *Record Collector*, Dec, 2007
Simmons, Sylvie, "The Who: Sweat, Bollocks & Guts", *Sounds*, 2 September, 1978
Stewart, Tony, *Quadrophenia* soundtrack review, *NME*, Oct, 1979
Sutcliffe, Phil, "The Who: Lifehouse", *Q*, April, 2004
Sutcliffe, Phil, "Long Live Rock", *Mojo Classic*, June, 2006
Svenson, John, "Mod 'Quad'", *Rolling Stone*, 15 November, 1979
Svenson, John, "Who Story: 30 Years Of Maximum R&B" review, *Rolling Stone*, Issue 690, 8 September, 1994
Townshend, Pete, "Meaty, Beaty, Big & Bouncy", *Rolling Stone*, 9 Dec, 1971
Various, "The 100 Best Albums Of The Last 20 Years", *Rolling Stone*, Issue 57, 27 August, 1987
Webb, Robert, "Cult Classics: The Kinks Are The Village Green Preservation Society," *The Independent*, 22 February, 2008
Welch, Chris, "The Who Sell In", *Melody Maker*, 27 January, 1979
Welch, Chris, "Rick Wakeman: Liszten To Rick!" *Melody Maker*, 16 August 1975
Welch, Chris, "Roger Daltrey: Who Am I?" *Creem*, March 1986
Other quotes come from *NME*, *Sounds*, *Melody Maker*, *Disc*, *Creem*, *Rolling Stone*, *Mojo*, *Uncut*, *Q*, *Record Collector*, *The Sunday Times*, though the source of a few oft re-quoted lines is lost in the mists of time...

Sleevenotes

Altham, Keith, "Who, Me? The Who In Britain", *Thirty Years Of Maximum R&B* booklet, 1994
Carr, Roy, *The Kids Are Alright* soundtrack CD liner, 2000
Charlesworth, Chris, "Anyway, Anywhere, Anyhow", *Thirty Years Of Maximum R&B* booklet, 1994
Kent, Matt, "Two Nights At The Opera", *Tommy And Quadrophenia Live* DVD set booklet, 2005
Marsh, Dave, "The Who In America", *Thirty Years Of Maximum R&B* booklet, 1994
Neill, Andy, "About My Generation", *My Generation* Deluxe Edition liner, 2002
Neill, Andy, "The Who At The BBC", *The Who BBC Sessions* (notes 1999, CD release 2000)
Neill, Andy, *Smash Your Head Against The Wall* by John Entwistle (expanded CD edition, liner notes 2005)
Resnicoff, Matt, *Who Are You* CD liner, reissue, 1995

Shaw, Mike, "How My Generation Came About", *My Generation* Deluxe Edition liner, 2002
Stamp, Chris, "A Quick One", *A Quick One* CD liner, 1995
Talmy, Shel, "On The My Generation Sessions And Album", *My Generation* Deluxe Edition liner, 2002
Townshend, Pete, *Who's Missing,* vinyl LP
Various, *1st Singles Box Set*, booklet includes a series of archive reviews of the singles, drawn from the original issues of the *NME* by a number of different writers
Welch, Chris, *Whistle Rhymes*, liner notes, 1996 CD reissue

DVD
Quadrophenia, The Making of...
Who's Next, The making of...
The Kids Are Alright
Amazing Journey: The Story Of The Who

About The Authors

Steve Grantley is a musician and currently plays drums for Stiff Little Fingers and the Alarm. He also writes for various drummer publications including the online drum magazine *mikedolbear.com*. Steve is a songwriter and producer and has been a professional musician since he was 19. Artists he's worked with include: Julian Lennon, Oleta Adams, Mike Peters' Electric Band, Billy Duffy, Craig Adams, Coloursound, Pete Wiley, Glen Matlock, Raf Ravenscroft, John Deacon, Kirk Brandon, the Thames TV Big Band, Horse, Jake Burns and the Big Wheel, Percussion Orgy, RTZglobal and Eighth Wonder. He is a life-long Who fan. This is his second book.

Previous books by Steve Grantley
Slade: Cum On Feel The Noize with Alan Parker (Carlton Books) 2006

Alan Parker is resident in the Maida Vale area of London and works as a consultant at EMI Records and Secret Music. His magazine work has included *Record Collector*, *Mojo*, *ICE*, *Bizarre*, *Rolling Stone* (USA), *Spiral Scratch* and *NME*. He is respected as an authority on all things punk and new wave, while his comedy obsession (effectively the work of the Monty Python team and the Carry On movies) has recently taken a major career turn, seeing him working on nine CD releases with the Monty Python team in 2005. In 2004 his book *Vicious: Too Fast To Live* (Creation Books) became a best seller and was voted into the Top 10 books of the year by *NME*. His spare time is spent watching bands play live and generally getting to know more about London and New York.

Previous books by Alan Parker
Satellite: The Sex Pistols with Paul Burgess (Abstract Sounds Publishing) 1999 (Also available in Japanese & German)
Sid's Way: Sid Vicious with Keith Bateson & Anne Beverley (Omnibus Press, London) 1990 (Also available in Japanese)
Song By Song: Stiff Little Fingers with Jake Burns (Sanctuary Publishing) 2003
Vicious: Too Fast To Live (Creation Books, London) 2004 (Also available in Japanese)
John Lennon & The FBI Files with Phil Strongman (Sanctuary Publishing, London) 2003 (Also available in Japanese)
The Great Train Robbery Files with Bruce & Nick Reynolds (Abstract Sounds Publishing) 2002
Rat Patrol From Fort Bragg: The Clash (Abstract Sounds Publishing) 2002
Hardcore Superstar: Tracy Lords (Private Publishing) 1992 (USA only)

And Now For Something Completely Digital: Monty Python with Mick O'Shea (Disinformation/USA) 2006
Sid Vicious: No One Is Innocent (Orion Books) 2007
Slade: Cum On Feel The Noize with Steve Grantley (Carlton Books) 2006
Lewd, Crued & Heavily Tattooed: The Official Biography Of Vince Neil with Vince Neil (Grand Central) 2009

Acknowledgements

This book would not have been at all possible without reference to the brilliant research and writing of the following people: Dave Marsh, Tony Fletcher, Andy Neill, Matt Kent, Richard Barnes, Terry Rawlings, Chris Charlesworth, "Irish" Jack Lyons, Ed Hanel, John Atkins, Chris Welch and Joe McMichael.

For our part we would like to thank the following people for their time, sense of humour and belief in this project: Sean Body and the team @ Helter Skelter, Robert Kirby & Charlotte Knee @ United Agents UK, Steve Woof @ EMI Records, Donna and Stephen @ Rex Features. And last but by no means least we would like to thank the Who for the inspiration to do this in the first place.

Official web site: www.thewho.com

Steve would like to personally thank the following:

Elsie and Norman, my long-suffering parents for just about everything. Sarah Vauls for support, advice, research, extensive archive material and proof-reading. Danny Vauls for computer expertise. Stevie "Nightrider" Jones for expert guitar information and technical advice. Steve Phypers for specialist drum information, "Who" history and proof-reading. Tracy Grantley for computer advice and proof-reading. Mike Peters for extra material and Mac advice. Grateful thanks to Lee Beauchamp for comments and encouragement. Cheers to Graham Willmott, "if you can do it, anyone can mate!" Many thanks to the late Sean Body to whom I owe a huge debt for his advice, support, excellent editing, cross-referencing and additions. I miss you, dear boy...

Alan would like to thank:

Alexa Morris, my incredible business partner (diamonds are forever). KT Forster, my wonderful agent. Amandine Clemintine, my sister from another mother! Margarita Doyle & John Osbourne, for nothing but good advice. Steve Diggle; Jake Burns; Mike Peters; Ian McCallum; Don Letts; Ali McMordie; Jon McCaughey; Chris Remington; Darrell Milnes; Mick O'Shea; Graeme Milton, for his sheer commitment to this project; Darryl & Gino, plus everyone @ Diamond Jacks Tattoo Studio, Soho, London. Frank Lea, who never stopped believing. Mum & David Parker, finally a book you can put out on the coffee tabel!! Steve Gowans @ Channel 5. Andy Street @ Universal Records, for the right bits of advice. All @ The Spice, The Phoenix & The Arts (after this number of books you know who you are by now!). And finally to the late, great Sean Body who never lost faith or sight of anything he started...

Forthcoming Titles From Helter Skelter Publishing

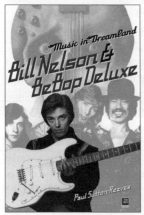

Music In Dreamland: Bill Nelson & Be Bop Deluxe
by Paul Sutton Reeves
ISBN 978-1-905139-29-3 PB 320pp B/W Illustrated
Throughout 234 x 156mm **£14.99 $19.95**
Be Bop Deluxe's Axe Victim – a timeless classic just waiting to be sung back to life, children. To William Nelson and his slow riders of the Wake Field, please raise your overflowing cup... and sup! **Julian Cope**
Music In Dreamland is the authorised biography of Bill Nelson, best known as guitarist, singer and songwriter with 70s art rock band, Be Bop Deluxe. Be Bop came to prominence through a combination of rock theatrics and Nelson's flamboyant guitar work, moving from glam rock to new wave, via the band's art rock masterwork, *Sunburst Finish*. After Nelson split Be Bop Deluxe he formed the acclaimed but short-lived Red Noise with whom he recorded the new wave classic, *Sound On Sound* before embarking on a solo career. Draws on hours of new interviews with Bill Nelson and other members of the band as well as admirers such as David Sylvian, Stone Roses producer John Leckie, Steve Harley and Reeves Gabrel.

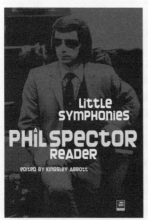

Little Symphonies: A Phil Spector Reader
edited by Kingsley Abbott
ISBN 978-1-905139-01-9 PB 256pp B/W Illustrated
Throughout 198 x 129mm **£9.99 $14.95**
Currently convicted of murder and beginning a life sentence in a Californian prison, Phil Spector is the reclusive maverick producer who invented the 'Wall Of Sound'. This collection gathers together the best articles, interviews and reviews about the enigmatic man and his revolutionary music. At the forefront of the sixties pop explosion, Phil Spector was the man who raised the profile of the record producer to undreamed of heights. Using a combination of imagination, musicality and sheer chutzpah, his records became as important and influential as any from that exciting decade. His 'Wall Of Sound' was widely imitated, but never bettered, and the records he made with the Righteous Brothers, the Ronettes, the Crystals and Ike & Tina Turner are amongst the most played to this day. Kingsley Abbott is the acclaimed writer of the well-received books, *Calling Out Around The World: A Motown Reader*, *Pet Sounds: The Greatest Album Of The 20th Century* and *Back To The Beach: A Brian Wilson And The Beach Boys Reader*.

Rush: Chemistry
by Jon Collins
ISBN 978-1-905139-28-6 PB 288pp B/W Illustrated Throughout 234 x 156mm **£14.99 $19.95**

It's hard to believe that a better biography will be written about the boys during their lifetimes. **Goldmine**

The first truly in-depth biography of one of the most enduring and successful cult bands in rock; now coming in paperback. Acclaimed Marillion biographer Collins draws on hundreds of hours of new interviews to tell the full in-depth story of the enduring Canadian trio, who refused to compromise their music and avoided the typical rock'n'roll lifestyle. From early days in Canada, to platinum albums, stadium shows and the world's stage, taking in tragedy, triumphs and a wealth of great music, this is the meticulous and definitive study of one of rock's great enigmas. From early triumphs such as classic concept album *2112*, on to their first hit single 'Spirit of Radio' and beyond to *Moving Pictures*, 'Tom Sawyer', and more pop-oriented 90s material, Rush have continued to make groundbreaking and original music that has sold in the millions.

Recent Highlights And Bestsellers

Steve Marriott: All Too Beautiful
by Paolo Hewitt & John Hellier
ISBN 978-1-905139-27-9 PB 352pp B/W Photo Section 234 x 156mm **£14.99 $19.95**

Revised and updated edition of one of the most acclaimed music books of recent years: bestselling account of the Small Faces and Humble Pie mainman. *The story of Steve Marriott is almost too awful to be true. Born in London's East End, he went from being fed jellied eels in his pram to teenage stardom as the lead singer of one of the most popular groups of the sixties, the Small Faces. After that there was success in America with his band Humble Pie and all the drugs and drink he could consume, three marriages and countless girlfriends and groupies and ever increasing penury. At the end he was to die at 44, if not penniless, poor, having generated millions for other people, burned to death in a fire at his home.*
Daily Mail

The Sharper Word: A Mod Anthology

edited by Paolo Hewitt

ISBN 978-1-900924-88-7 PB 224pp 198 x 129mm

£9.99 $14.95

Expanded and updated edition of 'unparalleled' Mod anthology. Paolo Hewitt, celebrated former *NME* scribe and acclaimed biographer of Steve Marriott, the Jam and Oasis, collects the best ever writing on the original, and peculiarly British, cult of Mod. Hewitt's hugely readable collection documents the clothes, the music, the clubs, the drugs and the faces behind one of the most misunderstood and enduring cultural movements. Includes: hard to find pieces by Tom Wolfe, bestselling novelist Tony Parsons, poet laureate Andrew Motion, disgraced Tory grandee Jonathan Aitken, Nik Cohn, Colin MacInnes, Mary Quant, and Irish Jack. Paolo Hewitt is a writer, broadcaster and journalist whose other books include *Forever The People: Six Months On The Road With Oasis* (Boxtree, 1999) and *Paul Weller: The Changing Man* (Bantam Press, 2007).

Poison Heart: Surviving The Ramones

by Dee Dee Ramone with Veronica Kofman

ISBN 978-1-905139-18-7 PB 224pp B/W Illustrated Throughout 198 x 129mm **£9.99 $14.95**

Poison Heart takes the reader on a breakneck tour from a dysfunctional childhood, heroin, punk rock and the heyday of the Ramones to internal wrangling, gruelling tours and methadone clinics. Along the way, Johnny Thunders and Stiv Bators succumb to their addictions, Dee Dee's own girlfriend overdoses, Sid Vicious shoots up with toilet water, and Phil Spector holds the band at gun-point in his Beverly Hills mansion. The Ramones were one of the first bands responsible for punk – wearing torn jeans, black leather jackets and playing short, loud trashy rock'n'roll songs. This is Dee Dee Ramone's harrowing tale of 15 years of life on the road with the band. A story both tragic and comic, littered with many of the colourful characters that made up the New York punk scene. Dee Dee lived the rock'n'roll lifestyle to the full, wrote the band's best songs and Sid Vicious openly modelled himself on him. A gripping story from the now sadly deceased Ramone. Hey! Ho! Lets Go!

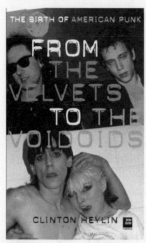

From The Velvets To The Voidoids
by Clinton Heylin
ISBN 978-1-905139-04-0 PB 288pp 234 x 156mm
£12.99
No other book or account succeeded so well in accurately bringing the period to life. **Richard Hell** (of Television, the Heartbreakers and the Voidoids)
This is a great story, and before Heylin no one saw it whole. **Greil Marcus**
Exhaustively researched and insight packed with insight, *Velvets To The Voidoids* is the definitive story of American punk rock. From 1960s roots, through to the arrival of 'new wave', with a cast that in addition to the Velvet Underground and the Voidoids, includes Patti Smith, Pere Ubu, Television, Blondie, the Ramones, the MC5, the Stooges, Talking Heads, as well as legendary venues like CBGB's and Max's Kansas City, this is a vividly drawn account of an extraordinarily diverse musical scene.

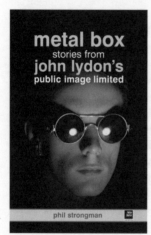

Metal Box: Stories From John Lydon's Public Image Limited
by Phil Strongman
ISBN 978-1-900924-66-5 HB 224pp Colour Photo Section 216 x 138mm **£14.00 $23.95**
John 'Rotten' Lydon, Jubilee 'Public Enemy No. 1', quit the Sex Pistols at the height of their commercial success and formed Public Image Limited, the ultimate cult band, as anarchic and out-of-control as the Pistols but making groundbreaking music that finally lived up to punk's year zero rhetoric. Often living communally in the seedy, druggy haze and malevolent occult atmosphere of Lydon's Gunter Grove flat, amid a regular succession of police raids, PiL harnessed their disparate personnel to somehow produce three albums: *First Edition*, *Metal Box* and *Flowers Of Romance*, that were as original as any ever issued. The group's corporate styling and innovatory sound were unique: dub-sonic bass overlaid with haunting guitars and Lydon's banshee-type wailing, combining elements of punk, reggae and dance. Lydon's confrontational approach led to riots at gigs and more tabloid outrage, as well as hit singles, further albums and some remarkably durable music. Drawing on extensive new interviews with band members Jah Wobble, Keith Levene, Martin Atkins and Jim Walker as well as pivotal figures such as Don Letts and Dennis Morris, *Metal Box* is the first time that those who were actually there amidst the madness have borne witness to Lydon's long strange trip. *Metal Box* also features a selection of rare and previously unseen Dennis Morris photos as well as a foreword by the late Tony Wilson.

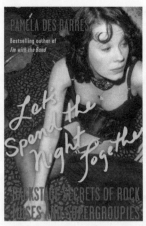

Let's Spend The Night Together
by Pamela Des Barres
ISBN 978-1-905139-17-0 HB 400pp B/W Illustrated Throughout 229 x 153mm **£17.99**
This intimate account of 24 legendary groupies reveals what went on behind the closed doors of rock stars from Elvis to Marilyn Manson. Consisting of Pamela Des Barres's revealing interviews with and profiles of other supergroupies, this book offers first-hand glimpses into the backstage world of rock stars and the women who loved them. The groupies - such as Miss Japan Beautiful, who taught Elvis how to dance; Cassandra Peterson (Mistress of the Dark), who tangled with Tom Jones in Sin City; Cynthia Plaster Caster, who redefined the art of Jimi Hendrix; and Rebecca Bayardi, who revealed Kurt Cobain's penchant for lip gloss - tell tales that go well beyond an account of a one-night stand to become a part of music history.

I'm With The Band
by Pamela Des Barres
ISBN 978-1-900924-61-0 PB 304pp 198 x 129mm **£9.99**
A kiss-and-tell that doesn't make you want to go and wash your hands. **Music Week**
One of the most likeable and sparky first-hand accounts. **Q**
Shag and tell bean-spilling about rock's biggest names... Pamela's mix of hippie enlightenment and teenage lust is terrific. **The Guardian**
B-format outing for the ultimate story of sex, drugs and rock'n'roll – the definitive groupie memoir from the ultimate groupie, now updated again. Frank and engaging memoir of affairs with Keith Moon, Noel Redding and Jim Morrison, travels with Led Zeppelin as Jimmy Page's girlfriend, and friendships with Robert Plant, Gram Parsons – with whom she was particularly smitten, and Frank Zappa.

www.helterskelterpublishing.com

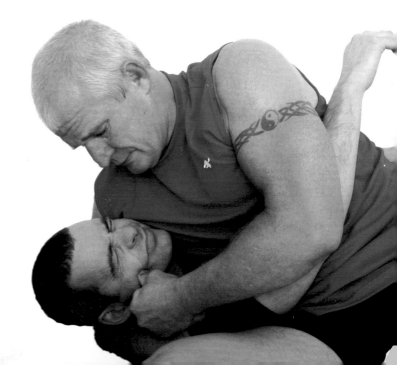

Marc McFann

Ground Fighting

A comprehensive guide to
throws, holds, chokes, locks,
submissions and escapes

❄ snowbooks

The advice and training techniques in this book should only be undertaken by martial arts students who are supervised by a qualified teacher. Neither the author nor the publisher will be held responsible for any injury or damage incurred through the application of techniques described in this book.

© Marc McFann 2007

Photographs by Pete Drinkell
Edited, designed and typeset by Emma Barnes, Snowbooks

First edition

Proudly published in 2007 by
Snowbooks Ltd
120 Pentonville Road
London
N1 9JN
0207 837 6482
www.snowbooks.com

ISBN: 9781905005246

Cataloguing in Publication data: a catalogue record for this book is available from the British Library.

→ CONTENTS

➲ INTRODUCTION

Fighting – combat of any type – must take place in one of seven ranges. From the farthest to the closest distance, they are:

➲ Projectile Weaponry Range: Includes all firearms (pistols, rifles, shotguns, cannons) rockets, missiles, as well as such weapons as spears and bow & arrows, slingshots and throwing knives.

➲ Handheld Weaponry Range: Includes swords, knives, clubs, staffs, chains, nunchaku, shields, sticks and all manner of striking weapons that are held in one hand or two.

➲ Kicking Range: Striking with the feet, shins and knees regardless of style or system of origin.

➲ Punching Range: Striking with the hands, fists, forearms or elbows regardless of style or system of origin.

➲ Trapping Range: A range where the arms, hands and feet of the opponent are trapped, circumnavigated or moved in order to allow you to strike or close the distance between you.

➲ Standing Grappling Range: This range allows for the grabbing of limbs, head and torso to apply locks, chokes, levers, throws and takedowns.

➲ Ground Fighting Range: Where at least one person is on the ground during combat.

I like to think of these ranges more like classifications of combat rather than distances of exact measurement. They have no clear-cut boundaries. They overlap and change during the course of the fight. You could throw a knife at a close distance (projectile weaponry range) and then swing a long stick (handheld weaponry range) without moving. Similarly, you can punch in the kicking range and you can also use a hand-held weapon while on the ground. I believe that to properly prepare for combat or self-defence you must acknowledge and address these ranges. You don't always get to choose how the fight happens or at what range. You may have the best round-house kick in the world but it will do you little good in a phone booth, against a rifle or when someone is sitting on your chest. I think multi-range training is what cross-training in the martial arts should be all about.

The content of this book stays within the framework of the Standing Grappling and Ground Fighting ranges. While we will look at the throws in a somewhat sterile environment, always remember that

the throw that is set up with a head-butt, knee or elbow will work better than one that is not. The same is true for the ground submissions. Once you have the position, the lock or choke is almost always easier to achieve if preceded by several blows to your opponent's face.

➲ THROWS AND TAKEDOWNS

In one-on-one, unarmed combat, there is a propensity for the combatants to draw closer together. Think about the number of times the referee has to separate boxers during a fifteen-round match. Often, it is the bigger, stronger or more aggressive person who closes the distance. It is also true that it is sometimes the one who is getting his ass kicked in the punching and kicking range that decides to close the distance, in the hope of changing his luck. The following fifteen techniques are designed to get the other guy down. After you have him down and have gained a controlling position, it will be time to consider holds, locks, chokes and submissions.

For simplicity's sake we will use a defence against the right punch as an entry to most of the throws. For example, when the attacker throws the wide right punch, step in and block it with your left forearm as shown. That will provide the opportunity for each of the throws.

In all cases you will need to break your opponent's balance before throwing. Again, to keep it simple, we will show the throw without a follow-up. However, you would normally want to follow the attacker down to the ground and secure a superior position. Many of the throws in this book are shown with me, the thrower, remaining in the standing position after the throw. This is for demonstration purposes only. Throws executed with force and commitment will almost always end up with you on the ground – on top of your opponent. Remember that the ground, in conjunction with your body, can be a powerful impact weapon at the end of the throw.

1: SHOULDER THROW

- ⊃ From the blocking position, grab the opponent's right wrist with your left hand.

- ⊃ Step your right foot across in front of his body and turn your body so you face the same direction as your opponent and you have him behind you.

- ⊃ Bring your right arm under his right arm while bending down and pulling him onto your back.

- ⊃ Straighten out your legs to lift your opponent and turn your upper body to the left to throw him down.

- ⊃ Always maintain a grip on the opponent after the throw. Notice how the right knee is poised and ready to drop into his ribs.

2: DROPPING SHOULDER THROW

- From the blocking position, grab the opponent's right wrist with your left hand.

- Step your right foot across in front of his body and turn your body so you face the same direction as your opponent and have him behind you.

- Bring your right arm under his right arm and drop to your right knee pulling him onto your back. Your right leg is on the outside of his right leg (not shown).

- Turn your upper body to the left, drop your right shoulder to throw him down.

- Again, keep a grip on the opponent after the throw and scramble quickly to gain a top controlling position.

3: OVER THE LEG DROP

- From the blocking position, grab the opponent's right wrist with your left hand.

- Grab him around the neck with your right arm. At the same time, step your right foot across and in front of his body so that your right foot is in front of his right foot.

- Place the weight on the ball of your right foot and turn your right knee toward the ground. You should be facing the same direction as your opponent.

- Pull him down and over your leg as you turn your head and body to the left. You have landed in the perfect position to control with kesa gatame (see page 30).

4: WINDING THROW

- ➲ From the blocking position grab the opponent's right wrist with your left hand.

- ➲ Step your right foot across in front of his body and turn your body so you face the same direction as your opponent and have him behind you.

- ➲ Step so your right foot is across and on the outside of his right foot. Simultaneously bring your right arm over his right arm and

hug it tight to your body.

- ➲ Drop to your right knee while pulling his right arm and twisting your body to the left. He will land on his left side and you should follow him to the ground and use your weight to add to the force of the throw.

- ➲ I was thrown hard with this throw during a Judo contest in 1973. The guy landed on me. It separated my shoulder.

5: HIP THROW WITH WAIST

- ➲ From the blocking position grab the opponent's right wrist with your left hand.

- ➲ Step your right foot across and in front of his body. Turn your body so you face the same direction as your opponent and have him behind you as your right arm snakes around his waist. The picture here shows an alternative with the arm around the neck.

- ➲ Bend your knees and let your hip be lower and a little past his hips.

- ➲ Straighten out your legs and lift him onto your right hip.

- ➲ Turn to the left and pull him over and down.

6: HIP THROW WITH ARM HOOK

- ⊃ From the blocking position grab the opponent's right wrist with your left hand.

- ⊃ Step your right foot across and in front of his body. Turn your body so you face the same direction as your opponent and have him behind you as your arm hooks under his left arm.

- ⊃ Bend your knees and let your hip be lower and a little past his hips.

- ⊃ Straighten out your legs and lift him onto your right hip.

- ⊃ Turn to the left and pull him over and down.

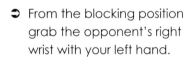

7: HIP THROW WITH OUTSIDE SWEEP

- From the blocking position grab the opponent's right wrist with your left hand.

- Step your right foot across and in front of his body. Turn your body so you face the same direction as your opponent and have him behind you while grabbing his neck with your right hand.

- Pull his body into and against your body.

- Sweep your right leg to the rear, just above his knee, as you turn your body to the left and drop your right shoulder downward. You could remain standing after the throw or land on their chest as shown here.

15

8: HIP THROW WITH BENT KNEE LIFT

- From the blocking position grab the opponent's right wrist with your left hand.

- Step your right foot across and in front of his body. Turn your body so you face the same direction as your opponent and have him behind you. Pull his body as in Technique #7.

- Instead of sweeping your right leg to the outside, leave it bent and in front of his right leg. Your right foot should be off the ground, knee bent and toes pointing out to the right. This allows your right leg to act as a lever to lift your opponent.

- Lift your right leg back against his right leg as you turn to your left and throw him over and down.

9: HIP THROW WITH INSIDE SWEEP

➲ From the blocking position grab the opponent's right wrist with your left hand.

➲ Step your right foot across and in front of his body. Turn your body so you face the same direction as your opponent and have him behind you as you grab him around the neck with your right arm.

➲ Sweep your right leg back between his legs, getting your thigh as far between his legs as possible.

⮡ Lift your right leg as you turn to your
left and drop your right shoulder
as you throw him over and down.

10: BIG OUTSIDE LEG SWEEP

- From the blocking position grab the opponent's right wrist with your left hand.

- Step your left foot in close to the right side of his body and let your right arm move across his neck and hook over his left shoulder.

- Bend him backwards by pushing your right arm across his throat.

- Bring your right leg behind his right leg. Your chest should be against his chest. Sweep backward with your right leg as you drive your chest and arm into his upper body.

- Turn slightly to the left as you throw.

11: BIG INSIDE LEG SWEEP

➲ From the blocking position grab the opponent's right wrist with your left hand.

➲ Hook his neck with your right hand. Pull him forward so he steps with his left leg.

➲ As he steps forward, sweep inside his left leg with your right leg as you drive him to the rear and down.

12: SMALL INSIDE LEG THROW

➲ From the blocking position grab the opponent's right wrist with your left hand.

➲ Step your right foot across in front of his body and pull him forward as if you were going to throw the Shoulder Throw (Technique #1).

➲ As he steps forward with his right foot to catch his balance, hook inside his right leg with your right leg.

➲ Secure his leg by holding it with your right hand. Push off your left leg, drive your right shoulder into his body and drive him to the ground. As you follow him down, turn immediately so you don't get caught in his guard.

23

13: SCISSORS THROW

- ⮞ From the blocking position grab the opponent by the neck or wrap the upper arm with your left hand.

- ⮞ Turn your body so that you are beside your opponent, on his right side and facing in the same direction.

- ⮞ Throw your left leg across his waist and your right leg behind his legs while simultaneously supporting yourself on your right hand.

- ⮞ Turn your body to the left so he will be tripped backwards. His legs are easily accessible for a leg lock from this position. Check out "Killer Leg Locks" by Erik Paulson.

14: DOUBLE LEG TAKE DOWN

(Not done off the Punch Defence)

- ⮑ Fake a grab or a punch at your opponent's head. Be close enough to touch your opponent. Shooting in for the legs from too far away will most likely not work.

- ⮑ Dive deep into his legs with your head up, right knee on the ground and chest against his body while grasping both his legs.

- ⮑ Drive your shoulder against his body while pulling and lifting his legs, tipping him over to the left.

- ⮑ Keep your head close to his body.

25

15: REAR ROLLING THROW

(Not done off the Punch Defence)

⮞ When the opponent lowers his head in his attempt to attack you legs, grab him around the neck with your right arm.

⮞ Pull his head down as you sit and bring your right leg between his legs.

⮞ Sit down and roll backwards, lifting him over with your right leg.

⊃ Come up on top of him, sitting into the mount position. You can keep hold of the neck and try for the choke or let it go and just start punching.

In order to apply most chokes, locks and submissions you need to have a base from which to apply them. There are many methods of controlling or holding an opponent once you are in the ground-fighting arena. We will consider the four most common ground fighting holds: Scarf Hold, Cross Body, Mount and the Guard.

The **scarf hold** (kesa gatame), is commonly found in Judo, Jujitsu and wrestling as well as other grappling arts around the world. It is a simple, yet effective, method of not only controlling your opponent but also in providing a platform for ending the confrontation through submission.

The **cross body hold** (yoko shiho gatame), also called the 'side control' or 'side mount' is an excellent hold and offers great versatility. In addition to providing access to many submissions it is also an exceptional hold for moving into other holds such as the knee mount and mount.

The **mount** (tate shiho gatame), is considered one of the most desirable holds in ground combat. The main reason for this is due to its stability as a striking platform. It is when your opponent attempts to defend against these strikes that the opportunity for a submission often presents itself.

The **guard** differs from the three holds above because it controls from the bottom position rather that the top. It is a deceptive hold in that being on bottom is often seen as being controlled. The guard provides excellent opportunities for all sorts of submissions.

After examining some guidelines to help hold the opponent in each of these positions we will look at some ways to disable, submit, impair or otherwise diminish the opponent's ability to resist.

PRINCIPLES OF HOLDING & CONTROLLING

The following guidelines are general in nature and not limited to one specific hold.

Keep your body relaxed and mind calm. This allows you to better "listen" with your body and feel what your opponent's intentions might be.

Keep your body close and tight to his body. Keep your hips low to the ground to help prevent his efforts to gain a lever beneath your body. Place as much weight on him as you can. Leave as little space between your body and his body as possible.

Maintain the same position relative to your opponent. If he turns or slides clockwise then you also must move in that direction to maintain control of your hold. Letting your opponent change his position while you remain in the same position is dangerous.

Do not continue to maintain a hold once it has begun to disintegrate. Clinging to a sinking ship in this manner is a classic sign of the novice ground fighter. Learn to switch from one hold to another when the time is right.

HOLDING THE HOLD

For continuity, we will hold our opponent on the right side.

Sit on your butt, next to your opponent, facing him and on his right side. Your right leg should be straight and placed well to the front

while your left leg should be bent at an angle and placed behind you. Place your right arm around the back of his head and hold his right arm by the triceps with your left hand while tucking his right arm under your left arm.

Let your right hand grip his shoulder while your left hand grips the back of his upper arm. Keep your head down and close to his head to keep him from placing his left hand in your eyes or throat.

Pull upward with your left arm and tighten the grip on his head with your right arm. Lift your butt and your left knee slightly off the ground in order to place more weight on your opponent. Try to pull yourself down and into your opponent. Squeeze his head tight.

⊃ CHOKES, LOCKS AND SUBMISSIONS

1: TRIANGLE NECK LOCK

⊃ This technique can be used as another variation of the initial hold or in some cases as a submission technique. The opportunity to work this technique occurs when he frees his right hand and pushes or strikes your face, eyes or throat.

⊃ When this happens, push his arm, at the triceps, across his face.

⊃ Then lower your head so that your neck and shoulder press against his arm, holding it tightly to his head.

⊃ Clasp your hands, and turn the bone of your right forearm (thumb side) into the muscles of his neck. Squeeze his neck! The pain is in the back of his neck.

⊃ I have used this hold in the street on more that one occasion. One time I was able to move my right leg close to his head and grab my leg with my hand. This freed up my left hand to help encourage him not to pull my hair (which I used to have) with his left hand.

⊃ This technique can easily render your opponent unconscious. Push your right index finger against his cheek where the back teeth come together. You do this to turn his head and chin to his left.

⊃ Slide your left hand across his throat and grasp your right triceps. Drop your left elbow to the ground, inside your right arm. SQUEEZE his neck hard!

⊃ With his head locked over to his left side it makes it very hard for him to use his legs against you or to shrimp out.

3: STRAIGHT ARM LOCK OVER THE LEG (LOW)

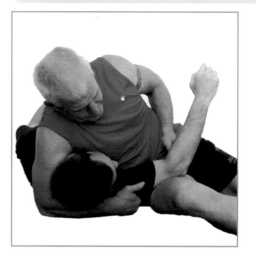  

- ⮑ He has managed to escape your grip on his right arm or you were unable to achieve control of his arm during the scuffle.

- ⮑ Rather than pushing his arm toward your face he carelessly places it out to his right side. Use your left hand to grasp his right wrist and push it over your right leg.

The right leg acts as the fulcrum as you push down and stress his elbow joint. The little finger of his right hand should be on the bottom and his thumb on the top.

- ⮑ While you may gain compliance with just the right amount of pressure you may also damage the elbow joint with a ballistic motion.

4: STRAIGHT ARM LOCK OVER THE LEG (HIGH)

- Resisting the above arm lock, he uses his biceps strength to keep his arm from straightening.

- As he raises his arm, switch your legs, bringing your left knee up and under his arm to apply the lock.

- The little finger of his right hand should be on the bottom and his thumb on the top.

5: STRAIGHT ARM LOCK OVER THE LEG (DROPPING)

➲ If he is still too strong for you to apply the lock, switch the legs back to the original position and drop his arm over the right leg.

➲ The little finger of his right hand should be on the bottom and

his thumb on the top. The added momentum from the drop will break his resistance… and possibly his arm.

➲ I find techniques 3, 4, and 5 work quite well and quite often when applied right after the throw, when your opponent has not yet regained his wits.

6: BENT DOWN ARM LOCK (UNDER LEG)

- His arm bends down in an attempt to avoid the straight-arm lock.

- Tuck it under your left leg, as close to 90 degrees as possible, and press your left knee into the mat to secure it.

- Push down on his shoulder with your left fist and lift your right leg. This causes pain in the shoulder joint.

7: STRAIGHT ARM LOCK WITH THE LEGS

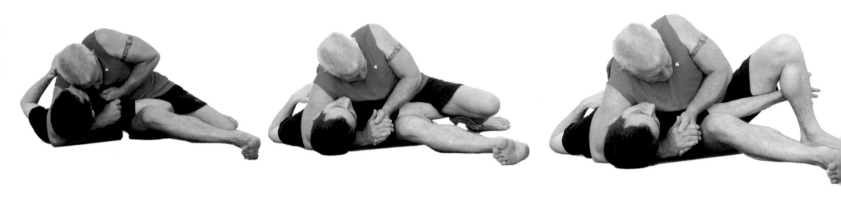

- If technique #6 above is not working or his arm seems to be slipping out you can apply a straight arm lock by shifting your leg position. With his arm over your right leg and under your left leg, move your right knee so it is pointing straight up. His right arm is trapped between the top of your right leg and the back of your left leg.

- Hold his head with both of your hands and lift up. Place both butt cheeks on the ground.

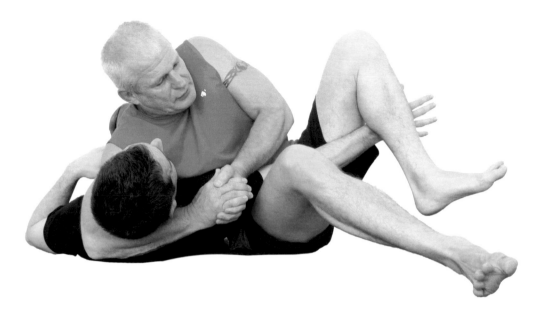

Ⓒ Use the back of your left thigh to
apply forward pressure to his lower
arm and make the straight elbow
lock. This pain is in his elbow joint.
Pushing your left leg ballistically
may cause his elbow to dislocate.

- If he bends his arm up to avoid the straight arm lock (technique #7) you have the opportunity to apply the Bent Up Arm Lock.

- Seize his right wrist with your left hand and place it under your right leg.

⊃ Lock your left leg over your right at the ankle and lift his head up and to your right to apply the lock. Your right leg and knee should be flat on the ground, as in the original hold. The pain is in his shoulder.

41

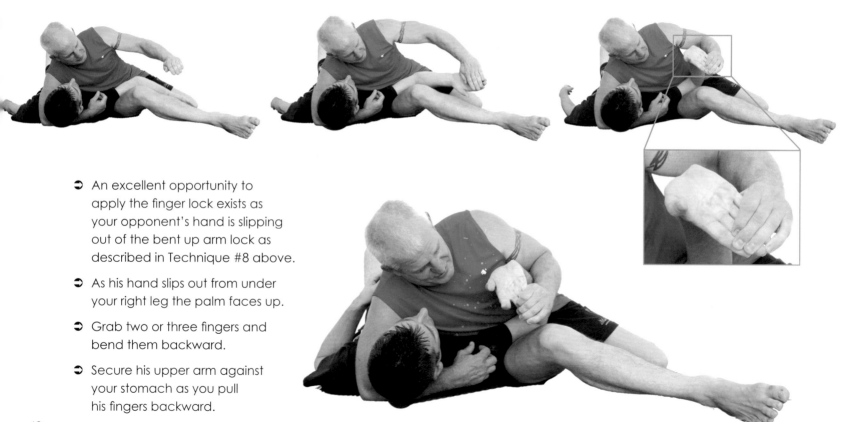

- An excellent opportunity to apply the finger lock exists as your opponent's hand is slipping out of the bent up arm lock as described in Technique #8 above.

- As his hand slips out from under your right leg the palm faces up.

- Grab two or three fingers and bend them backward.

- Secure his upper arm against your stomach as you pull his fingers backward.

10: THE BENT WRIST LOCK

- ➲ When your opponent is resisting your finger lock as described above he will turn his hand palm down. This is an excellent opportunity to apply the wrist lock.

- ➲ While his arm is bent, snap his hand down so the palm is being pushed downward. Trap the back of his arm against your right leg. Push on the back of his hand.

NOTE: Techniques 11-17 are applied in a variation of the hold commonly known as the "Telephone Position." It is held in much the same way as the basic hold.

⊃ Grab his right wrist with your left hand and feed it into your right. Capture his right arm by holding the wrist in your right hand and trap his arm against his head. Hold it there with your head and neck.

⊃ This can be accomplished easily from the basic hold when you are attempting to apply any one of the locks listed above. When he moves his hand toward his head, grab his right wrist with your left hand and guide it to the side of his head. Switch his wrist to your right hand.

⊃ Now that you have his right elbow pointing up, push it against his head with your left hand and trap it there with the right side of your head.

⊃ With your right hand holding his right wrist, and your head holding his upper arm against his head, your left hand is relatively free to help set up the following locks (11-17).

11: WRIST LOCK (FINGERS POINT UP)

- Holding his right wrist with your right hand, take the back of his right hand in the palm of your left hand. His palm should be facing up. Pull upward and into his forearm.

- You can also use the ground as a third hand and push his upper arm forward and down with your right shoulder. This force against the back of his hand makes the lock. The pain is in the wrist.

12: WRIST TWIST

⮕ With his right hand still in the above position take his hand with your left hand, much in the same way you would shake hands with someone. Twist his hand counter-clockwise. Twist it slowly as the son-of-gun is very painful. The pain is at the wrist.

➲ When his hand turns over (palm down) in an attempt to avoid one of the above locks, slide your hand (palm up) under his hand and grab two or more of his fingers. You can push his hand down into the ground and then pull up on the fingers or you can lift up the entire hand while pulling the fingers up.

14: WRIST LOCK (FINGERS POINT DOWN)

⮫ As he jerks his hand around to avoid the finger lock his hand will again be facing palm up but the fingers will be pointing down toward his feet. Grab the back of his hand with both hands and pull up applying the wristlock.

15: BOW & ARROW LOCK

⊃ Grab his wrist with your left hand. Cup his head with your right hand and hold his elbow firmly against his head with your neck, head and right shoulder. Pull his head to the right with your right arm and pull his hand out to your left with your left hand. The pain is in the shoulder.

16: STRAIGHT ARM LOCK

⮕ When he straightens out his arm, in an attempt to escape the telephone position, pull his wrist and duck your head down so that his elbow is behind your neck. Apply the lock against the back of your neck by pulling down and across your neck with your left hand.

➲ If he bends his arm back to avoid the straight arm lock, pull his arm across his face and wrap it around his head. Your forearm will be around his neck. Grip your left arm with your right hand to create a circle around his neck and face. Squeeze hard as you turn the thumb side of your right forearm into the back of his neck to create extra pain.

Techniques 18-21 are leg locks. They work when your opponent tries to encircle your rear (left) leg with his left leg in an attempt to make an escape. In all cases, when he tries to insert his leg, you must grab his foot with your left hand and move it between your legs, deep in your crotch, so he loses any leverage advantage with his leg.

18: LEG STRETCH

- ⮑ With the leg captured pull his foot with your left hand and move it toward his head.

- ⮑ Use your left leg to continue pushing his foot toward his head. The pain comes from the odd angle and the severe stretch on his hip.

55

- ➲ While pulling his foot forward with your left hand, place your left elbow into the soft spot inside of his shin.

- ➲ Pull his foot inward, while simultaneously digging the elbow into the side of his shin. The pain comes from the twist of the ankle and the pressure of the elbow into the pressure point on his shin.

20: THE ANKLE TWIST WITH FEET

- With his foot caught over your left leg, take your right foot and push against his left ankle.

- Trap it with your left foot.

- With his foot trapped by your left foot, place your right foot against your left foot and push his foot backward.

- The sole of your right foot is against the inside of his left foot. Your left foot hooks over the top of your right foot to force his right foot back and twist the ankle. The twisting causes pain in his ankle.

21: THE ANKLE STRETCH

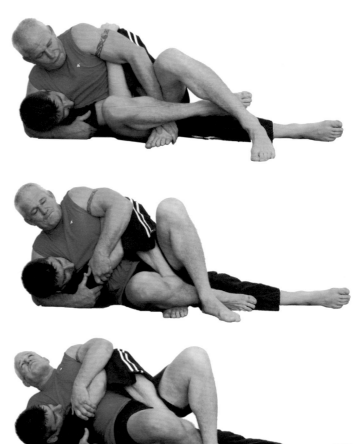

- ⊃ With his left leg still over your left leg trap his left foot under your right leg by bending your right leg toward your butt.

- ⊃ Lock your left foot over your right foot to more tightly secure the position.

- ⊃ Lift your hips upward and into the knee of his trapped leg and cause pain by stretching the back of his lower leg.

22: BUNDOCK A&B

This technique is done when your opponent pulls his right elbow down to the floor while trying to escape or trying to avoid a straight-arm lock.

➲ "Bundock A" – Insert your right shinbone against his forearm. Pull on his wrist to allow your shinbone to apply pressure to the nerves and muscles of his forearm.

➲ "Bundock B" – Insert your left shinbone against his forearm. Pull on his wrist to apply pressure to the nerves and muscles of his forearm. This variation is more powerful and more painful.

- The name comes from the method used to wrestle down a steer as seen in most rodeos. This technique is done when he pulls his right elbow down to the floor while trying to escape or trying to avoid a straight-arm lock.

- Push his arm down with your left hand until it is flat against the floor. Move toward his head and slide your butt over his arm so you are now holding only his head and neck.

- Push into his cheek or jaw to move his chin to the right.

- Slide your right hip in against his neck and tighten the hold. SQUEEZE! Unconsciousness can come quickly!

⊃ ESCAPING THE SCARF HOLD

1: THE BRIDGE AND ROLL

⊃ This may be the most common escape to the basic hold. With practice it can be done easily. Turn on your right side and move your body into his body trying to fill any spaces that may exist. Grasp your hands together tightly around his waistline – not around his chest.

⊃ Bump his body upward with your hips and arch straight back on your shoulders.

⊃ Then pull him up and over your body to your left side.

2: THE UP-HILL TURN

- The time to use this escape is when you feel he has relaxed his grip on your right arm. With a quick jerking move, pull your right arm out as you move your right shoulder away from your opponent.

- Twist and get to your knees. You can pull his clothing with your left hand to help get to your knees.

- Place your left hand over his shoulder and into the side of his face to brace yourself as you pull your right arm and head free. Use quick, jerking, pulls as opposed to one all-out effort.

- IMPORTANT NOTE: You must make sure to pull your elbow back, beyond your opponent's

right leg, so you will not be susceptible to the straight arm lock as described earlier.

- Use your left hand to push into his throat or face in order to get his head up.

- Quickly bring your left leg up and hook his head.

- Continue to push him backward and pull your right leg out from under his body so you can take the top position.

4: THE SIT UP

⭗ This escape is used when you can see both of his feet are near your head and to the front of his body. He has failed to keep his left leg back to use as a rear post. This means that he has no 'rear post' to stabilise his position.

⭗ Bring both of your feet in the air.

⭗ Use your legs as a counter weight and push off the ground with your left hand (or push your thumb into his neck as shown above) to sit up. Finish on top.

- When his left leg is too far back you can capture it with your legs by turning on your side, using your left leg to hook his left leg.

- Pull your right leg through and under his left leg. Lock your feet at the ankles and scissor his leg above his knee. You must do this quickly to avoid his attempt at a leg lock on you.

- Stretch your legs out and arch your back. This will put pressure on his hip and cause his head to rise. Take your left hand and grab his chin or below his nose and pull him over to your left.

6: THE PINCH TO THE FIGURE FOUR CHOKE & STOCK

- This one may take some setting up to achieve but is well worth the effort. Pinch his side with the hand of the arm he is holding... that would be your right hand.

- Make small, twisting pinches until he reaches back with his left hand to grab your wrist and make you stop.

- Then capture his left hand with your left hand from around his back. If he still grips your right hand, twist your right hand counter clock wise (palm up) to break his grip.

Push into the side of his face or throat with your right hand and pull his left hand until it is now between your legs. Scissor his

left arm. Hold his right arm and shoulder with both hands. Use your right index knuckle to grind in his ribs to help free his right arm from around his neck.

- **Figure Four Choke:** Turn slightly on your right side to get his weight off of you. From this position switch your legs so his left arm is held mainly with your right leg.

- Bring your left leg up over his head and place your left foot behind your right knee.

- Lift his face up by his nose so you can place your leg deeper under his chin and into the throat.

- **Stocks:** From the same position as above, insert your left leg over his left arm and your left arm over his right arm.

- Push your body upward until you are on your hands and knees. Keep your body tight against his head.

- Lift the right side of your body up and lean into his neck.

⮕ Push your hips as far away from his body as you can, as you turn on your right side.

⮕ Slide your right knee as high as you can between your bodies. Try to get your knee as close to your own right armpit as possible.

⮕ Grasp your hands together and rock your opponent back and forth as you push your knee through to the other side.

⮕ Secure the rear hooks position with both legs by hooking both of your legs around his body.

⮕ Be patient and work your head out by pulling it back while pushing his right arm with your left hand.

⮕ Once your head is free you will be in the perfect position to apply the rear choke.

➲ THE CROSS BODY HOLD

HOLDING THE HOLD

You can hold this position in several different ways. You must move your body, arms, and legs in response to the way your opponent moves. Your body may need to move towards his body as he moves away, or away from his body as he attempts to move into you.

Leg combinations can include: both legs in tight, left leg in tight, right leg in tight, legs turned forward like in the kesa gatame hold or turn the legs in the opposite direction.

Arm variations could include: both arms on far side, left arm on near side & right arm on far side, and left arm on far side & right arm on near side.

There is a time to use each of the above combinations. Your opponent's actions will dictate when and how to vary your hold. Practicing with many different opponents is the best way to get a feel for this.

However, for the purpose of this text, we will use the following method to hold Cross Body. Approach from the side and place your chest on his chest. You body should be at a 90-degree angle to his. Place both hands on the far side of his body. Bring your elbows tight against his body. Bring your right knee tight against his near side with your left leg back. Stay close and be as heavy as possible.

Let's look at **chokes, locks, & submissions.**

1: STRAIGHT ARM LOCK - NEAR ARM

⊃ Holding his right arm tightly against your body with your left arm, lift his arm so it is straight as you move your left knee over to the far side of his head. This traps his right arm between your thigh and the back of your arm.

⊃ Push his right arm backward with the back of your left arm, applying pressure to the elbow joint.

⟳ Move your left hand under his head and over his left arm. Secure a grip in his arm pit. Apply pressure by pulling his arm toward you while lifting his head upward with your left forearm. Use your arm as a lever to push his arm backward while lifting his head upward.

3: NECK CRANK WITH LEFT LEG (FAR SIDE)

⮕ From the position described in Technique #2, move up on your knees and slide your left foot behind his head and over his arm (replacing your arm with your left leg).

⮕ Apply the lock by pushing your shin into the back of his neck. Instead of using your arm as the lever, as above, you are using your shin in the same way.

4: STRAIGHT ARM LOCK

⊃ NOTE: TECHNIQUES 4, 5 and 6 are done while holding the position described in TECHNIQUE #3.

⊃ Wrap your right arm around his right arm. Secure the lock by grasping both your hands together just behind his elbow. Hyper-extend the joint by lifting and leaning back.

5: BENT-UP ARM LOCK

➲ NOTE: TECHNIQUES 4, 5 and 6 are done while holding the position described in TECHNIQUE #3.

➲ If, or when, he bends his arm upward, let your left arm go under his arm and then secure your grip. Lean a little forward so as not to lose the arm and turn to your left. The pain is in the shoulder.

6: BENT-DOWN ARM LOCK

➲ NOTE: TECHNIQUES 4, 5 and 6 are done while holding the position described in TECHNIQUE #3.

➲ If, or when, his arm bends downward, move your right arm under his arm and secure your grip.

➲ Lean a little forward so as not to lose the arm and turn to your right. The pain is in the shoulder.

7: STRAIGHT ARM LOCK (FAR ARM)

- While lying across his body, grab his left wrist in your right hand. Slide your left arm under his left arm and bring it up onto his stomach. Secure it by grabbing anything you can: pants, shirt, whatever.

- With the little-finger side of his hand pointing down toward the floor, press down with your right hand and apply the straight arm lock.

83

⮑ As he bends his arm to resist the straight arm lock, press down on the back of his hand. Push his wrist toward the floor, making the wristlock.

9: THE FINGER LOCK

➲ As he twists his hand around
to avoid the bent wristlock
his palm will be facing up.
Grab two or three fingers with
your right hand and pull them
backward toward the ground.

10: THE BENT-DOWN ARM LOCK

➲ Holding his left wrist in your
right hand, push his arm down
on the ground so his hand is
close to his leg and his arm is
bent at a 90-degree angle.

➲ With your left hand gripping your
right wrist, lift his arm and upper
body up so there is room for
you to bend his arm backward,
against the shoulder joint.

➲ Step your left leg over his head
to keep him from sitting up.

⊃ While trying to get the bent-down arm lock above he often tries to twist his arm out to avoid the pain. Keeping your left arm under his left arm '(under his elbow) push his wrist out and away until you have the straight-arm lock. This is much the same as Technique #7.

12: THE BENT-UP ARM LOCK

- In trying to escape the above straight-arm lock he bends his arm up.

- Quickly switch your hands. Grab his wrist with your left hand and slide your right hand under his upper arm.

- Pull his upper arm tight against his body and then apply the lock by holding his wrist down and lifting his elbow up.

87

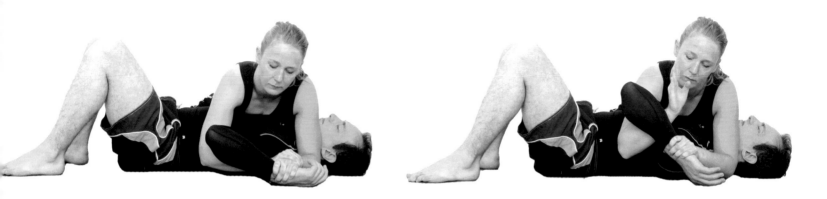

- Cut the Chicken A: Using the same position as above, move your right wrist up and deep into his elbow pit so that the bone (on the little finger side of your wrist) is against his forearm.

- While pulling his wrist in tight with your left hand, push your right wrist across and down onto his arm. The pain comes from the cutting motion of your wrist bone on his arm.

⮑ Cut the Chicken B: As he tries to resist, encircle your left arm under his head. Apply the technique from this position as described above.

From the 'Cut the Chicken B' position above, your left hand is still under his head and holding his left wrist in a bent-up position. Switch your grip of his left hand to your right hand.

Hold his head tight with your left hand. Raise his elbow with your right forearm and push his left wrist away from his body. Pull his head toward you with your left hand. The pain is in the shoulder joint.

15: THE REVERSE TRIANGLE LOCK

- Move your left elbow so it is on the lower side of his left arm.

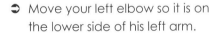

- Move your left arm in a backward circle, pushing his left arm across his face.

- Bring your left hand around under his head and grip your other hand. Press down with all your weight.

- Shift your legs, as if holding 'kesa gatame' as described on page 30.

- Push his right arm down. Move your head and body further across his chest.

- Bring your left foot over his right arm and head and push your foot back under his neck.

- Place the ankle of your left leg behind the knee of your right leg. This traps his head and arm in a triangle. Squeeze your legs tight.

- ➲ You have the Fig. 4 choke as in the preceding technique.

- ➲ To add the arm bar to this hold, pull his left arm up and pull it straight as you lay on your back.

- ➲ His left arm is trapped between your neck and right shoulder. Cup his elbow with both hands and pull down toward your chest.

18A: THE STRAIGHT ARM LOCK ON THE FAR ARM TRAPPED AT THE SHOULDER (VARIATION A)

➲ **Variation A:** When he twists into you and tries to escape by pushing with his left arm you may apply this lock. As he pushes, pull his left arm straight until it rests on your shoulder and against the side of your head.

➲ Move your right knee up and place it in his stomach. Move

your left shin against his neck. Sit backward and apply the lock by cupping both of your hands around his left elbow and pulling it in toward your chest.

95

➲ **Variation B:** Proceed as above, but instead of sitting backwards move forward across his body (left shin in his throat and right shin in his stomach). Post out on the top of your head.

➲ Apply the arm-lock by cupping the elbow and pulling it into your chest.

19: SPINNING ARM LOCK ON THE FAR ARM (VARIATION A)

⮑ **Variation A: ELBOW IN STOMACH:**
Grab his left elbow with your
right hand and pull his arm up so
your elbow rests in his stomach.

⮑ Keeping his left arm tight
against your neck, bring
your left knee up and over
to the far side of his head.

⮑ Lift your right knee and place
your right foot on the ground.

⮑ Lift his arm and pivot your body
so your left knee and shin pushes
close against his left side and
your right leg is across his neck.
Lean back and straighten out
his arm to apply the lock.

➲ **Variation B: KNEE IN STOMACH:**
Move your body up, and quickly place your right knee in his stomach. Keep your left leg out to the side. As he tries to escape and pushes against your knee, scoop under his left arm with your right hand and grasp his triceps.

➲ Step across or around his head with your left foot and turn 180 degrees into the arm-lock as described above.

20: STRAIGHT KNEE BAR

- ⟳ Move your right shin across his stomach.

- ⟳ Place your right hand inside of his left thigh.

- ⟳ Pull your left leg across his body and sit on the other side.

- ⟳ Bring your right leg up and between his legs as you straighten out his left leg.

- ⟳ Secure his foot on the left side of your head. Squeeze his leg tight to your chest and straighten out your body.

- When he turns his leg in defence against the straight knee bar, grab his left foot, near the toes, with your right hand.

- Bring your left hand under his left leg and grab your right wrist.

- Twist his ankle inward toward his body.

1: SHRIMP TO HALF-GUARD/GUARD

➲ To perform the shrimp movement, place your right hand on his left hip. Your left hand will be on his right shoulder. Pushing with both hands, drive your butt out to the left while turning onto your right side. The purpose

is to create space between you and your opponent.

➲ With this space, slide your right knee under his right leg and work your right foot around his leg. Cross your left leg over your right at the ankles.

➲ Push on his left hip and bring your right knee under his left leg and around his body. You now have the Guard.

- Shrimp in toward your opponent in the exact way you did in the above technique.

- Bend your right knee and bring it all the way under your opponent's body. Your right knee should extend beyond the left side of your opponent's body.

- Grab with your left hand as far as you can across his body. Try to reach under his armpit if you can.

- Pull with your left hand and lift his body onto your right shin. Turn to your left side and pull him over your body.

- As he falls onto his back, take the mount position.

3: BRIDGE AND ROLL

- ➲ This technique works well only when your opponent holds you with both of his legs close to your body.

- ➲ Work your right elbow under his left hip.

- ➲ Grasp across his back with your left hand as far as you can.

- ➲ Lift upward with your right elbow and turn to your left.

- ➲ Roll your opponent over to your left side.

- ➲ Come up to your knees and assume the cross body hold.

- This technique works best when your opponent is high on your chest and close to your head.

- Move your left arm around his neck.

- Position your right arm so that it is straight, palm up, under both of his legs.

- Place your feet flat on the floor with your knees up. Lift with your right arm and shoulder, while driving with your feet.

- Slide your body downward and out from under his body as you drive his body up and over your head.

- Come up to your knees and assume the cross body hold.

⊃ THE MOUNT

HOLDING THE POSITION

You can hold this position in several different ways. One person basically sits astride the chest of the other. How you move and position your arms and legs will depend on how your opponent moves and resists. The holder can just hold and wait for opportunity for a technique or punch, strike, and elbow to create such an opportunity.

The person on bottom has limited ability to strike back and attempting to turn or roll leaves the neck and arms vulnerable to attack. Even if the person manages to turn you over, you will most likely maintain some sort of guard.

Hold your mount high. Move up so your knees are in, or as close to, his armpits as possible.

Keep your arms spread and mobile. Place as much of your weight on him as possible. Avoid holding his head with both hands.

Again, let's start with chokes, locks, & submissions.

⊃ CHOKES, LOCKS AND SUBMISSIONS

1: STRAIGHT ARM WRAP

- ⊃ When his left arm is pushing against you and is nearly straight, wrap your right arm (clock wise) around it and grab your left hand so as to grip behind his elbow joint.

- ⊃ His arm is trapped under your right armpit.

- ⊃ Lean back to hyper-extend his arm.

113

⊃ **Variation A: Against the arm:** Grab the upper part of his left arm, from underneath, with your right hand.

⊃ Overlap your left hand over your right hand.

⊃ Twist his arm counter-clockwise and trap his wrist, in your elbow joint, between your forearm and the side of your upper right arm.

⊃ Turn your body slightly to the left and apply the straight-arm lock.

- **Variation B: Against the neck:** Grab the upper part of his left arm, from underneath, with your right hand.

- Overlap your right hand with your left hand.

- Twist his arm counter-clockwise and trap his wrist against the side of your neck.

- Turn your body slightly to the left and apply the straight-arm lock.

- Grab his left wrist with both of your hands.

- Pull his arm up to straighten it out. Rise up on your left knee and bring your right foot against the left side of his head. Most of your weight is off his body at this time.

- Force your right shin across his face and into the back of his left arm. Pull back on his wrist and hyper-extend his elbow.

4: STRAIGHT ARM LOCK AGAINST LEG, FAR SIDE OF HEAD (WEIGHT OFF)

- Grab his left wrist with both of your hands as in Technique #3.

- Pull his arm up to straighten it out. Rise up on your left knee and bring your right foot over his head and place it on the floor tight against the right side of his head. Again, most of your weight is off his body at this time.

- Force your right shin across his face and into the back of his left arm. Pull back on his wrist and hyper-extend his elbow.

- ➲ From the position described in Technique #5, let your weight fall onto his midsection as you let your right knee bend.

- ➲ Wrap your right arm clockwise around his left arm and clasp your hands together. This will secure his wrist under your armpit.

- ➲ Lift upward to hyper-extend the elbow.

6: BRANCH-UP ARM LOCK WRAP (WEIGHT ON)

- From the position described in Technique #5 above, his arm bends up while he attempts to resist the straight-arm wrap.

- Bend slightly at the waist and pull his arm to the left. Keep this arm tight and continue lifting his arm until he submits. The pain is in the shoulder.

7: CHOKE WITH LEG (WEIGHT ON)

- From the position described in Techniques #5 & #6, lift his head and move your foot under his head. Let your right ankle push into his throat.

- Cross your left arm across his throat and grab the toe of your right foot.

- Force your left forearm into his throat as you pull upward on your own foot.

- The choke comes from the pressure of your right lower shinbone being pulled into his neck.

8: BRANCH DOWN ARM LOCK #1 (A & B)

➲ **Variation A:** With his left arm on the right side of your body, secure it by grabbing his upper arm from underneath with your right hand.

➲ Overlap your hands and pull his arm upward so his left arm is caught at the wrist on your right side.

➲ Apply the lock by continuing to force his arm across his body.

➲ The pain is in the shoulder.

- ⊃ **Variation B:** If, when applying the above lock, you cannot trap his wrist or it slips off of your right side, secure his left wrist against your left upper arm.

- ⊃ Let your left hand slide under his left arm at the bend.

- ⊃ Grasp your hands together and apply the lock as described above.

9: BENT-UP ARM LOCK

- ○ When your opponent's left arm is out to his side and bent upward, grab his left wrist with your left hand, slide your right hand under his upper arm and hold your own left wrist.

- ○ Pull his upper arm tight against his body and then apply the lock by holding his wrist down and lifting his elbow up.

10: JUJI GATAME (CROSS ARM LOCK)

- This is one of the most common and recognisable techniques in grappling. While he is protecting his arms close to his body, place both of your hands on his left forearm.

- Shift your weight onto your hands and take the weight off of your legs.

- Lift your body up and bring your right leg across his face as you move your body to a 90-degree angle to his.

- Sit close to him, clamp his arm tight to your chest and lean back.

- Clamp your legs close together, lift your hips and arch your back.

- NOTE: While attempting to complete the final part of the Juji Gatame above, your opponent quite often grabs his hands together in defence. A strong man can still wage a fair battle from this position. We will look at three methods to break his grip and complete the lock and also

show three follow-up submissions
(techniques 11, 12 & 13) from the
Juji Gatame Lock-up Position.

BREAKING HIS GRIP:

- ➲ **Method A** – Insert one of your feet against his far biceps and push or kick his arm until his grip breaks free.

- ➲ **Method B** (not pictured) – Insert one of your knees against his arm so that your shin pushes against his forearm. Use this as a lever to break his grip.

⊃ **Method C** – Cup his far arm at the elbow and pull it across his body toward your chest. This takes away his leverage. When his arm is close and tight against your body, his grip will break easily.

11: THE CRUSH (A & B)

- **Variation A:** Move your right forearm into the inner elbow joint and pull it in tight with your left hand.

- Grab your left bicep with your right hand. Grab his right wrist with your left hand.

- Twist your right forearm so that the "thumb side" bone digs into his inner forearm as you press down hard.

- **Variation B:** Move your right forearm into the inner elbow joint and pull it in tight with your left hand as in variation A.

- Bring the back of your right calf across and over his right forearm.

- Lock your left leg over your right ankle, behind your left knee.

- Push down with your legs as you pull with both arms, digging the "thumb side" bone into his arm.

129

- The most common grip to use in this defensive technique is with the left hand gripping the right wrist.

- Grab the back of his right hand with your right hand then overlap your left hand onto your right.

- Keep his arm bent and the back of his upper arm against your chest.

- Pull toward your chest to apply the gooseneck.

13: FIGURE FOUR CHOKE

- ➲ Move your right leg between his arm so it lays between his head and left shoulder.

- ➲ Grab his head and lift it as you roll onto your back.

- ➲ Hook your left leg over your right ankle. Make sure your right ankle is behind your left knee.

- ➲ Pull his head down and squeeze with your legs.

➲ ESCAPING THE MOUNT

1: DOUBLE HOOK AND ROLL

- ➲ This is the most basic escape to the mount.

- ➲ Hook your opponent's leg with your left leg by stepping your foot over her right leg.

- ➲ Hook your opponent's right arm with your left arm by wrapping it around her upper arm with a counter-clockwise motion.

- ➲ Lift upward into her left arm pit with your right hand as you lift your hips as high in the air as possible.

- ➲ Turn hard to your left as you roll your opponent over and come up into her guard.

2: SHRIMP TO HALF/FULL GUARD

- Place both of your hands on her right knee.

- Push her right knee down as you push yourself onto your left side and bring your left knee through. Scissor her right leg with both your legs.

- Place both of your hands on her left knee.

- Push her left knee down as you push yourself onto your right side. Bring your right knee through and assume the guard position.

3: KNEE UP THE MIDDLE FOR ANKLE LOCK

- ➲ Place both of your hands on her hip bones.

- ➲ Thrust your hips high into the air. Then press upward with both hands so your opponent is above you and bring your right knee up between her legs.

- ➲ As her weight comes down she will be resting on your right shin.

- ➲ Now you are able to move to your left and secure her right leg for the ankle lock.

➲ THE GUARD

The scarf hold, cross body hold and the mount can be found in every judo book that covers ground techniques (ne waza). They are pure judo holds. The guard is not. I am not familiar with all the changes in sport judo rules over the years but in the past you were not allowed to hold the guard during competition, at least not for very long. Holding the guard would most likely get you a warning for 'non-combatively' with a subsequent penalty for repeat offences.

In the days before judo there were many styles of ju-jitsu. Judo founder Jigoro Kano studied several systems including Seigo Ryu, Yagyu Ryu, Jikishin Ryu and Kito Ryu. Kano preferred the standing throwing techniques over ground techniques.

In 1900, the Kano students were beaten in a contest with students from a school of Fusen Ryu ju-jitsu. Fusen Ryu specialized in ground fighting techniques. They would often throw themselves on their backs and pull the opponent between their legs to avoid being thrown.

Today, the guard is a well-known and significant position in all forms of grappling. It is an excellent method for controlling an opponent from the bottom. Its growth and refinement can be attributed to the development and advancement of Brazilian Jujitsu, most notably by members of the Gracie and Machado families and their students.

HOLDING THE POSITION

While on your back, keep your legs high up and around his upper body. Monitor his arms at all times. Crossing your ankles in the back keeps him in tight. This is a good method to stall for time with, or catch a small rest, or force him to make a mistake while attempting to escape. But over-using the guard in this way is often considered lazy, and simply delays the eventual outcome of the fight. In order to execute a choke, lock or submission, you must first uncross your legs.

⊃ CHOKES, LOCKS AND SUBMISSIONS

1: FIGURE FOUR CHOKE (WITH HANDS)

⊃ While described as a choke, people most often submit from the pain and pressure on the neck when this technique is applied.

⊃ With her right arm pulled far across to her left side, insert your right arm under her right arm and around her neck.

⊃ Grab your left bicep with your right hand.

⊃ Place your left hand on her forehead. Wrap your legs around your opponent's legs and stretch her out as you squeeze her neck.

2: FIGURE FOUR CHOKE (WITH LEGS)

- As she moves to pass your guard, she moves her left hand under your right leg.

- Lift your body and straighten your right leg up in the air.

- Move your body and head to your right and bring your right leg down and across the back of her neck.

- Lift your left leg up and place your right foot behind your left knee.

- Use your hands to pull her right arm across your body and pull her head down low.

- Squeeze tight with your legs!

141

3: CROSS-ARM LOCK "JUJI GATAME"

- ⊃ Pull her right arm across her body.
- ⊃ Move your head and body out to your right side.
- ⊃ Bring your left leg around the front and over her head.

- ⊃ Cross your legs at the ankles and squeeze your heels to your butt.
- ⊃ Straighten out her arm by pulling with both hands while lifting your hips.

142

143

⊃ Execute the cross-arm lock as described in technique #3.

⊃ She escapes the lock by pulling her right arm free from your grip.

⊃ Move your left leg and place it on the far side of her head while keeping a hold on her left arm.

⊃ Move your body and head to your left. Place your left leg across the back of her neck.

⊃ Bring your right leg up and over your left ankle.

⊃ Pull her left arm and head into your body and squeeze with your legs.

- When her left hand is on the floor, grab it at the wrist with your right hand.

- Sit up to the right and reach your left hand over her left arm.

- Let your left hand go under her left arm and grab your right wrist.

- Fall back onto your left side as you bend her arm up his back.

- Grapevine her left leg with your right leg to keep her from rolling as you apply the lock up her back.

6: BRANCH DOWN #2 (WITH THE LEG)

- ⊃ When her left hand is on the floor, grab it at the wrist with your right hand as in the above technique.

- ⊃ Push the back of your right knee against the back of her left arm, to cause it to bend.

- ⊃ Move your head to the right as you bring your right foot over her left shoulder.

- ⊃ Push her head to the side with your left hand to give you plenty of room to get by her head.

- ⊃ Pull your left leg from under her body as you sit up.

- ⊃ Pull her waist with your right hand as you scoot to the side, pulling her off her base.

- ⊃ Switch your left leg back so the knee is forward and your foot is to the rear. Lean forward and up toward her head to apply the lock.

- ➲ When her head is down, sit-up into her hip and wrap your right arm, clock-wise, around her head and under her throat.

- ➲ Grip your right hand with your left.

- ➲ Grapevine her legs and pull back.

- ➲ Stretch out your legs and arch your back.

- **Variation A: Trapped on the arm**
  Cup her left elbow with your right hand from underneath.

- Overlap your left hand over your right hand.

- Move to your right and turn on your left side.

- Her left arm is caught on your upper right arm.

- Insert your right knee into her side to add power and help keep the arm straight.

- **Variation B: Trapped on the neck**
  Cup her left elbow with your right hand from underneath.

- Overlap your left hand over your right hand.

- Move to your right and turn on your left side.

- Her left arm is caught on the right side of your neck.

- Insert your right knee into her side to add power and help keep the arm straight.

9: DOUBLE ARM LOCK

- ⊃ Attempt this technique when your opponent keeps both arms on your chest.
- ⊃ Grab both of her wrists with your hands.
- ⊃ Bring both of your feet up and onto her shoulders.

- ⊃ Hold her arms tight as you arch your back and lift your hips off the ground.
- ⊃ Grab, with both hands, whichever arm is on top.
- ⊃ Lock the top arm.

- ➲ Move your right leg over her left leg and let your right foot slide under her ankle.

- ➲ Push her left arm over to her right, allowing both of your hands to be on her left side.

- ➲ Sit up on her left side while pulling her left foot toward you with your right foot.

- ➲ Grab it with both hands.

- ➲ Pull her foot so your right shinbone digs into her calf and Achilles tendon.

- From the position described in Technique #10: when she reaches back to pull off your grip from her ankle, grab her right hand and wrap it so it is secure under your left armpit.

- Cross your legs to hold her tighter.

- Place both hands around her neck.

- Pull her head toward you as you stretch out your legs.

- The pain is in the lower back and hip joint.

- Grasp your hands together around his neck.

- Have the left palm up and the right palm down.

- Lower your left leg so as to offer a path for your opponent to pass your guard over your left leg.

- As he moves over your leg, twist your body and left arm inward, closing your arms on his neck.

- Keep twisting and bring both arms in tight against his neck.

⊃ When he attempts to pass your guard by lifting your right leg across your body, bend your right leg so that your shin is against his body for the half guard position.

⊃ He tries to get past your half guard by inserting his left arm under your calf, in order to lift or push your leg to the side.

⊃ Lean forward and grab the back of his left arm with both hands (your left hand goes under his armpit and your right hand over your own right shin).

⊃ His left forearm is trapped between your right calf and thigh.

⊃ Pull his arm toward you and down while driving your right shin into his left bicep.

14: ROLLING ARM LOCK

➲ The opportunity for this technique can arise from several different circumstances. One is when he pulls his arm free from your juji gatame attempt (technique #3). Another is when you are unable to bend his arm in your branch-down arm lock attack (techniques #5 and #6).

- Drop your left leg off of his head and onto the floor in front of him.

- Turn onto your left side and bring your right knee up and on top of the back.

- Grab his left hand with your right hand.

(continued over)

⮑ Lift yourself up onto your left
   elbow and bring your body up so
   you are on your left knee. (You
   should now be supported on your
   left elbow and your left knee)

⮑ Place your right shin across the
   back of his neck and push down.
   Let your body turn onto your right
   side. Continue applying pressure
   to the back of his neck as you turn.

⮑ His left arm can now be
   pulled straight and the
   cross-arm lock applied.

⮡ However, most often he will roll forward and onto his back… trying to escape the lock.

⮡ Roll with him and bring your right leg across his neck to apply the lock.

1: GOING UNDER THE LEGS

⮑ Place your left arm under her right leg.

⮑ Lift her right leg with your arm and push your shoulder into the back of her leg. Drive it across her body.

⮑ Slide your body around the outside of her leg and take the cross-body position.

⮑ NOTE: Great care must be used to not to get caught in the Figure 4 Choke (Technique #2 above).

167

- Push her right leg down flat on the ground using your left hand or elbow.

- Slide your left shin across her right thigh, applying as much pressure as possible.

- Move your right foot to the outside of her right leg.

- Slide your body to the outside of her right leg and assume the cross-body position.

3: THE STACK

- Keep your arms bent and close to your chest.

- Get to your feet and drive your opponent's legs up and over her shoulders.

- As her legs come up, place your hands on the floor, one on each side of her head, so her body cannot slide back.

- Walk forward until her legs loosen, then twist your body around to the left until you pass her right leg and assume the cross-body position.

- Care must be taken to avoid the arm lock. (See Technique #3: The Cross Arm Lock, Juji Gatame p.142)

171

- Slide both your arms between her legs and under her thighs.

- Hook your arms around her thighs and lift her butt off the ground, letting her upper body slide toward you.

- Drive her to one side, letting her legs fall to the side and take the top position.

THOUGHTS ON
TRAINING

It is a well-known fact that most fights end up on the ground. Gaining control of your opponent is the first step to victory in the ground fighting range. If you are a martial artist and concerned with self-defence you must train on the ground. Those martial artists who claim they need not train in grappling due to their extraordinary striking skills are deluding themselves.

I would like to comment on three topics that I think are important; drilling, sparring and attribute development.

DRILLING – There are literally hundreds of drills out there. Learn the drills and put in the time on your reps. Proper repetition of technique is key to developing skill.

SPARRING or "Rolling" – You must spar. You need as many different partners as possible…different sizes, weights, skill levels and body types. Don't always spar to win or tap out your partner. Don't let your ego rob you of a valuable training session. Try to use as little strength as possible. While strength and size are invaluable attributes in ground fighting our first focus should be on developing skill. An over-emphasis on using strength in our training retards the growth of our skill.

With thoughtful and methodical training you should be able to train in ground fighting for many, many years. Many ground-fighters enjoy it well into their 70s and even 80s.

ATTRIBUTE DEVELOPMENT – You are the machine. Don't neglect the machine. Flexibility, strength, sensitivity, speed, timing, agility, tenacity, endurance and technical skill are all of equal importance in fighting. Volumes have been written about how to develop the attributes listed below. This list is far from conclusive. I will only offer a brief comment as to how my experience has influenced my view of each one.

ATTRIBUTES

Flexibility: I cannot add to the knowledge of all the books and videos on how to be more flexible. I will say that I believe that it is the first attribute to be neglected by the martial artist over a long period of time. I no longer stretch to be flexible; I stretch to reduce the possibility of injury to my body. Also, I have found that it was much easier to stretch in my teens, 20s and 30s than it is now in my 50s.

Cardiovascular Endurance: This is the next most neglected attribute over time. All of us have "run out of gas" during sparring or a match. Consider this: look at this entire list of attributes. Let us say that you could grade yourself very high in each one. If you "run out of gas" what good do they do you?

Strength: Sooner or later you will hear all grappling teachers say you are using too much strength, and to try to relax. Strength is a valuable attribute but should never be favoured over skill...even if it works. Beginners often get the idea that if their opponent taps then they must have done the technique correctly. No: sometimes it was just lots of strength carrying a poor technique that did the job. And eventually there will always be someone stronger than you. World-renowned grappling champion Jean Jacques Machado once made a sensible comment on this. We were training at the Inosanto Academy in Los Angles. Jean Jacques was watching students grapple on the mat. It was a battle of strength and little skill. Jean Jacques said, in his infectious Brazilian accent, "You guys look like you are lifting weights. If you want to lift weights, that is ok but I think I would go to the gym. I would try to do jujitsu now...but that's just me."

Speed: A truly priceless attribute that unfortunately lessens with age. However, speed, unless paired with timing and skill, is of little use.

Timing: Timing can only be developed in relationship to another moving body. You must spar and drill with a variety of partners to improve your timing.

Sensitivity: Like timing, sensitivity must be developed in concert with another person. It's very important to spar with different body types (tall, short, fat, skinny, heavy, light) in order to feel the different types of energies you may need to respond to.

Technical Skill: Over the years I have had the privilege to train with my good friend and Light Heavy-Weight World Shooto Champion, Erik Paulson. Once, at a seminar he said something that has always stuck with me. He said, "Practice does not make perfect; practice makes habit." Take

the time to get the technique right, then drill it in every way you can think of. Then spar it.

Muscle Endurance: I remember a judo match I was in during my mid 20's. At that time I was lifting weights a lot and could bench-press 300 pounds. I felt very strong. The match proved to be mostly about fighting for a superior grip. My opponent and I gripped, counter gripped and re-counter gripped for the entire match. There was no score. We were given a short rest and then an overtime period. During the break I realized I could not work my hands. They would neither open nor close. My forearm and wrist strength was completely gone. I could not hold his gi. The overtime period went much the

same as the earlier match. I lost the decision. My 300-pound bench press was of no help.

Mental Calmness & Mental Tenacity: These two may seem like opposites but I feel like they are different sides of the same coin. When you fight, spar and sometimes even when you drill, you will get hurt. I said hurt, not injured. Little thing like accidental and incidental elbows to the eyes, busted lips, bloody noses and so on are part and parcel of contact training. Beginners are very challenging in this area. Strive to develop the mental calmness not to get upset during practice and the mental tenacity not to give in to these small annoyances during a match.

➲ About Marc McFann

MARC MCFANN is an internationally-recognised expert with 40 years of martial arts experience. He is a certified full instructor in Filipino and Jun Fan/JKD martial arts under Guro Dan Inosanto. He also holds instructorships in Muay Thai under Ajarn Chai Sirisute, Mande Muda Silat under Pendekar Herman Suwanda and in JKD Grappling under Sifu Larry Hartsell. He has studied several other martial arts and holds a 4th degree black belt in Okinawan Kempo, a 2nd degree black belt in Judo and a 1st degree black belt in Hapkido. He is retired from the U.S. Armed Forces and has studied the martial arts all over the world.

He runs McFann's Academy of Martial Arts in Fayetteville, Arkansas, USA. Mr. McFann teaches seminars throughout the U.S. and Europe and has produced a series of highly acclaimed martial arts DVDs.

➲ Models

Sincere thanks go to the models featured in this book who gave their time and enthusiasm to a very challenging photo-shoot.

Marc McFann

Joe Kerr

Stephanie De Howes

Peter Newton

Austin Plunkett

Julian Gilmour

Carl Greenidge

Sairs Capell

Ewen Campbell

➲ Notes

Use this space for your training notes.